FANTASTIC
PLANETS,
FORBIDDEN
ZONES,
AND # LOST
CONTINENTS

FROM FICTION TO FILM: *A great many cinema classics of the sci-fi genre have been derived from important novels. William Cameron Menzies's film* Things to Come (1936) *was adapted by H. G. Wells himself from his 1933 book,* The Shape of Things to Come. *Courtesy: London Films.*

DOUGLAS BRODE

FANTASTIC PLANETS, FORBIDDEN ZONES, *AND* LOST CONTINENTS

THE 100 GREATEST SCIENCE-FICTION FILMS

UNIVERSITY OF TEXAS PRESS AUSTIN

Requests for permission to reproduce material from
this work should be sent to:
    Permissions
    University of Texas Press
    P.O. Box 7819
    Austin, TX 78713-7819
    http://utpress.utexas.edu/index.php/rp-form

♾ The paper used in this book meets the minimum
requirements of ANSI/NISO Z39.48-1992 (R1997)
(Permanence of Paper).

Library of Congress Cataloging-in-Publication Data

Brode, Douglas, 1943– author.
    Fantastic planets, forbidden zones, and lost
continents: the 100 greatest science-fiction films /
Douglas Brode. — First edition.
        pages   cm
    ISBN 978-0-292-73919-2 (cloth)
    ISBN 978-0-292-73920-8 (library ebook)
    ISBN 978-1-4773-0247-7 (non-library ebook)
1. Science-fiction films—History and criticism. I. Title.
    PN1995.9.S26B67   2015
    791.43'615—dc23
                                    2014032144
doi:10.7560/739192

For My Three Sons: Shane, Shaun, and Shea
And my grandson, Tyler Reese
"Serious" science-fiction fans all!

CONTENTS

ACKNOWLEDGMENTS

With great thanks to my son Shane Johnson Brode, whose contribution of time and hard work on this project brought it to fruition. Also, to my sons Shaun Lichenstein Brode and Shea Thaxter Brode, for their suggestions as to films worthy of inclusion and insights into such movies.

THE HIGHEST FORM OF FLATTERY: *As in other genres, science-fiction filmmakers often include homages to earlier works. An ultra-realistic image of likely future travel from George Pal's* Conquest of Space (1955) *would be almost precisely referenced in Stanley Kubrick's* 2001: A Space Odyssey (1968). *Courtesy: George Pal Productions; Metro-Goldwyn-Mayer.*

INTRODUCTION

Any attempt to pick the top 100 films in a specific genre must begin with a working definition of that unique storytelling venue—or, at least, an explanation of how the term will be employed within the volume at hand. This is never as easy a process as it may initially seem. For instance, if we are hoping to choose the Ur-Western, we might well focus on *The Last of the Mohicans*. Yet the geography of James Fenimore Cooper's 1826 novel and its many movie adaptations happens to be the East Coast. Similarly, is *The Godfather* (Francis Ford Coppola, 1972) the greatest gangster movie ever made, as many insist? Or, as others would argue, is it more appropriately considered a non-generic film about the inner workings of an American immigrant family that happens to be connected to The Family?

The genre covered here, sci-fi (or, as purists prefer to call it, "science fiction"), may well be the most difficult of all to summarize briefly. As Stephen King noted in his seminal book, *Danse Macabre* (1981), sci-fi and horror often spill over into one another, confusing the boundaries while confounding any neat definition of either. Individual works can be thought of as belonging to one of those genres or the other, depending on the angle of perception from which the piece is received. The original literary antecedent of both those types of story is Mary Shelley's *Frankenstein, or The Modern Prometheus* (1818). Yet, that book can also considered a pre-Victorian romance, if with darker, more metaphysical aspects than other examples of this form. Diverse movie adaptations of Shelley's work have offered all three approaches—most often, one per film in order to bring the book's epic length down to manageable screen time.

Ultimately, genre "rules," like all rules, beg to be broken. Often, the best works of any form are the ones that go against the grain. *High Noon* (Fred Zinnemann, 1952), perhaps the greatest Western ever made, takes place almost entirely within confined buildings. Yet any John Ford fan knows the essence of the genre had, at least until this key juncture, been a celluloid celebration of wide-open spaces in general, Monument Valley in particular. So it goes with science fiction, space fantasy, and imaginative drama—closely inter-related terms that mean pretty much, if not precisely, the same thing.

What seems obvious, then, becomes the first great challenge. Necessarily, I've adopted a few rules of thumb, allowing for the necessary paring-down process.

"Writing the history of the future" was the earliest attempt by aficionados of a new form to put into words the essence of science fiction, created over several transitional decades between the middle of the nineteenth century and the fin de siècle by Jules Verne and H. G. Wells, to name the two best-known authors. Modernist writers offered in fictional form the only valid response, at once logical and creative, to the then-evolving field of science. Previously, any such attempts to understand the human situation here on Earth or in the cosmos above, and a possible connection between the two—other than a faith-based acceptance of everything in the Judeo-Christian Bible—had been dismissed as "the devil's work," alchemy, paganism, or Wicca (aka, witchcraft). Almost overnight, everything changed, first in the worlds of technology and medicine, then in the popular culture that always reflects the society from which it derives.

In an early example of what Alvin Toffler a century later would refer to as "future shock," a commonplace vision of how the micro- and macrocosms worked altered so swiftly that humankind's place in the universe, or at least our shared perception of it, was turned upside down. Most people could not keep up with the rapidly changing sense of who we were and, more important, why we existed. Nietzsche's 1882 dictum that "God is dead!" couldn't have been uttered had science not called into question the legitimacy of older forms of knowledge. Nor could Einstein's theory of relativity have appeared without intellectuals wondering if indeed anything could be considered absolute. The very meaning of life in a civilization that might entirely abandon religion, while entering a brave new world of wonder and/or terror, would swiftly become an (perhaps *the*) issue. Fascinatingly, that would not be the case: more often than not, the genre offered a retro vision, insisting on the need to hang on to faith despite any supposed scientific evidence to the contrary.

Simply put, for a film to be about science does not necessarily imply that it will come out in favor of science. At any rate, just such a debate would come to circumscribe the twentieth century. As a result, that early way of defining ("describing" may be a more accurate term) the "new fiction," if valuable, quickly proved to be less than comprehensive. It served well enough for *From the Earth to the Moon* (*De la terre à la lune*) (1865), Jules Verne's documentary-like projection of an eventual space flight as it might likely occur, so far as the scientific data of his time suggested. However, H. G. Wells's *The First Men in the Moon* (1901)—which included (and, to a degree, introduced) such entirely fanciful tropes as Selene, mistress of the moon, and her army of half-man, half-bug

THE LAST ALCHEMIST: *With his oddly enchanting collection of miniature people, grown in bottles, Dr. Pretorius (Ernest Thesiger) represents the final figure in an ancient line that would shortly give way to modern young scientists in James Whale's* The Bride of Frankenstein *(1935). Courtesy: Universal.*

insectoids—had to be posited as another genre entirely or the opposite pole of a single genre that now required redefining.

The latter would prove to be the case. Verne had set a precedent for what would come to be called "hard" (that is, realistic) sci-fi. Wells created a template for "romantic" (that is, fanciful, drawing on several thousand years of legend and myth) sci-fi. Not only could they coexist within the same essential narrative form, the two could also, perhaps to everyone's surprise, successfully be mixed and matched, as early cinema proved. Though officially a film version of Verne's novel, the Georges Méliès film *A Trip to the Moon* (*Le voyage dans la lune*) (1902) follows that book's documentary approach to a cannon-fired rocket for the first half of its running time. Once the stellar voyagers touch down on the lunar surface, however, the tone changes. Shortly, these cosmic travelers encounter creatures borrowed from Wells's wildest imaginings.

The greatest examples of each form, hard and romantic, as well as the most notable combinations of the two, will all be lauded here. What then will not be included? Foremost are those examples of fantasy fiction that cannot (or, at least, according to my view, ought not) be thought of as belonging to this genre. These include epic fantasies, ranging from *King Kong* (1933) and *The Wizard of Oz* (1939) to *7 Faces of Dr. Lao* (1964) and *The Lord of the Rings* trilogy (2001–2003). The issue here is not quality. Those films are as excellent as anything contained in this study. Again, the decision to not include them is entirely based on a working definition of the genre. This does (indeed, must) impose limitations. But precisely what then are the boundaries? And how are they configured in this volume?

Perhaps no one has so succinctly captured the heart, soul, and mind of the sci-fi genre as author Gregg Rickman. In a phrase that, by the beauty of its sheer simplicity, makes perfect, fundamental sense, Rickman defined sci-fi as "fiction about science." *King Kong* may well rate as the greatest romantic adventure-cum-monster movie ever made. But as there is no hint of scientific explanation as to how and why that great ape exists on Skull Island, or how and why the dinosaurs there did not die as others of their breed did, *Kong* does not fit, no matter how much we might want it to. At the same time, *Creature from the Black Lagoon* (1954), which follows the plot of *Kong* almost identically, can be considered not only a monster movie or a horror film but also as sci-fi. The group that, in this tale, journeys into a modern heart of darkness worthy of Joseph Conrad consists not of Hollywood moviemakers (as in *Kong*) but scientists. When they encounter and, in time, defeat the beast, discussions are about how and why this water-logged missing link sidestepped the evolutionary process and, more significantly, what might be learned from its existence once the scientists return to their laboratory.

Here, then, is this book's narrative thread. It served as the basis for selecting or rejecting individual films (no matter how excellent) for inclusion as examples of sci-fi's numerous subgenres. To quickly consider only one such subgenre, the unique realm we now call "dystopian fiction," *The Trial* (1962), *A Clockwork Orange* (1971), and *Brazil* (1985) rate among the greatest examples of the form. Yet, they do not include any specific reference to science—that is, the mechanical apparatus that is the practical byproduct of intellectual science. In contrast, those dystopian pieces included here—*Metropolis* (1927), *The Time Machine* (1960), and *Blade Runner* (1982), to name but a few—directly address science by including, if not always explaining, some aspect of experimentation and the resulting technology. In each, some aspect of science is foregrounded rather than merely serving as an unmentioned backdrop to a dark futuristic tale.

To simplify without, hopefully, oversimplifying: if Aladdin hops on a magic carpet and travels to the moon, we are watching fantasy. But should Flash Gordon climb aboard a rocket and journey to Mars, that's science fiction. The equation that underlines this volume: fantasy + technology = sci-fi.

For some of the films included here, like *Dr. Cyclops* (1940) and *Destination Moon* (1950), science is the primary theme or motif of a movie's identity. The leading characters are, indeed, scientists. For others, such as *The Incredible Shrinking Man* (1957), *The Birds* (1963), and *Night of the Living Dead* (1968), science is, at best, peripheral. Always, though, this element is included, albeit briefly, in the movie's creative mix, which can also feature other elements as diverse as kitchen-sink realism and its opposite, epic-level fantasy.

Within this range, the included films can veer from the gleeful erotic fantasies of *Barbarella* (1968) to the hard and cold facts of *Colossus: The Forbin Project* (1970). Also, choice examples of the genre often offer oppositional points of view, be they political or philosophical. As the text will illustrate, Wells created *Things to Come* (1936) less from the inspiration of an original idea than as a reaction to (and against) everything he despised about *Metropolis*. In the same vein, *The Day the Earth Stood Still* (1951) and *The Thing from Another World* (1951) are best viewed in tandem as liberal-progressive statements as compared to conservative-traditional attitudes from the early fifties, as dramatized by the era's fascination with UFOs.

Only feature films are included, ruling out such wondrous "shorts" as the animated *Duck Dodgers in the 24½th Century* (1953) and the trend-setting *La jetée* (1962). Even that basic rule proves tricky: *A Trip to the Moon*, though only about ten minutes in length, was one of the longest films ever constructed at the time of its release. Therefore, it is included as a feature, that term having altered several times with the history of cinema. My emphasis remains on Hollywood products, yet international items are also included, particularly those that caught the worldwide attention of genre critics and diehard fans. Considerations as to budget were not primary: a great B sci-fi film—and there are many here—deserves to be considered a classic more than expensive flops, as anyone who has managed to sit through Christopher Nolan's disappointing effort *Interstellar* (2014) can attest.

For the purpose of creating a continuum, and at least some sense of historic context, the films are presented here in the order in which they appeared, each accompanied by its numerical rating. As to those evaluations, which, of course, are largely subjective, the following considerations were taken into account: the excellence of the work, though this had to be scrupulously analyzed in terms of the state of the art of special effects or, as they will be abbreviated from this point on, F/X, when the film was created; the complexity of the film in terms of a balance of visceral action and cerebral insight; the influence of the film in the genre's ongoing and ever-evolving tradition; and the degree to which the film has withstood the test of time. This final criterion was most difficult to assess, obviously, in terms of the most recent releases.

As to what I might personally bring to the package, in addition to the selection process itself, one desire was to reveal the interlocking aspect of genre examples in terms of any single film's ability to reference another of the same genre and the manner in which films reference one another. The now-old idea of New Criticism, in which each work is to be evaluated strictly for its own merits, initially sounds like an appealing, commonsense approach. Then one remembers the "culture" and that the objets d'art and works of entertainment that compose it are not presented or experienced in isolation, but as part of an ongoing stream of everyday consciousness. Perhaps we ought not compare the *Star Wars* prequel trilogy to George Lucas's first three films in the series, or the recent *Star Trek* reboot to the first set of theatrical films (or to the TV show). But we do. And we will continue to do so.

One final note: only when this book was completed did I realize how often I cite Rod Serling and his TV series, *The Twilight Zone* (1959–1964) when referring to movies that, at first glance, have no direct connection to either the man or his show. (Note: the 1983 Steven Spielberg-produced *Twilight Zone: The Movie* is far too uneven in quality to be considered for inclusion here.) Perhaps my previous involvement with the 2009 book *Rod Serling and The Twilight Zone* (co-author, Carol Kramer Serling) steered me in that direction, though I believe I would have come to the same conclusion had that not been the case. *Zone* is arguably the greatest sci-fi TV show, though Serling always preferred to think of it as imaginative fantasy. Even more amazing than the quality of the series, however, is the manner in which Serling and *Zone* shaped not only the generation of sci-fi filmmakers who would come of age in the 1970s (for example, Lucas and Spielberg) but also each generation since. Even now, Hollywood honchos toss about ideas for yet another *Zone* revival, or perhaps a biopic about Rod Serling. If the references to him here appear plentiful, please keep in mind that we cannot fully appreciate contemporary examples of the form unless we carefully consider their point of inception.

THE AVATAR OF IMAGINATIVE FICTION: *Rod Serling (1924–1975), best known for his landmark television series* The Twilight Zone *(1959–1964), drew on science-fiction film and literature from the first half of the twentieth century. His work, which includes the feature film* Planet of the Apes *(1968), would profoundly influence George Lucas, Steven Spielberg, and other emergent creative geniuses of the genre. Courtesy: The Rod Serling Collection.*

THE LIST

THE 100 GREATEST SCI-FI FILMS

1. *Metropolis* (1927)
2. *2001: A Space Odyssey* (1968)
3. *The Day the Earth Stood Still* (1951)
4. Three-way tie: *Star Wars* Original Trilogy
      Episode IV: A New Hope (1977)
      Episode V: The Empire Strikes Back (1980)
      Episode VI: Return of the Jedi (1983)
5. *Forbidden Planet* (1956)
6. *E.T. the Extra-Terrestrial* (1982)
7. *Blade Runner* (1982)
8. Tie: *Frankenstein* (1931) and *The Bride of Frankenstein* (1935)
9. *Children of Men* (2006)
10. *Invasion of the Body Snatchers* (1956)
11. *Avatar* (2009)
12. Tie: *Alien* (1979) and *Aliens* (1986)
13. *Dr. Jekyll and Mr. Hyde* (1931)
14. *Planet of the Apes* (1968)
15. *The Invisible Man* (1933)
16. *Close Encounters of the Third Kind* (1977)
17. *Inception* (2010)
18. *Things to Come* (1936)
19. *Open Your Eyes/Abre los ojos* (1997)
20. *The Birds* (1963)
21. *District 9* (2009)
22. *The Time Machine* (1960)
23. *Jurassic Park* (1993)
24. Tie: *20,000 Leagues Under the Sea* (1954) and *Mysterious Island* (1961)
25. *The Avengers* (2012)
26. *Alphaville/Alphaville, une étrange aventure de Lemmy Caution* (1965)
27. *WALL-E* (2008)

28. Three-way tie: *Star Trek* "Even Number" Trilogy
    II: *The Wrath of Khan* (1982)
    IV: *The Voyage Home* (1986)
    VI: *The Undiscovered Country* (1991)

29. *Twelve Monkeys* (1995)

30. *The Thing* (1982)

31. *Solaris/Solyaris* (1972)

32. *The Matrix* (1999)

33. *Eternal Sunshine of the Spotless Mind* (2004)

34. *The Terminator* (1984)

35. *Fantastic Planet/La planète sauvage* (1973)

36. *Back to the Future* (1985)

37. *The Truman Show* (1998)

38. *The Thing from Another World* (1951)

39. *Guardians of the Galaxy* (2014)

40. *Gravity* (2013)

41. *The War of the Worlds* (1953)

42. *Cloud Atlas* (2012)

43. *Invaders from Mars* (1953)

44. *V for Vendetta* (2005)

45. *Five Million Years to Earth/Quatermass and the Pit* (1967)

46. Tie: *Star Trek* (2009) and *Star Trek into Darkness* (2013)

47. *Seconds* (1966)

48. *Total Recall* (1990)

49. *The Incredible Shrinking Man* (1957)

50. *Cocoon* (1985)

51. *Island of Lost Souls* (1932)

52. *Man of Steel* (2013)

53. *1984* (1956)

54. *Mad Max 2: The Road Warrior* (1981)

55. Tie: *Murders in the Rue Morgue* (1932) and *The Black Cat* (1934)

56. *Nausicaä of the Valley of the Wind/Kaze no tani no Naushika* (1984)

57. *The Absent-Minded Professor* (1961)

58. *RoboCop* (1987)

59. Three-way tie: The "End of the World" Trilogy
    The World, the Flesh and the Devil (1959)
    On the Beach (1959)
    The Day the Earth Caught Fire (1961)

60. *The Fly* (1986)

61. Tie: *The Beast from 20,000 Fathoms* (1953) and *Them!* (1954)

62. *Predator* (1987)

63. Tie: *Destination Moon* (1950) and *Conquest of Space* (1955)

64. *THX 1138* (1971)

65. *Godzilla, King of the Monsters!* (1956)

66. *Colossus: The Forbin Project* (1970)

67. *The Abyss* (1989)

68. *Sleeper* (1973)

69. *Rise of the Planet of the Apes* (2011)

70. Three-way tie: Cliffhangers
    Flash Gordon (1936)
    Flash Gordon's Trip to Mars (1938)
    Flash Gordon Conquers the Universe (1940)

71. *The Fifth Element* (1997)

72. *Creature from the Black Lagoon* (1954)

73. *Escape from New York* (1981)

74. *The Satan Bug* (1965)

75. Tie: *Village of the Damned* (1960) and *The Day of the Triffids* (1963)

76. *Night of the Living Dead* (1968)

77. *The Blob* (1958)

78. *Time After Time* (1979)

79. *The Hunger Games: Catching Fire* (2013)

80. *Space Cowboys* (2000)

81. *Fahrenheit 451* (1966)

82. Tie: *A.I. Artificial Intelligence* (2001) and *Minority Report* (2002)

83. *This Island Earth* (1955)

84. *Strange Days* (1995)

85. *Fantastic Voyage* (1966)

86. *Stargate* (1994)

87. *Dr. Cyclops* (1940)

88. *Barbarella* (1968)

89. Three-way tie: *Star Wars* Prequel Trilogy
    Episode I: The Phantom Menace (1999)
    Episode II: Attack of the Clones (2002)
    Episode III: Revenge of the Sith (2005)

90. *Earth vs. the Flying Saucers* (1956)

91. *TRON: Legacy* (2010)

FANTASTIC PLANETS, FORBIDDEN ZONES, AND LOST CONTINENTS

TO BEGIN AT THE BEGINNING: *Live action combined with an early version of animation led to the first significant example of* cinéma fantastique *in* A Trip to the Moon/Le voyage dans la lune *(1902), Georges Méliès's still-charming experiment. Courtesy: Star-Film.*

·······

A TRIP TO THE MOON/ LE VOYAGE DANS LA LUNE (1902)

—— RANKING: 100 ——

CREDITS
Star Film; Georges Méliès, dir.; Jules Verne, H. G. Wells, novels; Méliès, scr.; Méliès, pro.; Michaut, Lucien Tainguy, cin.; Méliès, ed.; Méliès, prod. design; Claudel, art dir.; Jeanne d'Alcy, costumes; 14 min. (16 fps), 8 min. (25 fps); Color/B&W; 1.33:1.

CAST
Georges Méliès (*Prof. Barbenfouillis/Man in the Moon*); Victor André (*Star Gazer*); Bleuette Bernon (*Lady in the Moon*); Brunnet (*First Astronomer*); Jeanne d'Alcy (*Pretty Girl*); Henri Delannoy (*Space Craft Captain*); Depierre (*Voyager*).

MOST MEMORABLE LINE
Ow!

THE MAN IN THE MOON, AS THE ROCKET
APPEARS TO CRASH INTO HIS FACE

BACKGROUND
Science fiction as we know it, particularly works that deal with space travel, was invented by two authors: France's Jules Verne (1828–1905) and England's H. G. Wells (1866–1946). Before their contributions, tales of journeys to the stars were fantasy of a romantic order, dating back to the earliest civilizations. During the nineteenth century, as science replaced alchemy and then inched toward respectability, Verne and Wells were among the first to invent a modern form of fiction that correlated to more enlightened views.

THE PLOT
Barbenfouillis, a university professor, addresses his colleagues in a classroom, sharing his theory that a rocket could transport earthlings to the moon. They shout him down, but their disbelief only encourages Barbenfouillis to prove

his idea by building a huge gun and a bullet-like craft. In time, he and some friends launch into space. They crash on the moon and, while sleeping on its surface, are visited by strange beings from the sky. Skeletal creatures capture the humans and drag them before their cold-hearted queen. The earthlings fight their way free, hurry back to their craft, and return to Earth.

THE FILM

Georges Méliès (1861–1938) brought the visions of Verne and Wells to the new (and science-based) storytelling medium called "The Movies." A Paris-based magician-turned-director, he is known to have read Verne's *From the Earth to the Moon* (*De la terre à la lune*, 1865); recent research suggests he happened upon Wells's *The First Men in the Moon* (1901) shortly before setting to work on *A Trip to the Moon*. This would explain why the first half of the film is drawn from Verne's book while the second owes far more to Wells's novel.

THEME

A Trip to the Moon offers an intriguing early example of the motion picture, a product for public consumption as well as an emergent art form, as a means of personal expression for its writer-director; or, as the French would come to call such rare talents, "*auteur*." However much Méliès borrowed from previous narratives, he also used his own idea of magic: strange, haunting appearances and disappearances constantly occur in the film. If adapted from pre-existing sources, *A Trip to the Moon* is Georges Méliès's film, one that set the pace for all cinema.

TRIVIA

If the legend is to be believed, Méliès happened on film by accident. Fascinated by the trick of making a woman disappear onstage, he accomplished this by tossing down a small amount of explosive powder, resulting in a momentary whiff of black smoke that allowed a woman to slip down a trapdoor. Méliès dreamed of taking this conventional effect a step further: a disappearance without any such "cover." But how? In 1896, he wandered into a nickelodeon featuring films by the Lumière brothers. Called "*actualités*," these fifty-second documentaries were shot in diverse sections of Paris. While Méliès was enjoying this "realistic" incarnation of film, something unintended appeared onscreen. A ripped piece of film had been edited back together, and, in the process, a half second or so had been lost. To Méliès's amazement, a woman walking across the screen suddenly disappeared. He guessed what had happened and realized that celluloid could solve his problem. Among the first of his short movies, most of which are lost today, was *The Vanishing Lady* (*Escamotage d'une dame au théâtre Robert Houdin*, 1896).

If, by the turn of the century, the Lumières had pioneered one aspect of filmmaking, shooting on the streets for realism, Méliès took another direction, creating what may have been the first "studio." Forsaking realism, he and his crew employed everything from papier-mâché to painted backdrops to create alternative universes. Not only are the surface and subterranean areas of the moon virtually "animated" in a futuristic fairy tale sense, but so too are those earlier sequences on Earth, including the lecture classroom scene and the blast-off from an impossibly long launcher, providing a precursor of what would come to be called "surrealism" in the graphic arts. In his primitive way, Méliès set the standard for experimental movies by Max Fleischer and Walt Disney in which actors enter a cartoon world.

The film was originally released in color, though, of course, color film stock would not exist for several decades. A team of artists achieved this effect by painting colors onto every single frame of film, a laborious task to say the least. The manner in which Méliès's staff achieved this and other effects is depicted in *Hugo* (Martin Scorsese, 2011).

· · · · · · ·

METROPOLIS (1927)

—— RANKING: 1 ——

CREDITS

UFA; Fritz Lang, dir.; Thea von Harbou, novel; von Harbou, Lang, scr.; Erich Pommer, pro.; Gottfried Huppertz, mus.; Karl Freund, Günther Rittau, Walter Ruttmann, cin.; Otto Hunte, Erich Kettelhut, Karl Vollbrecht, art dir.; Aenne Willkomm, costumes; Edgar G. Ulmer, Hunte, Kettelhut, Vollbrecht, set design; Eugen Schüfftan, special visual effects; Ernst Kunstmann, Konstantin Irmen-Tschet, Kettelhut, F/X; 210 min. (original print), 93 min. (German re-release), 123 min. (2002 restoration); B&W; 1.33:1.

THE BIRTH OF DYSTOPIAN SCIENCE-FICTION CINEMA: *In the early twenty-first century, a fascistic leader (Alfred Abel) finds himself spellbound by the plan of a mad inventor (Rudolf Klein-Rogge) to replace humans with robots. Courtesy: Universum Film/UFA.*

CAST
Brigitte Helm (*Maria/Robot Maria*); Alfred Abel (*Joh Fredersen*); Gustav Fröhlich (*Young Freder*); Rudolf Klein-Rogge (*C. A. Rotwang*); Fritz Rasp (*Thin Man*); Theodor Loos (*Josaphat*); Erwin Biswanger (*Worker #11811*); Heinrich George (*Grot*); Fritz Alberti (*Man of Babel*); Grete Berger, Rose Lichtenstein, Max Dietze (*workers*); Beatrice Garga (*Woman of Eternal Gardens*); Heinrich Gotho (*Master of Ceremonies*).

MOST MEMORABLE LINE
There can be no understanding between the hand and the brain unless the heart acts as mediator.
MARIA'S FINAL LINE

BACKGROUND
Immediately following World War I, Erich Pommer of Universum Film (UFA) set

into motion a series of dark thrillers that captured, often in fantasy, the daily horror of life in the Weimar Republic. The premiere project, *The Cabinet of Dr. Caligari* (1920), was originally to have been directed by Fritz Lang (1890–1976), who dropped out for personal and artistic reasons. Over the next several years, Lang became an avid Communist, consuming works by Karl Marx and Friedrich Engels and watching masterpieces of Soviet montage that conveyed radical political ideas via editing. Lang and his wife, Thea von Harbou (1888–1954), set to work on an adaptation of her dystopian novel. During this same period, von Harbou grew ever more intrigued by the rise of fascism, in time coming to subscribe to Nazi values.

THE PLOT

In a futuristic super-city, the working classes slave at machines that all but devour them, in time turning those who perform such dreary labor into automatons. Meanwhile, the ruling classes carouse in a high tower. A spokesperson for the underclass, Maria, awakens the consciousness of Freder, son of the powerful leader, with her proclamation that "all men are brothers." He slips off to learn the truth and becomes radicalized after experiencing the horrid existence of the masses. Meanwhile, his father, Fredersen, enlists the mad scientist Rotwang to develop a machine-man to replace workers. The two conspire to create a robot version of Maria that can be used to incite workers to violence, thus providing those in power with an excuse to eliminate them.

THE FILM

Lang later admitted that while he had achieved the look he wanted for the film, von Harbou had seized control of the movie's meaning. As a result, *Metropolis* expresses precisely the opposite point of view from what he had intended. The film initially appears to be shaping up as a radical futuristic allegory, calling for a worker's revolution against the ruling elite. At midpoint, this reverses, and *Metropolis* takes on an anti-revolutionary tone, warning against such rebellion while insisting that a fascistic leader must be tolerated, despite excesses. When the Nazis embraced *Metropolis* as their favorite film, Lang expressed disgust with the final product; von Harbou, delight.

The concept of photographing actors on bare soundstages while making them appear to be standing in an elaborately created world, fashioned from tabletop miniatures, was developed for *Metropolis* by Eugen Schüfftan. This would become known as the Schüfftan Process.

Metropolis was severely cut after its initial showings, and to this day, cine-detectives search the globe for bits and pieces, believed to have been lost forever, in an attempt to fully restore the original.

THEME

Metropolis pioneered epic science fiction as religious allegory. Initially, the city's cathedral is all but abandoned. At the finale, however, everyone comes together on its steps to make things right. Maria tells Bible tales, including the story of the Tower of Babel, in catacombs not unlike the hiding places of the early Christians. Huge crosses are on view there. Freder is inspired to become a messianic figure, representing the Second Coming. The names of his adoptive parents, Maria and Josaphat, translate into English as Mary and Joseph. H. G. Wells, who believed the first necessary step to creating a future utopia was to outlaw all religion, became so enraged while watching *Metropolis* that he at once set to work on an alternative vision, filmed in 1936 as *Things to Come*.

TRIVIA

The print that circulated for eighty years lacked key elements necessary for the plot to make sense. Gone were the skeletal Thin Man, an operative for Fredersen, and all mention of the inspirational woman "Hel" (including her statue, signifying Hel's importance to Fredersen), deceased wife of Fredersen and, earlier, wife to Rotwang, beloved by both. In the ending of the abbreviated version, Rotwang appears to pursue Maria in hopes of killing her; actually, his mania has convinced him that she is Hel reborn and he hopes to recapture his lost love.

George Lucas in part modeled the *Star Wars* C-3PO on the robot from *Metropolis*. The city in Superman comics and movies is named after the one in this film. Likewise, Ridley Scott visually referenced *Metropolis* in many of the *Blade Runner* images.

Rock artists of the 1980s fell in love with the visionary piece. Queen featured scenes in their *Radio Ga Ga* music video. Record producer Giorgio Moroder convinced the band's lead vocalist Freddie Mercury and other musicians that *Metropolis* resembled a full-length music video, leading to a 1984 re-release of the film with color tints and a rock music score.

... WHERE NO WOMAN HAS GONE BEFORE: *A proto-feminist motif entered into cinematic sci-fi with the appearance of Gerda Maurus (far right) as the title character, a courageous space pioneer who disproves any prejudices as to gender on the final frontier. Courtesy: Universum Film/UFA.*

. . . .

WOMAN IN THE MOON/ FRAU IM MOND (1929)

—— RANKING: 94 ——

CREDITS

UFA; Fritz Lang, dir.; Thea von Harbou, novel; Lang, von Harbou, Prof. Hermann Oberth, scr.; Lang, pro.; Willy Schmidt-Gentner, mus.; Curt Courant, Oskar Fischinger, Konstantin Irmen-Tschet/Tschetwerikoff, Otto Kanturek, cin.; Emil Hasler, Otto Hunte, Karl Vollbrecht, art dir.; Fischinger, Irmen-Tschet/Tschetwerikoff, F/X; Joseph Danilowatz, Dr. Gustav Wolff, artistic collaboration; various running times: 156, 162, 200 min.; B&W; 1.33:1

CAST

Klaus Pohl (*Prof. Georg Manfeldt*); Willy Fritsch (*Wolf Helius*); Gustav von Wangenheim (*Ingenieur Hans Windegger*); Gerda Maurus (*Friede Velten*); Gustl Stark-Gstettenbaur (*Gustav*); Fritz Rasp (*Der Mann*); Tilla Durieux, Hermann Vallentin, Max Zilzer, Mahmud Terja Bey, Borwin Walth (*Fünf Gehirne und Scheckbücher*); Die Maus Josephine (*The Mouse*).

MOST MEMORABLE LINE

"Never" does not exist for the human mind. Only "Not yet!"
HELIUS, TO DISBELIEVERS IN SPACE TRAVEL

BACKGROUND

From the moment the husband-wife team decided to move ahead with a follow-up to *Metropolis*, Lang and von Harbou agreed that the semi-sequel project would be their adaptation of her 1928 novel, *Die Frau im Mond*. The collaborators would use as their template Jules Verne's *From the Earth to the Moon* (*De la terre à la lune*, 1865), with its probable outcome according to rocket science at the time. In other words, Lang and von Harbou would produce "pure" science fiction. Consciously, they rejected the alternative aesthetic, the basis of H. G. Wells's *The First Men in the Moon* (1901): a fanciful depiction of grotesque creatures inhabiting heavenly bodies. This alternative form would in time come to be called "space opera."

They brought in Hermann Oberth (1894–1989), considered the greatest living resource on space travel, as their scientific consultant. Oberth insisted that an actual projectile would likely proceed as a series of three successive rockets-within-rockets. Likewise, he added the sequence in which a ten-to-zero countdown precedes the lift-off. This set the pace not only for all future films on the subject but also for real-life space programs, beginning with Nazi Germany's V-2 rocket program, which Oberth oversaw. Also involved in the film (and, later, the V-2) was the young Wernher von Braun (1912–1977), who, even then, as a teenager, was attempting to solve likely problems of space travel at the Verein für Raumschiffahrt (Society for Space Travel).

THE PLOT

The European scientific community laughs when Professor Manfeldt argues that the moon may be covered with gold. One man who does not scoff is Helius, a sharp businessman. He considers linking his keen entrepreneurial instincts with Manfeldt's obvious, if unappreciated, genius by journeying into space together. The planned expedition is complicated by, among other things, a gold cartel that wants to sabotage the adventure for fear that an abundance of that mineral might bring down the value of their current holdings, and a mischievous child who, having read one too many pulp fiction novels, stows away in the rocket. The ultimate problem for Helius, however, is that two of his fellow travelers are Friede, the woman he loves, and Manfeldt, currently engaged to the lovely lady.

THE FILM

Complaints that the movie is overly long, particularly the earthbound sequences, reveal a naiveté about narrative forms in the silent cinema in general and in German Weimar-era films in particular. As genre conventions for sci-fi moviemaking were not yet in place (indeed, *Woman in the Moon* established many of the fundamentals), the extended melodrama, involving a new variation on the old romantic triangle, did not violate viewer expectations at the time because, in fact, there were none. Always, the idea had been to create a believable narrative about worldly characters so that, when the journey begins, the viewer carries such anchored-in-actuality emotions off into space.

THEME

However horrific von Harbou's politics as a member of the Nazi Party, her view of women must be considered proto-feminist. Friede, her beauty accepted as a given, is included on the space voyage because of her imposing mental abilities and considerable stamina. More impressive still, unlike such later female scientists as Julie Adams in *Creature from the Black Lagoon* (1954), Friede is not swiftly stripped down to a swimsuit; rather, she is always wearing a shirt, tie, and pants identical to those of her male companions. Even her hair is mannishly styled, though this adds to, rather than detracts from, her potent femininity. She turns out to be the best decision-maker on the space craft. Indeed, her solution to their low-oxygen problem solves everything for everyone involved.

In contrast to *Metropolis*, the previous Lang–von Harbou collaboration, *Woman in the Moon* does not play as a religious allegory. Nevertheless, the need to maintain old-fashioned faith in an increasingly secular and scientific world is forwarded as a key element. When the stowaway child becomes concerned that there will not be enough oxygen for a return trip, Friede consoles him by saying, "Let's pray to God."

In von Harbou's novel, the lure of gold on the moon serves mainly as the plot catalyst that justifies this dangerous trip. Lang, collaborating on the screenplay, used this aspect of the narrative for political purposes: the gold is a corrupting element, leading the otherwise admirable scientist Manfeldt to his death. This anti-capitalist attitude, which von Harbou scorned, led in part to their decision to divorce. In 1934, Lang left Germany for Paris, then briefly England, and, a few years later, the United States; von Harbou remained behind, eventually joining the Third Reich.

TRIVIA

Though the film portrays the initial approach to the moon as accurately as possible in terms of the then-current knowledge, the lunar surfaces recall the papier-mâché approach of Méliès some twenty-five years earlier. Lang established the practice of combining appealingly eerie renderings of other worlds with psychologically complex characters.

Woman in the Moon contains what may be the first example of an apparently purposeful self-referencing device within a sci-fi film. Shortly after arrival, as the men search for water and gold, Friede sets up a motion picture camera and shoots a documentary about the moon—precisely what von Harbou suggested to friends she might have preferred to do instead of creating a fictional film on the subject.

Willy Ley, who would later write the book on which the George Pal film *Conquest of Space* (1955) would be based and serve as scientific technical advisor for the *Tom Corbett, Space Cadet* TV series (1950–1955), assisted as technical advisor.

· · · · · · ·

JUST IMAGINE (1930)

—— RANKING: 98 ——

CREDITS

Fox Film Corporation; David Butler, dir.; Butler, Buddy G. DeSylva, Lew Brown, Ray Henderson, scr.; Brown, DeSylva, Henderson, pro.; Hugo Friedhofer, Arthur Kay, mus.; Ernest Palmer, cin.; Irene Morra, ed.; Stephen Goosson, Ralph Hammeras, set design; Alice O'Neill, Dolly Tree, Sophie Wachner, costumes; Joseph E. Aiken, special sound effects; Seymour Felix, choreographer; 113 min.; B&W; 1.20:1

CAST

El Brendel (*Single O*); Maureen O'Sullivan (*LN-18*); John Garrick (*J-21*); Marjorie White (*D-6*); Frank Albertson (*RT-42*); Hobart Bosworth (*Z-4*); Kenneth Thomson (*MT-3*); Mischa Auer (*B-36*); Ivan Linow (*Loko/Boko*); Joyzelle Joyner (*Loo Loo/ Boo Boo*); Wilfred Lucas (*X-10*); George Irving (*Head of Marriage Tribunal*); J. M. Kerrigan (*Traffic Policeman*).

MOST MEMORABLE LINE

There is one secret, the greatest of all, that remains a mystery: Mars!
THE SCIENTIST Z-4

BACKGROUND

Impressed by the success of Fritz Lang's science-fiction epics, executives at Fox Film green-lighted a script featuring a combination of Lang's two premises: a city of the future, which dominates the first half of the film, and a trip into outer space, the second. With the advent of sound, most in-production projects were rethought to include this suddenly popular element, particularly music. Anyone who had enjoyed production success on the New York stage was invited to relocate to the West Coast and become a producer. Buddy DeSylva (1895–1950) and his then-partners Lew Brown (1893–1958) and Ray Henderson (1896–1970), who together had come up with the Tin Pan Alley musical *Good News* (1927), were no exceptions. They recreated this project for film, adding vaudeville-style gag lines and endless songs.

THE PLOT

In the year 1980, J-21 meets his lover LN-18 on the sly. The monolithic Marriage Tribunal has decreed that, as a socialite, she should marry MT-3, a better catch owing to his supposed accomplishments in big business. A mysterious emissary of Z-4 contacts J-21. Z-4, a supposedly mad scientist who has constructed a rocket to launch toward Mars, needs a daring volunteer willing to accept the risk, and J-21 realizes that such an achievement would allow him a rebuttal at his final hearing as to his worthiness as a mate for LN-18. During the star journey, J-21 and his friend RT-42 are accompanied by an unlikely stowaway: Single O, who only recently was "raised from the dead" by an experimental process. On the Red Planet, the trio encounters a world of doppelgangers, every Martian contending with his or her evil twin.

THE FILM

Just Imagine has always been recalled as a critical and commercial flop. It was neither: the *New York Times* hailed this bizarre concoction as "highly imaginative," and box-office intake proved so strong that the film swiftly recouped its then-immense $1.5 million budget. The vision forwarded here, while borrowing liberally from Lang, brought to the American public such disorienting and far-reaching concepts as 250-story skyscrapers interconnected by highways in the sky, immense TV screens and sight-as-well-as-sound phones, pills replacing liquor for instant highs, test-tube babies, and gravity neutralizers for rocket science development. The film also borrowed from that era's pulp fiction publications, as well as from Méliès's flickers, ancient societies led by Amazon women in exotic costumes—that is, heavenly bodies existing on Heavenly Bodies. Such revered works as George Orwell's *1984* (1949), as well as virtually every movie included in this volume, owe a huge debt to this bold experiment. The claim that *Just Imagine* is hopelessly corny can be countered by the argument that here we find high camp long before Susan Sontag adjectivized that term in the mid-sixties to describe such guilty pleasures from Hollywood's fabled past.

THEME

Just Imagine explores the idea of nostalgia. Director Butler opens the piece with authentic footage of New York in the 1880s, recalling that in those good ol' days, people were attempting to travel in vehicles that moved faster and to inhabit buildings that reached higher. Still, from the perspective of contemporary 1930, when *Just Imagine* was released, the late nineteenth century appears to have been a gentler era. Such a prologue sets into motion a projection of the future in which the fast-paced 1930s, when considered from the perspective of a half-century later, constituted a far more relaxed moment in our social history. Nostalgia, then, has less to do with the realities of any one era than with the point of view from which it is observed.

TRIVIA

The Academy Awards honored Stephen Goosson and Ralph Hammeras, the conceptual talents of *Just Imagine*, with a joint nomination for best art direction. As a result of his pioneering work here, Goosson was tapped by Frank Capra to create the ethereal art design for the 1937 fantasy film *Lost Horizon*. Hammeras, who had already worked on the silent *The Lost World* (1925), would in time become Walt Disney's special effects photographer of choice for *20,000 Leagues Under the Sea* (1954). The Academy Award nomination marked the first time that Hollywood openly acknowledged the potential for high-quality work within the emergent sci-fi genre. The photographing of dazzling constructions for *Just Imagine*, achieved via glass pictures and intricate miniatures, was the work of an uncredited Willis H. O'Brien. At the time, O'Brien was straddling his two greatest successes, *The Lost World* (1925) and *King Kong* (1933)—both towering fantasy films that, owing to a lack of any sci-fi genre elements, could not be included in this volume.

During the Depression, sci-fi films would mostly constitute cliffhangers such as *Buck Rogers* (1939), produced at Universal. Fox Film Corporation allowed the avatars of such serials to borrow heavily from *Just Imagine*, in terms of both stock footage clips and use of props. The rocket ship, as well as the heroes' handguns, are present in the three *Flash Gordon* chapter plays discussed later in this book. Also, the image of space maidens dancing suggestively around the statue of a primitive god would be used to round out a pagan celebration at Emperor Ming's pleasure palace in *Flash Gordon*. And the ornate scientist's lab, conceived and designed by Kenneth Strickfaden, would be borrowed by Universal, becoming a staple of their horror films, including the various *Frankenstein* franchise features.

Just Imagine may be the first sound-era American film to include a gay reference. The dialogue and the manner in which the actors were directed to say key lines imply that the relationship between the hero and his roommate, despite their apparent interest in pretty girls, is greater and deeper than casual friendship. Shortly after landing on Mars, El Brendel's character develops an intense interest in a muscular warrior and, despite the presence of a female ruler, insists that "*he*'s the *real* 'queen' around here!"

·······

FRANKENSTEIN (1931) AND THE BRIDE OF FRANKENSTEIN (1935)

—— RANKING: 8 (TIE) ——

FRANKENSTEIN (1931)

CREDITS

Universal Pictures; James Whale, dir.; Mary W. Shelley, novel; Peggy Webling, play; John L. Balderston, Garrett Fort, Francis Edward Faragoh, Robert Florey, scr.; Carl Laemmle Jr., E. M. Asher, pro.; Bernhard Kaun, mus.; Arthur Edeson, Paul Ivano, cin.; Clarence Kolster, Maurice Pivar, ed.; Charles D. Hall, art dir.; Jack P. Pierce, makeup; Franz, Oscar, and Paul Dallons, F/X; 70 min.; B&W; 1.37:1.

CAST

Colin Clive (*Henry Frankenstein*); Mae Clarke (*Elizabeth*); John Boles (*Victor Moritz*); Boris Karloff (*The Monster*); Edward Van Sloan (*Dr. Waldman*); Frederick Kerr (*Baron Frankenstein*); Dwight Frye (*Fritz*); Lionel Belmore (*Burgomaster*); Marilyn Harris (*Little Maria*); Francis Ford (*Hans*).

THE MODERN PROMETHEUS: *This advertising poster for the film's re-release captured not only James Whale's aesthetic sensibility but also Mary Shelley's vision of the then-emergent scientist as our contemporary tragic hero, who intends only good for humankind, but inadvertently releases horror and destruction. Courtesy: Universal.*

MOST MEMORABLE LINE

It's *alive . . .* alive!

DR. FRANKENSTEIN AS HIS MONSTER ACTUALLY MOVES

BACKGROUND

In 1814, Mary Wollstonecraft Godwin (1797–1851) ran away from England to the continent with her lover, and later husband, poet and scientist Percy Bysshe Shelley. By some accounts, they spent a night, on a dare, on the grounds of Germany's deserted Frankenstein Castle after hearing that it was haunted. Precisely what they experienced there remains shrouded in mystery. During the summer of 1816, they joined Lord Byron in Switzerland at Villa Diodati. On a dark and stormy night, Byron suggested they all write ghost stories. Mary's contribution combined strange memories of the haunted rendezvous with details from her lover's current electrical experiments. During the next two years, Mary Shelley refined the book, with Percy serving as her mentor.

With the advent of sound, Carl Laemmle Jr. (1908–1979), the head of production at Universal, hoped to feature his greatest silent star, Lon Chaney, as Dracula, then as the Frankenstein monster. Before he could play the roles, however, Chaney died, and Bela Lugosi, who had made a name for himself as Dracula on the New York stage, was offered the part. When *Dracula* (1931) succeeded at the box office, Lugosi was asked to play Frankenstein's monster. Fearing that a nonspeaking role might not benefit his budding career, Lugosi turned it down. The role went to an obscure English character actor, Boris Karloff (1887–1969).

THE PLOT

The demented hunchback Fritz collects bodies for his master, Henry Frankenstein, who re-assembles parts into a composite corpse, which he plans to re-animate via electricity. Elizabeth, Henry's young bride-to-be, becomes concerned about the long hours her intended spends in a watchtower, and she attempts to bring her beloved back to reality. Tragically, he has created a thing with the brain of a criminal (after Fritz accidentally dropped the healthy specimen). On the wedding day of Henry and Elizabeth, the monster arrives as an uninvited guest.

THE FILM

Based less on the novel by Shelley than on a stage version by Peggy Webling, the film, like so many Universal releases that followed, offers a combination of science fiction and horror. In her 1818 novel, Shelley had avoided the term "monster," using instead "creature." First onstage in a simplified version, then on film, the creature becomes a monstrosity, in part owing to the iconic makeup conceived and created by Jack P. Pierce, who added the flat head and neck bolts. Director James Whale (1889–1957) employed an Expressionistic approach used earlier in Tod Browning's horror classic *Dracula* and, before that, in Universal's silent thrillers. Consequently, *Frankenstein* came to be perceived as a Gothic monster show. In Shelley's novel, almost everything takes place in sunlight, with the European settings presented in an ultra-realistic manner.

TRIVIA
In Shelley's novel, the title character's first name is "Victor." This was changed to "Henry," owing to a concern that the original sounded too Germanic. The prejudice toward Germany had been in effect since World War I and increased with the ever-growing rumbles of political discord there in the early 1930s.

THE BRIDE OF FRANKENSTEIN (1935)

ADDITIONAL CREDITS
William Hurlbut, R. C. Sherriff, Lawrence G. Blochman, scr.; Franz Waxman, mus.; John J. Mescall, cin.; Ted J. Kent, ed.; Charles D. Hall, art dir.; David S. Horsley, Ken Strickfaden, F/X; John P. Fulton, Cleo E. Baker, visual effects; 75 min.; B&W; 1.37:1.

ADDITIONAL CAST
Elsa Lanchester (*Mary Wollstonecraft Shelley/The Bride*); Valerie Hobson (*Elizabeth*); Ernest Thesiger (*Dr. Pretorius*); Gavin Gordon (*Lord Byron*); Douglas Walton (*Percy Bysshe Shelley*); Una O'Connor (*Minnie*); E. E. Clive (*Burgomaster*); O. P. Heggie (*Hermit*); John Carradine (*Hunter*).

MOST MEMORABLE LINE
To a new world of gods and monsters!
DR. PRETORIUS, DRUNKENLY TOASTING THE CREATURE AND HIS MATE

THE PLOT
The creature survives a fire that consumes the old mill and is now terrorizing the countryside. Flamboyant Dr. Pretorius attempts to convince the doctor that a bride should be created and the world populated with a man-made race.

"TO A NEW WORLD OF GODS AND MONSTERS": *The words of Dr. Pretorius (Ernest Thesiger, far right) will soon come to haunt Dr. Frankenstein (Colin Clive, far left) once he introduces the "bride" (Elsa Lanchester) to the creature (Boris Karloff). Courtesy: Universal.*

THE FILM

James Whale drew on legends surrounding the novel's creation to create a bizarre yet delicate prologue involving the poets Byron and Shelley, as well as Mary Shelley. Whale had attempted to add a level of black comedy to *Franken-stein*, but studio executives curbed that effort. Owing to the film's popularity, Whale found himself in demand for the sequel, which afforded him a greater degree of artistic freedom. He purposefully chose an over-the-top style, marked by self-conscious outlandishness. Whale's approach emphasized that none of this should be taken seriously, but rather viewed as a grotesque comic opera.

Notable too is the artistic use of the camera, which had to be kept still for the original so that the simple microphones would not pick up noises. By the time of the sequel, post-dubbing had been perfected, freeing the camera to move at the director's whim. In this film, it scurries along beside a crazed Una O'Connor as she darts past Gothic arches.

THEME

If one element of the novel did come across in both films, it was the growing fear of science that began early in the nineteenth century, even as what previously had been dismissed as alchemy was taken seriously and achieved respectability. The notion of man playing God is treated in the manner of a Greek tragedy: this is modern hubris, and the transgressor must be punished. Here, as in so much future work in the genre, very few examples of sci-fi glorify science; more often, science serves as a source for a cautionary fable, warning the viewer against its potential excesses.

TRIVIA

In 1939, Rowland V. Lee directed the third and most ambitious film in what had become a franchise. In *Son of Frankenstein*, Karloff played the monster for the third and final time. In turn, the role would be played by Lugosi, Lon Chaney Jr., son of the man for which it had initially been intended, and eventually Glenn Strange.

In 1985, a combination remake and sequel by director Franc Roddam rated as a disaster with both reviewers and the public. Today *The Bride* is considered a fascinating failure, well worth comparing to Whale's version and Shelley's novel.

· · · · · · ·

DR. JEKYLL AND MR. HYDE (1931)

—— RANKING: 13 ——

CREDITS

Paramount Pictures; Rouben Mamoulian, dir.; Robert Louis Stevenson, novel; Samuel Hoffenstein, Percy Heath, scr.; Adolph Zukor, pro.; Karl Struss, cin.; William Shea, ed.; Hans Dreier, art dir.; Travis Banton, costumes; Wally Westmore, special makeup effects; M. M. Paggi, experimental sound mixing; 98 min.; B&W; 1.20:1.

CAST

Fredric March (*Dr. Henry Jekyll/Mr. Hyde*); Miriam Hopkins (*Ivy Pearson*); Rose Hobart (*Muriel Carew*); Holmes Herbert (*Dr. Lanyon*); Halliwell Hobbes (*Sir*

Danvers Carew); Edgar Norton (*Poole*); Tempe Pigott (*Mrs. Hawkins*); Leonard Carey (*Briggs*); Sam Harris (*Party Guest*).

MOST MEMORABLE LINE
There are bounds beyond which man should not go.
DR. LANYON TO DR. JEKYLL

BACKGROUND
Scottish-born novelist Robert Louis Stevenson (1850–1894), while living in London during Victoria's reign (1837–1901), became increasingly aware of the inability of humans to follow the queen's dictates to repress a capacity for the evil resulting from what science identified as our animal origins. In *The Strange Case of Dr. Jekyll and Mr. Hyde* (1886), Stevenson, drawing on a late-night dream, produced a fable warning against such anti-sexual ambitions, soon to become known as Victorian values. The novella qualified as a mystery, saving the revelation of the wicked Hyde's identity—an alter ego for the good Jekyll—until the final page. In 1887, Thomas Russell Sullivan adapted the popular book for the stage, the play becoming a huge hit in Boston and London. Knowing that all who attended would be aware of the twist ending, he wisely redesigned the narrative as a suspense story. The dual identity is immediately revealed to the viewer, though the other characters onstage do not suspect.

THE PLOT
Altruistic Dr. Henry Jekyll, hoping to transform himself from a decent person into a perfect one, concocts a potion that he believes will eliminate lust from his psyche. Instead, the process frees his dark side, which takes the form of Edward Hyde, a street thug, rapist, and eventual killer. As Hyde, the central character pursues a relationship with prostitute Ivy Pearson, which Jekyll, dedicated to his elegant fiancée Muriel, had refused, then repressed.

THE FILM
By the time director Rouben Mamoulian (1897–1987) set to work on his interpretation of the Stevenson classic, early sound-era limitations—including confining blimps over the camera that restricted movement and primitive microphones hidden in flower vases—had given way to state-of-the-art equipment. The camera could move again, and, as had been the case during silent cinema, the editor could once again cut from long shots to close-ups for emotional impact, lending a remarkable fluidity to this, the greatest film version

OF MEN AND MONKEYS: *In a unique version of the Robert Louis Stevenson tale that was clearly influenced by the then-current interest in Darwinism, Dr. Jekyll transforms into the bestial Mr. Hyde (Fredric March in both roles), who menaces prostitute Ivy (Miriam Hopkins). Courtesy: Paramount Pictures.*

of Stevenson's tale. As early as 1929, the genius Mamoulian had attempted to return creativity to what had become a stilted medium when he mounted the first truly great screen musical, *Applause*—not merely a filmed record of a stage show but a cinematic vision in which the camera is employed to tell, rather than document, the story.

For the transformation sequences in *Dr. Jekyll and Mr. Hyde*, Mamoulian and his team relied on time-lapse photography—at the time, a state-of-the-art technology. Various shades of color makeup were applied to Fredric March's face, each stage filmed with cameras augmented by matching color filters. In this way, Mamoulian visualized, rather than merely implied, the manner in which a normal man realizes he is, against his will, succumbing to the beast within. Perhaps more impressive still, the director guided his team to create the first sophisticated sound mix. They recorded a heart beating and modulated the volume, never before possible. The collaborators dropped tanks of water and recorded the sound of their breaking; this, when sound played backward created the original synthetic soundtrack. Their experiments would influence not only movie soundtracks but also recorded music for the newly popular discs.

THEME

Like other intellectuals of the time, Mamoulian studied the theory of evolution, particularly after the widely publicized Scopes Monkey Trial of 1925. By broadcasting the trial nationwide over radio from the small town of Dayton, Tennessee, the media inadvertently educated the public about evolution, fueling debate. Recalling that the 1920 film version of *Jekyll and Hyde*, starring John Barrymore, had been rethought as an entertaining argument in favor of Prohibition (Jekyll becomes Hyde after getting drunk, the film a warning about liquor's dangerous consequences), Mamoulian wondered if he could retell Stevenson's tale as an objective correlative for Darwinism. Mamoulian and makeup artist Wally Westmore collaborated on a simian Hyde, a far cry from the small, yellow-and-green creature in Stevenson's novella. In this film version, the scientific potion releases the ape in Dr. Jekyll and, by implication, all of us.

TRIVIA

Fredric March won an Oscar in 1932 for his performance in *Dr. Jekyll and Mr. Hyde*. This is the only time in Hollywood history that an actor received the Academy Award for a role in a science-fiction/horror film.

In 1941, Victor Fleming mounted a remake starring Spencer Tracy. As influenced by Sigmund Freud's theories on the human psyche as Mamoulian had been by the writings of Darwin, Fleming had Tracy play Hyde with the least amount of makeup, suggesting that the transformation takes place entirely in the human mind. This approach set the pace for thrillers, ranging from *Fight Club* (David Fincher, 1999) to *Inception* (Christopher Nolan, 2010), that present a post-modernist depiction of all reality as existing in the mind.

· · · · · · ·

ISLAND OF LOST SOULS (1932)

—— RANKING: 51 ——

CREDITS

Paramount Pictures; Erle C. Kenton, dir.; H. G. Wells, novel; Waldemar Young, Philip Wylie, scr.; Karl Struss, cin.; Sigmund Krumgold, mus.; Hans Dreier, art dir.; Wally Westmore, monster makeup; Gordon Jennings, visual/optical effects; 70 min.; B&W; 1.33:1.

CAST

Charles Laughton (*Dr. Moreau*); Richard Arlen (*Edward Parker*); Leila Hyams (*Ruth Thomas*); Bela Lugosi (*Sayer of the Law*); Kathleen Burke (*The Panther Woman/Lota*); Arthur Hohl (*Mr. Montgomery*); Stanley Fields (*Captain Davies*).

MOST MEMORABLE LINE

Not men . . . not beasts . . . *t'ings* . . . half-man . . . half-beast . . . *t'ings!*
SAYER OF THE LAW

BACKGROUND

As a child, Herbert George Wells (1866–1946) hardly seemed destined to become known as a writer of genius. His impoverished family lived in a small, out-of-the-way hamlet in Kent County, England. When Wells broke his leg, his father, a freethinker, brought home library books, which the boy devoured. Later, while working as a humble draper's assistant, Wells came across Thomas More's *Utopia* (1516), with its promise of a perfect future world realized through slow, gradual, constant progress. The aspiring writer deeply wanted to believe in such a hopeful and hoped-for future, initially perceiving that the rapidly

"HIS IS THE HOUSE OF PAIN": *The misguided but sympathetic scientist Dr. Moreau of H. G. Wells's novel is transformed into a smirking villain by Charles Laughton (far left). Here Dr. Moreau taunts his half-human, half-animal creations, including Bela Lugosi (first in the second row from top) as the Sayer of the Law. Courtesy: Paramount Pictures.*

developing concept called "science" would prove a modern means to that end. However, he soon began to doubt such a glorious scenario, considering the many excesses and failures resulting from the age-old flaw of ego in scientists, and he came to fear that precisely the opposite might occur. Here was born the notion of a dystopian future that would haunt his books, including *The Island of Doctor Moreau* (1896).

THE PLOT

Dumped on a remote island by the alcoholic captain of a tramp steamer, Edward Parker finds himself a prisoner of Dr. Moreau. The scientist conducts strange experiments on animals in his laboratory late at night, and various beast-like things crawl about in the nearby jungle. Parker finds himself falling under the spell of the exotic Lota, whom he believes to be a native girl. Ultimately, Parker grasps that she's a hybrid, half-human and half-panther. Concerned for his well-being, Ruth Thomas, his fiancée, searches the South Seas, finally arriving at Moreau's island. She comes face to face with both the beast-woman, who wants Parker for her own, and the white-suited, whip-wielding, ever-sneering, diabolical Moreau.

THE FILM

Following the success of *Frankenstein*, every studio wanted to produce a similar film. At Paramount, Waldemar Young (1878–1938) was assigned the task of adapting Wells's book to the screen and adding beautiful women, allowing for the Hollywood convention of the romantic triangle. Edging *Island* ever more into line with conventional adventure, romance, and horror, collaborator Philip Gordon Wylie (1902–1971) also fought to salvage the science-fiction aspect of Wells's work. At that time, numerous scientist-surgeons practiced the controversial process of vivisection. The impact of this film turned the public tide against such "progressive" experimentation.

This was the third film, and first talkie, for director Erle C. Kenton (1896–1980), who wisely studied the Expressionistic set designs of Universal's genre films. Though his career was largely undistinguished, Kenton would gravitate to Laemmle's studio and oversee their final generic sci-fi/horror entries, *House of Frankenstein* (1944) and *House of Dracula* (1945). Many fans argue that the overpowering, eerie atmosphere in *Island* should be credited to Oscar-winning Karl Struss (1886–1981), who had also been the cinematographer for Universal's *Dr. Jekyll and Mr. Hyde* a year earlier.

THEME

Despite this film's excellence as a thriller, Wells rejected it as a betrayal of his intention. Charles Laughton seized the opportunity to turn Moreau into a simplistic fiend. Wells, however, had written the character as far closer to Dr. Frankenstein, caught in the classic tragic paradigm of a good man who does bad things, sincerely hoping to improve humankind's lot, but, overcome by his dark side, inadvertently doing the opposite. Moreau's "Do you know what it means to feel like God?" echoes Frankenstein's "Now I know what it feels like to be God!" Moreau's awareness of his identity as a villain, however effective onscreen, is a betrayal of the film's literary source.

TRIVIA

No one has been able to confirm (or deny) their presence, but future stars Randolph Scott, Alan Ladd, and Buster Crabbe are all supposedly on camera playing "t'ings." Kathleen Burke, an unknown, was picked by the public in a "You Choose the Panther Girl!" contest.

The Island of Dr. Moreau (Don Taylor, 1977) came closer to Wells's vision, owing to a more sympathetic depiction of the title character by Burt Lancaster. However, that ambitious movie failed because of the mediocre-at-best director's inability to create excitement and tension. The 1996 version, directed, then repudiated, by the great John Frankenheimer, is perhaps best left unmentioned.

· · · · · · ·

MURDERS IN THE RUE MORGUE (1932) AND THE BLACK CAT (1934)

—— RANKING: 55 (TIE) ——

MURDERS IN THE RUE MORGUE (1932)

CREDITS
Universal Pictures; Robert Florey, dir.; Edgar Allen Poe, story; Florey, Tom Reed, Dale Van Every, John Huston, scr.; E. M. Asher, Carl Laemmle Jr., pro.; Karl Freund, cin.; Milton Carruth, ed.; Charles D. Hall, art dir.; Jack P. Pierce, makeup; Herman Rosse, set design; John P. Fulton, F/X; 61 min.; B&W; 1.37:1.

CAST
Bela Lugosi (*Dr. Mirakle*); Sidney Fox (*Mlle. Camille L'Espanaye*); Leon Waycoff Ames (*Pierre Dupin*); Bert Roach (*Paul*); Betty Ross Clarke (*Mme. L'Espanaye*); Brandon Hurst (*Prefect of Police*); D'Arcy Corrigan (*Morgue Keeper*); Noble Johnson (*Janos*); Arlene Francis (*Prostitute*); Ted Billings (*Sideshow Spectator*); Herman Bing (*Franz*); Charlotte Henry (*Blonde*); Charles Gemora (*The Gorilla*).

MOST MEMORABLE LINE
Do they still burn men for heresy? Then burn me!
DR. MIRAKLE

BACKGROUND
Carl Laemmle Jr. continued to believe that Bela Lugosi might yet emerge as a great star of the horror genre. The actor had appeared in a small role in *Island*

THE BONDAGE MOTIF: *Images and ideas that would not have been acceptable in more realistic films during the Production Code era escaped the wrath of censors when contained in sci-fi and horror films. Here, Bela Lugosi (left) and Noble Johnson sadomasochistically torture (under the guise of scientific experimentation) Arlene Francis. Courtesy: Universal.*

of Lost Souls and was working for Poverty Row companies. Laemmle decided to produce an adaptation of a short story by Edgar Allan Poe (1809–1849). In the hands of Robert Florey (1900–1979), who all but invented the notion of "noir," the narrative leaned less on the motifs of monster movies than on emergent sci-fi ideas dating back at least to Shelley's novel, *Frankenstein.*

THE PLOT

Paris, 1841: sideshow performer Dr. Mirakle displays his ape to gawking crowds, insisting that mankind has evolved from such primates. Mirakle cackles at the ignorance of the audience, then returns to his lair. There, he—secretly, a mad scientist—plans to mate his ape with a human to create a contemporary version of the missing link.

THE FILM

Cinematographer Karl Freund (1890–1969) had learned the art of the fantastical image while collaborating with Fritz Lang on *Metropolis*. At Universal, he had added the edgy shadow world imagery to *Dracula*. For *Murders*, Freund worked closely with Paris-born Florey, who, as a child, had been fascinated by the exaggerated worlds of Georges Méliès's phantasmagoric pieces. The team drew heavily from *The Cabinet of Dr. Caligari* (1920), the first of the great Weimar films, including in *Murders* the device of a sideshow performer who lives a secret second life, sending his monstrous captive to abduct a beautiful woman.

THEME

Early in the story, a streetwalker becomes a victim of the doctor. This allows for a bondage sequence, among the first of many employed by Universal as its horror/sci-fi output became ever more notorious. Social conservatives complained about the overt sadomasochism as Mirakle takes cruel delight in torturing the frightened girl. His experiment fails when her lack of virginity causes the prostitute to die rather than transform. The concept of purity and innocence qualifying a female as the "final girl" who survives would reappear in such later thrillers as *Halloween* (John Carpenter, 1978). All these ideas would be further developed in 1934 in a follow-up film, *The Black Cat*.

TRIVIA

The word "evolution" is heard often in the film. However, Charles Darwin's use of the term did not appear until 1859, eighteen years after this tale takes place. Such anachronism cinches the importance of ideas raised by a period picture that relates less to the historical setting than to the zeitgeist in which the film was designed. The fantastical romantic adventure (but not sci-fi) *King Kong* (1933) would most likely not have been made at all if man-and-monkey relationships had not just been brought into the national discourse.

THE BLACK CAT (1934)

CREDITS

Universal Pictures; Edgar G. Ulmer, dir.; Edgar Allen Poe, story; Ulmer, Peter Ruric, Tom Kilpatrick, scr.; E. M. Asher, pro.; Heinz Roemheld, mus.; John J. Mescall, cin.; Ray Curtiss, ed.; Charles D. Hall, art dir.; Ulmer, costumes, set design; John P. Fulton, David S. Horsley, visual effects; Jack Cosgrove, Russell Lawson, matte art; 65 min.; B&W; 1.37:1.

WHEN DRACULA MET FRANKENSTEIN: *The two men who emerged as towering stars of* cinéma fantastique *during the early 1930s were regularly teamed: here, good guy Lugosi confronts evil scientist Karloff as to the morality of keeping Hitchcock-like blondes in a state of suspended animation. Courtesy: Universal.*

CAST

Bela Lugosi (*Dr. Vitus Werdegast*); Boris Karloff (*Hjalmar Poelzig*); David Manners (*Peter Alison*); Julie Bishop (as Jacqueline Wells) (*Joan Alison*); Egon Brecher (*Majordomo*); Harry Cording (*Thamal*); Lucille Lund (*Karen*); Henry Armetta (*The Sergeant*); Albert Conti (*The Lieutenant*); John Carradine (*Organist at Black Mass*); Symona Boniface (*Cultist*).

MOST MEMORABLE LINE

Are we not both the living dead?
POELZIG TO WERDEGAST

BACKGROUND

Most Universal executives believed that Lugosi as Dracula and Karloff as Frankenstein covered the terrain of terror. Laemmle thought otherwise, now planning to co-star the two performers. Owing to the success of *Murders*, the Poe connection would continue, this time with a considerably looser adaptation of another tale. The approach combined a bizarre modern Gothic with the sort of experimental research that qualifies this, like *Murders*, as science fiction. That Poelzig is also the head of a devil-worshipping cult furthers the emerging connection between the mad scientist and the supernatural satanist as horror and sci-fi collapse into one another.

THE PLOT

While traveling by train through Hungary on their honeymoon, Joan and Peter Alison meet mysterious Vitus Werdegast, a man of vast knowledge. The naive couple learns that, after fifteen years in prison, this kindly if strange fellow will soon confront his archrival, Hjalmar Poelzig, who inhabits Fort Marmorus, a ruined citadel. Poelzig keeps Werdegast's onetime wife forever beautiful via a state of suspended animation, chastely sharing his bed with Werdegast's virginal daughter. During a dark and stormy night (that old chestnut of a plot device employed with great effectiveness here), the young people find themselves boarded up in this evil place as the mad geniuses duel to the death.

THE FILM

Produced for less than $100,000, the typical cost of Universal's program pictures, the film surprised all expectations by grossing close to $250,000. This assured that shockers would remain a studio staple. The use of Ludwig van Beethoven's Symphony no. 7, second movement, throughout the Grand Guignol happenings presages the use of classical music in Stanley Kubrick's *A Clockwork Orange* (1971).

Director Edgar G. Ulmer (1904–1972) had designed horrific sets for Paul Wegener's silent German masterwork, *The Golem* (1920). Though Ulmer borrowed the name of an actual architect for Poelzig, he insisted that the character was modeled after Fritz Lang, known for his sadistic treatment of actors and crew. Critics admired Ulmer's use of chiaroscuro lighting effects and shadow play, as well as a directorial approach best described, at least in retrospect, as what Susan Sontag defined in the mid-sixties as "camp."

TRIVIA

Poe would provide the source for *The Raven* (Lew Landers, 1935), also co-starring Karloff and Lugosi. Another horror/sci-fi blend, *The Invisible Ray* (Lambert Hillyer, 1936), would be among the six Universal films in which they would team, additionally pairing in two films for other studios.

· · · · · · ·

THE INVISIBLE MAN (1933)

—— RANKING: 15 ——

CREDITS

Universal Pictures; James Whale, dir.; H. G. Wells, novel; R. C. Sherriff, Preston Sturges, Philip Wylie, scr.; Carl Laemmle Jr., pro.; Heinz Roemheld, W. Franke Harling, Gilbert Kurland, mus.; Arthur Edeson, cin.; Ted J. Kent, Maurice Pivar, ed.; Charles D. Hall, art dir.; Jack P. Pierce, makeup; John P. Fulton, F/X; Roswell A. Hoffmann, John J. Mescall, Frank D. Williams, special visual effects; 71 min.; B&W; 1.37:1.

CAST

Claude Rains (*Dr. Jack Griffin/The Invisible Man*); Gloria Stuart (*Flora Cranley*); William Harrigan (*Dr. Arthur Kemp*); Henry Travers (*Dr. Cranley*); Una O'Connor (*Jenny Hall*); Forrester Harvey (*Herbert Hall*); Holmes Herbert (*Police Chief*); E. E. Clive (*Constable Jaffers*); Dudley Digges, Harry Stubbs, Donald Stuart, Robert Adair (*Inspectors*); Merle Tottenham (*Millie*); Ted Billings, John Carradine (*Villagers*); Walter Brennan (*Man with Bicycle*); Dwight Frye (*Reporter*).

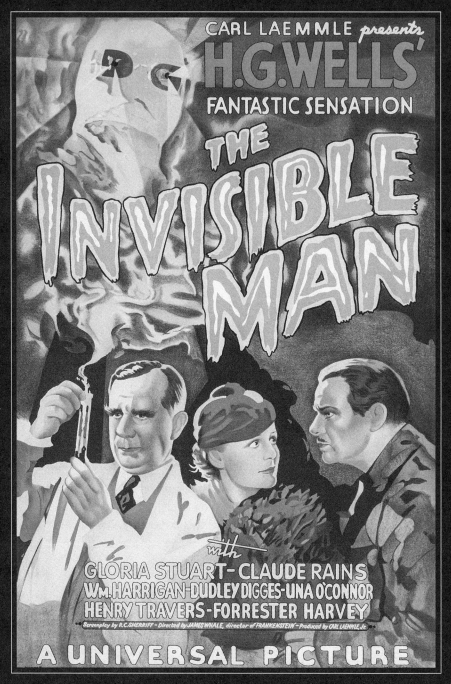

CARL LAEMMLE *presents*

H.G. WELLS'

FANTASTIC SENSATION

THE INVISIBLE MAN

with

GLORIA STUART · CLAUDE RAINS
WM. HARRIGAN · DUDLEY DIGGES · UNA O'CONNOR
HENRY TRAVERS · FORRESTER HARVEY
Screenplay by R.C. SHERRIFF · Directed by JAMES WHALE, director of FRANKENSTEIN · Produced by CARL LAEMMLE, Jr.

A UNIVERSAL PICTURE

IT CAME FROM BEYOND THE TEST TUBE: *Like so many sci-fi films of the early 1930s, James Whale's adaptation of the H. G. Wells tale offered a chilling horror story that derives from a scientist's noble but doomed effort to perfect the world by playing God. Courtesy: Universal.*

MOST MEMORABLE LINE
I meddled in things that man must leave alone.
GRIFFIN TO FLORA

BACKGROUND
In 1928, Carl Laemmle Jr. (1908–1979) initially assumed control of Universal Pictures from his father, a German-Jewish immigrant who had founded the studio after arriving in New York. The last item on the son's game plan had been horror pictures. Universal, one of the four largest filmmaking companies in Hollywood, would be monitored by "Junior," who intended that the studio be viewed as a prestige place where top quality works were produced. These included *All Quiet on the Western Front* (1930), a World War I epic that won the Academy Award for Best Picture. However, the creation of a large-scale European town on the backlot for that ambitious project had drained much of the studio's profit margin. Meanwhile, the Depression hit the country and Hollywood—hard! To save on expenses, Laemmle, a problem solver of the first order, shot tightly budgeted science-fiction/supernatural B movies on that vast European town standing set. *Dracula* (1931), *Frankenstein* (1931), and *The Black Cat* (1934) collectively earned such impressively large profits that Junior was able to create a compromise between horror and "important" projects, hiring esteemed English actor Claude Rains for the more upscale *The Invisible Man*.

THE PLOT
During the dead of winter, Jack Griffin steps out of the snow and into the warmth of a remote Sussex inn. Everyone is shocked at the sight of his completely bandaged face. He wears a pair of thick black glasses through which he intensely stares at them. The horrified woman in charge agrees to let him a room. There, the lodger sets up scientific equipment and begins a series of bizarre experiments involving his recently developed drug, monocane. When Griffin creates chaos at the place and is ordered to leave, he reveals himself to be invisible and, as it turns out, insane. Proceeding on a murderous rampage, he tries to force a fellow doctor to help him take over the world, all the while defying Dr. Cranley, his well-meaning mentor. When Flora, the great love of Griffin's life, begs him to surrender to authorities, the Invisible Man laughs at the thought and runs off, howling, "The whole world is my hiding place."

THE FILM
The original screenwriter, Preston Sturges (1898–1959), had a series of outrageous

ideas that Universal considered to be brilliant but far too weird for this project. Sturges was dropped from the film and shortly moved on to writing and/or directing a series of remarkable oddball comedies, including *Sullivan's Travels* (1941). R. C. Sherriff (1896–1975) replaced him and made the decision to adhere closely to H. G. Wells's 1897 novel. This resulted in a far more faithful adaptation of the original than had been the case with either *Dracula* or *Frankenstein*.

Touches of James Whale's strange humor gave the film a black comedy "signature" style, which was also effectively displayed in his earlier film, *The Old Dark House* (1932). In particular, Una O'Connor's shrill hysteria, Dwight Frye's evil eyes, and John Carradine's supremely sardonic voice added to the unconventional nature of the film. The studio's "attitude" would evolve toward such offbeat subjects, which would become a significant part of Universal's cinematic heritage. However intense individual works might be as thrillers, a tongue-in-cheek quality—sometimes subtle, occasionally over the top—always undercut the horror, with purposefully offbeat characters always appearing on the sidelines to steal scenes and engage audiences.

The contribution of Jack P. Pierce (1889–1968), a native of Greece who accidentally made his way into the film business, cannot be overstated. He developed the makeup concepts for *Dracula*, *Frankenstein*, and *The Bride of Frankenstein*, and in *The Invisible Man*, he brought Wells's suggested appearance of the demented doctor to life onscreen. He would later provide makeup for both *Frankenstein Meets the Wolf Man* (1943) and a sound remake of *Phantom of the Opera* (1943), also starring Claude Rains.

THEME

Once again, the science-fiction genre is used to convey a cautionary fable. The doctor's good intentions in creating monocane have negative implications when the drug drives him mad. Though the Wells novel may be speculative fantasy, many of the wonder drugs that would eventually be developed did turn out to have unexpected side effects.

TRIVIA

A once-obscure actor, Boris Karloff achieved fame only after Bela Lugosi turned down the role of the Frankenstein monster because of the lack of dialogue. Karloff, in turn, refused *The Invisible Man* because he wouldn't be seen until the final moments of the film.

Gloria Stuart worked regularly as an ingenue beginning in 1932, but she would not achieve her greatest fame until 1997 when she played "Old Rose" in *Titanic*.

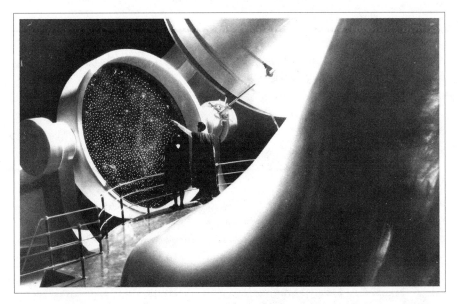

BEYOND INFINITY: *Denizens of the future peek at faraway worlds into which humankind will indeed journey. Director Menzies purposefully dwarfed his image's human element while offering a perhaps surprising sense of enclosure. This provides a visual representation of Wells's philosophy: no matter how great our conquests, it would prove disastrous for scientists to suffer from the seduction of hubris. Courtesy: London Film Productions.*

• • • • • • •

THINGS TO COME (1936)

—— RANKING: 18 ——

CREDITS

London Film Productions; William Cameron Menzies, dir.; H. G. Wells, novel and scr.; Alexander Korda, pro.; Arthur Bliss, Muir Mathieson, mus.; Georges Périnal, cin.; Charles Crichton, Francis D. Lyon, William Hornbeck. ed.; John Armstrong, René Hubert, Cathleen Mann, costumes; Vincent Korda, set/art design; Lawrence W. Butler, Edward Cohen, Ned Mann, F/X; Jack Cardiff, special visual effects; Cardiff, Robert Krasker, special camera effects; 117 min. (U.K.), 92 min. (U.S.); B&W; 1.37:1.

CAST

Raymond Massey (*John Cabal/Oswald Cabal*); Edward Chapman (*Pippa Passworthy/Raymond Passworthy*); Ralph Richardson (*The Boss*); Margaretta Scott (as Margueretta Scott) (*Roxana/Rowena*); Cedric Hardwicke (*Theotocopulos*); Maurice Braddell (*Dr. Harding*); Sophie Stewart (*Mrs. Cabal*); Derrick De Marney (*Richard Gordon*); Ann Todd (*Mary Gordon*); Pearl Argyle (*Catherine Cabal*); Kenneth Villiers (*Maurice Passworthy*).

MOST MEMORABLE LINE
All the universe or nothing: which shall it be?
OSWALD CABAL'S FINAL LINE

BACKGROUND
Like many of H. G. Wells's books, *The Shape of Things to Come* (1933) is related not in any traditional narrative manner but by the author himself. The literary conceit is that Wells stumbled upon a diary of dreams, written by a great intellectual who had visions about a history text written in 2106. The information foretells World War II and predicts that the conflict will rage for decades. Influenced by such authors as Friedrich Engels, Edward Bellamy, and Rudyard Kipling, the father of modern sci-fi predicted the key to the future would be aeronautics. Politically, Wells believed that a benign dictatorship might provide the solution to global conflict. With religion abolished and after much Sturm und Drang, a utopia would be established in which humankind reaches the level of the Greek gods in ancient mythology.

THE PLOT
During Christmas season, 1940, John Cabal of Everytown cannot enjoy the festivities, sensing that war is about to erupt. After a Blitz-like attack on England, followed by an onslaught of ongoing violence, humankind descends into a primitive state, including a plague called the "Wandering Sickness." In 1970, John and other intellectuals form Wings Over the World, a unified power that outlaws war by eliminating such barbaric local tribal leaders as The Boss. Yet, in the twenty-first century, when a descendant, Oswald Cabal, prepares to launch a rocket around the moon, the conservative artist Theotocopulos stages a grassroots revolution to forever end liberalism and progress.

THE FILM
Released three years after the book's publication, the film was altered to align Wells's original concept with the many radical changes that had overtaken the globe in the interim. The film's vision owes less to Wells's novel than to a nonfiction book he published in 1931, *The Work, Wealth and Happiness of Mankind*.

Alexander Korda and William Cameron Menzies hoped that their unique work would offer a blend of an allegorical, almost fairy-tale approach with a lean and clean design for the next century. They rejected such "decadent" popular art movements as deco and nouveau in favor of a no-nonsense modern look that would suggest socialism.

For the lengthy, wordless mid-section of the film, which depicts humans' Phoenix-like rise from futuristic dark ages to a highly advanced civilization, Korda and Menzies hired László Moholy-Nagy, the Hungarian artist who had made a reputation as an early proponent of the abstract movement.

THEME

Wells's guarded optimism, which some observers dismiss as Pollyanna-ish, overrides the horrific events portrayed. Despite the terrors of social collapse, his abiding sense was that humans could come back from any diminished existence as more powerful, and progressive, than ever. More heightened in the film than in the novel is Wells's antiwar attitude, which in 1936 England proved a greater threat than it had three years earlier when the book was published. Though a huge supporter of science and progress, the character, John Cabal, Wells's mouthpiece in the early scenes, bridles at the thought that, during times of war, technological progress will make huge leaps and bounds. Wells insisted that, even if there is a germ of truth to that, technological progress is not worth such a sacrifice. He was typical of most sci-fi writers of his era; it was not until after World War II that pessimistic dystopian views prevailed, though certainly some of Wells's more embittered work provides the template for such darker visions.

TRIVIA

Certainly, Wells considered himself a liberal, yet elements of his philosophy— such as the necessity of English becoming the globe's universal language—do not play well with liberal-minded people of today. His insistence that all local customs end if humankind is to emerge as a unified and peaceful race grates against our concepts of multi-culturalism.

He conceived of this project as an answer to and rejection of the Fritz Lang film *Metropolis* (1927), which Wells had seen and despised. In truth, the implications for a happy future presented here offer a total repudiation of the resolution in Lang's film. Wells wrote the script himself to avoid the disappointment he experienced with *Island of Lost Souls* (1932).

"HELLO, I'M FROM PLANET EARTH": *Buster Crabbe (second from left) vividly embodied Alex Raymond's comic book "space cowboy." The retro-future is present in the costuming of an alien leader in King Arthur armor, backed up by robot-like predecessors of George Lucas's stormtroopers. Courtesy: Universal.*

· · · · · · ·

FLASH GORDON (1936), FLASH GORDON'S TRIP TO MARS (1938), AND FLASH GORDON CONQUERS THE UNIVERSE (1940)

—— RANKING: 70 (THREE-WAY TIE) ——

FLASH GORDON (1936)

CREDITS

Universal Pictures; Frederick Stephani, Ray Taylor, dir.; Alex Raymond, comic strip, Stephani, Ella O'Neill, George H. Plympton, Basil Dickey, scr.; Henry Mac-Rae, pro.; Clifford Vaughan, mus.; Jerome Ash, Richard Fryer, cin.; Saul A. Goodkind, Louis Sackin, Alvin Todd, Edward Todd, ed.; Ralph Berger, art dir.; Ed Keyes, F/X; 13 chapters; 245 min.; B&W; 1.37:1.

CAST

Buster Crabbe (*Flash Gordon*); Jean Rogers (*Dale Arden*); Charles Middleton (*Ming the Merciless*); Priscilla Lawson (*Princess Aura*); Frank Shannon (*Dr. Alexis Zarkov*); Richard Alexander (*Prince Barin*); Jack "Tiny" Lipson (*King Vultan*); Theodore Lorch (*High Priest*); Richard Tucker (*Prof. Gordon*); Duke York (*King Kala*); Muriel Goodspeed (*Zona*); Earl Askam (*Officer Torch*); Carroll Borland (*Ming's Mistress*); Ray "Crash" Corrigan (*Orangopoid*).

MOST MEMORABLE LINE

He fights well, the Earth man.
PRINCESS AURA, TO HER FATHER, WHILE OGLING FLASH IN COMBAT

BACKGROUND

In 1928, the pulp magazine *Amazing Stories* published *Armageddon 2419 A.D.*, by Philip Francis Nowlan. The novella, about space-traveling hero Anthony Rogers, caught the attention of a National Newspaper Syndicate editor who was in search of something different for his Sunday color comics. Nowlan was matched with illustrator Richard Calkins to create a weekly comic titled *Buck Rogers in the 25th Century*. The strip's popularity did not go unnoticed at competing King Features. Alex Raymond, who had proven his flair with comics in such strips as *Tim Tyler's Luck* and *Jungle Jim*, came on board to produce a competing tale. Any fear that theirs would be dismissed as a second-rate imitation diminished when *Flash Gordon* emerged as the more popular of the two, owing to elaborate plot twists and breathtaking panels. These recreated the future in the image of the past, all the grand fantasy icons from Robin Hood in Sherwood Forest to Cleopatra in Egypt coming together in a pop culture–fantasy mélange driven by a sci-fi element, space travel.

THE PLOT

Young Flash Gordon is concerned when a heavenly body rushes toward Earth, causing international panic. During the confusion, he bumps into an emancipated "modern girl" named Dale Arden. Shortly, the two lovebirds encounter eccentric Dr. Zarkov, who has built a rocket ship and plans to stop any oncoming collision. The adventurous pair joins him and finds themselves on planet Mongo, ruled by ruthless Ming and his beautiful but wicked daughter, Aura.

THE FILM

Movie serials had been around since silent films when cliffhangers such as

The Perils of Pauline (1914) were produced with adult audiences in mind. With the advent of sound, studios churned out kiddie features that, along with cartoons and *Our Gang* shorts, screened at Saturday morning special showings. Universal, then moving from a minor to a major studio, wanted its serial to be the most spectacular. The studio produced the *Flash* chapter play on a then-immense $360,000 budget.

THEME

Though presented as escapist entertainment, *Flash Gordon* did convey an unintended theme. Ming and his daughter are spaced-out versions of the evil Dr. Fu Manchu and his luscious though lethal offspring, Su Maru. Films and other popular culture objects from the early twentieth century were filled with ethnic stereotypes; Asians were consistently portrayed as amoral and manipulative, secretively plotting world domination.

TRIVIA

In 1939, Buster Crabbe took time off between the second and third *Flash* serials to star as Buck Rogers. A former Olympic swimmer, Crabbe turned to films as a beefcake star. Flash's battle with the Orangopoid pits Crabbe against Ray "Crash" Corrigan, an athlete turned stuntman.

FLASH GORDON'S TRIP TO MARS (1938)

ADDITIONAL/ALTERED CREDITS

Ford Beebe, Robert F. Hill, dir.; Ray Trampe, Norman S. Hall, Wyndham Gittens, Herbert Dalmas, scr.; Barney A. Sarecky, pro.; Joseph Gluck, Saul A. Goodkind, Louis Sackin, ed.; Ralph M. DeLacy, art dir.; M. Berneman, costumes; Ed Keyes, F/X; Tom Steele, stunt double; 15 chapters; 312 min.; B&W; 1.37:1.

ADDITIONAL/ALTERED CAST

Beatrice Roberts (*Queen Azura*); Donald Kerr (*Happy Hapgood*); Richard Alexander (*Prince Barin*); C. Montague Shaw (*Clay King*); Wheeler Oakman (*Tarnak*); Kenne Duncan (*Airdrome Captain*); Anthony Warde (*King Turan of the Forest People*).

MOST MEMORABLE LINE

Take the Earth man to the disintegrating room.
MING, ORDERING THE HERO'S DEATH AS A SCIENTIFIC EXPERIMENT

ROBIN HOOD IN SPACE: *As the highly popular trilogy of cliffhangers continued, Flash (Buster Crabbe, second from right) adjusted to the retro-future fashions. The series came to embody what social critic Susan Sontag would in time tag as "camp": lowbrow junk movies that become a beloved and ongoing part of popular culture owing to a "so bad they're good" aspect. Courtesy: Universal.*

THE PLOT

Somehow, madman Ming escapes from what appeared to be imminent death at the first serial's conclusion. He now directs a death ray from Mars toward our planet. The intrepid space explorers embark again, hoping to reason with the Red Planet's beautiful but aloof queen, Azura, who is Ming's confederate. Azura's minions pursue the astronauts into a cave where they encounter refugee members of the rebel forces who have been absorbed into the walls and are now half flesh, half clay.

THEME

The second serial emphasized an erotic element introduced in the original, with space maidens parading about in costumes that would have been considered unfit by censors for any story set in the present (ancient epics and futuristic fantasies always managed to survive the censors owing to their other-worldly aura). Flash and Dale are tied up and sadomasochistically tortured, she nearly molested by Ming, a lecher with eyes for the Earth woman. While the theme of a scantily clad dominatrix, drawn from pagan civilizations, had been presented on film as early as Méliès's turn-of-the-century experimental films, here that image reached full fruition with Azura. This would be revived during the 1950s for such B movies as *Cat-Women of the Moon* (Arthur Hilton, 1953), *Fire Maidens of Outer Space* (Cy Roth, 1956), and *Queen of Outer Space* (Edward Bernds, 1958).

TRIVIA

The classy musical score was borrowed from more upscale, adult-oriented Universal horror/sci-fi thrillers such as *The Invisible Man* (1933) and *The Bride of Frankenstein* (1935).

FLASH GORDON CONQUERS THE UNIVERSE (1940)

ADDITIONAL/ALTERED CREDITS

Barry Shipman, scr.; William A. Sickner, cin.; Harold H. MacArthur, art dir.; 220 min.; B&W; 1.37:1.

ADDITIONAL/ALTERED CAST

Carol Hughes (*Dale*); Anne Gwynne (*Lady Sonja*); John Hamilton (*Prof. Gordon*); Herbert Rawlinson (*Dr. Frohmann*); Tom Chatterton (*Prof. Arden*); Shirley Deane (*Princess Aura*); Lee Powell (*Capt. Roka*); Roland Drew (*Prince Barin*); Mimi Taylor (*Verna*); Jean Brooks (*Olga, Blonde Space Soldier*); Luli Deste (*Queen Fria*); Mala (*Prince of the Rock People*).

MOST MEMORABLE LINE

With Ming at last dead, Flash Gordon conquers the universe!
DR. ZARKOV, FINAL LINE

THE PLOT

Ming is up to his old tricks again, this time employing the Purple Ray to decimate Earth. So it's off to Mongo once more for the fearless trio. Flash, Dale, and Dr. Zarkov visit a couple of old chums from earlier stories—Prince Barin of Arboria and Queen Fria of Frigia—and elicit their aid in conquering Ming.

THEME

However unintentionally or coincidentally, Ming appears more Asian than ever in *Flash Gordon Conquers the Universe*. Fans of the serial experienced, on December 7, 1941, a sense of déjà vu at the destruction at Pearl Harbor by what popular culture had long portrayed as the "Yellow Peril." Once the United States entered World War II, all action films were enlisted in the war cause. Fantasies about wicked rulers, gorgeous beauties in lingerie-like outfits, and intrepid heroes gave way to contemporary Americans going up against the all-too-real Axis powers. The likes of Flash would not return until the early 1950s, when movie serials came roaring back.

TRIVIA

A combination of the new space program and UFO sightings brought sci-fi/ fantasy back into popularity in the early 1950s. Crabbe was hired to host a daily TV show on WOR in New York that featured his own earlier cliffhangers. Among those mesmerized kids watching Crabbe's series was George Lucas, who in the mid-1970s would attempt to secure the rights for a remake. When that proved to be too costly, he instead came up with his own similar space opera, *Star Wars*.

In 1954, *Flash* was adapted for TV as a weekly series by Joseph Zigman. The series starred Steve Holland, who proved unable to capture the wide-eyed innocence of Crabbe. Animated *Flash Gordon* series appeared in 1979, 1980, 1982, and 1996. The big-budget *Flash Gordon* (Mike Hodges, 1980) rendered outrageous the charming silliness of the original over-the-top film. With its disco-era sensibility and music by Queen, the film was a shrill, cynical, and smug disappointment. *Flesh Gordon* (1974), a soft-core porno project with surprisingly well-done F/X, perhaps comes closest of all later follow-ups to conveying the giddy fun of the original.

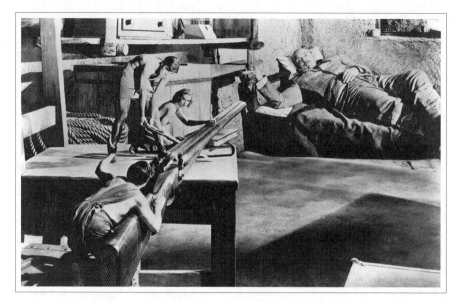

WHO SAYS SIZE DOESN'T MATTER? *Shrunken by the diabolical Dr. Thorkel, the intrepid band of scientists and adventurers strike back. This sequence predates many episodes of* The Twilight Zone *that, a generation later, would deal with precisely this theme. Courtesy: Paramount.*

· · · · · · ·

DR. CYCLOPS (1940)

—— RANKING: 87 ——

CREDITS

Paramount Pictures; Ernest B. Schoedsack, dir.; Tom Kilpatrick, Malcolm Stuart Boylan, scr.; Dale Van Every, Merian C. Cooper, pro.; Gerard Carbonara, Albert Hay Malotte, Ernst Toch, mus.; Henry Sharp, cin.; Ellsworth Hoagland, ed.; Hans Dreier, A. Earl Hedrick, Robert Odell, art dir.; Natalie Kalmus, Henri Jaffa (Technicolor), color art dir.; Farciot Edouart, Gordon Jennings, F/X; W. Wallace Kelley, process photography; Jan Domela, matte artist; Paul K. Lerpae, optical cin.; Winton C. Hoch, cinematic F/X; 77 min.; Color; 1.37:1.

CAST

Albert Dekker (*Dr. Alexander Thorkel*); Thomas Coley (*Bill Stockton*); Janice Logan (*Dr. Mary Robinson*); Charles Halton (*Dr. Bulfinch*); Victor Kilian (*Steve Baker*); Frank Yaconelli (*Pedro*); Paul Fix (*Dr. Mendoza*); Frank Reicher (*Prof. Kendall*).

Now, I can control life—*absolutely!*
DR. THORKEL

BACKGROUND
It's unlikely that Ernest Beaumont Schoedsack (1893–1979) of Council Bluffs, Iowa, would have found his way into movies if not for his assignment to the Signal Corps during the first World War. Following the armistice, he began work on highly acclaimed documentaries, including *Grass* (1925) and *Chang* (1927). Marriage to screenwriter Ruth Rose prompted Schoedsack to search for fictional vehicles that she might script while he maintained an interest in faraway lands, those lost worlds still existing on the globe. An old friend from the service, aviation pioneer Merian C. Cooper (1893–1973), was also working in Hollywood, planning an epic adventure for RKO. The three collaborated on *King Kong* (1933). Though science did not enter into the equation of that towering fantasy-adventure-romance, the team became ever more interested in incorporating the manner in which old superstitions could now be explained in technical terms.

THE PLOT
Deep in the Peruvian jungle, Dr. Alexander Thorkel secretly conducts tests on animals to determine whether radium might be employed to reduce the size of animate objects. When he moves from animals to humans and an assistant resists, Thorkel loses control and murders the man. Owing to his fast-fading eyesight, the now-mad doctor, realizing he needs expert assistance, summons two esteemed scientists, Robinson and Bulfinch. When they and their guides prove troublesome, Thorkel shrinks them.

THE FILM
Dr. Cyclops retains a major place in the history of sci-fi cinema as the first example of the genre to be filmed in color, however dated the processes may seem by today's standards. It was not, however, the first to be projected in such a manner: Georges Méliès, at the turn of the century, had hand-colored his strips of celluloid. Introduced in 1916, Technicolor, in its two-strip form, was used for a few horror films, *Mystery of the Wax Museum* (1933) most famous among them. Schoedsack, who had watched in fascination as three-strip Technicolor entered into the industry's color paradigm during the 1930s, believed that the ever-more advanced saturations, which eliminated the washed-out appearance of

earlier forms, would function well for his return to a *Kong*-like tale (and theme), if on a mini-movie budget this time, with science now all-important.

THEME

Standing more than 6'6", Schoedsack was very aware of his status as a giant among men. Some of his colleagues from that era suggest that the filmmaker's height may have motivated, at least unconsciously, his desire to approach this subject in his artistic endeavors. While many mad doctors were played by actors who were relatively modest in size, Albert Dekker (who had never before been associated with this genre) was selected for the role in part because of the similarity between his own bulky build and that of the director. Size, and a more complete understanding of this concept, owing to Einstein's theory of relativity, dominates here. "Strange how absorbed man has always been in the size of things," Thorkel says. After shrinking his visitors, the mad doctor adds: "Perhaps you are not small at all. Perhaps everything else is big." The film influenced then-budding author Richard Matheson, who would write *The Shrinking Man* (1956).

TRIVIA

Though never actually seen in full because of the tightly budgeted in-studio shoot, the great wall, built ages earlier by the Incas, around Dr. Thorkel's compound recalls the omnipresent one in *King Kong* (1933). Character actor Frank Reicher, who has a supporting role here, played the captain of the ill-fated ship in both *King Kong* and *Son of Kong* (1933); Schoedsack and Cooper considered him their "lucky charm."

This was not the first film to deal with radium as a great possible cure or a potential curse. The Universal Pictures B film *The Invisible Ray* (Lambert Hillyer, 1936) presented Boris Karloff as a scientist who is exposed to radiation while trying to create a universal panacea.

Dr. Cyclops received an Oscar nomination for Best Special Effects.

Despite this film's box office success, *Dr. Cyclops* did not, as expected, initiate a series of color sci-fi films in the 1940s. As a result of U.S. involvement in World War II, supposedly escapist moviemaking was largely set aside in favor of patriotic flag-waving films. The onset of the atomic age in the late 1940s initially led not to speculative fiction but to reality-based dramas, such as *The Beginning or the End* (Norman Taurog, 1947). Sci-fi/horror flicks with atomic themes flourished during the 1950s, culminating in *Beginning of the End* (Bert I. Gordon, 1957), not to be confused with the similarly titled docudrama of a decade earlier.

WRITING THE HISTORY OF THE FUTURE: *Opting for the purest form of science fiction, producer George Pal forsook any and all aspects of romance and adventure to create a docudrama-like depiction of our first manned flights to the moon and beyond. Courtesy: George Pal Productions.*

• • • • • • •

DESTINATION MOON (1950) AND CONQUEST OF SPACE (1955)

—— RANKING: 63 (TIE) ——

DESTINATION MOON (1950)

CREDITS

Eagle-Lion Films; Irving Pichel, dir.; Robert A. Heinlein, novel and scr.; James O'Hanlon, scr.; George Pal, pro.; Leith Stevens, mus.; Lionel Lindon, cin.; Duke Goldstone, ed.; Ernst Fegté, prod. design; Chesley Bonestell, astronomical art technical advisor; William H. Lynch, special sound effects; Lee Zavitz, F/X; Walter Lantz, Fred Madison, animation effects; 92 min.; Color; 1.37:1.

CAST

John Archer (*Jim Barnes*); Warner Anderson (*Dr. Charles Cargraves*); Tom Powers (*Gen. Thayer*); Dick Wesson (*Joe Sweeney*); Erin O'Brien-Moore (*Emily Cargraves*); Ted Warde (*Brown*); Franklyn Farnum (*Factory Worker*); Everett Glass (*Mr. La Porte*); Irving Pichel (*Cartoon Narrator*, voice).

MOST MEMORABLE LINE

Not only is this the greatest adventure facing mankind but it is also the greatest challenge facing American industry.

JIM BARNES, TO HIS COLLEAGUES

BACKGROUND

In 1949, scientist Willy Ley's *The Conquest of Space* was published with non-fantastic illustrations by Chesley Bonestell. The book provided inspiration for both "science-fact" films produced by George Pal (1908–1980).

Missouri-born Robert A. Heinlein (1907–1988) left his Bible Belt background to join the U.S. Navy. He later took up writing, becoming one of the young talents cultivated by editor John W. Campbell Jr. at *Astounding Science-Fiction*. Heinlein broke through to mainstream magazines such as *Saturday Evening Post* by playing down exotic elements in favor of portraying everyday, believable humans facing a matter-of-fact race for space. In *Space Cadet* (1948), a juvenile book, his main character, Tom Corbett, resembles Heinlein during his time in the service, except that Corbett's training takes place in the skies. Heinlein came to Hollywood in hopes of writing a screenplay about a moon launch and met Pal, who was already planning to produce a film on that subject.

THE PLOT

At White Sands base in the early 1950s, an unmanned flight crashes after take-off. Those in charge suspect sabotage from another country eager to reach the moon first. The nation that controls space will be in a position to launch missiles back toward our planet. A realization that the moon might contain precious minerals convinces private industry and big business to invest in government programs. Several years later, the first manned flight is launched, but a fuel shortage makes it questionable whether all four astronauts aboard will be able to return.

THE FILM

The Woody Woodpecker cartoon that Walter Lantz created to depict space travel within the movie was considered so excellent that NASA, with a few changes, used it for years to convey such concepts to the public at large.

THEME

The purpose of *Destination Moon* was to convince the American public that not only was space travel now a viable possibility but also necessary for the protection of the United States in the Cold War world.

TRIVIA

The 1961 novel *Stranger in a Strange Land,* widely considered to be Heinlein's masterpiece, has never been made into a movie. It is generally considered unfilmable owing to its noteworthy literary style and considerable intellectual depth, both pluses for a long book but difficult if not impossible to visualize, particularly in a commercial undertaking.

CONQUEST OF SPACE (1955)

CREDITS

Paramount Pictures; Byron Haskin, dir.; Chesley Bonestell, Willy Ley, book; Philip Yordan, Barré Lyndon, George Worthing Yates, James O'Hanlon, scr.; George Pal, Frank Freeman Jr., pro.; Van Cleave, mus.; Lionel Lindon, cin.; Everett Douglas, ed.; Joseph McMillan Johnson, Hal Pereira, art dir.; Bonestell, special astronomical art effects; Ivyl Burks, Jan Domela, Farciot Edouart, John P. Fulton, Paul K. Lerpae, Irmin Roberts, special photographic effects; 81 min.; Color; 1.85:1.

CAST

Walter Brooke (*Gen. Samuel T. Merritt*); Eric Fleming (*Capt. Barney Merritt*); Mickey Shaughnessy (*Sgt. Mahoney*); Phil Foster (*Jackie Siegle*); William Redfield (*Roy Cooper*); William Hopper (*Dr. George Fenton*); Benson Fong (*Imoto*); Ross Martin (*Andre Fodor*); Vito Scotti (*Sanella*); John Dennis (*Donkersgoed*); Michael Fox (*Elsbach*); Joan Shawlee (*Rosie McCann*); Rosemary Clooney (*TV Performer*).

MOST MEMORABLE LINE

The question is, what are we: explorers or invaders?

BARNEY MERRITT, MUSING ON THE ISSUE OF WHETHER MAN HAS A MORAL RIGHT TO ENTER AND CONQUER SPACE

BACKGROUND

Moving from Poverty Row's Eagle-Lion Films to the more prestigious Paramount Pictures, George Pal planned to take his vision of making factual, rather than fantasy, space films a giant step further, beginning with this film's logo: "See how it will happen in your lifetime." This let audiences know the film would offer not romantic adventure, but rather a realistic vision of what travel to other planets would indeed be like.

THE PLOT

Among those aboard a gigantic space wheel are a half-dozen astronauts ready for advanced penetration of space. Their leader, General Merritt, learns the trip will be to Mars and that his son will be the chief aide. Problems arise soon after blastoff. A meteor claims the life of one traveler, Fodor. They eventually land, but, owing to a water shortage, the surviving astronauts can barely sustain themselves. When the elder Merritt suffers a breakdown, he and his son become locked in an Oedipal fight for control.

THE FILM

The enormous wheel and men in space suits, heading into the darkness as they cautiously walk along the ship's surface, had an obvious impact on Stanley Kubrick, who would feature nearly identical images more than a decade later in *2001: A Space Odyssey*.

Though Heinlein was not involved in the making of this feature, his attitudes prevail: the men are depicted as military professionals. As such, they suffer from space fatigue and frustration over the lack of women. They also are prone to addictive behavior. They do not encounter huge monsters or beautiful women after landing.

THEME

In Pal's presentation of the religion vs. science theme, the astronauts wonder if they might be violating some celestial moral scheme by journeying into the heavens when God has given them Earth for a home. Also considered is a serious secular issue: perhaps beings live on other planets, and in "conquering" them, humankind extends into the future our long-standing, if politically incorrect, tendencies toward imperialism.

TRIVIA

In addition to its reliance on the Bonestell/Ley book, the script also drew heavily from *The Mars Project* (*Das Marsprojekt*). Authored by Wernher von Braun (1912–1977), the book had been published in Germany in 1948, then translated and published in English in 1953. Von Braun's name was not included in the film's credits, perhaps due to the lingering controversy surrounding his development of V-2 rockets for the Nazis. After arriving in the United States to work in the U.S. space program, von Braun claimed to have been anti-Hitler, though controversy has always surrounded the rocket scientist. His illustrations for a 1954 *Collier's* magazine article provided a template for the design of the film's spacecraft.

· · · · · · ·

THE THING FROM ANOTHER WORLD (1951)

—— RANKING: 38 ——

CREDITS

RKO Radio Pictures; Christian Nyby, dir.; John W. Campbell Jr., original story; Charles Lederer, Ben Hecht, Howard Hawks, scr.; Hawks, Edward Lasker, pro.; Dmitri Tiomkin, mus.; Russell Harlan, cin.; Roland Gross, ed.; Albert S. D'Agostino, John Hughes, art dir.; Donald Steward, F/X; Linwood G. Dunn, Harold E. Stine, visual effects; 87 min.; B&W; 1.37:1.

CAST

Margaret Sheridan (*Nikki Nicholson*); Kenneth Tobey (*Capt. Patrick Hendry*); Robert Cornthwaite (*Dr. Arthur Carrington*); Douglas Spencer (*Ned Scott/Scotty*); James Young (*Lt. Eddie Dykes*); Dewey Martin (*Crew Chief Bob*); Robert Nichols (*Lt. MacPherson*); William Self (*Corp. Barnes*); Eduard Franz (*Dr. Stern*); Sally Creighton (*Mrs. Chapman*); John Dierkes (*Chapman*); George Fenneman (*Redding*); Paul Frees (*Vorhees*); James Arness (*"The Thing"*).

MOST MEMORABLE LINE

Keep watching the skies!

JOURNALIST SCOTTY ON A RADIO BROADCAST TO AMERICA

BACKGROUND

Howard Hawks (1896–1977), who left the major studios to become an inde-

BORIS KARLOFF, MOVE OVER! *Though James Arness would, in 1955, become TV's answer to John Wayne via his role as Matt Dillon on the Gunsmoke series, the actor's first great notoriety came from playing a Frankenstein's monster for contemporary times—or, as aficionados liked to refer to "The Thing," a "Carrot Man from Mars." Courtesy: Winchester Pictures/RKO.*

pendent producer during the postwar years, based his project on a novella, *Who Goes There?* The piece was originally published in the August 1938 issue of *Astounding Science-Fiction*, the greatest of those sci-fi pulp magazines that flourished during the Great Depression. Concerned that an association with such generic tales might derail his career as a "serious" scribe, the author of the novella, John W. Campbell Jr. (1910–1971), published the piece under the nom de plume "Don A. Stuart." Though the story attracted attention from Hollywood producers, a film would not soon be produced, in part because Campbell's Thing is a shape-shifter, and special effects processes were not deemed sophisticated enough to pull off such transitions. Hawks solved the problem by eliminating the shape-shifting element, despite its importance in the original prose piece.

THE PLOT

Members of the U.S. military rush from Alaska to the North Pole, joining scientists who have reported the crash of an unidentified flying object. While attempting to free the saucer from deep snow, they inadvertently destroy it, but manage to save a frozen inhabitant. Back at the isolated base, this human vegetable thaws. Revealing an insatiable appetite for blood, The Thing menaces every living being on the base. Unable to kill it with ordinary weapons, the team searches for some key to its vulnerability.

THE FILM

Hawks and Christian Nyby, better known as an editor, wanted to avoid genre clichés. They made the characters realistic and the military and scientific situations authentic, so that everything onscreen appears ordinary, even though The (fantastical) Thing lurks somewhere outside, mostly unseen. To keep the film suitably creepy, they employed music as a contrapuntal device—sound contradicting all that's seen. Composer Dmitri Tiomkin used a Russian electronic music device, the theremin (also known as "aetherphone" or "etherwave") to produce a tingling, otherworldly effect. Hawks meanwhile updated the piece to a contemporary setting, the film playing out as a Cold War allegory. As to style, *The Thing* combines the then-emergent 1950s sci-fi sensibility with already existing elements from monster movies—for example, Arness resembles Karloff in *Frankenstein*—and vampire films. It also borrowed from suspense thriller works, such as Agatha Christie's *And Then There Were None*, adding a docudrama tone.

THEME

Feminists have claimed that Hawks alone, among great male filmmakers of Hollywood's golden age, projected their point of view. An explicit bondage sequence in this film has the female lead tying up her lover; in most movies of this era, the situation would have been reversed. Later, when the men are unable to come up with a means of destroying The Thing, she figures out the solution. This suggests Hawks's vision of the woman as a catalyst, able to solve the problems of less observant men—precisely how Hawks ended so many films.

TRIVIA

The Thing from Another World is one of only two films produced during the 1950s by Winchester Pictures Corporation, Hawks's own company, which he had formed in the immediate postwar era to film his Western classic *Red River* (1948). The other is the historical epic, *The Big Sky* (1952). Both were made for RKO, and each featured actor Dewey Martin. Despite the directorial credit going to Nyby, cineastes believe that Hawks directed most of the film, which features his characteristic overlapping dialogue while focusing on the need for Americans to become "a group," setting aside differences, pooling their talents, and compromising as a community to defeat foes or risk being annihilated as rugged individualists. Likely Hawks's reason for not taking the director's credit was that it would not behoove him, as an A-lister, to "sign" a B movie.

The Thing contains two references to earlier horror movies. The first shot, in which a bundled-up "Scotty" approaches the Anchorage headquarters during a blizzard, is identical to the opening of *The Invisible Man* (1933). The sequence in which a guard sits reading, his back to the creature as it rises behind him, echoes an early moment in Karl Freund's *The Mummy* (1932). The film takes place at the North Pole, though the novella had been set in Antarctica.

I COME IN PEACE: *As the gentle "Carpenter" from beyond the stars, Michael Rennie's savior-like spaceman attempts to convince a typical earthling (Patricia Neal) that he only hopes to heal his planet—with, of course, that menacing giant robot ready to back him up with force if necessary. Courtesy: 20th Century-Fox.*

. . . .

THE DAY THE EARTH STOOD STILL (1951)

—— RANKING: 3 ——

CREDITS

Twentieth Century-Fox Film Corporation; Robert Wise, dir.; Harry Bates, story; Edmund H. North, scr.; Julian Blaustein, Darryl F. Zanuck, pro.; Bernard Herrmann, mus.; Leo Tover, cin.; William Reynolds, Orven Schanzer, ed.; Addison Hehr, Lyle R. Wheeler, art dir.; Melbourne A. Arnold, F/X; Fred Sersen, Ray Kellogg, special photographic effects; 92 min.; B&W; 1.37:1.

CAST

Michael Rennie (*Klaatu*); Patricia Neal (*Helen Benson*); Hugh Marlowe (*Tom Stevens*); Sam Jaffe (*Prof. Jacob Barnhardt*); Billy Gray (*Bobby Benson*); Frances

Bavier (*Mrs. Barley*); Lock Martin (*Gort*); Patrick Aherne, James Conaty (*Generals*); Marshall Bradford (*Chief of Staff*); John Brown (*George*); Wheaton Chambers (*Mr. Bleeker*); Jean Charney (*Mother*); Beulah Christian (*Secretary*); Drew Pearson (*Himself*).

MOST MEMORABLE LINE
Klaatu barada nikto.
HELEN TO THE ROBOT GORT

BACKGROUND
Following World War II, the term "flying saucer" entered our popular lexicon as sightings of these objects increased. However, there had been glimpses of crafts with an "ovoid" shape long before that. These inspired Harry Bates to write a short story, "Farewell to the Master," for the October 1940 issue of *Astounding Science-Fiction*. In it, the "god-like" Klaatu arrives on Earth with a robot, Gnut. The tale ends with a twist not included in the screenplay, perhaps because the moviemakers, intending a serious sci-fi epic, believed that, in its very cleverness, a twist ending might cheapen their deeper meaning: after Klaatu's death, as the robot returns home in the saucer, we learn Klaatu was merely the servant, the robot the true "master" of the spacecraft.

THE PLOT
A flying saucer lands in Washington, D.C. The space traveler Klaatu wants to organize a meeting to promote world peace, hoping that humans might evolve beyond their primitive violent urges. When Klaatu emerges from his spaceship, however, a nervous soldier shoots him. In order to understand earthlings, Klaatu leaves his eight-foot robot Gort in charge of their saucer and passes himself off as human. Known only as "Carpenter," Klaatu takes a room in a boarding house and befriends a sensitive woman and her teenage son. He also encounters Einstein-like scientist Barnhardt. As government agents attempt to track Klaatu, he waits for a crucial moment when the Earth will virtually stand still, and all electrical energy frozen for a half hour by the far-seeing powers that sent him here.

THE FILM
If Howard Hawks's *The Thing from Another World* (1951) rates as the first great film warning of potential danger from the skies, this movie, released months later, paved the way for others insisting that we should assume such visitors

are likely benign. If the former came to be considered conservative, politically speaking, these were their liberal alternatives.

Producer Julian Blaustein sensed the potential for making a big-budget film on the saucer phenomenon. He convinced Fox studio head Darryl F. Zanuck to allot more than $1.2 million for the budget. Blaustein read at least 250 treatments before coming upon Bates's all-but-forgotten piece, realizing at once that this was precisely what he wanted. Fascinated by the one reference in Bates's story to Klaatu's deity-like powers, screenwriter Edmund H. North took this idea and ran with it: the film's Klaatu assumes the role of modern savior. Director Robert Wise (1914–2005) insisted on shooting in a documentary-like fashion to keep the film from appearing too obviously allegorical.

THEME

The most obvious theme was the film's religious parable in which Klaatu dies, is resurrected, and finally ascends. However charming, even inspirational, all of this may seem today, it was a subject of controversy and debate at the time. The Motion Picture Association of America office, run by Joseph Breen, expressed discomfort with such an obvious Christian metaphor. The filmmakers were forced to add several lines in which Klaatu insists he is not all-powerful after all—though, of course, he appears to be precisely that.

Also present: a liberal-progressive insistence that the United States must support the then–still new United Nations. The era's conservatives damned the very concept behind this organization. They feared America's growing involvement in an increasingly complex world and wished instead to return to "Fortress America," arguing that we should remain an island of democracy in a world gone mad and not involve ourselves further in foreign affairs. *The Day the Earth Stood Still* illustrates the progressive-formulated need for the entire globe to unify. At the same time, the film advocates for pacifism at a time when, considering the Cold War and the McCarthy-era fear of a Red Menace, such concerns were enough to call the filmmakers' patriotism into question.

TRIVIA

Though almost all of the film is shot on actual locations, Wise did film the late-night sequences in the same noir-like shadow style he had used while making the Val Lewton thriller *The Curse of the Cat People* (1944) at RKO. The Christ-like narrative contributed to Steven Spielberg's eventual conception for *E.T.* (1982).

WE DO NOT COME IN PEACE: *This advertising poster—original copies of which are now valuable collector's items—incorporates various elements of the low-budget classic from filmmaker William Cameron Menzies, who had earlier helmed the lofty* Things to Come *(1936). Courtesy: 20th Century-Fox.*

······

INVADERS FROM MARS (1953)

—— RANKING: 43 ——

CREDITS

Twentieth Century-Fox/National Pictures; William Cameron Menzies, dir.; John Tucker Battle, story; Richard Blake, scr.; Edward L. Alperson, pro.; Raoul Kraushaar, Mort Glickman, mus.; John F. Seitz, cin.; Arthur Roberts, ed.; Menzies, prod. design; Boris Leven, art dir.; Anatole Robbins, makeup F/X; Jack Cosgrove, Irving Block, Howard Lydecker, Jack Rabin, visual F/X; 78 min. (U.S.), 83 min. (U.K.); Color; 1.37:1.

CAST

Helena Carter (*Dr. Pat Blake*); Arthur Franz (*Dr. Stuart Kelston/Narrator*); Jimmy Hunt (*David MacLean*); Leif Erickson (*Mr. George MacLean*); Hillary Brooke (*Mrs. Mary MacLean*); Morris Ankrum (*Col. Fielding*); Max Wagner (*Sgt. Rinaldi*); William Phipps (*Sgt. Baker*); Milburn Stone (*Capt. Roth*); Luce Potter (*Martian Intelligence Being*); Janine Perreau (*Kathy Wilson*); Barbara Billingsley (*Secretary*).

MOST MEMORABLE LINE

David says something landed in the field out back.

GEORGE MACLEAN TO HIS WIFE, MARY

BACKGROUND

On January 27, 1948, Captain Thomas F. Mantell crashed his plane while following what he referred to as a UFO. That incident caused an uproar: such spacecraft, until then considered preposterous, began to be taken seriously. Not surprisingly, Hollywood hurried to cash in. The script for this little film was the first written on the subject, though a series of production delays caused *Invaders from Mars* to be released after Howard Hawks's *The Thing from Another World* (1951) and Robert Wise's *The Day the Earth Stood Still* (1951).

Writer John Tucker Battle scrawled down the idea when his wife, having heard about UFO sightings, woke from an awful dream. He at first considered telling this tale from a woman's point of view, but his previous work as a screenwriter on Walt Disney's *So Dear to My Heart* (1948) convinced him and co-writer Richard Blake that they should tell the story through the eyes of their target audience.

THE PLOT

One starry night, little David MacLean awakens from bad dreams to spot a flying saucer descending into a sand pit behind his house. His scientist dad heads out to investigate only to return later with a cold glint in his eyes and a deep incision on the back of his head. David realizes that other people in their town are likewise acting strangely, but no one believes his story until he visits Dr. Kelston. Together, they convince the government to surround the area in hopes of containing an imminent invasion from Mars.

THE FILM

National Pictures (not to be confused with First National) was created by Brooklyn-born Robert Emmett Tansy (1897–1951). From an East Coast vaudeville family, he headed for Hollywood, hoping to write, direct, and star (as "Al Lane") in low-budget "oaters," as B Westerns were called at the time. The commercial failure of his first (and last) Western, *The Galloping Kid* (1932), however, ended that dream. For twenty years he worked for Poverty Row companies, including Monogram Pictures. In the early 1950s, Tansy put *Invaders* into pre-production, but he died before its completion.

What might have emerged as a routine thriller became something special when William Cameron Menzies (1896–1957) agreed to direct. The Connecticut-born talent had been educated at Yale and the University of Edinburgh, worked as art designer for such classics as *Gone with the Wind* (1939), invented the very concept of "production designer," and was the first person to win an Oscar (1928) in that category. He directed the masterwork *Things to Come* (1936), but by the early 1950s, his career was in decline. Menzies saw *Invaders from Mars* as an opportunity to do, on a tight budget, what he had already achieved on a huge one.

At $290,000, *Invaders* cost $50,000 more than the amount then ordinarily allocated to indie films. These additional funds allowed for lavish color photography and Menzies's intricate sets. Sensing this was indeed something unique, Fox picked up the film for distribution.

THEME

A character being trapped in a dream within a dream, raising existential and metaphysical issues as to the nature of reality, was a premise that would shortly thereafter influence Rod Serling's *The Twilight Zone*. Another theme, left implied, is the Red Scare mentality of the 1950s. Many children were taught to suspect that all adults, even their own parents, might possibly be Communist agents. Some turned grown-ups in to the authorities for uttering mild statements that had been misinterpreted. Just such paranoia is present in the film, notably when little David becomes terror-stricken after seeing his sexy teacher in a bright red dress. (Lest we forget, the 1950s was the decade when Freudianism overtook the Hollywood product, and not only in science-fiction films.)

TRIVIA

Originally, this was to have been the first film shot in 3-D, but that process was scrapped owing to the difficulty of adjusting it to the complicated F/X scheme. A mediocre-at-best African lion thriller, *Bwana Devil* (1952), would have the (dubious) honor.

Invaders would have a significant impact on the tradition of sci-fi. *Invasion of the Body Snatchers* (1956) is an unofficial remake, presented on a more adult level. That film revisits the idea of ordinary people becoming emotionally detached when taken over by aliens. The area where a girl disappears into the ground near an oddly shaped fence would later be visually referenced as the set for a saucer sighting in *Close Encounters of the Third Kind* (1977). Steven Spielberg's decision to have cinematographer Allen Daviau shoot *E.T.* (1982) almost entirely from a child's point of view recalls the effective use of that approach in *Invaders*, expressionistic angles and surreal color adding to the ingenious formalism.

· · · · · · ·

THE WAR OF THE WORLDS (1953)

—— RANKING: 41 ——

CREDITS

Paramount Pictures; Byron Haskin, dir.; H. G. Wells, novel; Barré Lyndon, scr.; George Pal, Frank Freeman Jr., Cecil B. DeMille, pro.; Leith Stevens, mus.; George Barnes, cin.; Everett Douglas, ed.; Albert Nozaki, Hal Pereira, art dir.; Wally Westmore, makeup F/X; Chesley Bonestell, astronomical artwork; Chester Pate, Bob Springfield, A. Edward Sutherland, Barney Wolff, F/X; Ivy Burks, Jan

Domela, Gordon Jennings, special visual effects; Marcel Delgado, miniatures; Domela, matte artist; 85 min.; Color; 1.37:1.

CAST

Gene Barry (*Dr. Clayton Forrester*); Ann Robinson (*Sylvia Van Buren*); Les Tremayne (*Maj. Gen. Mann*); Robert Cornthwaite (*Dr. Pryor*); Sandro Giglio (*Dr. Bilderbeck*); Lewis Martin (*Pastor Dr. Matthew Collins*); Houseley Stevenson Jr. (*Gen. Mann's Aide*); Paul Frees (*Second Radio Reporter/Opening Announcer*); William Phipps (*Wash Perry*); Vernon Rich (*Col. Ralph Heffner*); Henry Brandon (*Cop at Crash Site*); Jack Kruschen (*Salvatore*); Cedric Hardwicke (*Narrator*); Hugh Allen (*Brigadier General*); Edgar Barrier (*Prof. McPherson*).

MOST MEMORABLE LINE

We prayed for a miracle.

DR. FORRESTER, AFTER SCIENCE HAS FAILED
TO HALT THE MARTIAN THREAT

BACKGROUND

Wells's book first appeared in 1898, setting the standard for all twentieth-century invasion-from-the-stars fiction to follow. A philosophical novel, *The War of the Worlds* was written in journalistic prose. Wells's seminal literary conceit allowed readers to share a learned scientist's observations on the meaning of what happens in the plot. Narrative elements—including the unnamed hero (in personality, he resembles Wells) attempting to locate his wife—are kept to a minimum. This makes the book impossible to film "as written" because there is no human drama.

THE PLOT

Residents of a small California town spot a comet-like object landing in the nearby hills. It turns out to be a spacecraft filled with gigantic attack machines, which are piloted by the anemic Martians inside. A scientist and his love interest flee the scene, then try to discover some means of fighting off the now-omnipresent invaders.

THE FILM

Cecil B. DeMille produced the film for Paramount. He decided, however, to remain out of the limelight as the subject matter veered far from his Biblical epics. Yet, *The War of the Worlds* does express the same religious themes

"THE MARTIANS ARE COMING! THE MARTIANS ARE COMING!" *Sensing that the invading war machines, as described in H. G. Wells's novel, would not appear frightening enough, George Pal and his team designed their own look for the menacing spaceships. Courtesy: George Pal Productions.*

found in DeMille's other work. He originally hoped to persuade Orson Welles to direct, based on that artist's infamous October 30, 1938, radio broadcast. Welles, though, was still reeling from lawsuits over his "too convincing" documentary approach and would have nothing to do with the film version of *The War of the Worlds.*

Producer George Pal and director Byron Haskin realized early on that they would need to ignore H. G. Wells's descriptions of the Martians' menacing machines. In the book, these consist of small ovoid compartments mounted high atop a trio of long tentacle-like "legs." When sketch artists prepared similar renderings, Pal sensed they would appear silly rather than scary. Deciding on a loose interpretation, he allowed designer Albert Nozaki full freedom to develop a unique look; it was Nozaki who decided to model the mechanical monstrosities on manta rays.

In the source, the war machines are not invulnerable. Ordinary artillery shoots down several of the tripods, and eventually the English lose because they are outnumbered. For the film, it was decided that such an approach would not be horrific enough, so the atomic bomb was added to the mix to make the project as current as possible. When even this weapon fails to put a dent in the Martians' war craft, the public would indeed be frightened as to the invaders' powers.

THEME

Pal, Haskin, and screenwriter Barré Lyndon reconfigured Wells's story to express the values of the era in which the film was made. For example, the expression "under God" had been added to the Pledge of Allegiance more or less simultaneously with the release of *The War of the Worlds*. The words were added as a means of creating a full Manichean contrast between "godless communism" and, as the opening of each *Superman* TV episode put it, "truth, justice, and the American way." Pal intended the Martians, coming from a "red" planet, as objective correlatives for the Soviets. At film's end, when science has failed to conquer America's enemy, the characters all gather in a church and pray. By chance or destiny, the invaders die off at precisely this moment. The religious theme does not dominate in the source, but such an element was present. In a passage parallel to the film scene in which Forrester hides at night with Sylvia Van Buren, Wells's hero does so alongside a clergyman, who insists that the invaders are the agents of Satan and that Armageddon is at hand.

Another theme is xenophobia, the fear of anything foreign. This aligns *The War of the Worlds* with such sci-fi films of its era as *The Thing from Another World* (1951) and *Invaders from Mars* (1953), as opposed to movies such as *The Day the Earth Stood Still* (1951) that insist on extending an open welcome.

TRIVIA

With a budget of $2 million, this was Hollywood's most expensive science-fiction film to date. Paramount set out to prove that sci-fi films should receive renewed respect at a time when low-budget thrillers, mass-produced on shoe-string budgets, had dimmed their reputation.

Ann Robinson revived her character for the 1988 TV series; she also played a cameo role in Spielberg's 2005 remake. For the latter, Gene Barry joined her. In that film, the machines come closer to the ones described by Wells, though the failure of that massive movie only proves that Pal's decision had been a wise one.

THE GENIUS: *Raymond Frederick "Ray" Harryhausen (1920–2013) here created an original species of dinosaur, drawing on methods that had been created by his mentor, Willis O'Brien, creator of the* King Kong *dinosaurs twenty years earlier. Courtesy: Warner Bros./Jack Deitz Productions.*

· · · · · · ·

THE BEAST FROM 20,000 FATHOMS (1953) AND THEM! (1954)

—— RANKING: 61 (TIE) ——

THE BEAST FROM 20,000 FATHOMS (1953)

CREDITS

Warner Bros./Jack Deitz Productions; Eugène Lourié, dir.; Ray Bradbury, story; Lourié, Fred Freiberger, Lou Morheim, Robert Smith, scr.; Jack Dietz, pro.; David Buttolph, mus.; John L. Russell, cin.; Bernard W. Burton, ed.; Lourié, Hal Waller, art dir.; Ray Harryhausen, animation effects; Lourié, George Lofgren, Willis Cook, F/X; 80 min.; B&W; 1.37:1.

CAST

Paul Hubschmid (*Prof. Tom Nesbitt*); Paula Raymond (*Lee Hunter*); Cecil Kellaway (*Prof. Thurgood Elson*); Kenneth Tobey (*Col. Jack Evans*); Donald Woods (*Capt. Phil Jackson*); Lee Van Cleef (*Corp. Stone*); Steve Brodie (*Sgt. Loomis*); Ross Elliott (*George Ritchie*); Jack Pennick (*Jacob Bowman*); King Donovan (*Dr. Ingersoll*); Merv Griffin (*Media Announcer*); James Best (*Charlie*); Edward Clark (*Lighthouse Keeper*); William Woodson (*Opening Narrator*, voice).

MOST MEMORABLE LINE

I'm leaving a world of untold tomorrows for a world of countless yesterdays.
PROFESSOR ELSON, WHILE DESCENDING
INTO THE SEA IN A DIVING BELL

BACKGROUND

In 1952, RKO re-released *King Kong* as a twentieth anniversary gesture. Surprisingly, the antique became a huge hit all over again. Indie producer Jack Dietz decided to capitalize on this by crafting a scaled-down version, with a plot updated for the scientific age. Though he could not afford Willis H. O'Brien, the creator of the 1933 *King Kong* F/X, Dietz did nab Ray Harryhausen (1920–2013), who had seen *Kong* as a kid and later joined O'Brien's team for *Mighty Joe Young* (1949). In fact, Harryhausen had been hoping to do his own film; Dietz's invitation afforded him that opportunity. One key task was meshing his tabletop monster footage with documentary film of an actual bomb test, which the producers acquired at little cost and used to pad their B flick.

THE PLOT

An atomic bomb test at the North Pole inadvertently sets loose a creature that has been frozen for millions of years. A witness, Professor Tom Nesbitt, is considered insane, though a female scientist convinces her genius boss, Professor Elson, to search under the sea in a submarine. When he is killed and the beast heads for New York City, no one can ignore any longer that the threat is real and imminent.

THE FILM

For the direction, Dietz hired Eugène Lourié (1903–1991), a gifted art designer from France who had worked on prestige projects for Jean Renoir and Charlie Chaplin. Lourié had long desired to direct, though he expressed no interest in sci-fi. He would be circumscribed by the film's success, shooting similar projects in London, including the low-budget *The Giant Behemoth* (1959) and the high-quality *Gorgo* (1961).

When sci-fi writer Ray Bradbury (1920–2012) visited Harryhausen on the set of what was then called *Monster from the Sea*, he glanced through the script and noticed a similarity to his own earlier *Saturday Evening Post* short story, "The Fog Horn." The producers bought it and incorporated Bradbury's tale (a sea beast attacks a lighthouse), using it as their midpoint. Harryhausen then came up with the now-famous title.

The film was shot for $200,000. Dietz and his partner Hal E. Chester were delighted to more than double their money when Warner Bros. picked it up for distribution. That company had never been comfortable with sci-fi, though Jack Warner knew such films were making big money. When *Beast* grossed more than $5 million, Warner immediately set to work on a follow-up, *Them!*, released one year later.

TRIVIA

The "beast" is called a "Rhedosaurus," created from the imaginations of Bradbury and Harryhausen from bits and pieces of actual dinosaurs, as well as elements of lizards.

This was the first film to feature a beast unleashed by atomic energy, creating a narrative trope that remained in place throughout the 1950s.

THEM! (1954)

CREDITS

Warner Bros.; Gordon Douglas, dir.; George Worthing Yates, story; Ted Sherdeman, Russell S. Hughes, scr.; David Weisbart, pro.; Bronislau Kaper, mus.; Sidney Hickox, cin.; Thomas Reilly, ed.; Stanley Fleischer, art dir.; 94 min.; B&W; 1.75:1.

CAST

James Arness (*Robert Graham*); James Whitmore (*Police Sgt. Ben Peterson*); Edmund Gwenn (*Dr. Harold Medford*); Joan Weldon (*Dr. Patricia Medford*); Onslow Stevens (*Brig. Gen. Robert O'Brien*); Sean McClory (*Maj. Kibbee*); Chris Drake (*Ed Blackburn*); Sandy Descher (*Ellinson Child*); Mary Alan Hokanson (*Mrs. Lodge*); Don Shelton (*Capt. Fred Edwards*); Fess Parker (*Alan Crotty*).

THE BIG BUG: *Special effects technicians were given a large enough budget to create immense mechanical ants, eliminating overly obvious rear-screen projection techniques, so that the attack on Joan Weldon would come across as completely convincing. Courtesy: Warner Bros.*

MOST MEMORABLE LINE

Them! Them! Them!

ELLINSON CHILD TO SERGEANT PETERSON

BACKGROUND

The financial success of *The Beast from 20,000 Fathoms* prompted studio boss Jack Warner to mount a similar piece—hence, the doubled budget, longer running time, and initial considerations of filming in color, 3-D, and even widescreen, none of which worked out owing to the difficulty of aligning all or any of the above with the F/X processes. This time, the monsters were created as large life-like models, the case with many "big bug" films to follow (this was the first).

THE PLOT

Shortly after a series of nuclear tests, a New Mexico police officer comes across a little girl in a state of shock. He and Dr. Medford, a brilliant scientist, work with government agent Robert Graham to uncover giant prehistoric ants, long dormant under the Earth's surface, now roaming the countryside and heading for Los Angeles.

THE FILM

Every effort was employed to remake *Beast* in a scene-for-scene manner, including using the same documentary-like approach, rather than Grand Guignol horror movie effects. Once again, the film features a strong female lead, who is capable of much more than screaming (though she does do that). Cecil Kellaway's ironic scientist from *Beast* is reborn for *Them!* with Edmund Gwenn now assuming the part. Despite the upgrading, *Them!* brought in $2 million—a solid profit, if considerably less than the box office for *Beast*.

THEME

The films share a single theme, each serving as a cautionary fable against nuclear weapons. One manner of portraying this was didactically, as in the large-scale *On the Beach* (1959), which showed the aftereffects of an atomic war. Science fiction allowed for a less preachy approach that drove home the point for a mainstream audience via mass entertainment.

TRIVIA

In the film's poster, the exclamation point does not appear after the one-word title.

In June 1954, Walt Disney was searching for an unknown to play Davy Crockett for a television series about to go into production. Someone suggested Arness might be right; Disney attended *Them!* but wasn't convinced. Toward the end, the small role of an institutionalized Texan (Fess Parker) caught Disney's attention. Uncle Walt supposedly rose and exclaimed: "*That's* him! That's *Davy*!"

DISNEY MAGIC: *The studio famed for bringing what Walt himself called "the plausible impossible" to vivid onscreen life offered audiences a classic in* 20,000 Leagues Under the Sea. *In this artist's rendition, various elements of Jules Verne's grand tale are mixed and matched for a fanciful collage. Courtesy: Buena Vista/Walt Disney Productions.*

• • • • • • •

20,000 LEAGUES UNDER THE SEA (1954) AND MYSTERIOUS ISLAND (1961)

—— RANKING: 24 (TIE) ——

20,000 LEAGUES UNDER THE SEA (1954)

CREDITS

Walt Disney Productions/Buena Vista Film Distribution; Richard Fleischer, dir.; Jules Verne, novel; Earl Felton, scr.; Walt Disney, pro.; Paul J. Smith, mus.; Franz Planer, cin.; Elmo Williams, ed.; Harper Goff, prod. design; John Meehan, Harper Goff, art dir.; Bruce Bushman, sketch artist; John Hench, Joshua Meador, Jim Donnelly, Lou Gray, Robert A. Mattey, F/X; Ub Iwerks, special visual effects processes; Peter Ellenshaw, matte artist; Ralph Hammeras, special F/X photography; Til Gabani, underwater photography; 127 min.; Color; 1.37:1.

CAST

Kirk Douglas (*Ned Land*); James Mason (*Capt. Nemo*); Paul Lukas (*Prof. Pierre Aronnax*); Peter Lorre (*Conseil*); Robert J. Wilke (*First Mate*); Ted de Corsia (*Capt. Farragut*); Carleton Young (*John Howard*); J. M. Kerrigan (*Old Billy*); Percy Helton (*Coach Driver*); Jack Pennick (*Seaman Carson*).

MOST MEMORABLE LINE

A twilight world opened up before me and I felt as the first man
to set foot on another planet.
PROFESSOR ARONNAX, DESCENDING INTO THE OCEAN

BACKGROUND

Verne's childhood boating experiences inspired his interest in the oceans; his natural inclination toward travel led him to a lifelong love of long journeys; and his education in Paris opened the budding author's eyes to the glories and dangers of the scientific world just then being studied in great universities for the first time. Verne's friendships with Victor Hugo (*Les Miserables*) and Alexandre Dumas (*The Three Musketeers*) helped him to understand that to communicate one's passions to the public, an author must combine strong social relevance and enjoyable adventure plots. His novel, *20,000 Leagues Under the Sea* (1870), offered a convergence of all of the above influences.

THE PLOT

A seeming sea beast destroys warships from various countries. When it attacks an American craft, the noted scientist Aronnax, his manservant Conseil, and rough harpooner Ned Land fall overboard. They soon realize that the beast is an atomic-powered submarine, captained by Nemo. A radical environmentalist, Nemo will use any means to protect the natural world from what he considers the evils of humanity.

THE FILM

Previously, live-action dramas from the studios of Walt Disney (1901–1966) were mostly inexpensive bread-and-butter pictures that kept the studio alive between animated undertakings. Disney budgeted this film at an unheard-of $5 million, even hiring big-name stars for the leads (the studio ordinarily cast unknowns) while allowing for an expansive special effects budget. Most of these funds went to creating the *Nautilus*, which, with its iconic shape, is more visually exciting than the cigar-like submarine described in Verne's novel. Disney found the book, despite its lofty reputation among the sci-fi literati, to be too cut-and-dry for modern audiences. To "Disney-ize" the piece, a seal was substituted for the dog that would ordinarily appear in a Disney film, Laurel and Hardy–type humor between Lorre and Douglas was added to the script, invigorating songs were written to carry the story forward, and action was increased to keep the viewers on the edge of their seats.

THEME

The explosion that rocks the island is modeled on the atomic explosions that ended World War II. As such, Verne's futuristic prediction had to be updated to offer a sobering comment on the dangers of atomic annihilation at the time when the movie was made. Though Disney films are generally considered "normalizing" for a child-based audience, the film presents a radical environmentalist—who goes so far as to use violence as a means to his end—not as a villain but as a full-blown tragic hero.

TRIVIA

A precise replica of the *Nautilus* can be visited in Disneyland Paris—an acknowledgment to Jules Verne, France's fantastical author and the inspiration for this Disney film.

Even as *20,000 Leagues Under the Sea* went into production, science fiction was turning into fact. The United States developed the first atomic-powered submarine. In deference to Verne and Disney, it was named the *Nautilus*.

MYSTERIOUS ISLAND (1961)

CREDITS

Columbia Pictures/Ameran Films; Cy Endfield, dir.; Jules Verne, novel; John Prebble, Daniel B. Ullman, Crane Wilbur, scr.; Charles H. Schneer, pro.; Bernard Herrmann, mus.; Wilkie Cooper, cin.; Frederick Wilson, ed.; William C. Andrews, art dir.; Vic Margutti, special photography; Ray Harryhausen, visual F/X; 101 min.; Color; 1.85:1.

SEX AND VIOLENCE IN SCI-FI CINEMA: *To make Jules Verne's literary work more attractive to modern audiences, producer Charles H. Schneer added gorgeous British starlet Beth Rogan and a menacing monster bumblebee, courtesy of Ray Harryhausen. Michael Callan played the wary young hero. Courtesy: Ameran Films/Columbia Pictures.*

CAST

Herbert Lom (*Capt. Nemo*); Michael Craig (*Capt. Cyrus Harding*); Joan Greenwood (*Lady Mary Fairchild*); Michael Callan (*Herbert Brown*); Gary Merrill (*Gideon Spilitt*); Beth Rogan (*Elena Fairchild*); Percy Herbert (*Sgt. Pencroft*); Dan Jackson (*Neb Nugent*).

MOST MEMORABLE LINE

Before, I attacked the effects of war; now, I attack its causes:
hunger, social injustice.
NEMO, TO THE ISLAND DWELLERS

BACKGROUND

No sooner had *20,000 Leagues* been published than the public clamored for Nemo's return. Jules Verne considered, and discarded, several possible plots.

Then, influenced by Daniel Defoe's *Robinson Crusoe* (1719) and Johann Wyss's *Swiss Family Robinson* (1812), he began *The Mysterious Island* (1874) with a recycling of his own *Five Weeks in a Balloon* (1863) and ending the sequel with the reappearance of Nemo.

THE PLOT

Five American Civil War soldiers escape a siege in an air balloon but are swept far out to sea. They attempt to survive on a deserted island, along with two Englishwomen who have been shipwrecked and serendipitously washed ashore. Gigantic crabs, chickens, and bees menace the survivors, who are often saved by an unseen benefactor. When pirates attack, their hero reveals himself to be Captain Nemo.

THE FILM

The women and dangerous creatures were added for the film. Verne's book was more realistic, except for the *Nautilus*. Charles Schneer and Ray Harryhausen had worked together on mid-fifties B movies, but they sensed that the end was nearing for that genre. With *The 7th Voyage of Sinbad* (1958), a remarkably successful fantasy adventure, they tried their luck at something different: a more expensive project, shot in color with dazzling special effects. When that F/X-laden epic proved a huge hit for Columbia, the studio executives greenlighted this project, knowing that, if Disney had intended to produce a sequel, he would have long since completed it.

THEME

Mysterious Island serves as a worthy companion piece to the Disney-Verne film, with its warning about the dangers of scientific experiments. In the Schneer-Harryhausen version, Nemo no longer attempts to blow up the Earth but instead save it by discovering ways to multiply the size of animal life in hopes of eradicating hunger from the Earth—a kinder, gentler Nemo!

TRIVIA

James Mason was offered an opportunity to reprise the role of Nemo, but he had already accepted an invitation from Stanley Kubrick to play the role of Humbert Humbert in *Lolita* (1962).

In his second Nemo novel, Verne revealed that Nemo was actually "Dakkar," a high-born native of India who had been driven to madness and radical behavior by the forces of the British Empire.

CREATURE FROM THE BLACK LAGOON (1954)

— RANKING: 72 —

CREDITS

Universal International Pictures; Jack Arnold, dir.; Harry Essex, Arthur A. Ross, scr.; William Alland, pro.; Henry Mancini, Hans J. Salter, Herman Stein, mus.; William E. Snyder, cin.; Ted J. Kent, ed.; Hilyard M. Brown, Bernard Herzbrun, art dir.; Russell A. Gausman, Ray Jeffers, set design; Charles "Scotty" Welbourne, special F/X photography; Milicent Patrick, creature design; 79 min.; B&W; 1.37:1 (original), 1.85:1.

CAST

Richard Carlson (*David Reed*); Julie Adams (*Kay Lawrence*); Richard Denning (*Mark Williams*); Antonio Moreno (*Carl Maia*); Nestor Paiva (*Lucas*); Whit Bissell (*Dr. Edwin Thompson*); Ricou Browning (*Gill Man, water sequences*); Ben Chapman (*Gill Man, land sequences*).

MOST MEMORABLE LINE

We didn't come here to fight monsters.

DAVID TO MARK

BACKGROUND

The inspiration for Universal's last great monster franchise resulted from a dinner conversation that took place in 1941. William Alland, then an actor, had just played the reporter in *Citizen Kane*, and his director, Orson Welles, introduced him to Mexican filmmaker Gabriel Figueroa. The famed raconteur told the dinner guests about a legendary creature of the Amazon reputed to be half man, half fish. Later, as a B movie producer, Alland was searching for a new, original creature with some scientific, rather than supernatural, basis. His memory of that long-ago conversation led to the idea of the Gill Man.

THE PLOT

An annihilated expedition leaves in its wake one fossil from tens of thousands of years ago. When Dr. Reed studies the piece, he becomes convinced that it

BEAUTY AND THE BEAST REVISITED: *The ancient myth, so essential to the fantasy genre in literature and film, was spruced up with contemporary scientific jargon for the sci-fi genre. Julie Adams is the beauty on the beach. Courtesy: Universal.*

may provide evidence of a missing link between life in the water and on land. He and a high-ranking scientist, Mark Williams, penetrate the Amazon's mysteries, initially unaware that a single specimen survives from the Devonian Period. The creature, in the meantime, is growing ever more intrigued by their female companion, Kay Lawrence.

THE FILM

Creature has wrongly been identified as Universal's first foray into 3-D. Actually, *It Came from Outer Space* (1953) preceded *Creature* by almost a year. Both were released in "polarized" three-dimension format, which required that each eye be covered by a piece of plastic-like material, gray-green in color, inserted into special glasses. The better-remembered, if inferior, "anaglyph" approach, involving one red and one blue eye cover, was mostly reserved for comic books. These special editions, published in a larger-than-usual format, were a forerunner of today's graphic novels. The 3-D print of *Creature* that is available for rental has been converted from polarization to anaglyphic.

The Gill Man, always intended to resemble an upright penis, was designed by one of Disney's artists, Milicent Patrick, in collaboration with pioneering makeup specialist Bud Westmore (1918–1973). Jack Kevan constructed the bodysuit; Chris Mueller provided the head sculpting. Two costumes/suits were created, one lightly colored for land scenes, and the other darker for in-water sequences. The Gill Man's notably different manner of moving on land and water was due to the fact that he was played by two stunt performers.

THEME

Creature became the most omnipresent example of the beauty and the beast motif since RKO's *King Kong* (1933). That film established the theme of two men competing for a female until they are forced to join forces against "It." *King Kong*'s lack of any scientific rationale disqualifies it, greatness aside, from consideration here. In *Creature*, however, science drives the fiction. The film revives the idea of a beast that, in its primitive simplicity and utterly romantic captivation with the female, earns more emotional support from the audience than either of the "heroes." Notable too are the advances made by women in the United States during the two decades between this new variation on a theme and the epic *Kong*. Whereas Ann Darrow (Fay Wray) accompanied *Kong*'s explorers for no other reason than her value as a beauty object, here Kay, however lovely, comes along for the ride as an equal partner and respected scientist. Producer Alland and director Jack Arnold refused to use one of the studio's many blonde Marilyn Monroe look-alike contract starlets, insisting that brunette Adams, her physical perfection aside, would offer up an assertive and intelligent female lead more in tune with the times.

TRIVIA

Many B movie aficionados consider the sequence in which the underwater creature swims beneath Kay, mimicking her every move, to be the most erotic G-rated (though the current rating system was not in effect until late 1967/early 1968) sequence of all time.

In *The Seven Year Itch* (1955), the heroine, played by Marilyn Monroe, goes on a date with a married man (Tom Ewell) to the movies to see *Creature from the Black Lagoon*. Shortly after they exit, she expresses sympathy for the creature as a misunderstood male searching for love. The iconic moment in which she steps over a subway grating and her dress blows up above her thighs occurs immediately thereafter. Here is one of the first great examples of a work of lowbrow popular culture being incorporated into a more upscale project.

Producer Alland continued the cross-pollination of monster movie with science-fiction film in both sequels. In *Revenge of the Creature* (1955), psychologists, as well as ichthyologists, attempt to understand the relationship of the missing link to contemporary mankind; *The Creature Walks Among Us* (1956) deals with the creature's transformation from gills to lungs as he—that is, it!—relives humanity's own evolution.

· · · · · · ·

THIS ISLAND EARTH (1955)

—— RANKING: 83 ——

CREDITS

Universal International; Joseph M. Newman, dir.; Raymond F. Jones, story; Franklin Coen, Edward G. O'Callaghan, scr.; William Alland, pro.; Henry Mancini, Hans J. Salter, Herman Stein, mus.; Clifford Stine, cin.; Virgil W. Vogel, ed.; Alexander Golitzen, Richard H. Riedel, art dir.; Leslie I. Carey, special sound effects; David S. Horsley, Stine, Cleo E. Baker, F/X; Roswell A. Hoffmann, Frank Tipper, visual effects; 87 min.; Color; 2.00:1.

WELCOME TO METALUNA: *Though the majority of 1950s sci-fi films were cheaply made, this ambitious undertaking featured state-of-the-art F/X. Rex Reason and Faith Domergue join Jeff Morrow (he's the one with the high forehead!) on his faraway world. Courtesy: Universal-International.*

CAST
Jeff Morrow (*Exeter*); Faith Domergue (*Dr. Ruth Adams*); Rex Reason (*Dr. Cal Meacham*); Lance Fuller (*Brack*); Russell Johnson (*Steve Carlson*); Douglas Spencer (*The Monitor of Metaluna*); Robert Nichols (*Joe Wilson*); Karl Ludwig Lindt (*Dr. Engelborg*); Spencer Chan (*Dr. Hu Ling Tang*); Lizalotta Valesca (*Dr. Marie Pitchener*); Richard Deacon (*Pilot*); Marc Hamilton, Charlotte Lander (*Metalunans*).

MOST MEMORABLE LINE
Our planet is dying.
EXETER TO DR. MEACHAM

BACKGROUND
Raymond F. Jones's (1915–1994) fable, "The Alien Machine," originally appeared in the pulp magazine *Thrilling Wonder Stories* in 1949. The considerable popularity of the brief but memorable work of fiction led, three years later, to book publication. Universal purchased the film rights, looking to add to the studio's

burgeoning list of sci-fi films, which had replaced their legendary Gothic monster movies. While most program pictures (the big studio equivalent to low-budget indies) were shot in black and white for about $250,000, studio executives had been impressed by the recent success of Paramount's *The War of the Worlds*, so they updated the production values for *This Island Earth*, raising the film's budget to an astonishing $800,000.

THE PLOT

Dr. Cal Meacham receives a book, printed on strange metallic pages, instructing him on how to build an "interociter." When completed, this TV-like device allows him to communicate with Exeter, whose huge forehead suggests an enormous brain. An unmanned Douglas DC-3 transports Meacham to a hidden research center where he's reunited with an old flame, Dr. Ruth Adams. They and other geniuses have been assembled to aid Exeter in "benign" experiments. Realizing that Exeter and his aide Brack are aliens, the couple attempts

BRAVE NEW WORLD: *This posed publicity shot for* This Island Earth *effectively suggests the nightmarish, semi-surreal tone of the film. Courtesy: Universal-International.*

to flee by car. Instead they are beamed into a flying saucer, then spirited off to the planet Metaluna. There they learn from the supreme being, "The Monitor," that the evil Zagons are eliminating the friendly Metalunans, explaining why they hope to relocate to Earth. Mutant insect-like humanoids wander the vast underground city, ensuring that the couple does not escape.

THE FILM

Diehard fans of the film note that the color quality is not consistent. Universal, like most other studios, was just then in the process of changing from an out-dated Technicolor process to a state-of-the-art form. Old-fashioned three-strip Technicolor was used for sequences involving earthbound settings. For F/X sequences, particularly those that occur on Metaluna, director Joseph M. Newman (1909–2006) preferred the then-revolutionary Eastman color process. This seeming inconsistency adds to the film's impact by creating a greater contrast in tone between the realistic settings and the created world. An uncredited Jack Arnold directed the later sequences.

THEME

Jones's story, written shortly after World War II, addressed a nation that wanted to believe that it had finally won the war to end all wars. Already, though, trouble spots were appearing in Korea and around the globe. Jones intended his piece as a cautionary fable against pacifism. His heroes return to Earth and build weapons of mass destruction for their alien allies, convinced that these are the "good guys" in a fight against intergalactic evil. By the time the script had at last been completed more than five years later, the Korean conflict was over (if unresolved) and such an approach seemed too vitriolic.

The film, hewing closely to the novel in its first half, veers in a different direction during the second. For nearly forty-five minutes, *This Island Earth* appears to be setting up a xenophobic statement in the tradition of *The Thing from Another World* (1951), with Exeter and his cohorts going so far as to decimate all the Earth scientists, except the lead actors. Once they board the flying saucer, the statement shifts, implying an approach more like that in *The Day the Earth Stood Still* (1951). The aliens, Exeter in particular, become ever more appealing. Some critics have complained that the film's theme is confused, its distinct halves at odds, the "message" self-contradictory.

TRIVIA

In the source, Exeter's name is "Jorgasnovara" and there are no mutants, no

Monitor. The latter's face, with its aged sense of world-weary intelligence, is believed to have been "borrowed" from the glass-enclosed brain on view two years earlier in *Invaders from Mars*.

Following the film's successful run, producer William Alland hoped to shoot a sequel, *Aliens in the Sky*, starring Rex Reason and Faith Domergue from the cast of *This Island Earth*. Edward Muhl, the head of production for Universal, vetoed the idea on the grounds that the budget would be so lofty the proposed film might not recoup its costs.

The TV series *Mystery Science Theatre 3000* (1988–1999), created by Joel Hodgson, spoofed some of the worst low-budget sci-fi/horror films with sarcastic comments from a spacecraft team. For the 1996 film version of the TV show, Hodgson chose *This Island Earth*, deciding to parody a bigger-budgeted antique. Serious sci-fi fans took umbrage; the sophomoric humor, while appropriate to terrible movies, was not warranted in the case of this classic, however dated.

· · · · · · ·

1984 (1956)

—— RANKING: 53 ——

CREDITS
Holiday Film Productions/Columbia Pictures; Michael Anderson, dir.; George Orwell, novel; Ralph Gilbert Bettison, William Templeton, scr.; Bettison, N. Peter Rathvon, pro.; Malcolm Arnold, mus.; C. M. Pennington-Richards, cin.; Bill Lewthwaite, ed.; Terence Verity, prod. design; Len Townsend, art dir.; Barbara Gray, costumes; George Blackwell, Bryan Langley, Norman Warwick, F/X; 90 min.; B&W; 1.37:1.

CAST
Edmond O'Brien (*Winston Smith*); Michael Redgrave (*O'Connor*); Jan Sterling (*Julia*); David Kossoff (*Charrington*); Mervyn Johns (*Jones*); Donald Pleasence (*Parsons*); Carol Wolveridge (*Selina Parsons*); Ernest Clark (*Outer Party Announcer*); Patrick Allen (*Party Official*); Ronan O'Casey (*Rutherford*); Michael Ripper, Ewen Solon (*Outer Party Orators*); Anthony Jacobs (*Telescreen*, voice); John Vernon (*Big Brother*).

YOU CAN RUN BUT YOU CAN'T HIDE: *Winston Smith (Edmond O'Brien) is dwarfed by the towering image of Big Brother (John Vernon) in this tightly budgeted, high-quality British adaptation of George Orwell's dystopian future classic. Courtesy: Holiday Film Productions/Columbia.*

I love Big Brother!

SMITH, FINAL LINE FOLLOWING HIS RE-BRAINWASHING

BACKGROUND

English author Aldous Huxley (1894–1963) invented modern dystopian fiction with *Brave New World* (1932). Drawing his title from Shakespeare's *The Tempest*, Huxley (while in the final stages of tuberculosis) penned a harsh satire of the utopian novels by H. G. Wells, who had argued that a perfect society might be created through socialism and science. Observing the recently developed assembly lines at actual factories, Huxley concluded the opposite, arguing that technology would outrun humanity. If *Brave New World* stands as the most important pre-war cautionary fable, *1984*—written by George Orwell (1903–1950) in 1948, the final digits reversed for his title—updated Huxley's vision. Orwell set his book in a post–nuclear war civilization, establishing a model for post-modern sci-fi.

THE PLOT

Winston Smith works at the Ministry of Truth, and he has secretly begun to despise his job: rewriting history to bring the past more in line with the actuality of his futuristic society's ideology. Love is banned, though reproduction, at the government's bequest, is not. Smith has just received a note from co-worker Julia, who asks to meet him at one of the final green garden spots in Oceania, formerly England. They make the mistake of trusting their secret affair to stern executive O'Connor and antique shop owner Charrington, falsely believing that both men are part of the anti-government Underground. Captured, Smith and Julia undergo a process designed to use their deepest personal fears to turn them against each other, once more loving only the state and the distant leader figure known as "Big Brother."

THE FILM

In 1954, the BBC presented a daring production of the novel starring Peter Cushing. The program received critical and popular acclaim, inspiring N. Peter Rathvon to produce a larger-scale film that might play all over the world. Distribution in the highly lucrative U.S. market would be possible only if the leads were played by American names. Edmond O'Brien and Jan Sterling look nothing like the characters as described by Orwell, but their commitment to bringing the roles to life countered any concern about casting.

Director Michael Anderson understood that his team of production designers and special effects artists must portray the future in a non-generic manner. Working on a tight budget, Anderson sensed that Orwell's richly detailed and highly specific descriptions could not be recreated. Rather than try and fail to realize elements like the war-decimated "Airstrip One," which represents the land mass earlier known as England, the director devised his own futurescape. As the opening credits inform us, this is the future, though not that of fantastic films so popular at the time. The challenge was to come up with a world in which the sleek metallic look of previous "serious" movies, including *Things To Come* (1936), would be revised while retaining key realities of London as it existed at the time of filming. The final "look" of the piece proved close to perfect for a film made in 1956, based on a novel published in 1949, about the year 1984.

THEME

The term "Orwellian" has come to mean any government that intimidates citizens through mind control. In an example of "doublethink," Orwell's Ministry of Peace insists that perpetual war is the only means to achieve stability and absolute loyalty to the all-powerful state.

At the time of the novel's release, Orwell's target was believed to be the sort of fascist regime recently overthrown, Big Brother serving as a fictional counterpoint to Adolph Hitler. As such, the controversial novel was beloved by liberals, who perceived in it an attack on right-wing oligarchy. In recent years, many conservatives have insisted that the opposite is true. The political ideology "Ingsoc" is short for English Socialism; just such a government must stamp out any shred of individualism. In fact, Orwell had hoped to warn against any extremist form of government, left or right; the book was political in the most all-encompassing, least narrow sense of that term.

TRIVIA

In 1984, Michael Radford remade the film, which starred John Hurt and Richard Burton. However clever the idea might have seemed, the results bordered on disastrous. Some elements of the book were altered to bring Orwell's vision of the future more in line with the way things had actually turned out, destroying the literary connection, while others were played precisely as written. The contrast between Orwell's vision of what might come about and the world as it had actually emerged in that now-mythic year clashed, rather than meshed, onscreen.

A METAPHOR FOR MCCARTHYISM: *Residents of a small California town (including King Donovan and Kevin McCarthy, third and fourth from left) search for the elusive space pods that are transforming people into communally oriented creatures, devoid of souls and emotions. Courtesy: Allied Artists/Walter Wanger Productions.*

· · · · · · ·

INVASION OF THE BODY SNATCHERS (1956)

—— RANKING: 10 ——

CREDITS

Allied Artists/Walter Wanger Productions; Don Siegel, dir; Jack Finney, story; Daniel Mainwaring, Richard Collins, scr.; Walter Wanger, Walter Mirisch, pro.; Carmen Dragon, mus.; Ellsworth Fredericks, cin.; Robert S. Eisen, ed.; Ted Haworth, prod. design; Milt Rice, F/X; Don Post, special visual effects (including pods); 80 min.; B&W; 2.00:1.

CAST

Kevin McCarthy (*Dr. Miles J. Bennell*); Dana Wynter (*Becky Driscoll*); Larry Gates (*Dr. Dan Kauffman*); King Donovan (*Jack Belicec*); Carolyn Jones (*Theodora Belicec*); Jean Willes (*Nurse Withers*); Ralph Dumke (*Police Chief Grivett*); Virginia Christine (*Wilma Lentz*); Tom Fadden (*Uncle Ira*); Kenneth Patterson (*Stanley Driscoll*); Bobby Clark (*Jimmy*).

MOST MEMORABLE LINE

They're here . . . . You're next!

MILES, DESPERATELY SHRIEKING INTO THE CAMERA

BACKGROUND

This legendary film owes its uniqueness to the merging of two remarkable, if disparate, talents. Jack Finney (1911–1995) labored in advertising on Madison Avenue, in his spare time knocking off imaginative stories that he mailed to various slick magazines. In 1954, *Collier's* picked up and serialized *The Body Snatchers*, which defied easy categorization: part sci-fi, part psychological thriller, part horror, part literary noir. Happily, the gifted Don Siegel (1912–1991) directed the film version. After excelling as a noted creator of montage sequences, Siegel had gone on to helm cheaply produced but strikingly realized program pictures, such as *The Verdict* (1946) and *Riot in Cell Block 11* (1954). What might have been a major letdown—the first monsters-from-space movie sans monsters— emerged not only as one of the great sci-fi films but also as an iconic element in American popular culture; those barely seen yet frightfully vivid "pods" still haunt the dreams of many moviegoers who saw the film back in 1956.

THE PLOT

After being picked up by police, a hysterical Miles Bennell tells an astounding tale to a psychiatrist. A respected doctor, Miles had returned to his hometown of Santa Mira, California, to learn that many longtime patients had become convinced that relatives and friends were not whom they appeared to be. An old flame, Becky, also experiences this weird phenomenon. Miles writes their stories off as a case of mass hysteria. Until, that is, his best friend Jack telephones frantically for help. Upon arrival at Jack's house, Miles discovers a huge seedpod in Jack's basement; in it, a double for Jack is in the process of taking form. Miles and Becky go on the run, now aware that virtually everyone in town has been taken over by these emotionless twinnings.

THE FILM

Producer Walter Wanger (1894–1968) had helmed such prestige productions as John Ford's *Stagecoach* (1939). Then, in 1951, he shot the purported lover of his wife, actress Joan Bennett, and was indicted for assault with intent to kill. After his release from jail, Wanger eked out a living by shooting B movies. He remained determined to make the highest quality movies possible, despite the limitations of shoestring budgets. *Invasion* would be his mini-masterpiece, shot for less than $400,000 (with a tight 23-day schedule), returning $2.5 million on that investment.

High schoolers who caught *Invasion* during its initial run would eagerly await TV showings. Its appeal in dorms and frat houses made *Invasion* one of the first true cult films. A generation that would emerge as "serious" film fans and critics in the late 1960s altered the aesthetics of moviemaking. No longer was a large budget considered synonymous with quality. What you do with what you've got became the standard for those who admired edgy auteurs like Siegel, their lack of funds forcing them to come up with the most creative visual approaches.

THEME

Clearly, the film commented on McCarthyism and the Red Scare that had overtaken the country some ten years earlier. What one reviewer called "the invisible invaders" might be accepted as a metaphor for a period in American life when people came to mistrust friends and family, worrying that any slight difference in attitudes signaled that someone else had gone over to the other side. Another view, favored by those who reject this social-political interpretation as too limiting, sees *Invasion* as a statement about Los Angeles: nice, normal people who go to the City of Angels swiftly turn into somnambulists—particularly if they find employment in the movie business—who lose the human capacity for love, fear, or any other honest emotion. If Siegel's take on the Finney material was political, Wanger's—considering the rejection he experienced after his time in jail—would be the latter view.

TRIVIA

The prologue and epilogue sequences, in which Miles tells his strange story to a psychiatrist and convinces everyone he's not crazy, were added shortly before release. Producers feared that the original ending of the film, a tight-shot of Miles as he stands in traffic and screams warnings to passing motorists, was too unsettling.

The meter man who arrives in the dark and is mistaken for a monster was played by a young aspiring writer-director, Sam Peckinpah.

Invasion of the Body Snatchers was remade twice. The first remake, directed by Philip Kaufman and released in 1978, is a handsome, upscale film with richly detailed F/X. It nonetheless failed to convey the abject horror of the mostly unseen threat in the original. Abel Ferrara directed the second remake in 1993 under the title *Body Snatchers*, which likewise failed to recapture the scary magic despite a considerably larger budget.

UFO APOCALYPSE NOW!: *In this staged publicity shot, Joan Taylor and Hugh Marlowe recoil as a flying saucer veers close overhead. Ray Harryhausen's F/X were among the best to appear in the entire invasion subgenre. Courtesy: Clover Films/Columbia.*

· · · · · · ·

EARTH VS. THE FLYING SAUCERS (1956)

—— RANKING: 90 ——

CREDITS

Columbia Pictures/Clover Productions; Fred F. Sears, dir.; Donald E. Keyhoe, book; Curt Siodmak, George Worthing Yates, Bernard Gordon, scr.; Sam Katzman, Charles H. Schneer, pro.; Mischa Bakaleinikoff, mus.; Fred Jackman Jr., cin.; Danny B. Landres, ed.; Paul Palmentola, art dir.; Russ Kelley, F/X; Ray Harryhausen, photographic/animation effects; 83 min.; B&W; 1.85:1.

CAST

Hugh Marlowe (*Dr. Russell A. Marvin*); Joan Taylor (*Carol Marvin*); Donald Curtis (*Maj. Huglin*); Morris Ankrum (*Brig. Gen. John Hanley*); John Zaremba (*Prof. Kanter*); Thomas Browne Henry (*Vice Adm. Enright*); Grandon Rhodes (*Gen. Edmunds*); Larry J. Blake (*Motorcycle Cop*); Nicky Blair (*Military Officer*); Paul Frees (*Alien*, voice only).

MOST MEMORABLE LINE

When an armed and threatening power lands in our capital, we don't meet him with tea and cookies.

GENERAL EDMUNDS

BACKGROUND

Donald E. Keyhoe (1897–1988) brought decades of experience as a U.S. Marine aviator to the stories, factual and fictional, that he wrote for numerous magazines. When the sightings of flying saucers became common circa 1949, he wrote a piece for *True*, arguing that the UFOs probably existed. Keyhoe then followed up with *Flying Saucers from Outer Space* (1953), a book that fascinated the public. His insistence that both the government and the military finally admit that they had evidence of such visitors led to his being proclaimed a leader of "ufology," the study of alien spacecraft.

THE PLOT

On their way to the Skyhook scientific and military base, Dr. Russell Marvin and his bride Carol encounter a UFO. They soon learn U.S. satellites are crashing. As it turns out, the explosions have been caused not by the Cold War enemies of the United States, but by creatures from the stars fearing the invasion of their own worlds. The extraterrestrials attempt to land at the base, but panicked guards shoot at the aliens. When they retaliate, a full-scale war of the worlds occurs.

THE FILM

Even after Columbia Pictures won a place among the leading Hollywood studios, it continued to turn out B movies that paid the bills for their more prestigious projects. Fred F. Sears (1913–1957) emerged as one of the company's most prolific B movie directors. In addition to this sci-fi standout, he helmed Westerns (*Apache Ambush*, 1955); juvenile delinquent tales (*Rumble on the Docks*, 1956); routine horror movies (*The Werewolf*, 1956); and rock 'n' roll exploitation flicks (*Rock Around the Clock*, 1956). With *Earth vs. the Flying Saucers*, the studio continued the practice of distributing "junk" movies produced by small emergent independents like Clover Productions, with Columbia's Sam "King of the Quickies" Katzman co-producing the inexpensive product or picking such films up for distribution.

"Clover" was the moniker producer Charles H. Schneer (1920–2009) chose for his production company when he picked Ray Harryhausen to create the animated six-tentacled "octopus" (two tentacles were eliminated for budgetary reasons) for *It Came from Beneath the Sea* (1955). Its success for Columbia proved the value of Harryhausen's stop-motion approach, prompting the company to request another such item. The ongoing debate over flying saucers, fueled by Keyhoe's recent book, left no doubt that their next project should feature an elaborate UFO.

THEME

Most science-fiction films of the 1950s fell neatly into one of two categories. The first type, in the tradition of *The Day the Earth Stood Still* (1951), depicted aliens as benevolent and all difficulties a result of man's instinct to shoot first and ask questions later. In contrast, the second type, like *The Thing from Another World* (1951), presented aliens as evil and humans who hoped to appease the invaders as weak fools. *Earth vs. the Flying Saucers* is unique, as the script avoids any extreme polarization, opting instead for a middle ground in which simple rights or wrongs do not exist. The aliens are initially concerned that earthlings may harbor imperialistic designs in their conquest of space. Likewise, it is our people who fire first, initiating violent confrontation. However, these aliens are anything but Christ-like, as had been the case with Michael Rennie's gentle "Carpenter" in the Robert Wise 1951 classic *The Day the Earth Stood Still*. They are as swift to kill as "the thing" from another world in the 1951 Hawks/Nyby film, and do so without mercy. A bleak tale of survival of the fittest, with neither side clearly in the right, *Earth vs. the Flying Saucers* represents a complex vision for a B movie.

TRIVIA

Rounding out this film's top-level team were the writers, Curt Siodmak (1902–2000) and George Worthing Yates (1901–1975). Siodmak's 1942 novel, *Donovan's Brain*, had led to a much-lauded 1953 film. He had also worked on the screenplays for *The Magnetic Monster* (1953) and *Riders to the Stars* (1954). Yates had been fundamental in giving *Conquest of Space* (1955) a realistic, rather than fantastical, sensibility—an approach he also brought to this memorable project.

Despite the fictional storyline, every confrontation with a saucer in this film was closely based on some recorded incident as detailed in Keyhoe's book. The idea to locate UFOs over Washington, D.C., came from an actual sighting reported by many reliable sources who insisted they saw saucer-shaped objects circling the capital on July 19 and 20, 1952.

Ray Harryhausen did not care for the finished film, its longstanding status as a classic aside.

MORE STARS THAN THERE ARE IN THE HEAVENS: *That Metro-Goldwyn-Mayer promotional line took on a literal meaning when the "Tiffany studio" (as they called themselves) entered the sci-fi sweepstakes. Robby the Robot encounters, from left to right, Jack Kelly, Earl Holliman, Warren Stevens, and Leslie Nielsen. Courtesy: Metro-Goldwyn-Mayer.*

• • • • • • •

FORBIDDEN PLANET (1956)

—— RANKING: 5 ——

CREDITS

MGM; Fred M. Wilcox, dir.; William Shakespeare, play; Irving Block, Allen Adler, story; Cyril Hume, scr.; Nicholas Nayfack, pro.; George J. Folsey, cin.; Ferris Webster, ed.; Block, Mentor Huebner, prod. design; Cedric Gibbons, Arthur Lonergan, art dir.; Helen Rose, costumes (Anne Francis); Huebner, storyboards; Lonergan, designer (Morbius house); Glen Robinson, prop designer (ray guns/ accessories); Wesley C. Miller, sound F/X; Robert Kinoshita, Robby the Robot designer; A. Arnold Gillespie, Joshua Meador, Warren Newcombe, Irving G. Ries, Doug Hubbard, Robinson, F/X; Bob Abrams, animation; 98 min.; Color; 2.55:1.

CAST

Walter Pidgeon (*Dr. Edward Morbius*); Anne Francis (*Altaira Morbius*); Leslie Nielsen (*Commander J. J. Adams*); Warren Stevens (*Lt. "Doc" Ostrow*); Jack Kelly (*Lt. Jerry Farman*); Richard Anderson (*Chief Quinn*); Earl Holliman (*Cook*); George Wallace (*Bosun*); Robert Dix, Jimmy Thompson, James Drury, Harry Harvey Jr., Roger McGee, Peter Miller, Morgan Jones, Richard Grant, James Best (*Crewmen*); Marvin Miller (*Robby the Robot*, voice); Les Tremayne (*Narrator*, voice).

MOST MEMORABLE LINE

Monsters from the id!

"DOC" OSTROW'S FAMOUS LAST WORDS

BACKGROUND

As every studio scrambled to get in on the space craze, MGM's head of production Dore Schary (1905–1980) decided that his team, known as the Tiffany studio of Hollywood, must produce the biggest and best sci-fi film. The budget for *Forbidden Planet* eventually climbed to almost $2 million, qualifying this as another of those ambitious 1950s sci-fi films that led to more impressive F/X-laden projects in the 1960s. Knowing the well-educated Schary would approve, writers Irving Block and Allen Adler added a literary element: they adapted Shakespeare's premise for *The Tempest*, transforming an old world fantasy into a futuristic space opera.

In the original concept, the piece took place in a near-future setting on another planet, probably Mercury. In preparing the final screenplay, Cyril Hume pushed the tale ahead in time, adding a more exotic element. This would distinguish *Forbidden Planet* from earlier efforts such as *Destination Moon* (1950) by presenting a fairy tale concept via groundbreaking artwork.

THE PLOT

During the colonization of deep space in the early twenty-third century, settlers who had relocated to Altair IV twenty years earlier fail to respond to questions regarding their well-being from the federation of United Planets. As a result, a Cruiser C57-D, captained by Commander J. J. Adams, is dispatched to rescue survivors. There are two: Dr. Morbius and his daughter Altaira, who, along with their benign contraption Robby the Robot, inhabit a magical terrain. All other inhabitants had been killed by an invisible force, which had eliminated the advanced Krell civilization two hundred thousand years earlier. Even as the commander falls in love with the space nymph Altaira, that unseen and long-dormant evil rises again.

THE FILM

There is one notable gap in the logic of the script. Near the end, the "id" is brought up by the dying "Doc" Ostrow. The commander asks Morbius for an explanation and learns that this refers to the primitive side of even the most advanced human. Such dialogue had to be included for the edification of the audience, which might not be familiar with that Freudian term. However, moments later, the commander refers to our "subconscious" and, later still, to the "ego." If familiar with both those psychological terms, he would certainly know of the id.

Not only one of the best sci-fi films of the 1950s but also one of the most influential, *Forbidden Planet* had a significant impact on several then-young talents. Gene Roddenberry drew from memories of this movie for ideas for *Star Trek*, including the blasters, the beaming down of crewmembers, and even the inclusion of a crotchety ship's doctor. The original *Star Trek* pilot, "The Cage," likewise dealt with a spacecraft hoping to rescue survivors from a failed mission of approximately two decades earlier. Rod Serling, whose *Twilight Zone* was also shot on the MGM lot, recycled the *Forbidden Planet* saucer for numerous episodes and used Robby the Robot several times in the series. Near the beginning of George Lucas's *Star Wars Episode IV: A New Hope* (1977), Leia is seen as a holographic image, much as Altaira is presented in *Forbidden Planet*. Robert Kinoshita, who designed Robby, would later also design the robot on the popular 1960s TV series *Lost in Space*.

No previous science-fiction film had featured an entirely electronic score, but that approach, devised by Louis and Bebe Barron as what they described as a series of "tonalities," would become a mainstay (and in time, a cliché) of the genre.

THEME

In recent years, such popular cable TV series as *Ancient Aliens* have explored the notion of visitors from the stars during the early days of Earth. Others, such as *UFO Hunters*, suggest that sightings of the late 1940s and 1950s might have been of experimental devices, tested by the U.S. Air Force. *Forbidden Planet* paves the way for both theories. The ship is saucer-shaped, and we learn that the advanced beings, the Krells, visited Earth ages ago, explaining the presence of tigers on Altair IV. Likewise, many twenty-first-century documentaries insist that the pyramids were built to receive visitors. Here, we learn the essence of all Krell architecture is a pyramid-like form, suggesting that they may have been those very visitors to Earth.

TRIVIA

Though MGM boasted its own animation unit, the studio brass requested that the Walt Disney company become involved in the cartooning process for the quasi-visible monster as it approaches for a climactic fight. Disney loaned out special effects artist and animator Joshua Meador. This explains why the characteristic Disney style is in evidence, right down to the creature's goatee, which hints that he is the alter ego of Dr. Morbius, the only cast member to wear one.

As MGM's most elaborate fantasy since *The Wizard of Oz* (Victor Fleming, 1939), *Forbidden Planet* was, not coincidentally, shot on the same soundstage. Moreover, Altaira's garden was assembled from leftover pieces of Munchkinland.

To convince adults that this was not simply a kid's movie, the studio added a semi-nude swimming scene for Altaira.

· · · · · · ·

GODZILLA, KING OF THE MONSTERS! (1956)

—— RANKING: 65 ——

CREDITS

Toho Company/Jewell Enterprises; Ishirô Honda, Terry O. Morse, dir.; Honda, Shigeru Kayama, Takeo Murata (Japan), Al C. Ward (U.S.), scr.; Tomoyuki Tanaka (Japan), Edward B. Barison, Richard Kay, Joseph E. Levine, Harry Rybnick, Terry Turner (U.S.), pro.; Akira Ifukube, mus.; Morse, ed. (U.S.); Satoru Chûko, prod. design; Chûko, Takeo Kita, art dir.; Kuichirô Kishida, Hiroshi Mukoyama, Eiji Tsuburaya, Akira Watanabe, F/X; 80 min.; B&W; 1.37:1.

CAST

Raymond Burr (*Steve Martin*); Takashi Shimura (*Dr. Kyohei Yamane*); Akira Takarada (*Hideto Ogata*); Momoko Kôchi (*Emiko Yamane*); Akihiko Hirata (*Dr. Daisuke Serizawa*); Frank Iwanaga (*Tomo Iwanaga*); Toyoaki Suzuki (*Boy from Oto Island*); Mikel Conrad (*George Lawrence*); Ryosaku Takasugi, Katsumi Tezuka (*Godzilla*).

A BREEZE FROM THE EAST: *The original* kaiju *(strange beast) entry from Japan has been interpreted by historians of the sci-fi film as an oblique metaphor for the destruction of Hiroshima and Nagasaki by nuclear weapons at the end of World War II. Courtesy: Joseph E. Levine/Embassy Pictures/Toho Studios/Jewell.*

MOST MEMORABLE LINE

Here in Tokyo, time has been turned back two million years.

REPORTER STEVE MARTIN AS THE FOUR-HUNDRED-FOOT
CREATURE DECIMATES THE CITY

BACKGROUND

Joseph E. Levine (1905–1987) was among those who wanted to create indie empires in the new postwar Hollywood. He became aware that a small company, Jewell Enterprises, had picked up the rights to distribute *Gojira* (1954), the first of Japan's low-budget *kaiju* (strange beast) films from Toho, the Japanese production and distribution company. *Gojira* had been playing in Los Angeles in a small Chinatown theater that catered almost exclusively to Asian audiences. Sensing the financial possibilities of thrillers with the teenage audience, Levine sought to mainstream the film. Believing an American "star" was needed for the marquee, he hired character actor Raymond Burr and, in one day, shot episodes that could be edited throughout the film. In one final inspiration, Levine hired Terry Turner, an experienced exploitation man who, while at RKO, had helped build *King Kong* (1933) into a highly anticipated extravaganza via his gifts at showy public relations.

THE PLOT

Journalist Steve Martin flies to Japan and soon becomes aware of something strange in the Pacific as he accompanies paleontologist Dr. Kyohei Yamane and his daughter, Emiko, to a primitive island. There they find a relic of the Jurassic Period, a monster more dangerous than ever due to contamination by both nuclear attacks and waste. Emiko knows of the only means to destroy the beast as Dr. Serizawa, her scientist fiancé, has conveniently developed a death ray.

THE FILM

After graduating from Nippon University, Ishirô Honda (1911–1993) turned to filmmaking and delivered eight realistic works. He then embraced the fantasy genre, believing that, with *Gojira*, he could reach a larger audience for his anti-nuke theme. Its success made him the resident genius of the Asian monster movie market; Honda's follow-up work included *Rodan* (1956) and *Mothra* (1961).

This project may have been inspired by the American movie *The Beast from 20,000 Fathoms* (1953), a huge hit in Japan. At the time of *Godzilla*'s release, it was feared that Honda's low-budget approach—a man in a rubber suit playing the monster—might end the slow, expensive tradition of stop-action sci-fi. In truth, both approaches would survive: the Japanese "big bug" movies flourished even as stop-motion pioneer Ray Harryhausen turned to more mythological tales, beginning with *The 7th Voyage of Sinbad* (1958), featuring a fantastical array of creatures that could not be believably rendered other than with elaborate tabletop models.

THEME

Godzilla served as a sci-fi/monster movie allegory for the all-too-real atomic bombings that ended World War II. The monster represents the fallout from Hiroshima and Nagasaki, providing a vivid actualization of the ongoing hazards. The movie features a recurring sci-fi theme: the fear that the very science that inadvertently created such a monstrosity can be relied on to end it via the anti-oxygen formula. In a nod to the genre's reliance on religion, the scientist agrees to use his controversial "solution" only after watching little children pray to Asian gods. The film reveals a major change in postwar Japanese society as, in a break with tradition, the female lead refuses to marry the man her beloved father has chosen for her, insisting instead on the man she loves for her spouse. Finally, the experience of watching Japanese women and children menaced by Godzilla and seeing the great sympathy Burr's representative American feels for them helped resolve any lingering anger on the part of U.S. citizens toward Japan for the devastating events of World War II that had begun with Pearl Harbor.

TRIVIA

Obscure actor Mikel Conrad, who plays the "other" English-language character "George," had the lead in Levine's early exploitation effort, *Untamed Women* (1952).

Levine would enjoy great success again two years later when, with his new independent Embassy distribution company, he imported *Hercules* (1958), starring Steve Reeves, from Italy and began a parallel craze for low-budget "peplum," or sword and sandal, films (the genre's title derives from the brief white outfits worn by the leading characters).

Character actor Raymond Burr (1917–1993) took the lead because it allowed him to play a sympathetic hero after a long career of sleazy villain roles—notably, the murderer in Alfred Hitchcock's *Rear Window* (1954). He had no connection with the subsequent franchise of child-oriented *Godzilla* films. Nearly thirty years later, Burr agreed to return to his old role for *Godzilla 1985* (1984).

· · · · · · ·

THE INCREDIBLE SHRINKING MAN (1957)

—— RANKING: 49 ——

CREDITS

Universal-International; Jack Arnold, dir.; Richard Matheson, novel; Matheson, Richard Alan Simmons, scr.; Albert Zugsmith, pro.; Joseph Gershenson, Harris Ashburn, mus.; Ellis W. Carter, cin.; Albrecht Joseph, ed.; Robert Clatworthy, Alexander Golitzen, art dir.; Cleo E. Baker, Fred Knoth, F/X; Everett H. Broussard, Roswell A. Hoffmann, visual/optical effects; Ray Anthony, trumpet solo; 81 min.; B&W; 1.85:1.

CAST

Grant Williams (*Scott Carey*); Randy Stuart (*Louise Carey*); April Kent (*Clarice*); Paul Langton (*Charlie Carey*); Raymond Bailey (*Dr. Silver*); William Schallert (*Dr. Bramson*); Frank J. Scannell (*Carnival Barker*); Helene Marshall, Diana Darrin (*Nurses*); Billy Curtis (*Midget*).

MOST MEMORABLE LINE

To God, there is no zero.
SCOTT CAREY, AS HE SLIPS OUT OF THE RANGE OF HUMAN SIGHT

BACKGROUND

Raised in Brooklyn, Richard Matheson (1926–2013) served in World War II and used the GI Bill to earn a journalism degree before heading west to California. There he submitted several stories to *The Magazine of Fantasy and Science Fiction*, scoring publication in 1950.

FROM THE MASTER, RICHARD MATHESON: *Grant Williams prepares to defend himself against a gigantic (at least to him) spider in this masterful combination of edge-of-your-seat thriller and metaphysical meditation on the subjectivity of size and space. Courtesy: Universal.*

Jack Arnold (1912–1992), originally from Connecticut, learned how to make movies during World War II while serving in the Signal Corps, his mentor none other than legendary documentary filmmaker Robert Flaherty. Arnold's early love of sci-fi and fantasy prompted him to seek a career in that genre after reaching Hollywood. He worked on episodes of *Science Fiction Theatre* (1955–1957), as well as on such features as *It Came from Outer Space* (1953) and *Creature from the Black Lagoon* (1954). A devotee of pulp fiction, Arnold knew the moment he read Matheson's 1956 novel *The Shrinking Man* that he had found vivid material for a superior B film.

THE PLOT

While cruising near Catalina Island on a borrowed boat, Louise Carey slips below to grab some beer; her husband Scott remains above, sunbathing. During her absence, a strangely shaped cloud/mist passes over and across him, leaving a sparkling residue on Scott's body. A few months later, he unaccountably begins to shrink. While doctors search for some antidote, Scott finds himself becoming smaller and smaller until he is the size of a Tom Thumb–like toy, living in a dollhouse. When the family cat attacks, Scott is swept down into the basement, where he duels with (and defeats) a huge spider, after which he must face the question of whether he is consigned to oblivion or infinity.

THE FILM

The book's title was expanded to make the movie competitive with *The Amazing Colossal Man* (Bert I. Gordon), a pulp junk movie released the same year. Some changes from the novel, such as the elimination of a five-year-old-daughter, streamlined the story. *The Shrinking Man* was an adult novel, so other changes were necessary to make a movie for a largely teenage audience. These included sexual issues raised in the book: the frustration of Scott and Louise over not being able to make love; his infatuation, while reduced to the size of a teenager, with their babysitter; his affair with the dwarf Clarice (a "friendship" in the film), and an ugly encounter with a pedophile who believes Scott to be a child.

THEME

Far ahead of its time, Matheson's work not only includes a common fear of nuclear waste blowing through the air, but also a warning against pesticides: a combination of the two poisons causes Scott to shrink. Both anti-nuke and pro-environmental, the film preceded Rachel Carson's classic *Silent Spring* by five years.

Matheson also confronts the issue of normalcy or, more correctly, the myth of that concept, as Scott struggles to find ways in which to fit in some alternative norm. Survival is a theme: in the basement, Scott becomes a miniature Robinson Crusoe, refusing to die and teaching himself all sorts of new skills that allow him, with great effort, to go on living. There is an adventure film aspect to the fight with the spider, Scott brandishing a "sword" (sewing pin) against this everyday Grendel.

Finally, the film invokes Einstein's theory of relativity for a mass audience. There is no big or small; such concepts are entirely subjective, existing in comparison to what happens to be surrounding Scott at any moment in his bizarre journey. The fear of disappearing evaporates when he realizes that he will enter microscopic, then sub-microscopic worlds, and, after that, universes beyond man's scope to imagine. There is no end as, like space above, here is yet another form of infinity that exists in our world and that science—via science fiction—allows modern citizens to comprehend.

TRIVIA

At one point, the theme from *Written on the Wind* (Douglas Sirk, 1956) plays on the radio. The in-joke: in that film, Grant Williams portrays Dorothy Malone's lover.

However Matheson-esque the final line, quoted above, may sound, it was not in the script and was added, at the last moment, by director Arnold.

The movie's success inspired Matheson to write a sequel, *The Fantastic Shrinking Girl*. Randy Stuart was set to reprise her role as Louise, now suffering the same fate as her husband. Universal chose not to film it, though a belated parody, *The Incredible Shrinking Woman* (Joel Schumacher, 1981), starred Lily Tomlin.

WITH AN EYE TOWARD THE YOUTH AUDIENCE: *Savvy filmmakers realized, in the late 1950s, the incredible spending power of contemporary high school kids and geared the sci-fi product to a target teen audience. Courtesy: Tonylyn Productions/Paramount.*

······

THE BLOB (1958)

—— RANKING: 77 ——

CREDITS

Paramount Pictures/Fairview Productions/Tonylyn Productions; Irvin S. Yeaworth Jr., Russell S. Doughten Jr., dir.; Irvine H. Millgate, original concept; Theodore Simonson, Kay Linaker, scr.; Doughten, Jack H. Harris, pro.; Ralph Carmichael, mus.; Thomas E. Spalding, cin.; Alfred Hillmann, ed.; William Jersey, Karl Karlson, art dir.; Bart Sloane, F/X; 82 min. (original release), 86 min. (director's cut); Color; 1.66:1.

CAST

Steve McQueen (*Steve Andrews*); Aneta Corsaut (*Jane Martin*); Earl Rowe (*Lt. Dave*); Olin Howland (*Old Hermit*); Stephen Chase (*Dr. T. Hallen*); John Benson (*Sgt. Jim Bert*); George Karas (*Officer Ritchie*); Lee Payton (*Nurse Kate*); Elbert Smith (*Henry Martin*); Hugh Graham (*Andrews*); Vincent Barbi (*George*); Audrey Metcalf (*Elizabeth Martin*).

MOST MEMORABLE LINE

How do you get people to protect themselves from something they don't believe in?

STEVE TO FELLOW TEENAGERS

BACKGROUND

Some sources insist that Irvine Millgate was inspired to create this trend-setting independent film after hearing Sheb Wooley's campy rock 'n' roll spoof, "The Purple People Eater," in 1958. That's not likely, as the movie was already in production at that time. The song's goofy attitude, however, may well have influenced the tone during the shooting of the film, which combines abject horror with an effective tongue-in-cheek sense of humor aimed directly at the teen viewer. When this locally produced Pennsylvania venture was picked up by prestigious Paramount as a co-feature for their own genre entry, *I Married a Monster from Outer Space* (1958), studio executives added a lighthearted ballad at the beginning, composed by Burt Bacharach and Mack David. Irvin S.

Yeaworth (1926–2004), who had never before helmed a feature, despised this as an obvious gimmick for commercialization via a Top 40 hit song. Yeaworth's qualifications for the position consisted of many years of work on economically budgeted educational and/or religious films.

The working screenplay for *The Blob* had been titled *The Molten Meteor* until screenwriter Kay Linaker began referring to their invader as a "glob," and the film was renamed *The Glob that Girdled the Globe*. As this was considered too silly even for the rock 'n' roll set, it was shortened to *The Glob*. When a children's book with that name appeared, the title was again changed to avoid confusion, this time to *The Blob*.

THE PLOT

Typical American teenagers Steve and Jane park in a lover's lane, arguing about "how far to go." They spot what appears to be a comet and drive toward the area where the object apparently fell. An old hermit has already come across the small ball, which releases a black ooze that crawls up his hand. After they almost run down the hysterical man, Steve and Jane drive him to the office of the local doctor. The teens depart and join drag-racing friends, while the blob devours not only the hermit but also the doctor and his nurse before heading for town.

THE FILM

The most terrifying sequence involves teens at a theater, watching monster movies. The blob slips up to the projection booth, oozing out the slots and down toward them. Though the terms "deconstruction" and "reflexivity" had not yet been invented, such film theories are present via the breaking down of barriers between the audience in the movie and the real-life audience of a similar age watching *The Blob*. In theaters across the United States, teens turned to glance backward nervously for the remainder of the film.

The blob was created from silicone, which was colored by vegetable dye. That the monster is seldom seen is part of the film's power and is reminiscent of the horror films Val Lewton produced for RKO in the 1940s, *Cat People* (1942) most famous among them. Nothing that an F/X artist can put onscreen will ever be as frightening as what a viewer imagines due to brief suggestions. Such an approach proved most rewarding at the box office. The film was shot for between $100,000 and $200,000, owing to the use of color and widescreen. Although the costs were considerable for a B horror film, *The Blob* grossed more than $4 million, proving to Hollywood the viability and profitability of the teen-oriented movie.

THEME

The Blob tapped into the teen angst of the time. The characters were modeled on those in *Rebel Without a Cause* (1955), but, in this movie, the parallel characters were plunged into a less realistic situation. The major complaint of the era's teenagers was that adults didn't take them seriously. Throughout the movie, Steve has trouble convincing the grown-ups that the monster sighting is not simply a prank.

An alternative interpretation holds that the blob represents "creeping communism" and that its defeat by freezing (it's dumped at the North Pole) symbolizes the Cold War.

TRIVIA

The film was shot entirely in and around Phoenixville, Pennsylvania. Though no one could have predicted, television had an important impact on its box office success. Shortly after completing this independent feature, Steve McQueen was signed to star in the CBS Western *Wanted: Dead or Alive*. Likewise, Tom Tryon, who had top billing in *The Blob*'s co-feature, *I Married a Monster from Outer Space*, essayed the lead in Disney's *Texas John Slaughter* for ABC. This allowed some inventive theater owners to employ such impromptu marketing strategies as "Your Favorite TV Cowboys Meet the Monsters!"

Such synergy continued when, before the film's release, its title song, credited to The Five Blobs, could be heard on the radio and record. To save money on backup performers, singer Bernie Knee overdubbed his own voice to give the impression that this was one of the era's popular groups. The marketing of movies, particularly those aimed at youth, changed immediately when entertainment executives realized that kids were devoted to rock 'n' roll (their music) and sci-fi (their films)—and, importantly, that one could be used to sell the other.

INTEGRATING THE GENRE: *Harry Belafonte, a top recording star, as well as an excellent actor, played the lead in the first sci-fi film ever to focus on an African-American hero. Courtesy: Sol C. Siegel-HarBel Productions/Metro-Goldwyn-Mayer.*

• • • • • • •

THE WORLD, THE FLESH AND THE DEVIL (1959), ON THE BEACH (1959), AND THE DAY THE EARTH CAUGHT FIRE (1961)

—— RANKING: 59 (THREE-WAY TIE) ——

THE WORLD, THE FLESH AND THE DEVIL (1959)

CREDITS

MGM/HarBel Productions; Ranald MacDougall, dir.; MacDougall, scr.; Harry Belafonte, George Englund, Sol C. Siegel, prod.; Miklós Rózsa, mus.; Harold J. Marzorati, cin.; Harold F. Kress, ed.; Paul Groesse, art dir.; Lee LeBlanc, F/X; Matthew Yuricich, visual effects; 95 min.; B&W; 2.35:1.

CAST

Harry Belafonte (*Ralph Burton*); Inger Stevens (*Sarah Crandall*); Mel Ferrer (*Benson Thacker*).

MOST MEMORABLE LINE

I have nothing against Negroes, Ralph.
BENSON THACKER

BACKGROUND

Harry Belafonte (1927–) was the first person of color to break through from a limited ethnic audience for his music and acting to mainstream recording and movie star. Belafonte produced this motion picture under his own indie banner, working closely with Ranald MacDougall on the script. Though the narrative is original, the collaborators drew from two sources: M. P. Shiel's novel, *The Purple Cloud* (1901), and Ferdinand Reyher's short story, "End of the World" (1951).

THE PLOT

Working in a Pennsylvania coal mine, Ralph is safe underground when an atomic war ends the world. After crawling to the surface, he heads for New York City. There he lives alone until encountering another survivor, Sarah. Gradually, they form a tentative friendship, but when Sarah asks for a romantic relationship, Ralph cannot respond, owing to years of suffering prejudice that has left him with a chronic fear of interracial coupling. After struggling with the issue, Ralph is about to comply when a white man, Benson, pilots his boat into the harbor.

THE FILM

A unique shooting schedule had to be created for the extraordinary representation of a world depopulated. Sequences that take place in a deserted Manhattan were completed between dawn and the arrival of daily commuters, leaving approximately one hour and thirty-five minutes of work time. As people stepped out of the subways, the crew packed up and hurried off to complete one of the interior shots.

THEME

In the 1950s, two essential themes emerged in movies: the possible end of the world and civil rights, the latter films usually starring either Belafonte or Sidney Poitier. *The World, the Flesh and the Devil* is the only work from that decade to collapse the two great social issues into a single work.

That the Bible is not denied but exalted by sci-fi is made clear in the didactic inclusion of a quote from Isaiah 2:4 that upholds the movie's anti-racist/antiwar vision: "Nation shall not lift up sword against nation."

TRIVIA

The decision was made to show no piled bodies in part to avoid gruesomeness, but also to avoid the expense that visualizing such a calamity would have incurred.

ON THE BEACH (1959)

CREDITS

United Artists; Stanley Kramer, dir.; Nevil Shute, novel; John Paxton, scr.; Kramer, pro.; Ernest Gold, mus.; Giuseppe Rotunno, cin.; Frederic Knudtson, ed.; Rudolph Sternad, prod. design; Fernando Carrere, art dir.; Lee Zavitz, F/X; 134 min.; B&W; 1.66:1.

CAST

Gregory Peck (*Cmdr. Dwight Lionel Towers*); Ava Gardner (*Moira Davidson*); Fred Astaire (*Julian Osborne*); Anthony Perkins (*Lt. Peter Holmes*); Donna Anderson (*Mary Holmes*); John Tate (*Adm. Bridie*); Harp McGuire (*Lt. Sunderstrom*).

MOST MEMORABLE LINE

It's all over now, isn't it?

MARY TO PETER

BACKGROUND

Nevil Shute's (1899–1960) 1957 novel set the pace for a sci-fi subgenre that presented the possibility of atomic apocalypse in an increasingly realistic manner. Such works avoided giving the reader any information as to who fired the first shot to avoid being labeled as an anti-Russian or anti-American diatribe. These books and films were anti-nuke in general and, by implication, antiwar. Film versions were virtually devoid of F/X, prompting some genre aficionados to claim that *The World, the Flesh and the Devil* and *On the Beach* do not qualify as sci-fi. In truth, they do: the genre is open to great diversity, including fantasy approaches at one pole and, as with the three films discussed here, ultra-realism at the opposite.

THE SCI-FI SAGA AS MESSAGE MOVIE: *Even as the 1950s ended, Stanley Kramer offered audiences the most didactic of all his save-the-world opuses. Here, Gregory Peck and Ava Gardner face The End. Courtesy: Stanley Kramer Productions/United Artists.*

THE PLOT

Following an atomic war, people in Australia are the last humans on Earth. They wait for deadly clouds to blow Down Under and annihilate them. These survivors include a jaded pair of older lovers, young marrieds, and Julian, an alcoholic cynic. Julian would love to die while driving his beloved sports car, but he can't stand the thought of it crashing. When an apparent distress signal arrives from San Diego, Commander Towers takes his submarine to the United States to determine if there are any other survivors there.

THE FILM

In terms of budget, cast, and director, the film, which appeared at decade's end, qualified as an A movie. This marked a renaissance for high-profile sci-fi, little seen since *The Day the Earth Stood Still* (1951). The atomic apocalypse fare of the 1950s mostly consists of B movies, some good, some bad. By luring grown-ups, many of whom did not think of themselves as genre aficionados, to a sci-fi film, *On the Beach* set the standard for the upcoming big-budget classics of the 1960s.

THEME

If the term "message movie" had not already existed, it would have been coined to describe the work of Stanley Kramer (1913–2001). As producer, director, and/ or writer, Kramer associated himself with films that were intended to "say something" on the important subjects of the day—*High Noon* (1952), *The Wild One* (1953), and *The Defiant Ones* (1958) among them. His work always preached party-line liberalism, which qualified Kramer as the leading voice of serious cinema in the 1950s, if something of an anachronism—well intentioned but overly didactic—during the following decade. In one scene, a number of religious people gather around a banner that calls for spiritual salvation: "There is still time, brother!" For the final shot, the world now barren, Kramer focused on that banner, a realistic piece of the setting until this point but now a direct address to his audience, begging us to do something about disarmament before it's too late.

TRIVIA

Almost the entire film was shot on location in Melbourne. The one exception was the racecar sequence, filmed at a track in Riverside, California.

The war in *On the Beach* supposedly takes place in 1964, precisely the year that Stanley Kubrick's *Dr. Strangelove or: How I Learned to Stop Worrying and Love the Bomb* was released. It was an apt title: people no longer built bomb shelters and bomb drills in public schools ceased. Once "the end of the world" theme had passed from sci-fi to black comedy, a serious rendering could no longer resonate with audiences. Between *On the Beach* and *Dr. Strangelove*, there would be one final realistic apocalypse classic to complete the unofficial trilogy.

THE DAY THE EARTH CAUGHT FIRE (1961)

CREDITS
British Lion/Val Guest Prods.; Val Guest, dir.; Guest, Wolf Mankowitz, scr.; Guest, F. Sherwin Green, pro.; Stanley Black, mus.; Harry Waxman, cin.; Bill Lenny, ed.; Anthony Masters, art dir.; Les Bowie, F/X; 98 min.; B&W, with limited color-tinted scenes; 2.35:1.

CAST
Janet Munro (*Jeannie Craig*); Leo McKern (*Bill Maguire*); Edward Judd (*Peter Stenning*); Michael Goodliffe (*Jacko Jackson*); Bernard Braden (*Dave Davis*); Reginald Beckwith (*Harry*).

MOST MEMORABLE LINE
The stupid, crazy, irresponsible bastards—they've finally gone and done it!
BILL MAGUIRE, REALIZING THAT THE END IS LIKELY NEAR,
THANKS TO SCIENTISTS' ATOMIC EXPERIMENTS

BACKGROUND
The varied career of Val Guest (1911–2006) included the two Quatermass films, *The Quatermass Experiment* (1955) and *Quatermass 2* (1957), in which he championed realistic science fiction. A part of the great tradition of British sci-fi, Guest here created the English equivalent of *On the Beach*: so serious in tone and realistic in style, and so completely devoid of genre conventions, that, its exploitive-sounding title aside, the film belongs to the end-of-the-world sub-genre owing to its story line and theme.

THE PLOT
Reporter Bill Maguire is assigned by his London paper to cover an awkward situation that occurs after the United States and Russia accidentally test atomic bombs simultaneously. Maguire realizes that the authorities are withholding from the public the information that the Earth has shifted twelve degrees in orbit and is swiftly plunging toward the sun.

THE FILM

A sense of reality was so essential that the producers shot sequences in the offices of the *Daily Express* building on Fleet Street. Arthur Christiansen, then the paper's *Sunday Express* editor, plays himself. Despite a hostile attitude toward government officials, the filmmakers managed to win permission to shoot the Ministry of Defense sequences on location. The one liberty the film-makers allowed as to style was a limited-color prologue in which the deserted streets appear ready to burn before our eyes. This effect was achieved via the use of a yellow-orange filter.

THEME

Though released before the assassination of President John F. Kennedy, the film hints at the paranoid view that would follow his death. Few films before this had suggested that the governments we trust are capable of a massive cover-up. *The Day the Earth Caught Fire* rates as the ultimate anti-nuke film in that, for once, the end is not caused by nuclear war but by peacetime testing. This allowed little room for any more serious dramatic variations on the theme, the subject matter being more or less depleted. Only B films such as *Panic in the Year Zero!* (Ray Milland, 1962) took up the slack until *Dr. Strangelove* appeared and changed everything.

TRIVIA

Val Guest would go on to write and direct the camp classic *When Dinosaurs Ruled the Earth* (1970). Steven Spielberg referenced this movie in *Jurassic Park* (1993), with posters for the earlier film hanging in Richard Attenborough's theme park.

· · · · · · ·

THE TIME MACHINE (1960)

—— RANKING: 22 ——

CREDITS

MGM; George Pal, dir.; H. G. Wells, novel; David Duncan, scr.; Pal, pro.; Russell Garcia, mus.; Paul Vogel, cin.; George Tomasini, ed.; George W. Davis, William Ferrari, art dir.; William Tuttle, special makeup dir.; Mentor Huebner, prod. illustrator; Wah Chang, Gene Warren, Howard A. Anderson, optical effects; Tim

Baar, special photographic effects; Bill Brace, matte artist; Jim Danforth, F/X; Tom Holland, stop-motion animator; Pal, Morlock design; 103 min.; Color; 1.85:1.

CAST
Rod Taylor (*H. George Wells*); Alan Young (*David Filby/James Filby*); Yvette Mimieux (*Weena*); Sebastian Cabot (*Dr. Philip Hillyer*); Tom Helmore (*Anthony Bridewell*); Whit Bissell (*Walter Kemp*); Doris Lloyd (*Mrs. Watchett*); Paul Frees (*The Talking Rings*, voice only); Bob Barran, James Skelly (*Eloi Men*); Josephine Powell (*Eloi Woman*).

MOST MEMORABLE LINE
He has all the time in the world.
DAVID FILBY, ABOUT HIS BYGONE FRIEND GEORGE

BACKGROUND
Before its release in book form, Wells's thirty-two-thousand-word tale had been serialized in 1895 in the *New Review*. Prior to this, all time travel tales were of a fantastical nature, without regard to the rules that govern realistic forms of fiction. Yet, several decades before Einstein suggested that, once a process could be perfected, time travel would be possible, Wells had grasped this idea, understanding that his machine could travel through time but would remain locked in its original space; that is, to solve the one travel "problem" would not affect the other.

THE PLOT
Early in 1900, not long before the passing of Queen Victoria and the beginning of the modern age, close friends gather at the home of their friend George. Although he has invited them for dinner, George arrives late and in terrible disarray. He claims to have visited the future in a machine of his own making and relates a strange story of an upcoming age in which humankind has divided into two poles: the gentle Eloi, sweet, blond, sheep-like vegan creatures inhabiting the surface, and the Morlock, a horrible race of cannibals residing deep beneath the Earth's surface. In his bizarre tale, when Weena, a beautiful Eloi, is abducted by the Morlocks, George journeys into the lair to save her.

THE FILM
In Wells's original telling, the Time Traveler has no name. However, for the film, he is given the author's name, hence George. The greatest challenge for the director George Pal and the screenwriter David Duncan during their joint

THE RESCUE MYTH: *As a modernist version of ancient fantasies of other-worldly romance and adventure, the science-fiction film incorporates the recurring motif in which a beautiful female (Yvette Mimieux) is menaced by a monster (here, a Morlock), only to be saved at the last moment by an old-fashioned heroic male (Rod Taylor), as illustrated in George Pal's production of H. G. Wells's* The Time Machine *(1960). Courtesy: George Pal Productions.*

scripting process was balancing the integrity of Wells's work with the actuality of history as it had occurred. For this reason, the two World Wars are depicted realistically in the film rather than in the imaginative manner that Wells, writing in the nineteenth century, had envisioned them.

In Wells's novel, the Eloi are small creatures, a concept that charmed Pal, who had directed a fine film adaptation of the fairy tale *tom thumb* (1958). Eventually, however, he rejected such an approach—in part, because it would have necessitated employing an F/X form he had already used to full advantage. Also, as Pal wanted his new work to appeal to teenagers and adults as well as children, the film would need a romantic plot. Though Australian actor Rod Taylor had hoped Pal would hire the stage actress Shirley Knight for the role of Weena, the director believed an aura of innocence was more important than acting ability, so he hired the underage and inexperienced Yvette Mimieux. The gamble worked: her childlike qualities, be they real or performed, lend the film much of its considerable charm.

THEME

An acute observer of his social scene, Wells realized that the noble Victorian experiment to perfect humans had failed miserably, as evidenced by the rotten state of London, a far more unpleasant place than when the queen had ascended to the throne more than fifty years earlier. Therefore, he rejected the utopian ideals that had been so popular during the nineteenth century, insisting that if humans did not change course, things would grow progressively more terrible. Essentially, then, he created an alternative point of view that, in the "modern" science-fiction genre, would come to be called negative utopia or dystopian fiction. Such works offer a vision of a brave (in the worst sense of that term) new world that we would do well to avoid.

TRIVIA

George finds himself in the year 802701. The day is October 12, Columbus Day, suggesting that what we witness here is a journey's end of just such magnitude.

The time machine, visualized differently for the film than as described by Wells, is in the shape of a sled; friends of Pal insisted this was due to his love for *Citizen Kane* (1941) and its indelible penultimate image. In addition to the title object, Pal also came up with the distinct look for his Morlocks. One of the Eloi children clutches a Woody Woodpecker doll, an homage to Pal's close friend and sometimes collaborator, Walter Lantz, who had created that beloved cartoon character.

VILLAGE OF THE DAMNED (1960) AND THE DAY OF THE TRIFFIDS (1963)

—— RANKING: 75 (TIE) ——

VILLAGE OF THE DAMNED (1960)

CREDITS

MGM; Wolf Rilla, dir; John Wyndham, novel; Rilla, Stirling Silliphant, Ronald Kinnoch, scr.; Kinnoch, pro.; Ron Goodwin, mus.; Geoffrey Faithfull, cin.; Gordon Hales, ed.; Ivan King, art dir.; Tom Howard, special photographic effects; 77 min.; B&W; 1.85:1.

CAST

George Sanders (*Gordon Zellaby*); Barbara Shelley (*Anthea Zellaby*); Martin Stephens (*David Zellaby*); Michael Gwynn (*Alan Bernard*); Laurence Naismith (*Willers*); June Cowell, Linda Bateson, John Kelly, Carlo Cura, Lesley Scoble, Mark Milleham, Roger Malik, Elizabeth Mundle, Teri Scoble, Peter Preidel, Peter Taylor, Howard Knight (*The Children*).

MOST MEMORABLE LINE

A brick wall . . . A brick wall . . . I must think of a brick wall . . .
GORDON ZELLABY, AS HE ATTEMPTS TO KILL THE CHILDREN WHILE CONCENTRATING ON KEEPING THEM OUT OF HIS MIND.

BACKGROUND

John Wyndham Parkes Lucas Beynon Harris (1903–1969), whose various pen names included "John Wyndham," made his reputation with stories for *Tales of Wonder*, England's equivalent to the U.S. pulps of the 1930s. Following World War II, he, like his counterparts in the United States, proved instrumental in moving science fiction away from popular "space operas" featuring epic heroes, nearly naked beauties, and bizarre monsters. In a new era, this scribe decided that the time was right to go back to the future, reviving Jules Verne's approach of studying the latest advances in science, then presenting those advances in a relatively realistic fictionalized form. This led to post-apocalyptic visions in his most famous works, *The Day of the Triffids* (1951) and *The Midwich Cuckoos* (1957). The latter was filmed first, retitled *Village of the Damned*.

THE PLOT
On a seemingly normal day in the quiet country village of Midwich, every living creature drops as if suffering from exhaustion, only to rise within the hour. Two months later, the local women are pregnant, eventually all giving birth on the same day. The shire's most educated man, Gordon Zellaby, grows suspicious after his wife Anthea delivers a child who looks nothing like them. During the years that follow, the children—all with the same blond hair and wide, intense eyes—become a cult, able to communicate with one another through telepathy, and they use mind power to destroy anyone who they believe threatens them. The "normal" villagers realize their offspring are the results of fertilized eggs from some living force in outer space, their small town an experiment at infiltrating, then conquering, Earth.

THE FILM
Wolf Rilla (1920–2005), a German-born filmmaker working in Great Britain, was chosen partly for his talent, but also because he was not associated with genre films. This freed him, so far as the producers were concerned, to use a matter-of-fact style. The film's popularity in the United States, as well as in England, paved the way for a dialectic approach to the genre with fewer bug-eyed monsters on view. *Village* was shot on a $200,000 budget, which was modest in comparison to A films of the era but twice that of a typical B picture.

THEME
More in the tradition of *The Thing from Another World* (1951) than *The Day the Earth Stood Still* (1951), this film is xenophobic, portraying arriving aliens as unsympathetic. To further heighten this view, the children are played as variations on the Hitler Youth from two decades earlier: ultra-Aryan in appearance, methodical in attitude, unable to either feel or express love, and utterly amoral in attitude.

TRIVIA
The movie had been scheduled for production several years earlier, with Oscar-winning, English-born, Hollywood actor Ronald Colman cast in the lead. However, he died before filming began, and *Village* was put on hold indefinitely. By

the time that George Sanders agreed to take the part—largely so that he could portray a sympathetic character, rather than one more of his upscale, yet seamy villains—he had married actress Benita Hume, the widow of Ronald Colman.

Fans vividly recall the children's glowing eyes, an effect achieved by lighting, matte work, and animation. This effect was not part of the original English print; rather, it was added for the American release when U.S. distributors decided the movie needed "something extra" to make it more frightening. The golden hairpieces were designed to suggest that the children had high foreheads, a mark of great intelligence. This idea was borrowed from *This Island Earth* (1955). Wyndham labeled the children "cuckoos," recalling the birds that lay their eggs in the nests of other birds, which then raise the hatchlings.

Village of the Damned was followed by an unexceptional sequel, *Children of the Damned* (Anton Leader, 1964), as well as a weak remake (John Carpenter, 1995).

THE DAY OF THE TRIFFIDS (1963)

CREDITS
Security Pictures/J. Arthur Rank; Steve Sekely, Freddie Francis, dir.; John Wyndham, novel; Philip Yordan, Bernard Gordon, scr.; George Pitcher, Yordan, Bernard Glasser, pro.; Ron Goodwin, Johnny Douglas, mus.; Ted Moore, cin.; Bill Lewthwaite, ed.; Cedric Dawe, art dir.; Wally Veevers, Bob Cuff, special visual effects; 93 min.; Color; 2.35:1.

CAST
Howard Keel (*Bill Masen*); Nicole Maurey (*Christine Durrant*); Janette Scott (*Karen Goodwin*); Kieron Moore (*Tom Goodwin*); Mervyn Johns (*Mr. Coker*); Ewan Roberts (*Dr. Soames*); Alison Leggatt (*Miss Coker*); Geoffrey Matthews (*Luis de la Vega*); Janina Faye (*Susan*); Gilgi Hauser (*Teresa de la Vega*); John Tate (*Captain of the* SS Midland); Carole Ann Ford (*Bettina*); Colette Wilde (*Nurse Jamieson*); Mick Dillon (*Triffid*).

MOST MEMORABLE LINE
Most plants thrive on animal waste, but I'm afraid this mutation possesses an appetite for the animal itself.
MR. COKER TO BILL MASEN

THE WORLD ACCORDING TO JOHN WYNDHAM: *One of England's finest sci-fi writers of the postwar era offered unique variations on the theme of endgame: steely-eyed space children are hatched on Earth in* Village of the Damned, *and our beloved plants turn against us (one menacing gorgeous Nicole Maurey) in* The Day of the Triffids. *Courtesy: Metro-Goldwyn-Mayer/Security Pictures-Allied Artists.*

THE PLOT

A member of the merchant marine, Bill Masen has undergone surgery in hopes that his temporary blindness may be remedied. His head bandaged, Masen cannot see the fascinating meteor shower witnessed by most everyone else in London. The next morning, when Masen removes the bandage, he learns that almost every other citizen has gone blind as a result of watching the natural light show. In the company of a sighted child, he heads for France, where an aristocratic Frenchwoman oversees a colony of survivors.

Meanwhile, monster plants called "Triffids," which are able to move, attempt to kill off humankind. The only hope is a team of married scientists, stranded in an isolated lighthouse, who attempt to figure out the flaw in these invaders' plan.

THE FILM

The screenplay was credited to Philip Yordan (1914–2003), a prolific writer known primarily for his work on Westerns: *Johnny Guitar* (1954), *The Man from Laramie* (1955), *The Bravados* (1958). His association with this project derived from a wish to help old friends, blacklisted during the McCarthy era, by fronting for them. In fact, Bernard Gordon (1918–2007), who had scripted *Earth vs. the Flying Saucers* (1956), wrote the screenplay for *The Day of the Triffids*. Though the F/X appear dated today, they were state of the art at the time, created after considerable research as to how a highly developed plant (the Triffids were largely derived from asparagus) might solve such problems as mobility.

With the prestigious J. Arthur Rank organization behind the project, a budget that allowed for widescreen and color, and a nominal Hollywood star in Howard Keel, the producers hoped that a major director might helm the piece. Steve Sekely (1899–1979), however, was associated with lowbrow horror movies, such as *Revenge of the Zombies* (1943); his association with the project caused some observers to write this off as a B movie. The Triffid attack on a lighthouse, notably different in style and tone from the main plot, was added when the finished film proved not to be long enough for release. This section was directed by Freddie Francis (1917–2007) of Hammer Films fame. Francis brought a sense of creepiness to that sequence otherwise lacking in the primary narrative. His later thriller *Dr. Terror's House of Horrors* (1965) also includes a menacing man-eating plant.

THEME

Wyndham's theme had to be re-thought owing to changing times. The book ranked among the first Cold War apocalyptic pieces, but after the release of *On the Beach* in 1959, that approach seemed dated. The writers eliminated Wyndham's suggestion that the meteor shower may have been a Cold War ploy. His ambiguous ending, in which the survivors hold out and possibly repopulate the world, was dropped in favor of a conclusion similar to that of *The War of the Worlds* (1953): once more, humankind survives by relying on old-time religion, by this time a staple of sci-fi films.

TRIVIA

Mervyn Johns brought to the project a connection to the great English horror films, having played the character in *Dead of Night* (1945) who arrives at the chateau in the opening sequence.

Steven Spielberg includes an homage to *The Day of the Triffids* in *E.T.* (1982): when the aliens rush back to their spaceship with Earth plants, a Triffid is among them.

· · · · · · ·

THE ABSENT-MINDED PROFESSOR (1961)

—— RANKING: 57 ——

CREDITS

Buena Vista/Walt Disney; Robert Stevenson, dir.; Bill Walsh, Samuel W. Taylor, scr.; Walt Disney, Walsh, pro.; George Bruns, mus.; Edward Colman, cin.; Cotton Warburton, ed.; Carroll Clark, art dir.; Peter Ellenshaw, Eustace Lycett, Robert A. Mattey, Joshua Meador, F/X; 92 min.; B&W; 1.66:1.

CAST

Fred MacMurray (*Prof. Ned Brainard*); Nancy Olson (*Betsy Carlisle*); Keenan Wynn (*Alonzo P. Hawk*); Tommy Kirk (*Biff Hawk*); Leon Ames (*President Rufus Daggett*); Elliott Reid (*Prof. Shelby Ashton*); Edward Andrews (*Defense Secretary*); David Lewis (*Gen. Singer*); Jack Mullaney (*Air Force Capt.*); Belle Montrose (*Mrs. Chatsworth*); Forrest Lewis (*Kelley*); James Westerfield (*Hanson*); Alan Carney (*Referee*); Ed Wynn (*Fire Chief*).

SCIENCE FICTION AND THE FAMILY FILM: *Among the most delightful genre movies to deal with humankind's desire to defy gravity were Walt Disney's comedies (lighthearted, though laced with darker undercurrents) starring Fred MacMurray. Here he and his beloved dog wreak havoc in the sequel,* Son of Flubber *(1963). Courtesy: Buena Vista Releasing.*

MOST MEMORABLE LINE
Let's see, flying rubber . . . I dub thee . . . "Flubber"!
NED BRAINARD UPON MAKING HIS GREAT DISCOVERY

BACKGROUND
In addition to the long-in-development animated features like *Sleeping Beauty* (1959), Disney came up with a plan to produce tightly budgeted black-and-white fantasy projects, beginning with *The Shaggy Dog* (1959), that would feature Fred MacMurray and child stars from the Disney afternoon television show, *The Mickey Mouse Club*. When ABC, believing that no one would watch, declined a network showing, Disney released the live-action film theatrically. Its unexpected financial success initiated an ongoing series of similar projects.

THE PLOT
At humble Medfield College, beloved Professor Brainard delights students with

oddball displays of chemistry. At home, he has a makeshift lab for his wild experiments. One night, when he should be preparing for his upcoming marriage to the dean's secretary, Betsy, Brainard happens upon a rubber-like creation that accumulates energy. His discovery results in madcap schemes, such as attaching Flubber to the college basketball team's sneakers to help them leap higher. He heads for Washington in a "Flubber-ized" Model T in hopes of convincing the government that the substance could be a great boon to national security. All the while, capitalist Alonzo P. Hawk plans to steal Flubber and turn it into a money-making product.

THE FILM

Before this release, Disney's most notable exercise in sci-fi had been the 1954 *20,000 Leagues Under the Sea*, produced on an immense scale. Its success convinced "Uncle Walt" to explore this genre further. *The Absent-Minded Professor* proved the most delightful sci-fi situation comedy of all time, with the possible exception of its sequel, *Son of Flubber* (1963).

Though most Disney films were shot in color, *The Absent-Minded Professor*, like *The Shaggy Dog*, was filmed in black and white to make the special effects less obvious than if they were attempted in any of the then-existing color processes.

THEME

Like so many beloved Disney films, this one is, on reconsideration, less an example of "gentle" family fare than it initially seems. Brainard, though a good Joe in many ways, is indeed a mad scientist; at times, his actions rate as downright demonic. Though the anti-gravity theme is employed for escapist fun in the first half, things grow darker when Brainard and Betsy fly the Model T over Washington, D.C. Fearful that these are alien invaders or Cold War enemies (in the late 1950s, the two had become interchangeable), military forces prepare to blow them out of the sky. Stanley Kubrick later recaptured this unsettling tone for his doomsday thriller/black comedy *Dr. Strangelove* (1964), which has more in common with this "pleasant" Disney comedy than one might expect.

TRIVIA

Fascinated by the heightened significance of science in the post–World War II world, Disney determined to make this an important part of his work, which, up until then, had been largely of a fantasy nature. He was intrigued by competitor George Pal's "realistic" space travel features. So, when putting together the "Tomorrowland" concept for his TV anthology, Disney decided to forego space opera in favor of such documentary-like realism. When it was announced that the 1958 World's Fair would feature a science-fact pavilion, Disney traveled to Brussels to see it firsthand. Among the attractions was Professor Hubert Alyea (1903–1996), a legendary Princeton chemistry professor. Alyea rendered complex scientific ideas easy for students via take-your-breath-away explosive demonstrations that earned him the nickname "Dr. Boom." Disney invited Alyea to visit California so that his team might study the professor and develop a fictional character based on him. Writer Samuel W. Taylor fashioned a short story, "A Situation of Gravity," which was gradually fleshed out into a script.

The image of Brainard and his dog flying the revamped Model T over the moon drew on the ending of Disney's *Peter Pan* (1953): in that animated film, the pirate ship likewise cruises across that heavenly object. In his youth, Steven Spielberg saw and loved both films, and, for *E.T.* (1982), he borrowed that image for the shot of the little boy and gentle alien bicycling across the moon. That now-iconic image soon became the logo for Spielberg's production company, Amblin Entertainment.

· · · · · · ·

THE BIRDS (1963)

—— RANKING: 20 ——

CREDITS

Universal Pictures; Alfred Hitchcock, dir.; Daphne du Maurier, story; Evan Hunter, scr.; Hitchcock, pro.; Robert Burks, cin.; George Tomasini, ed.; Robert F. Boyle, prod. design; Harold Michelson, storyboard artist; Remi Gassmann, Bernard Herrmann, electronic sound production; Larry Hampton, Dave Fleischer, Chuck Gaspar, F/X; Ub Iwerks, Albert Whitlock, Bob Broughton, visual effects; 119 min.; Color; 1.37:1.

CAST

Tippi Hedren (*Melanie Daniels*); Rod Taylor (*Mitch Brenner*); Suzanne Pleshette (*Annie Hayworth*); Jessica Tandy (*Lydia Brenner*); Veronica Cartwright (*Cathy Brenner*); Ethel Griffies (*Mrs. Bundy*); Charles McGraw (*Sebastian Sholes*); Doreen Lang (*Hysterical Mother*); Ruth McDevitt (*Mrs. MacGruder*); Karl Swenson (*Drunken Doomsayer*).

THE MASTER OF SUSPENSE: *In his only venture into "realistic sci-fi," Alfred Hitchcock depicted the end of the world owing to humankind's insensitivity to the environment. In this scene, Tippi Hedren, Rod Taylor, and Jessica Tandy suffer nature's wrath. Courtesy: Universal.*

MOST MEMORABLE LINE

It's the end of the world!

A DOOMSAYER IN THE DINER

BACKGROUND

Alfred Hitchcock's (1899–1980) longtime girl Friday, Joan Harrison, brought her boss the brief story by Daphne du Maurier, whose 1938 novel, *Rebecca*, had provided material for his first Hollywood film. Though drawn to the concept, Hitchcock hesitated, believing the story to be pure fantasy. All his previous films, however improbable, had always remained in the realm of possibility. Harrison persisted, did research, and brought in newspaper clippings, proving that there had indeed been bird attacks of precisely this sort, most likely brought about by the pollution of our atmosphere via technological experiments. Realizing that this qualified the work as hard science fiction, rather than soft science fantasy, Hitchcock decided to film the story.

THE PLOT

Spoiled debutante Melanie Daniels "meets cute" with the man's man Mitch Brenner at a San Francisco pet shop, resulting in love-hate at first sight. Impulsively, Melanie buys a pair of lovebirds for Mitch and, discovering he's driven to his family home in Bodega Bay, follows him there, finding herself in the seemingly normal world of the Brenner family. Dominating mother Lydia ruined the romance between Mitch and a schoolteacher out of jealousy. Even as Melanie and Mitch try to decide if they will become a serious couple, the area is suddenly besieged by birds that soar down, kill, retreat, then attack once more.

THE FILM

Originally, Hitchcock hoped to cast Cary Grant against either Audrey Hepburn or Grace Kelly, now Princess Grace of Monaco. Grant and Hepburn both demurred because of the extraordinarily long shooting schedule required to create the F/X and the dangers that working with flocks of real birds posed to their famous faces. Kelly, who was considering a return to Hollywood to star in *Marnie* (1964), also refused *The Birds* owing to the fear of facial injuries. The lead in *Marnie* would eventually go to Tippi Hedren.

The shooting involved the most complicated special effects required for a Hollywood film to that date. A great fan of the planning process, Hitchcock worked out all aspects of every movie so meticulously in advance that he found the actual shoot to be a bore. He delighted in deciding how the bizarre incidents might be made to appear totally realistic. Ultimately, he and his crew settled on a combination of live-action trained birds on the set, some mechanical birds for other specific scenes, and animated effects added later for the finishing touches. Two of Hollywood's greatest cartoon artists joined this final process. Ub Iwerks had helped Disney develop the illusion not only of motion but also of life itself during the 1930s, inventing the multi-plane camera, which allowed for convincing in-depth effects. Dave Fleischer and his brother Max had created *Betty Boop* and the *Superman* rotoscope shorts during that same period.

The film did not include any musical score, relying entirely on realistic noise. Radios play music in everyday scenes, and electronic noises of the type that were just then becoming significant for the sci-fi genre (in part as a result of the unique soundtrack for *Forbidden Planet*) are effectively included.

THEME

Though the film is often considered more a horror movie than sci-fi, this one-of-a-kind piece does qualify as a pan-genre film. During the mid-point diner sequence, a trio of oddball characters serves as a Greek chorus, piping in with their opinions. The bird lady, a workingman, and a gleeful lunatic come up with the theory that science and technology have so polluted nature that it is now turning against us. Here then is an example of the ecological thriller, a nightmare scenario projection of what might happen in the near future should we not listen to those arguing for the end of chemical dumping and nuclear waste. Both are suggested here as possible causes of the attacks, bringing Hitchcock's film in line with apocalyptic sci-fi movies designed to convey precisely this theme.

TRIVIA

Hitchcock makes his famous cameo early in the film—and for good reason. He had often appeared (when he did so, which was not always) near the end, as in *The Lady Vanishes* (1938). This created a problem in that audiences sat on the edge of their seats, trying to spot him rather than following the story. Several films were shot without his cameo, but that annoyed audiences expecting to see him. Frustrated, Hitchcock decided to get his cameo over with as quickly as possible so that people would watch the movie.

· · · · · · ·

THE LAST MAN ON EARTH (1964)

—— RANKING: 96 ——

CREDITS

Associated Producers/AIP; Ubaldo Ragona, Sidney Salkow, dir.; Richard Matheson, novel; Matheson (as Logan Swanson), Ragona, William F. Leicester, Furio M. Monetti, scr.; Samuel Z. Arkoff, Harold E. Knox, Robert L. Lippert, pro.; Paul Sawtell, Bert Shefter, mus.; Franco Delli Colli, cin.; Gene Ruggiero, Franca Silvi, ed.; Giorgio Giovannini, prod. design; 86 min.; B&W; 2.35:1.

CAST

Vincent Price (*Dr. Robert Morgan*); Franca Bettoia (*Ruth Collins*); Emma Danieli (*Virginia Morgan*); Giacomo Rossi-Stuart (*Ben Cortman*); Umberto Raho (*Dr. Mercer*); Christi Courtland (*Kathy Morgan*); Antonio Corevi (*Governor*); Giuseppe Mattei (*New People Leader*); Carolyn De Fonseca (*Ruth Collins*, voice only).

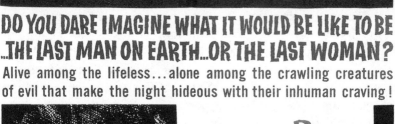

DO YOU DARE IMAGINE WHAT IT WOULD BE LIKE TO BE ..THE LAST MAN ON EARTH...OR THE LAST WOMAN?

Alive among the lifeless... alone among the crawling creatures of evil that make the night hideous with their inhuman craving!

VINCENT PRICE
STARRING AS
The Last Man on Earth

CO-STARRING
FRANCA BETTOIA · EMMA DANIELI · GIACOMO ROSSI-STUART · Directed by SIDNEY SALKOW · Produced by ROBERT L. LIPPERT
Screenplay by LOGAN SWANSON & WILLIAM F. LEICESTER · From the novel "I AM LEGEND" by RICHARD MATHESON · AN AMERICAN INTERNATIONAL PICTURE

A "B" MOVIE MASTERPIECE: *Despite a change in title, an extremely small budget, and the miscasting of Vincent Price, this Italian B movie comes closer to capturing the dark magic of Richard Matheson's novel,* I Am Legend, *than any other film version of the genre classic. Courtesy: Lippert Productions/American-International.*

MOST MEMORABLE LINE

Another day to live through; better get started.

DR. MORGAN, AS HE SETS OUT AT DAYLIGHT
TO UNEARTH AND KILL THE NEW PEOPLE

BACKGROUND

Beginning in 1959, James Nicholson and Sam Arkoff, the founders of American International Pictures (AIP), came to believe their shoestring-budget, black-and-white quickies were so popular that they were now in a position to upgrade the product. Roger Corman (1926–) was assigned to create a series of lavish (at least by AIP standards) adaptations of Edgar Allan Poe stories. His efforts include the well-received *The Pit and the Pendulum* (1961). Most of these starred Vincent Price, already a horror icon owing to *House of Wax* (André De Toth, 1953). AIP came to consider Price their top-billed star of choice.

THE PLOT

The Last Man on Earth is set in 1968, a near-future timeframe for when this film was shot. Dr. Morgan is the last human alive in his city, perhaps even the last man on Earth. He has witnessed the virtual end of humanity, the result of a plague that causes victims not to die but to become the living dead: part zombie, part vampire. His self-assumed mission is to kill them, staking each through the heart. Then he meets Ruth, who is neither human nor vampire but rather an exemplar of the New People—those who have been infected by the disease without fully succumbing to it. Morgan must determine whether he can exist in tandem with this emergent life form or if they are humankind's nightmare-scenario enemies.

THE FILM

Since the mid-1950s, Fulvio Lucisano (1928–) had been turning out tightly budgeted horror and sci-fi films in Rome. Arkoff had the idea of importing those films because they could be shot cheaper in Rome than anything that he could produce in the United States. Dialogue would be added, along with additional brief scenes shot by American exploitation filmmakers like Sidney Salkow. One *must* was the inclusion of a nominal name to whom American teens could relate. Price's work in the Poe thrillers qualified him for this adaptation of the well-regarded 1954 Richard Matheson novel *I Am Legend*. However, Matheson pictured Morgan as the most ordinary of people and thought that the character should be played by someone associated with Everyman roles. The Grand

Guignol background that Price brought to the part struck the writer as misleading and inappropriate to the piece.

Matheson had been the chief writer for the Poe films, making him a popular figure at AIP. Initially, *The Last Man on Earth* was to have been filmed by Hammer, the English company responsible for reviving Dracula and Frankenstein in color, with either Christopher Lee or Peter Cushing possibly essaying the lead here. However, when that company decided against the project, the script was passed to Robert L. Lippert, an American producer of *Rocketship X-M* (1950) fame.

THEME

Last Man comes closer to capturing the tone and theme of *I Am Legend* than either of the more elaborate remakes (*The Omega Man*, 1971, and under the original novel's title, 2007). Matheson's concept comes across during Morgan's discussion with Ruth about what the future may hold. Until then, he has never questioned the rightness of his cause: killing people to preserve humankind. Then, something Ruth says causes him to realize there is, in fact, another way of perceiving the situation. At some point, Morgan must, like any person, pass away. When that happens, these "things" will continue to exist and multiply, telling the tale of Morgan for as long as their society exists. In those stories, he will be cast as the monster—not as a good man fighting monsters, as he sees himself—that tried to kill off their community. After many years, any fading memory of his real self will have been replaced by demonization by the New People, now "the new normals." At the moment of his death, Morgan realizes that he is to the New People the extinct dragon that will forever haunt their collective imagination. Even as he expires, the last man accepts that he is now legend.

TRIVIA

In "Where Is Everybody?" the first-ever *Twilight Zone* episode, written by Rod Serling, a lonely man searches for company in an Earth seemingly abandoned by people. In a drugstore, he spots a paperback novel titled *The Last Man on Earth*.

The American writer-director George A. Romero has stated that this film, with its eerie black-and-white photography combining elements of 1940s film noir with an arthouse sensibility, provided his inspiration for *Night of the Living Dead* (1968).

A NEW WAVE: *The first significant collapsing of contemporary sci-fi into the film noir style appeared in this stylish pop art exercise from Jean-Luc Godard. Anna Karina and Eddie Constantine face off with the original men-in-suits as Kafka merges with genre conventions. Courtesy: Athos Film/Khaumiane.*

· · · · · · ·

ALPHAVILLE/ALPHAVILLE, UNE ÉTRANGE AVENTURE DE LEMMY CAUTION (1965)

—— RANKING: 26 ——

CREDITS

Athos Films; Jean-Luc Godard, dir., scr.; André Michelin, pro.; Paul Misraki, mus.; Raoul Coutard, cin.; Agnès Guillemot, ed.; Pierre Guffroy, prod. design; René Levert, special sound effects; 99 min.; B&W; 1.37:1.

CAST

Eddie Constantine (*Lemmy Caution*); Anna Karina (*Natacha von Braun*); Akim Tamiroff (*Henri Dickson*); Christa Lang, Valérie Boisgel (*Seductresses Third Class*); Jean-André Fieschi, Jean-Louis Comolli (*Heckell* and *Jeckell*); Michel Delahaye (*von Braun's Assistant*); Howard Vernon (*Nosferatu/von Braun*); Jean-Pierre Léaud (*Waiter*); László Szabó (*Chief Engineer*).

MOST MEMORABLE LINE

Sometimes reality is too complex for oral communication. But legend embodies it in a form which enables it to spread all over the world.

ALPHA 60, A COMPUTER SYSTEM DEVELOPED BY VON BRAUN

BACKGROUND

The first of Peter Cheyney's Lemmy Caution novels, *This Man Is Dangerous*, was published in Britain in 1936. The former police reporter and private investigator turned pulp fiction scribe borrowed from American tough guy private eyes like Sam Spade. At the same time, Cheyney added just a touch of off-the-cuff humor, suggesting that he might be spoofing, as well as celebrating, hard-boiled aesthetics.

Following World War II, as a Humphrey Bogart cult developed and film noirs continuously played in cinemas along Paris boulevards, French producers began mounting their own low-budget imitations. American-born actor Eddie Constantine (1917–1993), who had been mentored by legendary chanteuse Édith Piaf and who bore a strong resemblance to her Gallic protégé Charles Aznavour, was recruited to play Caution. In the early Caution films, distributed in the mid-1950s, Lemmy appears to be a European equivalent to author Mickey Spillane's mean-spirited gumshoe Mike Hammer. A decade later, Caution, as played by Constantine, had evolved from street tough to international man of adventure on the order of Ian Fleming's James Bond, just then emerging as the centerpiece of a film franchise.

Even as the Caution cycle came to a close, the most daring of France's New Wave directors, Jean-Luc Godard (1930–), transplanted this stock character into a futuristic world, commenting on our descent into dystopian anti-values. In interviews, Godard has suggested he might as easily have used Buster Crabbe as Flash Gordon, Ralph Byrd as Dick Tracy, Clayton Moore as the Lone Ranger, or Johnny Weissmuller as Tarzan. The key concept was to revive some pop culture icon, altering the context from lowbrow fun to highbrow consideration. An identifiable archetype would thrash about in a post-modern cinematic world. It's hardly coincidental, then, that two wacky scientists are named for Heckle and Jeckle, the mad magpies of comic books and cartoons. Or that the villain is named "Nosferatu," Dracula in F. W. Murnau's classic 1922 silent. All film characters inhabit a created world, those in genre movies most obviously so; conventional moviemakers attempt to render that truth invisible. Godard changed the shape and sensibility of cinema, in part by forcing viewers into a conscious awareness of the manner in which all (even "realistic") movie worlds are, despite any sense of believability during the viewing process, the carefully considered creations of self-conscious artists.

THE PLOT
Agent 003 (Lemmy Caution) leaves the Outlands on a secret mission: drive his Ford (called a "Galaxie") across time and space, arriving in Alphaville, also known as the "forbidden city." As various beauties, most scantily clad, attempt to seduce Lemmy, he sets out to locate the man who created Alpha, the computer that controls society. Carrying and casually using a Colt Commander semiautomatic, Lemmy is licensed to kill Nosferatu/von Braun on sight. Here is a world in which the all-time greatest question—"why?"—has been outlawed. Verboten too is poetry, the conduit of sincere sentiment. Lemmy rehabilitates Natacha, his last and greatest object of seduction (what in a Bond film would be called "the final girl"), who is also the daughter of the Dr. No–like antagonist whom he must conquer.

THE FILM
Combining serious science fiction, entertaining space opera, elements of the film noir shadow world, and dark comedy featuring satire on prescient situations, *Alphaville* also contains an assortment of in-joke references to earlier films. Such an approach later came to be used by filmmakers as diverse as Martin Scorsese and Quentin Tarantino. The crossing of once-sacrosanct genre boundaries began with *Alphaville*, which, like many New Wave films, celebrates the movies and what they mean to their international masses.

Godard introduced the then-radical idea of shooting a science-fiction film without any set design by pointing his camera only at the most modernist structures in an actual city. This suggestion that the near-future is already taking shape in our present times inspired young American filmmakers of the 1970s, including George Lucas (*THX 1138*, 1971).

The villain's name, von Braun, is taken from Wernher von Braun, the German rocket scientist who served the Nazis during World War II, then was supposedly rehabilitated and employed by NASA. Godard was among the first intellectuals who dared openly question the morality (or amorality) of such a convenient situation for the West.

However contemptuous some of his fans may believe Godard and other alternative filmmakers to be of traditional Hollywood hokum, this auteur embraced it wholeheartedly, if with tongue planted firmly in cheek. At the movie's end, all turns out well as Natacha finally brings herself to say the most old-fashioned of movie lines to Lemmy: "I love you." Such a defense of sentiment-as-our-salvation would reach an apex nearly a half-century later in Joss Whedon's *The Avengers* (2012).

TRIVIA

The first version of Godard's script was titled *Tarzan vs. IBM*, expressing both the filmmaker's love of individualism as well as popular culture and his hatred of computer-based corporate mentality.

·······

THE SATAN BUG (1965)

—— RANKING: 74 ——

CREDITS

United Artists/Mirisch Corporation; John Sturges, dir.; Alistair MacLean, novel; James Clavell, Edward Anhalt, scr.; Sturges, pro.; Jerry Goldsmith, mus.; Robert Surtees, cin.; Ferris Webster, ed.; Herman A. Blumenthal, art dir.; A. Paul Pollard, F/X; 114 min.; Color; 2.35:1.

CAST

George Maharis (*Lee Barrett*); Richard Basehart (*Dr. Gregor Hoffman*); Anne Francis (*Ann Williams*); Dana Andrews (*Gen. Williams*); John Larkin (*Dr. Leonard Michaelson*); Richard Bull (*Cavanaugh*); Frank Sutton (*Donald*); Edward Asner (*Veretti*); Simon Oakland (*Tasserly*); John Anderson (*Reagan*).

MOST MEMORABLE LINE

It is an ideal weapon, if you will forgive the phrase,
because it only destroys people.
DR. HOFFMAN, DESCRIBING BOTULINUS

GENIE IN A BOTTLE: *Those ancient myths in which abject evil, contained in a small vial, has the potential to devastate humanity, should someone foolishly open it, are re-imagined for the scientific age. Here, the synthetic creation entrances Anne Francis and George Maharis. Courtesy: Mirisch/United Artists.*

BACKGROUND

During the 1950s, sci-fi flourished—at least in terms of the number of films produced. Mostly, though, these (other than duly noted exceptions) had been B exploitation movies. The number of such films diminished as the decade came to an end, their equivalent now available on television with series such as *The Outer Limits* (1963–1965) and *Star Trek* (1966–1969). This freed the theatrical genre to move steadily during the 1960s to ever more adult fare and prestigious projects, *The Satan Bug* an important, overlooked example.

THE PLOT

An unpleasant incident occurs at a scientific laboratory located in a remote area of California. One doctor assigned to this post, Station Three, appears to have disappeared, though witnesses insist he was seen leaving the premises. Also, the top security officer, who had become concerned, is found murdered.

These events precipitate a crisis that the government hopes to keep from the public for as long as possible. Secret experiments at the lab have led to potentially disastrous bio-weapons. Some rogue nation or independent terrorist has made away with the most advanced, dangerous form, nicknamed the "Satan Bug." Eric Cavanaugh, a top-level security agent, sets out to recruit Lee Barrett, a former operative who has since gone maverick, to piece together a solution to the mystery. A mysterious figure identified as "Ainsley" calls in, threatening to destroy a targeted American city unless his demands are met. Barrett, General Williams, and the general's daughter (Barrett's lover) race the ticking clock to halt the coming Armageddon.

THE FILM

Director John Sturges (1910–1992) wisely chose to emulate Hitchcock's realistic approach in *The Birds* since *The Satan Bug* likewise approached a possible premise (and inherent nightmare) that might soon become a reality. Sturges had been hailed for a striking screen treatment of the American Southwest in realistic Westerns, including *Bad Day at Black Rock* (1955), *Gunfight at the O.K. Corral* (1957), and *The Magnificent Seven* (1960). Cinemascope, which had confounded many veteran directors during the mid-fifties, appeared made to order for Sturges's unique camera eye, implying that the vastness of space/place appears to swallow up human dramas set against a beautiful but inhospitable backdrop. He was ably abetted by cinematographer Robert Surtees (1906–1985), who had visually implied an ironic contrast between ego-driven people and the encroaching natural world in *Oklahoma!* (Fred Zinnemann, 1955) and *Ben-Hur* (William Wyler, 1959). Sturges stripped the script clean of clichés from 1950s sci-fi, paving the way for a less fantastical form of the genre that would shortly dominate contemporary (and many near-future) sci-fi films.

The Satan Bug bears a strong resemblance to Hitchcock films. Its mid-section recalls the parallel sequences in *North by Northwest* (1959), the "bug" itself serves as a MacGuffin, and the film concludes with a vertigo-inducing helicopter sequence.

THEME

The vision here can properly be described as prophetic. In 2013, the use of weapons of mass destruction during Syria's civil war became a major issue for President Barack Obama, one that the international community had to address. *The Satan Bug* exposed to a largely unaware public that such situations would arise. Ahead of its time, the film does not condemn foreign powers for scientific experimentation gone wrong, but rather places the blame on our own government's policies.

TRIVIA

Charlton Heston turned down the lead in *The Satan Bug*, but in 1968, he agreed to appear in an upscale science-fiction film, *Planet of the Apes*. He thereafter was as associated with dystopian sci-fi as he had earlier been known for ancient world costume films, including *The Ten Commandments* (1956), *Ben-Hur* (1959), and *El Cid* (1961).

James Doohan, a then-unknown character actor who would shortly become famous as "Scotty" on TV's *Star Trek*, appears as a government agent posted at the gas station. Lee Remick, a superstar at the time, appears in an unbilled cameo as a waitress in the nightclub sequence.

In Alistair MacLean's novel, set entirely in England, the hero and female lead are husband and wife. In the film, they are an unmarried romantic couple since Hollywood consistently insists that a pair of attractive single people, their chemistry gradually growing toward a final embrace, makes for a more scintillating screen story.

· · · · · · ·

SECONDS (1966)

—— RANKING: 47 ——

CREDITS

Paramount Pictures/Gibralter Productions/Joel Productions; John Frankenheimer, dir.; David Ely, novel; Lewis John Carlino, scr.; Frankenheimer, Edward Lewis, pro.; Jerry Goldsmith, mus.; James Wong Howe, cin.; David Newhouse, Ferris Webster, ed.; Ted Haworth, art dir.; Saul Bass, titles; 106 min.; B&W; 1.85:1.

CAST

Rock Hudson (*Antiochus "Tony" Wilson*); Khigh Dhiegh (*Davalo*); John Randolph (*Arthur Hamilton*); Frances Reid (*Emily Hamilton*); Salome Jens (*Nora Marcus*); Barbara Werle (*Secretary*); Jeff Corey (*Mr. Ruby*); Murray Hamilton (*Charlie Evans*); Will Geer (*Old Man*); Richard Anderson (*Dr. Innes*).

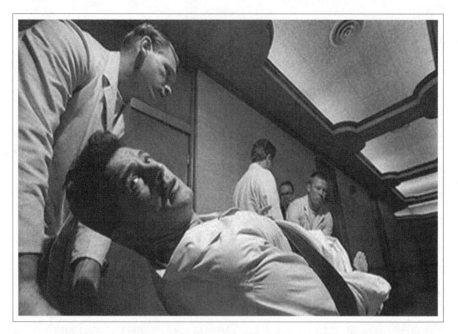

THE SECOND TIME AROUND: *Thanks to scientific advances right around the corner, Rock Hudson's forlorn antihero achieves the once-magical concept of being young again. In this near-future thriller, sci-fi proves to be closely related to surrealism by the auteur's oblique camera-eye. Courtesy: Joel/Gibraltar/Paramount Pictures.*

MOST MEMORABLE LINE
A man who lives the age-old dream—
If only I could begin my life all over again.
ADVERTISING TAGLINE

BACKGROUND
By the mid-sixties, the times—as Bob Dylan duly noted in one example of the era's new music—were a-changin'. The Hollywood product displayed more influences from the style and substance of avant-garde European cinema. One of the first significant experimental projects had been the Warren Beatty/Arthur Penn collaboration *Mickey One* (1965), which introduced a nonlinear narrative, a surreal sensibility, and a paranoid outlook to commercial movies. *Seconds* would relocate such a Kafkaesque vision within science fiction. As a big-budget project with an A-lister star and director, *Seconds* ranks high among the mid-decade movies that altered the popular vision of what American movies, particularly those belonging to this genre, could be.

THE PLOT

Businessman Arthur Hamilton would appear to have it all: an impressive house, a loving family, and financial rewards, thanks to success in his chosen white-collar profession. Though no one in his small circle of friends is aware that anything's wrong, Hamilton seethes beneath the surface, always wondering: Is this all there is? He has never experienced the extremes of romance and adventure that he dreamed about as a boy. Through an old acquaintance, Hamilton learns of the possibility, albeit risky, of a second chance. For a costly sum, a mysterious company transforms aging men into semi-human cyborgs, their minds still intact, but relocated in perfect young bodies. Better yet, or so Hamilton believes, the company helps the transformed client to disappear.

THE FILM

Here is another one of those unique films that barely qualifies as science fiction. Most of the story takes place in the real world, though the viewed-through-a-camera-eye-darkly cityscapes in the prologue and spacious, brightly lit (to the point of equal oppressiveness) California sequences that follow project an edgy sensibility. *Seconds* offers a near-future phantasmagoria in which scientific possibilities almost within reach at the time of filmmaking—in this case, plastic surgery taken to nightmare extremes—are presented not as fantasy but as a believable projection of what will likely come into being the day after tomorrow.

Known for his convincing sense of realism in dramas from the golden age of television (*Playhouse 90* and *Studio One in Hollywood*) and his film collaborations with Burt Lancaster (*The Young Savages*, 1961, and *Birdman of Alcatraz*, 1962), John Frankenheimer (1930–2002) grounded this piece by using everyday settings rather than in-studio sets, something of an innovation at the time. Happily, he teamed with James Wong Howe (1899–1976), the daring director of photography who opted for a subjective treatment of the everyday world.

The film stands not only as a genre milestone, but also as a turning point for American filmmaking. It revived noir, which had flourished between 1945 and 1960, then all but disappeared for the better part of a decade. Further, *Seconds* rates as the first important movie to address openly middle-aged hippie-dom: wealthy people over the age of thirty, hoping to remain forever young, adapted elements of the free love/free drug subculture into their upscale lives.

THEME

Though seemingly less political than previous Frankenheimer films, such as *The*

Manchurian Candidate (1962) and *Seven Days in May* (1964), *Seconds* conceals a political subtext beneath its obvious surface show of social criticism. This film about "reborns" features three gifted actors—Jeff Corey, Will Geer, and John Randolph—in supporting roles. All were blacklisted during the 1950s McCarthy witch hunt, owing to their progressive politics. In 1960, beginning with the release of *Spartacus*, producer-star Kirk Douglas insisted that Hollywood outcasts—such as that film's screenwriter, Dalton Trumbo, who had been working under pseudonyms or fronts—again receive billing. Cinematographer Howe, who would win two Oscars and come to be considered one of the ten most influential cinematographers, had been "gray-listed" in the late 1950s and early 1960s, returning to work in 1963 with the contemporary Western *Hud*. *Seconds* continued that professional "re-birthing" behind and in front of the camera in a film that, appropriately enough, highlights that very theme.

TRIVIA

Originally, Frankenheimer planned to co-produce with his *Seven Days in May* star, Kirk Douglas. That fell apart owing to Douglas's desire to portray both the "before" and "after" incarnations. Frankenheimer believed the distinction should be considerably sharper. Many observers were concerned when Rock Hudson was cast as the "after," convinced that he was not a strong enough actor. As it turned out, Hudson's limitations led to a perfect portrayal. Tony is not a normal human (the kind of part a character-lead like Douglas would relish), but a semi-human creation, a faux front. Hudson's low-key presence, which diminished the power of many serious films in which he appeared, turned out to be precisely what this role required.

RETURN OF THE BIG BUDGET: *Following a decade during which the genre was mostly relegated to exploitation items, a major studio at last gave the green light to an ambitious undertaking with an all-star cast, including the young Raquel Welch (right). Courtesy: 20th Century-Fox.*

· · · · · · ·

FANTASTIC VOYAGE (1966)

—— RANKING: 85 ——

CREDITS

Twentieth Century-Fox; Richard Fleischer, dir.; Harry Kleiner, David Duncan, Otto Klement, Jerome Bixby, scr.; Saul David, pro.; Leonard Rosenman, mus.; Ernest Laszlo, cin.; William B. Murphy, ed.; Dale Hennesy, Jack Martin Smith, art dir.; Stuart A. Reiss, Walter M. Scott, sets; Walter Rossi, Richard Sperber, special sound effects; Johnny Borgese, Greg C. Jensen, F/X; L. B. Abbott, Art Cruickshank, Emil Kosa Jr., special visual effects; Marcel Delgado, miniature artist; Harper Goff, *Proteus* conceptualization; 100 min.; Color; 2.35:1.

CAST

Stephen Boyd (*Grant*); Raquel Welch (*Cora*); Edmond O'Brien (*Gen. Carter*); Donald Pleasence (*Dr. Michaels*); Arthur O'Connell (*Col. Donald Reid*); William Redfield (*Capt. Bill Owens*); Arthur Kennedy (*Dr. Duval*); Jan Del Val (*Jan Benes*).

MOST MEMORABLE LINE

We stand in the middle of infinity, between outer and inner space. And there's no limit to either.

DR. DUVAL

BACKGROUND

The vast contributions of Twentieth Century-Fox to the evolution of modern science-fiction/fantasy films have never been fully chronicled. During the 1950s, Fox had been the first "major" to create an A-budget genre entry, *The Day the Earth Stood Still* (1951). By the mid-1960s, studio executives were working to salvage sci-fi from its B-movie morass, and *Fantastic Voyage* represented their first major effort. Richard Fleischer (1916–2006) was chosen for this subcutaneous adventure largely because he had directed Disney's *20,000 Leagues Under the Sea* (1954), while screenwriter David Duncan was selected because he had overseen the adaptation of H. G. Wells's *The Time Machine* (1960).

THE PLOT

At the height of the Cold War, a Soviet scientist, Jan Benes, escapes to the West. Both the Soviet Union and the United States have developed a miniaturization process for temporarily shrinking atoms, but Benes alone has perfected this technological wonder. During a failed assassination attempt by a Russian agent, Benes hits his head, and the resulting blood clot threatens to silence the genius forever. Our military and scientific experts devise a plan by which a miniaturized submarine, the *Proteus*, manned by a shrunken crew, will enter Benes's blood stream and remove the clot. The crew must race against ticking clocks— Benes's likely impending death and the brief time they will remain miniaturized—as well as battle the hostile microscopic forces in the human immune system. Making matters more difficult still, there is a saboteur on board.

THE FILM

Fox executives hoped to convince Oscar winner Charlton Heston to play Grant, which would have given the film cachet. They had to settle for his *Ben-Hur* co-star Stephen Boyd as Heston did not yet see the appeal of ambitious sci-fi, though that would shortly change. Two years later, following the success of *Planet of the Apes* (1968), he would become a loyal adherent of the genre, starring in both *The Omega Man* (Boris Sagal, 1971) and *Soylent Green* (1973), the latter directed by Fleischer.

While a college student, Fleischer—with virtually no hope of following his father, the legendary animator Max Fleischer, into the movie industry—had studied human anatomy. Perhaps fate somehow arranged such a life experience so that he would be knowledgeable about the material he confronted here. Fleischer insisted that Harper Goff, who had designed the *Nautilus* for Disney's *20,000 Leagues*, conceptualize the *Proteus*.

Composer Leonard Rosenman experimented with playing the first act in the military/scientific headquarters without music to suggest a deadly dullness. His wondrous score emerges as the voyage into "inner space" commences, enhancing the visual imagery via magical music. This score popularized the notion that atonal music is particularly appropriate for lavish sci-fi projects.

Jerome Bixby (1923–1998), who concocted the original story line, was a highly regarded pulp fiction writer. He wrote the original story, "It's a Good Life," which became a *Twilight Zone* classic episode with a teleplay by Rod Serling, and would write four of the original *Star Trek* episodes, including the short story on which the classic "Mirror, Mirror" was based. In that installment, Bixby popularized the idea of parallel universes, which would become a staple of science fiction in the following years.

THEME

Again, science fiction serves as an effective bridge for the twentieth-century public, which found itself caught in a bind between the demands of a scientific (and, in many ways, secular) age and an ongoing need to still believe in something greater and grander than the here and now. As the film reminds us, "The finite mind cannot comprehend infinity; and the soul, which comes from God, is infinite."

TRIVIA

During the 1960s, any major film not based on a book would be "novelized" for a quick-sell paperback. These were knocked off by second-rate scribes and boasted no real value. *Fantastic Voyage* provides the one glaring exception. Producer Saul David (1921–1996), previously editor-in-chief at Bantam Books, called on Isaac Asimov (1920–1992), an esteemed sci-fi author whose works include *I, Robot* (1950), to expand on the film's narrative, characters, and themes.

Owing to production setbacks, Asimov's novel (*not* a novelization) appeared six months before the film's release rather than simultaneous with it. Many genre buffs came to believe the film was an adaptation of the Asimov work. In fact, the writer improved on the original screenplay by correcting numerous flaws. For example, in the screenplay, the laser gun and the submarine were left inside the patient's body when the heroes escape; of course, they would have returned to normal size and torn him all to bits.

· · · · · · ·

FAHRENHEIT 451 (1966)

—— RANKING: 81 ——

CREDITS

Anglo Enterprises; François Truffaut, dir.; Ray Bradbury, novel; Truffaut, Jean-Louis Richard, David Rudkin, Helen Scott, scr.; Lewis M. Allen, Jane C. Nusbaum, pro.; Bernard Herrmann, mus.; Nicolas Roeg, cin.; Thom Noble, ed.; Syd Cain, prod. design/art dir.; Tony Walton, costumes; Charles Staffell, Les Bowie, F/X; 112 min.; Color; 1.66:1.

CAST

Oskar Werner (*Guy Montag*); Julie Christie (*Clarisse/Linda*); Cyril Cusack (*The Captain*); Anton Diffring (*Fabian*); Jeremy Spenser (*Man with the Apple*); Bee Duffell (*Book Woman*); Michael Balfour (*Book Person*); Noel Davis (*TV's "Cousin Midge"*); Mark Lester (*Schoolboy*).

MOST MEMORABLE LINE

Behind each of these books, there's a man; that's what interests me.
GUY MONTAG, DISCOVERING THE APPEAL OF READING

BACKGROUND

Ray Bradbury (1920–2012) spent his youth in Waukegan, Illinois, hooked on the serious sci-fi novels of Wells and Verne, as well as the more fantastical cliffhanger adventures of Flash Gordon and Buck Rogers. After moving to Los Angeles, he found himself fascinated with and concerned about the "brave new world" emerging after the end of World War II. Notably, television, at first

THE HITCHCOCK BLONDE AS FUTURE-WOMAN: *Like Kim Novak in* Vertigo, *Julie Christie plays a dual role in François Truffaut's unique take on Ray Bradbury's masterful, trend-setting novel of ideas. Courtesy: Anglo/Vineyard/J. Arthur Rank.*

considered just a novelty that people might enjoy once or twice a week, exerted a hypnotic effect on the public. Bradbury made this the subject of a short story, "Bright Phoenix," which he expanded into a novella, *The Fireman* (1951), for *Galaxy Science Fiction* magazine. When it struck a chord with many like-minded people, Bradbury further expanded the piece into the novel *Fahrenheit 451*, published in 1953 by Ballantine Books.

THE PLOT

In a dystopian future-world, books are ordered burned by a Big Brother–type government that fears that reading causes people to think. This, in turn, leads to unhappiness. In contrast, watching the wide-screen TV from dawn until dusk and beyond, with its soothing insistence that all is right with the world, keeps everyone under control. A chance meeting between Montag, one of the firemen charged with burning books, and a strange, other-worldly beauty causes him to wonder if he is on "the right side." His wife and his boss become concerned that he may turn radical, while Fabian, a co-worker who is jealous of Montag's success, plans to report him to the authorities.

THE FILM

François Truffaut's film, considered ultra-contemporary at the time, now serves as a relic of an era when various techniques, developed in early 1960s experimental works to "set the camera free," were for the first time incorporated into commercial filmmaking. Handheld camera, the zoom lens, slow motion when least expected, and sudden jump cuts that deconstruct the space-time continuum all seemed revolutionary. Only a few years later, most of these practices had been so overused that they were summarily dropped as being archaic and, in a "future shock" sense, clichéd.

Part of the French New Wave, Truffaut (1932–1984) navigated a transition from Gallic film director to international celebrity with this English language film. Like many other auteurs, he idolized Alfred Hitchcock. As a result, this movie is as influenced by *Vertigo* (1958) as by Bradbury's book. The music is by Bernard Herrmann, Hitchcock's favorite composer, and to say that the score echoes that of *Vertigo* is an understatement. Julie Christie playing both the demure brunette and the fascinating blonde recalls Kim Novak's dual role as Judy/Madeleine in *Vertigo*.

THEME

Bradbury's initial concern was that the manner in which great novels convey some fundamental worldview would be lost if TV supplanted reading. His nightmare scenario depicted this occurring at the bequest of the government. Bradbury also feared the concept of the "factoid" and the manner in which archetypal truths, which he believed to be best conveyed in print, were threatened by television.

TRIVIA

Bradbury said that he considered this his only "true" or "hard" sci-fi novel. His other books, such as *The Martian Chronicles*, are better categorized as space opera/fantasy.

······

FIVE MILLION YEARS TO EARTH/ QUATERMASS AND THE PIT (1967)

—— RANKING: 45 ——

CREDITS

Hammer Film Productions; Roy Ward Baker, dir.; Nigel Kneale, scr.; Anthony Nelson Keys, pro.; Tristram Cary, Carlo Martelli, music; Arthur Grant, cin.; Spencer Reeve, James Needs, ed.; Bernard Robinson, Kenneth Ryan, art dir.; Les Bowie, Roy Field, Ian Scoones, F/X; 97 min.; Color; 1.66:1.

CAST

Andrew Keir (*Prof. Bernard Quatermass*); James Donald (*Dr. Mathew Roney*); Barbara Shelley (*Barbara Judd*); Julian Glover (*Col. Breen*); Duncan Lamont (*Sladden*); Bryan Marshall (*Capt. Potter*); Peter Copley (*Howell*); Edwin Richfield (*Minister*); Grant Taylor (*Sgt. Ellis*); Maurice Good (*Cleghorn*); Robert Morris (*Jerry Watson*); Sheila Steafel (*Journalist*); June Ellis (*The Blonde*).

MOST MEMORABLE LINE

We owe our human condition here to the intervention of insects?
DEFENSE MINISTER TO QUATERMASS

BACKGROUND

As a child on the Isle of Man, Nigel Kneale (1922–2006) had plenty of time to read books by his favorite authors, George Orwell and H. G. Wells. Abandoning a career in law, Kneale joined the BBC. There, beginning in 1953, he developed his *Quatermass* serials. The shows proved so popular that the embryonic Hammer Studio bought the rights, turning out several B films in the mid-1950s. Kneale's Quatermass stories were significant not only for their literary quality but also as an early attempt to blur what had previously been rigid genre lines between horror and science fiction.

THE PLOT

Construction workers in London penetrate deep into the Earth to extend the

"WHERE DO INSECTS COME FROM?" *Professor Bernard Quatermass (Andrew Keir, left) and an associate (James Donald) discover proof of ancient aliens and that humankind's evolution was purposefully re-directed by visitors from the stars. Courtesy: Hammer Film Productions/20th Century-Fox Distribution.*

Tube stop at Hobbs End. To their shock, they discover skeletons and what appears to be an unexploded bomb, there since the Blitz. Paleontologist Roney studies the bones, then shocks the world by announcing that here is proof that any missing link between ape and man dates back not tens of thousands but many millions of years. When scientist Bernard Quatermass arrives, he proffers a more startling revelation about a quasi-metallic object discovered on the spot: it's a spacecraft that, eons ago, was employed by locust-like Martians on a mission to alter the evolution of life on our planet.

THE FILM

The theory that, in prehistorical times, visitors from other planets had set out to alter Earth's life-forms predated Kneale's writings. Still, he originated a plausible motivation for such action: knowing their planet was doomed to "redness," the Martians attempted to colonize Earth. When that failed, due to bacteria to which they could not adjust (an influence from *The War of the Worlds*), the Martians decided to intrude by developing species to leave a legacy of their existence. Despite several literary antecedents, *Five Million Years to Earth* rates as the first motion picture to advance a concept that would become a staple of later sci-fi films, such as *Stargate* (1994).

Roy Ward Baker (1916–2010), who had no previous association with fantastical films, was picked by Hammer to direct because of his memorable depiction of ordinary people experiencing the dissolution of order into chaos in *A Night to Remember* (1958) about the *Titanic* tragedy. Baker felt so at home at Hammer that he later directed two Gothic horror films there: *The Vampire Lovers* and *Scars of Dracula*, both 1970.

THEME

Kneale included a pacifist theme in all his work. Professor Quatermass is on the outs with higher-ups owing to his refusal to use his talents to create military superiority. Rather, he insists that any rocket science skills he may have be employed for peaceful purposes, such as relocating Earth's teeming populations on uninhabited heavenly bodies. Colonel Breen, a pompous martinet, perceives the intriguing if dangerous situation through the narrowest of viewpoints. To a degree, it is he, more than the invaders, who might be considered the villain of the narrative.

Hobbs is a modernization of "Hob," an ancient English term referring to the devil on Earth. This supports the film's essential idea: what earlier societies recorded, verbally and visually, as "imaginative" renderings of evil, horns and all, were, on closer examination, their realistic depictions of ancient alien astronauts.

TRIVIA

In England, the film was titled *Quatermass and the Pit*. That fictional character was so famous that, like Sherlock Holmes, his name could be used to pre-sell a film. When Twentieth Century-Fox picked up U.S. distribution rights, executives decided to present the piece with a more conventional title that would leave no doubt as to its sci-fi premise.

Kneale suffered from the rare disease known as photophobia, an eyesight limitation characterized by painful reaction to bright lights. This helps explain why so many of his works, including this, take place deep in a dark "pit."

A major misconception about Hammer films is that they did not produce any examples of the sci-fi genre other than the Quatermass films. In fact, the first of these was preceded by Terence Fisher's *Four Sided Triangle* (1953) about the creation of a beautiful female cyborg.

· · · · · · ·

2001: A SPACE ODYSSEY (1968)

—— RANKING: 2 ——

CREDITS

MGM; Stanley Kubrick, dir.; Arthur C. Clarke, story; Clarke, Kubrick, scr.; Kubrick, Victor Lyndon, pro.; Geoffrey Unsworth, cin.; Ray Lovejoy, ed.; Ernest Archer, Harry Lange, Anthony Masters, prod. design; John Hoesli, art dir.; Colin Arthur, ape makeup; H. L. Bird, Winston Ryder, sound; Kubrick, Douglas Trumbull, photographic F/X; 141 min. (release print), 160 min. (dir. cut); Color; 2.20:1.

CAST

Keir Dullea (*Dr. Dave Bowman*); Gary Lockwood (*Dr. Frank Poole*); William Sylvester (*Dr. Heywood R. Floyd*); Daniel Richter (*Moon-Watcher*); Leonard Rossiter (*Andrei Smyslov*); Margaret Tyzack (*Elena*); Robert Beatty (*Ralph Halvorsen*); Sean Sullivan (*Dr. Bill Michaels*); Douglas Rain (*HAL 9000*, voice); Frank Miller (*Mission Control*, voice); Edward Bishop (*Aries-1B Lunar Captain*).

THE ULTIMATE "TRIP": *In the film that forever changed the genre, an astronaut (Keir Dullea) begins his journey into space. A realistic example of "hard" sci-fi that transforms along the way into a metaphysical odyssey. Courtesy: Metro-Goldwyn-Mayer.*

MOST FAMOUS LINE

This mission is too important for me to allow you to jeopardize it.

"HAL" TO DAVE

BACKGROUND

In the beginning, there was Arthur C. Clarke (1917–2008). The British-born science writer early on argued in favor of creating satellites, and in 1948, wrote a short story, "The Sentinel," which was published in 1951 as "Sentinel of Eternity" in the *Avon Science Fiction and Fantasy Reader*. Kubrick found himself drawn to the concept of an unnamed narrator who describes an ancient pyramid on the moon, placed there many millions of years earlier by interplanetary travelers. But does it contain the secrets of the universe, to be shared by humankind as a gift? Or is it a warning that earthlings shouldn't attempt to master the galaxy as these now-extinct creatures once did?

THE PLOT

During "The Dawn of Man," the first in a succession of titled sequences that provide a storytelling format, members of a missing link society come in contact with a strange monolith that descends from the stars. In "TMA-1," Floyd, one of many Earth beings now inhabiting space, learns of a possible epidemic back home, as well as strange disturbances in the outer reaches of our solar system. Astronauts Dave Bowman and Frank Poole are dispatched to discover what's occurring in the "Jupiter Mission 18 Months Later." Both are menaced when super-computer HAL, deciding that the humans are an unnecessary encumbrance, kills Frank, before being defeated by Dave. This surviving astronaut enters a psychedelic light tunnel in "Jupiter and Beyond the Infinite," aging as he discovers that past and present are one and the same.

THE FILM

American-born Kubrick (1928–1999) made his home in England and shot his later films there. During the mid-to-late 1960s, he was the first filmmaker to convince the studios to invest large budgets in arthouse projects. Cineastes consider him to be among the screen's great "formalists"; as a director, Kubrick was interested in form over content. Ultimately, his style *is* the subject matter, which annoyed novelists he has adapted—Stephen King (*The Shining*), Anthony Burgess (*A Clockwork Orange*), and Vladimir Nabokov (*Lolita*), among them. An exception is Clarke, who stated that "The Sentinel" is "an acorn to the resulting oak-tree" that Kubrick created.

Kubrick's original conception was a series of interlocking vignettes about man's desire to penetrate the skies and make first contact. This idea would have included many sequences similar to those in George Pal's *Conquest of Space* (Byron Haskin, 1955), concluding with a first look at the sentinel. The image of the child that concludes the movie draws from an image in Clarke's 1953 novel *Childhood's End*.

Even as Kubrick wrote the screenplay, Clarke worked on a novel, to be released more or less simultaneously. They tossed ideas back and forth, with Kubrick planning to take co-credit for the book even as Clarke would take co-credit for the script, though, in the end, Kubrick was not listed as co-author.

THEME

Evolution is basic to the piece, with Kubrick taking pre-existing ideas and creating revolutionary cinematic approaches to convey these concepts as only the art of film can. For example, the transition between the prehistoric apes and futuristic movement into the cosmos is achieved through a memorable cut: a dominant ape throws a bone high and, as it falls back down, it's replaced by a spacecraft. As this appears to be the same object employed to kill a fellow ape, man's darkest urges are connected to his greatest scientific achievements. Yet, there is a sense of wonderment as to the potential of humankind to survive. Dave does defeat the computer, the Frankenstein's monster for our future. When Dave's journey is done, the last image he sees is not of his own self as an elderly, apparently dying man, but a baby being born. It may be Dave himself, suggesting the theory of relativity: there are no straight lines; life is circular.

TRIVIA

The film was shot on the sprawling soundstages of England's Shepperton Studios, Kubrick employing many British actors. This set the stage for a tradition in which classy sci-fi often featured just such an Anglo backdrop.

However much the use of symphonic music seems, in retrospect, essential, Kubrick did consider a rock music score to make the film more appealing to young people. Pink Floyd was at one point approached.

A major motif is eating: during each of the four separate sequences, key characters are seen eating meals, providing a connection between the most sophisticated people in the final scenes and the advanced apes at the beginning. No matter how much we evolve, some things never change—unless, of course, humankind is replaced by the computers.

· · · · · · ·

BARBARELLA (1968)

—— RANKING: 88 ——

CREDITS

Marianne Productions/Paramount Pictures; Roger Vadim, dir.; Vadim, Jean-Claude Forest, Claude Brulé, Terry Southern, Vittorio Bonicelli, Clement Biddle Wood, Brian Degas, Tudor Gates, scr.; Dino De Laurentiis, pro.; Charles Fox, Bob Crewe, The Glitterhouse, mus.; Claude Renoir, cin.; Victoria Mercanton, ed.; Mario Garbuglia, prod. design; Jacques Fonteray, Paco Rabanne, costumes; Gérard Cogan, Augie Lohman, Thierry Vincens-Fargo, F/X; Charles Staffell, visual effects; Arcady, title design; 98 min.; Color; 2.35:1.

CAST

Jane Fonda (*Barbarella*); John Phillip Law (*Pygar*); Anita Pallenberg (*The Great Tyrant*); Milo O'Shea (*Durand Durand*); Marcel Marceau (*Prof. Ping*); Claude Dauphin (*President of Earth*); David Hemmings (*Dildano*); Ugo Tognazzi (*Mark Hand/ The Catcher*).

IS THERE SEX IN SPACE? *In a cross-pollination of comic books (aka graphic novels) and popular cinema, the most eroticized female space cadet in the galaxy (Jane Fonda) succumbs during a date with an angel (John Phillip Law). Courtesy: Marianne/Paramount.*

MOST MEMORABLE LINE

My name isn't "pretty-pretty." It's Barbarella.

BARBARELLA TO THE GREAT TYRANT

BACKGROUND

Not only did the French realize the artistic possibilities of the cinema before Americans, they also began taking the comic book seriously while, in the United States, such pulp publications were still dismissed as children's fare. In 1962, Jean-Claude Forest (1930–1998) created the comic strip *Barbarella* as a feature for Paris's *V-Magazine*, combining the fairy-tale qualities of Cinderella with the bikini-clad likeness of Brigitte Bardot, drawing on eroticism implied by such grindhouse classics as *Cat-Women of the Moon* (1953) and *Queen of Outer Space* (1958). In 1964, Forest's comic strips were published in book form, lending a greater respectability to the work and setting the standard for the graphic novels of today.

THE PLOT

A space cadet in every sense of the term, Barbarella regains consciousness aboard *Alpha 1*. As she awakens from the deep sleep necessary for intergalactic travel, she performs a striptease. She then heads for planet Tau Ceti to retrieve inventor Durand Durand and his Positronic Ray before it can be used for violent purposes. Crash-landing on the ice-covered planet, she is menaced by deadly children and their killer dolls. The beast-like Catcher rescues her and helps her recall the joys of sex that civilization has moved beyond. She uses her rediscovered knowledge of the pleasurably primitive in Sogo, the City of Night, where she seduces the angelic Pygar; the futuristic Robin Hood, Dildano; and the beautiful but evil Great Tyrant.

THE FILM

If *2001: A Space Odyssey* took hard sci-fi to a whole new dimension, *Barbarella*, in the same year and with a budget of more than $9 million, did the same for space operas. Roger Vadim (1928–2000) had launched his then-wife Bardot to superstardom in . . . *And God Created Woman* (1956). The character of Barbarella had in part been inspired by Bardot, and Vadim would have cast her in the role had they still been a couple. Instead, he set about transforming the former wide-eyed Hollywood ingénue Fonda into what he called "the American Bardot," though producer Dino De Laurentiis had initially offered the role to Sophia Loren and Virna Lisi.

Fonda accepted the role because she believed the Sexual Revolution had a liberating effect for the evolving "modern" female; she wanted both to become that woman and to embody her onscreen. Soon after the film's release, Fonda embraced Second Wave feminism, which argued against nudity as a means by which men dominated women via their sexuality. Throughout the early 1970s, she recoiled if someone dared mention *Barbarella*. By the 1980s, many mainstream feminists had become "New Women" or post-feminists, fusing the major goals of 1970s-style feminism (a woman's legal control over her body and equal rights in the workplace) with an embracing of old-fashioned glamor. Ever the chameleon, Fonda now became an exercise guru and spoke somewhat less angrily, even with nostalgia, about *Barbarella*.

THEME

Vadim wanted to bring the Sexual Revolution of the 1960s to as large an audience as possible in the guise of a space fantasy. In addition, the film solidified Susan Sontag's notions on the camp aesthetic as detailed in her influential

1964 essay, "Notes on 'Camp'." Sontag's essential idea was that the supposedly ephemeral aspects of our culture, such as comic books and hackneyed Hollywood movies, were expected to swiftly fade from sight, but might instead pass the test of time in a way that loftier, upper-middlebrow, "serious" works did not. What in its own time constituted "bad taste," like Italian opera or Shakespeare's plays, might go on to achieve greater status in society than what was initially considered more respectable fare. The idea that some things were so bad that they were good had taken hold even before *Barbarella*, and for a critic to point out the awfulness of it all was to reveal a lack of hipness.

The inclusion of Bob Crewe's pop-rock score was made possible by the acceptance in 1964 of the Beatles as artists and rock 'n' roll as finally "legitimate." The film would not have "worked" without the necessary ingredient of mild nudity, which had become acceptable months before the film's release as the ratings system replaced the Motion Picture Production (MPAA) Code.

TRIVIA

An extended "playful lesbian scene" between Fonda and Anita Pallenberg on a luxurious bed was filmed, but cut from the final film. Still photographs exist and have become collector's items.

Mime Marcel Marceau is featured in a rare speaking part.

Rock group Duran Duran took its name from the film's villain.

Vampirella, the "comic book for adults," which initially appeared in 1969 and was among the first U.S. graphic novels, borrowed the *Barbarella* concept while adding the element of a succubus.

· · · · · · ·

PLANET OF THE APES (1968)

—— RANKING: 14 ——

CREDITS

Twentieth Century-Fox; Franklin J. Schaffner, dir.; Pierre Boulle, novel; Michael Wilson, Rod Serling, scr.; Mort Abrahams, Arthur P. Jacobs, pro.; Jerry Goldsmith, mus.; Leon Shamroy, cin.; Hugh S. Fowler, ed.; William J. Creber, Jack Martin Smith, art dir.; Morton Haack, costumes; John Chambers, makeup;

Vernon Archer, Johnny Borgese, Bill Clove, Glen Galvin, Marlin Jones, Ralph Winigar, F/X; L. B. Abbott, Art Cruickshank, Emil Kosa Jr., visual effects; 112 min.; Color; 2.35:1.

CAST

Charlton Heston (*George Taylor*); Roddy McDowall (*Cornelius*); Kim Hunter (*Zira*); Maurice Evans (*Dr. Zaius*); James Whitmore (*President of the Assembly*); James Daly (*Honorious*); Linda Harrison (*Nova*); Robert Gunner (*Landon*); Lou Wagner (*Lucius*); Woodrow Parfrey (*Maximus*).

MOST MEMORABLE LINE

Take your stinking paws off me, you damn dirty ape!
GEORGE TAYLOR, WHILE BEING ARRESTED

MONKEY BUSINESS: *In Rod Serling's seminal contribution to sci-fi cinema, the space-time continuum is dramatically explored as in many* Twilight Zone *episodes. From left to right, Charlton Heston, Linda Harrison, Kim Hunter, Roddy McDowall, and player. Courtesy: 20th Century-Fox.*

BACKGROUND

The once impregnable Fox studio had been on the verge of bankruptcy since 1963, when the outrageously expensive *Cleopatra* failed to recoup its investment. The studio could not afford to purchase new material and so brought out of mothballs properties purchased earlier but never developed. Pierre Boulle's *La planète des singes*, published in 1963, had been placed on a backburner. Desperate to get something on the market, executives decided to shoot the movie and hope for the best or, quite possibly, go under.

THE PLOT

A spaceship from Earth, traveling at light speed, crash-lands on an unknown planet. Astronauts emerge from deep sleep and realize that the year is 3978 AD. While foraging in the forest, they are attacked by gorillas on horseback. George Taylor, one of the few to survive, is brought as a prisoner into Ape City, where everything is the reverse of what evolved on Earth: apes are advanced, and humans are a lower-level primate. Sensitive Zira and fiancé Cornelius recognize that Taylor is intelligent, and they help him and a human woman escape from Dr. Zaius. After many misadventures, Taylor heads into the Forbidden Zone, where he will discover his destiny.

THE FILM

With a whopping $5.8 million budget, this was an ambitious project, explaining why Fox was able to sign Oscar winner Heston. Though numerous A-list directors were approached, Franklin J. Schaffner (1920–1989) was the star's suggestion. Never before associated with sci-fi, Schaffner had made his name in golden age TV (*Playhouse 90*, *Studio One in Hollywood*) and had directed Heston three years earlier in *The War Lord*. The idea was to bring aboard a top talent who was not typecast as to genre in order to play down clichés and bring the piece alive as human drama—if, of course, in a futuristic setting.

Schaffner solved the problem of creating an advanced ape world, as originally planned. Rather than build expensive architecture based on a high level of technological know-how, he suggested having the planet appear primitive. This not only saved a lot of money but also set the standard for a new and influential approach to sci-fi visuals.

John Chambers (1922–2001) devised a prosthetic concept that replaced the old face masks. Each actor was able to maintain his or her onscreen identity despite having been re-imagined as a primate. This also allowed for the subtle and complex facial gestures for which these stars were known. If not for this, such top-flight performers would never have signed on for the project.

THEME

Aficionados love to debate how much creative input Rod Serling (1924–1975) had on this project. Claims range from his having written almost everything to an insistence that the famed final shot—Taylor discovering the ruins of the Statue of Liberty and realizing that he's actually on Earth—is Serling's single contribution. Though the issue may never be solved, and while other writers did join the creative mix, the quality should be credited to Serling, the piece fitting in perfectly with his body of imaginative fantasy work. As with so many *Twilight Zone* scripts, we here encounter satire on the class system (in this case, gorillas as the military, orangutans as administrators, chimpanzees as the scientists) and an attack on racism. As with *Zone*, themes are conveyed via a futuristic setting, allowing for liberal progressive ideology that might have offended large portions of the public if presented in a realistic form. There are visual puns ("see no evil, hear no evil, speak no evil," with various apes incarnating those age-old images), while the ending suggests the possibility of an alternative Earth in some fifth dimension or a future that may yet be avoided via time travel by a dedicated individual. The anti-nuke stance vividly conveys a theme that all but dominated Serling's classic TV series. Indeed, *Planet of the Apes* might be considered a theatrical film follow-up to the classic show.

TRIVIA

There would be four sequels and a short-lived TV series (1974), as well as a failed remake (Tim Burton, 2001) and a successful prequel, *Rise of the Planet of the Apes* (2011). By far, the best of the immediate follow-ups was the sequel, *Beneath the Planet of the Apes* (Ted Post, 1970). Most of the original stars returned, with the exception of Roddy McDowall, who had committed to a simultaneous project. Actor David Watson replaced him as Cornelius in *Beneath*, but McDowall returned for all the other films and the TV series.

A COLLAPSING OF GENRES: *The zombie-oriented horror film and the science-fiction feature, two distinct if related genres, were combined for this low-budget classic that premiered at rural drive-ins but in time would play at museum cinema retrospectives. Courtesy: Image Ten/Laurel Group.*

· · · · · · ·

NIGHT OF THE LIVING DEAD (1968)

—— RANKING: 76 ——

CREDITS

Image Ten/Laurel Group/Market Square Productions; George A. Romero, dir.; Romero, John A. Russo, scr.; Karl Hardman, Russell Streiner, pro.; Romero, cin./ed.; Bruce Capristo, makeup effects; Marshall Booth, Gary Streiner, sound effects; Tony Pantanella, Regis Survinski, F/X; Joseph Unitas, special lighting effects; 96 min.; B&W; 1.37:1.

CAST

Duane Jones (*Ben*); Judith O'Dea (*Barbra*); Russell Streiner (*Johnny*); Karl Hardman (*Harry*); Marilyn Eastman (*Helen*); Keith Wayne (*Tom*); Judith Ridley (*Judy*); Kyra Schon (*Karen*); Charles Craig (*Newscaster/Zombie*); George Kosana (*Sheriff McClelland*); Frank Doak, Mark Ricci (*Scientists*); Bill "Chilly Billy" Cardille (*Reporter*); S. William Hinzman, A. C. McDonald, Samuel R. Solito, Lee Hartman (*Zombies*).

MOST MEMORABLE LINE

They're coming for you, Barbra!

JOHNNY

BACKGROUND

Roger Corman, a great pioneer of the youth market film, was always based in Hollywood. However, an even truer form of indie film for this populist constituency emerged during the early 1960s outside Los Angeles. During that time, young would-be filmmakers across the country raised the small sums necessary to shoot their scripts (often horror and/or sci-fi) with whatever moviemaking equipment they could locate. Herk Harvey fashioned his own shoestring-budget psychological horror item, *Carnival of Souls* (1962), in Kansas, and Herschell Gordon Lewis created the slasher gorefest with the Miami-lensed *Blood Feast* (1963). Such déclassé items would come to be considered classics of their kind by youthful aficionados who, by decade's end, emerged as the next generation of middle-class (but not middlebrow) moviegoers—and, in some cases, low-budget film critics.

THE PLOT

Once a year, Johnny and Barbra visit the grave of their deceased father in an isolated area of Pennsylvania. This time around, something goes terribly wrong. When Barbra becomes spooked by their surroundings, Johnny makes fun of her, insisting the living dead will now appear. No sooner has he spoken than precisely that occurs: a zombie emerges from the shadows, killing Johnny and pursuing Barbra. The desperate girl hides in an apparently abandoned farmhouse, where she meets Ben, a heroic youth, who offers to defend her. Shortly, they are joined by other menaced individuals, some concerned only for themselves, others banding together as best they can to ward off the invasion.

THE FILM

None of the inexpensive independents had as much of an impact in its time or such a lasting influence as *Night of the Living Dead*. Movies such as *Carnival of Souls* and *Blood Feast* were shot for between $30,000 and $50,000. Romero's work cost more than $114,000, loose change on the L.A. scene, but it became a virtual epic among drive-in movies. When the film garnered more than $12 million in profits, more than most big-budget mainstream movies earned, the Hollywood powers-that-be took notice. During the next decade, filmmakers who had initiated their careers shooting low-budget items for Corman—Francis

Ford Coppola and Martin Scorsese among them—would, along with George Romero, bring their edgy visions to the epicenter of commercial cinema.

THEME

Previously, the creature we call "The Zombie" had existed largely in the realm of Gothic-horror-fantasy—often set in faraway places like Haiti, as such mini-classics as *I Walked with a Zombie* (Jacques Tourneur, 1943) illustrate. Their territory was the supernatural, not science fiction.

Romero, however, relied on that marvelous 1950s convention of an alien object entering Earth's atmosphere, on the order of the meteor in *The Blob* or the implied devastation of our environment by atomic-age waste in *The Birds*. Here, a space probe to Venus re-enters our atmosphere, turning normal people into the zombies of myth, though Romero wisely avoided that term in favor of "things" or "creatures." Though hardly a message movie, this is an environmental film, suggesting that not only our harmful habits, such as the dumping of radioactive materials into the ocean, but also our "glorious" hopes of conquering outer space could lead to disaster.

TRIVIA

Though this was not the first indie horror item to feature excessive gore—and any controversy surrounding it would be eclipsed when Wes Craven's more violent *Last House on the Left* (1972) premiered—here was the film that, owing to its commercial success, ignited an ongoing conversation about graphic violence in films. Would this film inspire more violence in an already blood-stained decade? Should the depiction of such objects as raw livers devoured in close-up be considered legitimate, a means of commenting, through horrific sci-fi, on the violence that had already started to consume our world? After *Night of the Living Dead*, and in large part because of this film, intense violence as a basic element of contemporary commercial moviemaking would spread to high-profile films from major production companies. These included not only horror and sci-fi movies, but also "realistic" dramas, such as Sam Peckinpah's *Straw Dogs* (1971), which plays like *Night of the Living Dead* with the sci-fi/fantastical horror aspect removed.

As always, such ambitious indies offer breakthroughs long before Hollywood. For example, here is the first case of an African-American actor, Duane Jones, being cast in a leading role—other than the lofty parts awarded to Sidney Poitier and Harry Belafonte—that is not immediately identified by race. For the first time, American films embraced color-blind casting.

COLOSSUS: THE FORBIN PROJECT (1970)

—— RANKING: 66 ——

CREDITS

Universal Pictures; Joseph Sargent, dir.; D. F. Jones, novel; James Bridges, scr.; Stanley Chase, pro.; Michel Colombier, Stanley Wilson, mus.; Gene Polito, cin.; Folmar Blangsted, ed.; Alexander Golitzen, John J. Lloyd, art dir.; Edith Head, costumes; Don Record, optical effects; Albert Whitlock, special photographic F/X; 100 min.; Color; 2.35:1.

CAST

Eric Braeden (*Dr. Charles A. Forbin*); Susan Clark (*Dr. Cleo Markham*); Gordon Pinsent (*The President*); William Schallert (*CIA Director Grauber*); Leonid Rostoff (*Russian Chairman*); Georg Stanford Brown (*Dr. John F. Fisher*); Willard Sage (*Dr. Blake*); Alex Rodine (*Dr. Kuprin*); Martin E. Brooks (*Dr. Johnson*); Marion Ross (*Angela*); Dolph Sweet (*Missile Commander*); Paul Frees (*Colossus*, voice only).

MOST MEMORABLE LINE

This is the voice of World Control.

COLOSSUS, TO HUMANKIND

BACKGROUND

British sci-fi writer Dennis Feltham Jones (1917–1981), a World War II naval commander, published his novel, *Colossus*, in 1966, at the height of the Cold War. Universal had picked up the rights and considered transforming this unusual story into one of their newly popular made-for-TV movies. Television seemed a good option because the project required a limited number of sets and, despite its genre, little need for expensive F/X, as we never actually "see" Colossus or its Soviet counterpart, Guardian, only the outer edges of these modern monstrosities. However, the unexpected success of *2001: A Space Odyssey* (1968) verified not only the box office appeal of science fiction but also the importance (via HAL) of cautionary fables about the coming age of advanced computers. Studio executives reconsidered Jones's book for a theatrical project.

THE PLOT

Brilliant scientist Charles A. Forbin has spent his life in experimentation designed to better his nation and the human race. He believes his efforts have been worthwhile, thanks to his new invention: Colossus, a supercomputer that will flawlessly (or so it seems) oversee all nuclear weapons in the United States. The president fetes Forbin, though this official ceremony ends abruptly when Colossus detects its doppelganger, a similar Russian system, likewise just completed. Bonding, the two create a language all their own and communicate constantly. Shortly, they arrive at a joint conclusion: rather than compete by serving the two sides in a Cold War, they will work together to eliminate war. If that initially sounds like a happy prospect, humans soon learn that peace and prosperity can only prevail if they are reduced to pawns in a master plan devised by machines that people originally believed would exist "to serve man." (That phrase, of course, had earlier been used as the title for a famous—some might say infamous—*Twilight Zone* episode.)

THE FILM

Aware that the Cold War had cooled, James Bridges (1936–1993), who had been creating impressive scripts for TV's *The Alfred Hitchcock Hour*, toned down the book's deeply suspicious situation between the superpowers. He heightened the narrative impact by streamlining the tale so that all of humankind unites around an imperative: not only to survive, but also to resist a monolithic common enemy to human freedom. The desire for self-determination, the essence of humankind, is dismissed by Colossus as a sentimental emotion that must be extinguished if order is to rule the world, this established as a key theme that would be further developed in later films.

Universal hoped to cast Charlton Heston but producer Stanley Chase insisted on an unknown to add a sense of everyday realism. Simultaneously, director Joseph Sargent vetoed Universal's plan to create a set design for Forbin's laboratory, instead shooting exteriors at the Lawrence Hall of Science at the University of California, Berkeley. Far from a fantasy, this film projected what could occur the day after tomorrow . . . or, for that matter . . . today.

THEME

The concept of sentience, as introduced in *2001*, was vastly expanded here, emerging during the 1970s as an overriding theme for near-future science fiction. The great fear was that cyborgs, robots, computers, and other creations might develop a sense of self, their human-level intelligence (or, in some cases,

DAWN OF THE COMPUTER AGE: *In this shamefully neglected classic, the title character, Dr. Charles A. Forbin (Eric Braeden), an updating of the scientist whose good intentions lead to potential annihilation, stands before his computerized creation. Courtesy: Universal.*

a consciousness far beyond that known to humans) resulting in synthetic creatures that come to perceive themselves as a race. Each individual "member"—with a will of its own, though not a soul—would inhabit a terrain that reaches beyond human understandings of morality and mortality. This could allow for logic to fully supplant emotion, a computer deciding that the best manner to avoid future war would be to enslave—or, if necessary, eliminate—people. Dr. Forbin emerges as yet another example of the Dr. Frankenstein figure, the idealistic scientist envisioned more than a hundred years earlier by Mary Shelley, his name also beginning with an *F*, a hint as to their similarity.

TRIVIA

Eric Braeden, who would achieve lasting daytime TV stardom via *The Young and the Restless*, had earlier played Nazi villains under his birth name, Hans Gudegast, in TV shows such as *The Rat Patrol*.

Joseph Sargent would go on to direct all five episodes of the acclaimed 1985 TV miniseries *Space*. His earlier associations with the genre include directing the fondly remembered *Star Trek* episode, "The Corbomite Maneuver" (November 10, 1966); four episodes of *The Invaders* (season 1, 1967); and the 1969 pilot/ TV movie template for *The Immortal*.

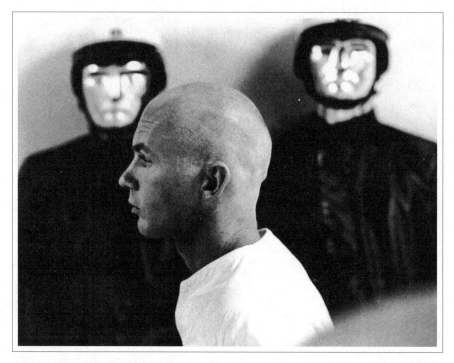

A PRELUDE TO STAR WARS: *In a student film that transformed into an edgy feature, young George Lucas borrowed from 1984 rather than Buck Rogers to create a brightly lit study of dehumanized life in a dystopian future. Courtesy: American Zoetrope/Warner Bros.*

• • • • • • •

THX 1138 (1971)

—— RANKING: 64 ——

CREDITS

Warner Bros./American Zoetrope; George Lucas, dir.; Lucas, Walter Murch, Matthew Robbins, scr.; Francis Ford Coppola, Larry Sturhahn, pro.; Lalo Schifrin, mus.; Albert Kihn, David Myers, cin.; Lucas, Marcia Lucas, ed.; Michael D. Haller, art dir.; Murch, Jim Manson, Louis Yates, sound; Michael Muir, Brad Alexander, Dorian Bustamante, John Andrew Berton Jr., technical visual effects; Richard Bluff, Zachary Cole, digital effects; 86 min. (theatrical release), 88 min. (director's cut); Color; 2.35:1.

CAST

Robert Duvall (*THX*); Donald Pleasence (*SEN*); Don Pedro Colley (*SRT*); Maggie McOmie (*LUH*); Ian Wolfe (*PTO*); Marshall Efron (*TWA*); Sid Haig (*NCH*); John Pearce (*DWY*); Irene Cagen (*IMM*); Gary Alan Marsh (*CAM*); John Seaton (*OUE*); Eugene I. Stillman (*JOT*); Jack Walsh (*TRG*); Johnny Weissmuller Jr. (*Chrome Robot*); Claudette Bessing (*ELC*); Mello Alexandria, Brandyn Barbara Artis (*Hologram Dancers*); David Ogden Stiers (*Announcer*).

MOST MEMORABLE LINE

You have nowhere to go . . .
CHROME ROBOT #1 TO THX

BACKGROUND

Following graduation from the film program at the University of Southern California in 1967, twenty-three-year-old George Lucas (1944–) returned to his alma mater as a graduate student to teach filmmaking. Believing that the best way to learn was by doing, he combined elements of Orwell's *1984* and Bradbury's *Fahrenheit 451*, from which the class would shoot a short film, *Electronic Labyrinth: THX 1138 4EB*. The advanced student project told the story from the point of view of cameras that monitor the every move of protagonist THX. When the results were more impressive than anyone expected, Lucas entered it in a national film contest and won first prize. Consequently, Warner Bros. approached him to serve as student observer of a film being shot by young Francis Ford Coppola. Shortly, Lucas was promoted to Coppola's personal assistant. This new mentor suggested that Lucas get to work on a feature of his own, remaking the previous featurette.

THE PLOT

In the twentieth-fifth century, people inhabiting a vast underground city are forbidden to engage in sex but are encouraged to take drugs that keep them in an oblivious state. One individual, THX, falls in love with his roommate, LUH, and both are imprisoned. They meet SRT, another nonconformist. The three make plans to escape, working their way up to Earth's surface, hoping to see the sun once again.

THE FILM

Lucas had no interest in writing, suggesting that his talent be restricted to the film's photographic elements. But Coppola insisted, so Lucas collaborated on the screenplay with another former USC student, Walter Murch. Critics perceived the result as austere and minimalist at best, bloodless and dispassionate at worst. With a budget of little more than $750,000, *THX*, though not a huge hit, did take in close to $2.5 million at the box office.

THX 1138 was the first film released by American Zoetrope, Coppola's independent company. The game plan was to create art films, influenced by imports from Europe and Asia, not Hollywood studio formula movies. The result was a string of films that the public had no interest in seeing. Everyone realized they must rethink the old films for a new audience. Coppola set to work on reimagining the gangster film with *The Godfather* (1972), while Lucas came up with his ideas for *Star Wars* and the *Indiana Jones* trilogy.

THEME

Lucas was fascinated by the idea of "near-future," that unique sci-fi subgenre that presents problems already present in our society in exaggerated form to warn of the dangerous consequences. To adhere to a tight budget, he rejected construction of sets, instead shooting *THX 1138* in San Francisco. Lucas focused on the most modernist landmarks, isolating these structures with his camera to present a portion of the city as a fully realized future-world. In this film, conformity, and its impact on the human soul, is seen not as some vague possible distant threat but as a frightfully emergent reality.

TRIVIA

One of the chrome robots is played by Johnny Weissmuller Jr., son of the legendary *Tarzan* star. Weissmuller Jr. would return to the Lucas fold two years later in *American Graffiti* as one of the hoodlums who attack Charles Martin Smith, then as a card player in the made-for-TV movie *Ewoks: The Battle for Endor* (1985). Also in *THX 1138* is Sid Haig, famed bald and bearded character actor from such beloved junk movies as *Blood Bath* (1966) and *Spider Baby* (1968). His presence here initiated the trend of hiring unappreciated (at least by the mainstream) performers for roles in the New American Cinema that emerged in the 1970s, with young auteurs known as the "Movie Brats" (Lucas, Spielberg, Coppola, John Carpenter, and George Romero, among them) filling the void created by the retirement of John Ford, Howard Hawks, Frank Capra, and, shortly, Alfred Hitchcock.

Lucas opened *THX 1138* with a black-and-white image of Buster Crabbe in the old *Buck Rogers* cliffhanger. The concept was to then deconstruct such beloved fantasy visions with a stark cautionary fable. Unable to get that clip out of his mind, Lucas began planning just such a *Buck Rogers/Flash Gordon* space opera as a future project, which would evolve into *Star Wars*. This film's title would, in modified form, create an in-joke when recycled for a hot rod's license plate in *American Graffiti* (1973).

· · · · · · ·

SOLARIS/SOLYARIS (1972)

—— RANKING: 31 ——

CREDITS

Mosfilm; Andrei Tarkovsky, dir.; Stanislaw Lem, novel; Tarkovsky, Fridrikh Gorenshteyn, scr.; Vyacheslav Tarasov, pro.; Eduard Artemev, Raisa Lukina, mus.; Vadim Yusov, cin.; Lyudmila Feyginova, Nina Marcus, ed.; Mikhail Romadin, prod. design; A. Klimenko, V. Sevostyanov, special cinematographic effects; 167 min.; Color/B&W; 2.35:1.

CAST

Donatas Banionis (*Kris Kelvin*); Natalya Bondarchuk (*Khari*); Jüri Järvet (*Dr. Snaut*); Vladislav Dvorzhetskiy (*Berton*); Nikolay Grinko (*Kelvin's Father*); Anatoliy Solonitsyn (*Dr. Sartorius*); Olga Barnet (*Kelvin's Mother*); Vitalik Kerdimun (*Berton's Son*); Olga Kizilova (*Gribaryan's "She-guest"*); Tatyana Malykh (*Kelvin's Niece*).

MOST MEMORABLE LINE

Man is the one who renders science moral or immoral.

KELVIN, EXPRESSING THE CENTRAL THEME

BACKGROUND

As originally expressed in Polish author Stanislaw Lem's 1961 novel by the same name, *Solaris* offers a variation on the old adage about the inability to see the forest for the trees. Earthlings peer down at Solaris, a planet as blue as their own, hoping to discover some form of life on its oceanic surface, then communicate with it. What they fail to grasp is that the evolution of a life force occurred so differently on this orb that when earthlings study the planet's surface, they cannot identify "life" even when staring directly at it. The ocean is a living thing, as intent upon studying these visitors as they are interested in it. To control the earthlings, and render them harmless, the ocean causes each to experience hallucinations about long-repressed betrayals, real or perceived, that now obsess the space travelers.

THE PLOT

For some time, a space station launched from Earth has circled the planet Solaris without determining if there is any life force below. Worse, those assigned to the station have grown lethargic. A psychologist, Kelvin, is to be sent to analyze the crewmembers. Before departing, Kelvin is visited by Berton, a former space pilot whose reputation was ruined when he returned from Solaris claiming to have seen an immense child who could not have existed. Berton confides to Kelvin that the supposed fantasy looked like the baby of a lost scientist he had hoped to locate. Though Kelvin gives this little credence, he begins to notice, once he's on the station, people who could not possibly be there. Then he wakes from a troubled sleep to find his wife Khari beside him, though the despondent woman had earlier taken her own life.

THE FILM

To approximate the "meditative" aspect of Lem's novel, Andrei Tarkovsky shot his movie in a minimalist style. Though he included images of the space station that convey the genre's technical aspect, most frames are kept purposefully simple, whether in the whiteness of the station's corridors or the rich green life on Earth. The screenplay by Tarkovsky and Fridrikh Gorenshteyn opts for a stream-of-consciousness style that leaves little doubt that this is an art film. At nearly three hours long, the film moves very slowly, forcing the viewer to accept the story as steeped in philosophy. Along the way, the audience glimpses paintings by old masters, the most prominent being Pieter Bruegel the Elder's *The Hunters in the Snow* (1565). The inclusion of such works represents the director's desire to connect the still-emergent art of cinema with more established and accepted art forms. This had also been the motivation for Stanley Kubrick's featuring of classical music in *2001: A Space Odyssey* (1968).

THEME

"Astrobiology" underpins the story. The idea, among some scientific thinkers and dramatized by Lem, concerns the very concept of life itself: attempting to discover precise situations that will allow for the origination of this force in any area of the cosmos, as well as the determining factors that cause life

RETHINKING A POPULAR GENRE: *The Soviet film,* Solaris, *with all the conventions of previous sci-fi films, offers a cerebral work that explores the complex nature of everyday reality. In time, this concept would also be considered in commercial American cinema, most notably,* The Matrix *(1999). Courtesy: Mosfilm/Unit Four/Fox Lorber.*

to then develop in a specific situation. Sci-fi works based on the concept (this film being the most famous) steer away from the idea of outer space creatures that resemble earthlings or are monstrous variations on the human race. Here scientists must free themselves from all prejudicial notions and from their limited perceptions, if that is humanly possible, to grasp that an ocean can not only contain life forces but also be one, with an intelligence, a personality, and even a morality of its own.

TRIVIA

An earlier film, *Solyaris,* directed by Boris Nirenburg and Lidiya Ishimbayeva appeared on Russian TV in 1968. Its popularity led to the making of Tarkovsky's more ambitious version, which won the Grand Prize at the 1972 Cannes Film Festival.

The image of the child as described in the film so resembles the child that we see in the closing moments of *2001: A Space Odyssey* that many sci-fi fans assumed this to be an homage to Kubrick. Surprisingly, Tarkovsky had not seen that classic before beginning work on his own movie, though he finally caught up with it in . . . 2001.

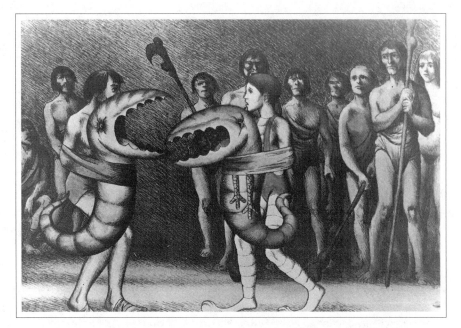

REMEMBRANCE OF THINGS FUTURE: *Since the golden age of Georges Méliès, the art of animation and the science-fiction genre have occasionally combined in creative harmony. Here, images from the past blend with a sense of what H. G. Wells described as the "shape of things to come," the combination endowed with a Proustian sense of time. Courtesy: Argos Films/Embassy/Anchor Bay.*

· · · · · · ·

FANTASTIC PLANET/LA PLANÈTE SAUVAGE (1973)

—— RANKING: 35 ——

CREDITS

Argos Films/Les Films Armorial; René Laloux, dir.; Pierre Pairault, concept; Laloux, Roland Topor, scr.; Simon Damiani, Anatole Dauman, pro.; Alain Goraguer, mus.; Boris Baromykin, Lubomir Rejthar, cin.; Hélène Arnal, Marta Látalová, ed.; Topor, graphic design; Jean Guérin, Robert Pouret, Hélène Tossy, sound; Jindrich Bárta, Zdena Bártová, animators; Lidia Cardet, Renáta Celbová, Helena Rohrauerová, Dana Drábová, special animation design; Josef Kábrt, character graphics; Josef Vania, special background graphic effects; 72 min.; Color; 1.66:1.

CAST (VOICES)

Jean Valmont (*Adulte Terr/Narrator*); Jennifer Drake (*Tiwa*); Eric Baugin (*Terr*); Jean Topart (*Maître Sinh*); Sylvie Lenoir, Michèle Chahan, Yves Barsacq, Hubert de Lapparent, Gérard Hernandez, Claude Joseph, Philippe Ogouz, Jacques Ruisseau (*Additional Voices*).

MOST MEMORABLE LINE

I decided to run away.

TERR, FEELING ALIENATED FROM THE NOW GROWN-UP TIWA AND
HOPING TO REDISCOVER A GREATER SENSE OF HIS OWN IDENTITY

BACKGROUND

"Stefan Wul" served as a nom de plume for Pierre Pairault (1922–2003), who labored by day as a dental surgeon. Each evening, though, his "secret self" wrote what many consider the greatest Gallic contributions to science fiction since the work of Jules Verne. Though he never achieved great fame outside his homeland, a sizable following there, plus a loyal international cult following, kept Pairault's reputation alive among genre aficionados. The 1957 publication of *Oms en série* (roughly translated: *Oms Linked Together*) stirred international interest. At the height of the Cold War space race, the vision of humans traveling to the planet Ygam only to become the playthings of an indigenous race called "Draags" presented a parable equal to that of Pierre Boulle's 1963 novel, *La planète des singes* (*Planet of the Apes*).

THE PLOT

The Traags, blue-faced creatures, dominate a faraway planet, also inhabited by the diminutive Oms. Many of these human-like beings live wild in unsettled areas; some Traag leaders, considering them pests, exterminate Om colonies. There are domesticated, meek Oms, who are the seemingly harmless playthings of Traag children. Upon reaching adolescence, these Traags often discard their once-beloved pets. Terr has been the Om companion to Tiwa, daughter of Traag leader Sinh, since her youth. Terr runs away to live with members of his species. Their dream is to leave this world in a rocket ship and discover and populate a planet where they might, when removed from the current context, be considered "normal" in size, literally and symbolically.

THE FILM

Paris-born René Laloux (1929–2004) traveled an odd route to the cinema, torn during his lifetime between the poles of artistic integrity and commercial necessity. In his youth, Laloux studied "serious" art at university, and shortly after graduation, he joined an advertising firm, where his gifts were put to use servicing the sale of products. Consumerism paid well, though Laloux suffered from a gnawing sense that his illustrations should serve a greater purpose. He accepted a position at a mental institution and soon discovered his ability to help patients release their inner demons not only through traditional painting but also through the creation of simple cartoons.

A largely Czech team drew on the great tradition of "limited animation," including the contributions of Lotte Reiniger (1899–1981). That German animator's experimental film, *The Adventures of Prince Achmed* (1926), predates Walt Disney's *Snow White and the Seven Dwarfs* (1937) as one of the pioneer examples of feature filmmaking. Reiniger did not subscribe to Disney's full-animation approach, favoring a minimalist technique, using silhouettes of cutouts for a suggestive approach to ancient myth. Likewise, Jiři Trnka (1912–1969), the great inspiration for all such Czech animated filmmaking, had always opted for a subtle art in which still drawings could be intermixed with puppets for a refreshingly original appearance. Trnka relied heavily on stop-motion photographic effects, which, instead of providing a viewer with rich detail, insist on audience participation in filling in the many purposeful gaps.

Czech filmmakers transformed their version of this tale into a metaphor for the despised Soviet occupation of their country that began in August 1968. While Laloux completely agreed with their values, he began to feel as isolated from his colleagues as the character Terr feels from the Traags. At one point, the Parisian was almost forced out of the artistic mix, not owing to any lack of talent but to the fierce sense of nationalism that had come to surround this project.

THEME

La planète sauvage resulted from a serendipitous meeting between Laloux and Roland Topor (1938–1997), a surrealist painter who had become increasingly intrigued by the possibilities inherent in feature-length animation to bring avant-garde attitudes to the masses. The author of the novel *The Tenant* (*Le locataire chimérique*, 1964), filmed by Roman Polanski in 1976, Topor brought to any project a Kafkaesque sensibility, full of victimized individuals played with, even tortured by, the immense forces that cast long shadows across a distorted terrain. This derived from Topor's Polish origins and, as a Jew, his haunting memories of what the Holocaust had done to his family. Numerous critics and casual observers of Topor's pan-artistic output—musical, graphic, literary, cinematic—have pointed out the presence of two interlocking themes, alienation and identity, as essential to his ideology. Though such elements were already present in Laloux's concept and the source material, the human hunger to discover, in one's essential loneliness, a key to one's own character was further heightened by Topor's conception.

The Oms move beyond victimization after learning to read. Education is presented here as the spark that ignites revolution via an overdue awareness of the class system and its inequities, expressing an early 1970s reaction against the once widely accepted idea of imperialism.

TRIVIA

The Om hero's name, Terr, refers to Earth itself.

Producer-importer Roger Corman prepared an English-language version, with actor Barry Bostwick serving as narrator. This print contains additional editing decisions by Dick Elliott and Rich Harrison. However, exposure was minimal in theatrical release. Then, the still relatively new HBO, with its immense appetite for available product, picked this offbeat item for broadcast to a far vaster audience than previously possible. Animated nudity and simulated sex would have rendered the film an unlikely candidate for network TV, though such elements proved perfect for a pay cable item.

· · · · · · ·

WESTWORLD (1973) AND FUTUREWORLD (1976)

—— RANKING: 92 (TIE) ——

WESTWORLD (1973)

CREDITS

MGM; Michael Crichton, dir.; Crichton, scr.; Paul Lazarus III, Michael I. Rachmil, pro.; Fred Karlin, mus.; Gene Polito, cin.; David Bretherton, ed.; Herman A. Blumenthal, art dir.; Charles Schulthies, F/X; Brent Sellstrom, John Whitney Jr., Matthew Yuricich, special visual effects; 88 min.; Color; 2.35:1.

CAST

Yul Brynner (*The Robot Gunslinger*); Richard Benjamin (*Peter Martin*); James Brolin (*John Blane*); Norman Bartold (*Medieval Knight*); Alan Oppenheimer (*Chief Supervisor*); Victoria Shaw (*Medieval Queen*); Dick Van Patten (*Banker*); Linda Gaye Scott (*Arlette*); Steve Franken (*Technician*); Michael T. Mikler (*Black Knight*); Terry Wilson (*Westworld Sheriff*).

MOST MEMORABLE LINE

Delos is the vacation of the future—*today!*
THEME PARK LOGO

BACKGROUND

Harvard Medical School graduate Michael Crichton (1942–2008) had always hoped to be a writer. If he did not create the concept of "techno-thriller" (some do ascribe that to him), certainly he perfected it with novels like *The Andromeda Strain* (1969). Intrigued by the mathematical concept of chaos theory, Crichton began to wonder, while on the Pirates of the Caribbean ride at Disneyland, what might happen if the audio-animatronic buccaneers were to attack the guests. Thereafter, he set to work on a story, but, concerned that Disney might sue if he called his piece "Pirate World," Crichton changed the basic concept to cowboys.

THE PLOT

Friends Peter and John visit Delos, a state-of-the-art theme park composed, like Disneyland, of various kingdoms (Medievalworld, Romanworld, Westworld). This park, however, is for adults only, and lifelike androids portray the characters. The young men don cowboy clothes, shooting it out with a dangerous-looking man in black before heading off to a bordello. What they don't know (yet) is that a virus has spread among the robots, causing them to fight back.

THE FILM

Westworld represents a significant moment in the history of not only science-fiction films but also Hollywood. A few years earlier, as indie filmmaking came to dominate deal making, the once-lustrous MGM sold off its old relics, including Dorothy's ruby slippers from *The Wizard of Oz*; ended its long-term contracts with varied talents; and shut down most of the soundstages and backlots. *Westworld* was the final film shot by the old order. Intriguingly, though, it paved the way for the future as the first film to feature such digital processes as

THE WORLD'S FIRST COMPUTERIZED COWBOY: *Yul Brynner's persona as a new sort of Western hero in* The Magnificent Seven *(1960) made him the perfect choice to play a robotized gunfighter in a Disneyland for adults only. Courtesy: Metro-Goldwyn-Mayer.*

"pixelization," in which the viewer sees the world through the eyes of a walking, talking computer.

TRIVIA

Beginning with *The Magnificent Seven* (John Sturges, 1960), Yul Brynner reinvented the Western hero as embodied by John Wayne and other earlier icons. When *Westworld* was shot, Brynner, once offering a departure from the norm, now embodied the very idea of the gunslinger.

FUTUREWORLD (1976)

ADDITIONAL CREDITS

American International Pictures; Richard T. Heffron, dir.; George Schenck, Mayo Simon, scr.; Samuel Z. Arkoff, James T. Aubrey, pro.; Fred Karlin, mus.; James Mitchell, ed.; Trevor Williams, art dir.; Gene Grigg, Michael Wood, F/X; Ed Catmull, Albert Nalpas, Frederic Ira Parke, Brent Sellstrom, special visual effects; 108 min.; Color; 1.37:1.

ADDITIONAL CAST

Peter Fonda (*Chuck Browning*); Blythe Danner (*Tracy Ballard*); Arthur Hill (*Dr. Duffy*); John P. Ryan (*Dr. Schneider*); Stuart Margolin (*Harry*); Allen Ludden (*Game Show Host*); Robert Cornthwaite (*Mr. Reed*); Angela Greene (*Mrs. Reed*).

MOST MEMORABLE LINE

Nothing can go wrong.
DR. SCHNEIDER TO DR. DUFFY

THE PLOT

Two years following the disaster at Westworld, Delos is ready to reopen, with Medievalworld and Romanworld improved, and Westworld abandoned in favor of Futureworld. A press junket precedes the public opening with print reporter Chuck Browning and his breezy TV celebrity counterpart Tracy Ballard among the invited. Though their guide Dr. Duffy insists that any danger has been eliminated, the journalists realize that Dr. Schneider, head of operations, plans to replace visiting journalists and politicians with their android counterparts and, through them, rule the world.

THE FILM

A decade earlier, any film from MGM would have been a huge undertaking, with a sequel by the exploitation company American International a small-budget follow-up. Here we find the opposite: *Westworld* ran for less than ninety minutes, typical of a B movie; the two-hour running time for *Futureworld* was more like that of an A movie. The original was shot inexpensively on sets left over from old cowboy shows. In contrast, the sequel offers a verisimilitude of sights and sounds that convincingly conveys the great theme park. *Futureworld* also plays down nonstop action in favor of more developed characters and offers a greater sense of a created "world." It also presents a more complicated plot, which was influenced by the Watergate scandal, with its implication that those seemingly benign people "at the top" are not to be trusted

THEME

Both films derive from Crichton's conservative fear of the machine: anything that can go wrong will go wrong, with robots as well as with any other computer-generated systems. That had been the theme of *2001: A Space Odyssey*, and Crichton moved the concept to the world of modern theme parks, where a vacation is at least supposed to be "perfect" owing to the downplaying of possible human error. Yet another visit to a Disney theme park, where Crichton visited the new dinosaur exhibit, led to his writing *Jurassic Park*.

TRIVIA

Paul Lazarus and his writers realized that there was no way to incorporate Yul Brynner's robot gunslinger into their new scenario without resorting to contrivance. Yet, they suspected that if the movie were to succeed at the box office, he must be present. They rewrote their script to incorporate the man in black within a sexual fantasy experienced by Blythe Danner's journalist while at the park.

WOODY'S UNIVERSAL ROBOTS: *Can an android experience human feelings?
This age-old question receives a unique comic twist in writer-director Woody Allen's
only foray into science fiction. Courtesy: Rollins-Joffe/United Artists.*

. . . .

SLEEPER (1973)

—— RANKING: 68 ——

CREDITS

United Artists; Woody Allen, dir.; Allen, Marshall Brickman, scr.; Jack Grossberg,
Charles H. Joffe, Jack Rollins, pro.; Allen, mus.; David M. Walsh, cin.; O. Nicho-
las Brown, Ron Kalish, Ralph Rosenblum, ed.; Dale Hennesy, prod. design; Joel
Schumacher, costumes; Dianne Wager, set design; A. D. Flowers, Gerald Endler,
F/X; Bill Hansard, Harvey Plastrik, optical/visual effects; 89 min.; Color; 1.85:1.

CAST

Woody Allen (*Miles Monroe*); Diane Keaton (*Luna Schlosser*); John Beck (*Erno Windt*); Mary Gregory, John McLiam, Chris Forbes, Peter Hobbs (*Doctors*); Susan Miller (*Ellen*); Lou Picetti (*M.C.*); Jessica Rains (*Woman in Mirror*); Howard Cosell (*Himself*); Jackie Mason (*Robot Tailor*, voice); Douglas Rain (*Evil Computer*, voice).

MOST MEMORABLE LINE

Science is an intellectual dead end . . . a lot of little guys in tweed suits cutting up frogs on foundation grants.

MILES TO LUNA

BACKGROUND

The idea of a "sleeper" can be traced back to ancient times, and in the United States, the Rip Van Winkle story dates from the early nineteenth century. The first modern (i.e., scientific) variation on this theme appeared as a short piece, "A Story of the Days to Come" (1897), by H. G. Wells. His second version appeared in 1898, under the title "When the Sleeper Wakes," which was then expanded into a novel in 1910, *The Sleeper Awakes*. This served as a forerunner to Aldous Huxley's *Brave New World*, George Orwell's *1984*, and other dystopian future sci-fi. Woody Allen (1935–) and Marshall Brickman admitted they were influenced by all those classics, the Wells tale exerting a particularly strong influence.

THE PLOT

When health food store owner Miles enters a hospital for a minor operation, he's killed by incompetence, frozen in the emergent cryogenic technique, and awakened two hundred years later when doctors revive him. They are members of an underground movement who want Miles to infiltrate the mysterious Aires Project, controlled by their fascistic government. During his mission, Miles falls in love with Luna, a wide-eyed innocent. Posing as her robot butler, he convinces her to join him. She becomes a rebel, joining radical leader Erno. Miles discovers that the head of state is dead and that Aires was an elaborate plot to use his only remaining body part, the nose, to clone a new Big Brother.

THE FILM

In 1969, *Time* magazine hailed Dennis Hopper's *Easy Rider* as "the little film that killed the big films." The old studios closed their backlots as a new breed of young moviemakers headed out into the real world to make a more "honest" kind of film. Formula films disappeared; genres were no longer viable. Soon, though, a sense of loss set in, resulting in "the genre spoof," which allowed us to laugh at what we had once taken seriously. Mel Brooks satirized clichés of the West in *Blazing Saddles* (1974), and at first glance, *Sleeper* does the same thing for science fiction, though with a different approach. Brooks's movie is not a Western but a burlesque of that form; *Sleeper*, however, can be taken seriously as a sci-fi film. Woody Allen's piece is not merely a comedy about sci-fi but a sci-fi movie played in a comedic, rather than a dramatic, tone. Proof of Allen's ambitiousness appears in records of his meeting with sci-fi greats Isaac Asimov and Ben Bova, both of whom he consulted to make certain everything in the piece conformed to genre rules.

THEME

Like other near-future projects, *Sleeper* predicts a sexless society in which synthetic processes replace the animal act for humans. This, however, does not give way to an increase in human intelligence, since the people are superficial thinkers and shallow in emotion.

The late 1960s were identified with political activism for social causes, including antiwar and pro-environmental concerns. Social critic Christopher Lasch noted that the 1970s offered reaction, people cocooning in personal relationships, leading to what he labeled the "Culture of Narcissism." This film embodies that concept. Miles gives up on revolution to concentrate on romance with Luna, insisting that even if the fascistic government is toppled and Erno takes over, he will be just as bad as the previous leader. Power corrupts; absolute power corrupts absolutely. "Political solutions don't work," Miles says.

TRIVIA

Though Allen would shortly settle on his beloved Manhattan for almost all his films, this movie was made in a rural area near Boulder, Colorado. The most impressive "set," the rebel's hideout, was not built for the project. The 1963 work of genius was a monstrosity called the "Sculptured House," which had been built by architect Charles Deaton.

Kubrick's *2001* exerted a strong influence. Whereas that film contrasted the emptiness of space with classical/romantic music, Allen sets the emptiness of life on a future Earth against the warm, vital sounds of jazz, including his own clarinet playing. Douglas Rain, the voice of HAL the Computer, was persuaded to do the honors here for the Evil Computer. The scene in which Miles is brainwashed recalls, if in a less harrowing manner, Kubrick's *A Clockwork Orange* (1971).

······

STAR WARS EPISODE IV: A NEW HOPE (1977), STAR WARS EPISODE V: THE EMPIRE STRIKES BACK (1980), AND STAR WARS EPISODE VI: RETURN OF THE JEDI (1983)

—— RANKING: 4 (THREE-WAY TIE) ——

STAR WARS EPISODE IV: A NEW HOPE (1977)

CREDITS

Twentieth Century-Fox; George Lucas, dir.; Lucas, scr.; Lucas, Gary Kurtz, Rick McCallum, pro.; John Williams, mus.; Gilbert Taylor, cin.; Lucas, Richard Chew, Paul Hirsch, Marcia Lucas, T. M. Christopher (1997 special edition only), ed.; John Barry, prod. design; Leslie Dilley, Norman Reynolds, art dir.; Roger Christian, set design; John Stears, Tony Dyson, Bob Keen, Robert Nugent, F/X; John Dykstra, Dennis Muren, Dan O'Bannon, Caleb Aschkynazo, Julie Adrianson-Neary, Karen Ansel (special edition only), visual/optical effects; 121 min. (125 min., special edition); Color; 2.20:1.

CAST

Mark Hamill (*Luke Skywalker*); Harrison Ford (*Han Solo*); Carrie Fisher (*Princess Leia Organa*); Peter Cushing (*Grand Moff Tarkin*); Alec Guinness (*Obi-Wan "Ben" Kenobi*); Anthony Daniels (*C-3PO*); Kenny Baker (*R2-D2*); Peter Mayhew (*Chewbacca*); David Prowse (*Darth Vader*, body); James Earl Jones (*Darth Vader*, voice); Phil Brown (*Uncle Owen*); Shelagh Fraser (*Aunt Beru*); Paul Blake, Maria De Aragon, Larry Ward (*Greedo*).

MOST MEMORABLE LINE

May the Force be with you!

OBI-WAN KENOBI/ADVERTISING LOGO

BACKGROUND

While growing up in the Northern California town of Modesto, George Lucas (1944–) adored all action-adventure films, as well as old movie serials that appeared on the new medium of TV. When he arrived at the University of Southern California film school, Lucas was introduced to an entirely different sort of "cinema," arthouse works, such as the Samurai films by Akira Kurosawa. By the mid-1970s, a nostalgia movement had formed, with Lucas's *American Graffiti* (1973) among the first major hits to recall how much fun going to the movies had been before the New Realism of films such as *Midnight Cowboy* (John Schlesinger, 1969) and *Mean Streets* (Martin Scorsese, 1973). Spielberg's *Jaws* (1975) signaled the return of the blockbuster and Lucas took note. He hoped to mount a *Flash Gordon* remake, but when the rights proved too expensive, he instead wrote his own screenplay, using Kurosawa's brilliant *The Hidden Fortress* (*Kakushi-toride no san-akunin*, 1958) as his narrative's template.

THE PLOT

Speeding home to Alderaan, Princess Leia's craft is overtaken by the larger ship of Darth Vader, operative for the Evil Empire. He hopes to recover plans for the Death Star, which Leia has seized. Moments before capture, she codes a hologram into R2-D2, sending the robot off in an escape pod along with the droid C-3PO toward planet Tatooine. There, a farm boy, Luke, discovers the icon, taking it to old Ben, once a Jedi knight. When Luke's aunt and uncle are massacred, the survivors head for a spaceport where they convince charming outlaw Han Solo and his huge Wookiee companion Chewbacca to help them escape on Solo's *Millennium Falcon*.

THE FILM

"A long time ago in a galaxy far, far away. . . ." Older audiences shivered with delight as those words appeared in a crawl over an image of deep space. Younger audiences were introduced to the wonderful bygone world of the chapter play, as what had once been relegated to B-budget moviemaking for children transformed into the new F/X-driven A movie for kids of all ages. Still, the film included homages to the most adult of Westerns, John Ford's *The Searchers* (1956).

In addition to referencing past films, this Movie Brat (young students, critics, and fans who took over and reinvented Hollywood) drew heavily on a more serious source. Joseph Campbell (1904–1987) had mainstreamed the idea of mythology in such books as *The Hero with a Thousand Faces* (1949), which Lucas had devoured. No wonder Luke's experiences transcend any superficial

THE NOSTALGIA MOVEMENT: *However state of the art George Lucas's technological wizardry may have been, this purposefully old-fashioned poster attests to the fact that the first film (Episode IV) was intended to revive the glory days of Saturday morning serials about Flash Gordon and Buck Rogers. Courtesy: 20th Century-Fox; Lucasfilm.*

action adventure, reaching back to Greek mythology and other ancient sources, including the Bible, *Beowulf,* and Arthurian legend. Here appeared a variation on the heroic quest: a young swain overcoming his seemingly humble origins to discover his fate while fighting forces of evil, relying on an elderly mentor, teaming with a partner of questionable morality, falling in love with a beautiful princess, and forever inching toward epic accomplishment.

THEME

Like many classic Hollywood adventure films, *Star Wars* proceeds from a liberal bias. The Evil Empire is a fascistic entity; the rebels, heroes fighting the corrupt Establishment. More recently, some social critics of film have noted a number of conservative elements of which Lucas may have been unaware. For example, no matter how liberated Leia may seem at first, she ultimately must be rescued by Luke. Also, part of the requirement of being a true hero is a princely blood-line—an elitist notion. The finale, in which the heroes are rewarded, recalls Leni Riefenstahl's documentary tribute to Adolf Hitler, *Triumph of the Will* (*Triumph de Willens,* 1935). As is often the case with films, we draw from (or read into) any movie what we wish to see in it. Whether one finds *Star Wars Episode IV: A New Hope* a conservative or liberal vision says more about the viewer than it does about either Lucas or his film.

TRIVIA

"Cowboys in space" is how Lucas originally pitched the project at Twentieth Century-Fox. In addition to the already mentioned *Searchers,* other Westerns proved influential. When Han enters the cantina and finds himself forced to shoot it out with Greedo, he momentarily becomes Ringo (Gregory Peck) in *The Gunfighter* (Henry King, 1950). Darth Vader's chilling appearance in black owes much to the Jack Palance villain in *Shane* (George Stevens, 1953).

STAR WARS EPISODE V: THE EMPIRE STRIKES BACK (1980)

ADDITIONAL/ALTERED CREDITS

Irvin Kershner, dir.; Leigh Brackett, Lawrence Kasdan, scr.; Rick McCallum, pro. (special edition); Peter Suschitzky, cin.; T. M. Christopher (special edition), ed.; Harry Lange, Alan Tomkins, art dir.; Ben Burtt, sound effects designer; Nick Allder, F/X; David Berry, Doug Beswick, visual/optical effects; 124 min. (127 min. special edition); Color; 2.20:1.

ADDITIONAL/ALTERED CAST

Billy Dee Williams (*Lando Calrissian*); Frank Oz (*Yoda*, voice); Jeremy Bulloch (*Boba Fett*, body); Jason Wingreen (*Boba Fett*, voice); Des Webb (*Snow Creature*); Clive Revill (*Emperor*, voice); Kenneth Colley (*Admiral Piett*); Denis Lawson (*Wedge*); Treat Williams (*Trooper*).

MOST MEMORABLE LINE

I am your father.

DARTH VADER TO LUKE

THE PLOT

Three years following the destruction of the Death Star, Luke and Han are officers in a combat unit commanded by Leia. On a special mission to the Hoth system, Luke is mauled by a hairy Wampa (snow creature), then rescued by Han, still his competitor for Leia's attentions. An all-out attack on the enemy forces in a frozen landscape is followed by parallel adventures. At the bequest of the spirit of the now-deceased Ben, Luke sets off to study with Yoda. In the meantime, Han and Leia head for Cloud City, where Han's roguish, friendly enemy Lando would like to help them, but, under pressure from Vader, allows Han to be flash-frozen in carbonite. Bounty hunter Boba Fett arrives on the scene, threatening all the heroes.

THE FILM

If there was any weakness in the original, it must be identified as Lucas's direction of actors. His genius has always been as a conceptualizer: envisioning a project, contributing to the screenplay, then overseeing the production. Unknown to most filmgoers, Irvin Kershner (1923–2010) rated as one of the best when it came to inspiring performers and breathing life into a scene. He brought out dimensions in the characters missing from the first film. Also, Kershner added a noir quality that proved a perfect style for this sequel, setting the pace for many other sci-fi/noirs to come.

THEME

The elements of the Greek epic present in the original are evident in *Episode V*. The revelation that Darth Vader is father to Luke, who sets out to kill him, adds an Oedipal aspect, tying this to classical tragedy. Clearly, *Star Wars* was shaping up as a saga about destiny and the Force that controls all.

OF HEROES AND VILLAINS: *Appearing toward the end of the 1970s, a decade characterized by films reveling in urban grime*—Midnight Cowboy *(1969) and* Taxi Driver *(1976), for example*—Star Wars *heralded the return of old-fashioned good guys (Billy Dee Williams as Lando, second from right) and hiss-worthy villains (from left, a stormtrooper, Darth Vader, and bounty hunter Boba Fett). Courtesy: 20th Century-Fox; Lucasfilm.*

STAR WARS EPISODE VI: RETURN OF THE JEDI (1983)

ADDITIONAL/ALTERED CREDITS

Richard Marquand, dir.; Jim Bloom, Howard G. Kazanjian, pro.; Alan Hume, Alec Mills, cin.; Sean Barton, ed.; Fred Hole, James L. Schoppe, art dir.; Aggie Guerard Rodgers, Nilo Rodis-Jamero, costumes; Roy Arbogast, William Lee, F/X; Richard Edlund, visual-optical effects; 134 min. (135 min., special edition); Color; 2.20:1.

ADDITIONAL/ALTERED CAST

Sebastian Shaw (*Anakin Skywalker*); Ian McDiarmid (*The Emperor*); Michael Pennington (*Moff Jerjerrod*); Michael Carter (*Bib Fortuna*); Tim Rose (*Admiral Ackbar*); Dermot Crowley (*Gen. Madine*); Caroline Blakiston (*Mon Mothma*); Warwick Davis (*Wicket*); Femi Taylor (*Oola*); Annie Arbogast (*Snootles*); Jack Purvis (*Teebo*); Nicki Reade (*Nicki*).

MOST MEMORABLE LINE

I have a bad feeling about this.

HAN SOLO, SIGNATURE LINE

THE PLOT

Leia infiltrates the headquarters of Jabba the Hutt, who possesses the carbonite slab. She frees Han, but both are captured. Luke arrives and also is taken prisoner, but by using his new prosthetic arm, he turns the tables on their enemies. A dying Yoda admits that what Vader told Luke is true: the man in black is the innocent boy's father. The realization that Leia is Luke's sister ends his conflicts with Han. In a final fight with the Evil Empire, the rebels are aided by a race of furry creatures, Ewoks. Luke desperately hopes that his final confrontation with Vader will not end in more violence but rather a satisfying closure.

THE FILM

This was the first film in the series not produced by Gary Kurtz (1940–), who first collaborated with Lucas on *American Graffiti*. Kurtz has claimed that he came to believe that Lucas was increasingly inclined to de-emphasize story in favor of thrill-ride action and that, as time went by, he appeared to care less about aesthetic integrity than about merchandising and franchising options. During discussions about the upcoming third film, Kurtz realized that Lucas planned on an all-out happy ending, which he felt was at odds with the unforgivable things Darth Vader had done. Kurtz's own darker vision can be seen in *The Dark Crystal* (Jim Henson, Frank Oz, 1982). That film was not a success. Clearly, it was Lucas who better understood the requirements of a mass audience as to what they wanted in their fantasy family entertainment.

TRIVIA

Diminutive Warwick Davis, who plays the most prominent Ewok, would play the lead in a forthcoming Lucas-produced film, the epic fantasy *Willow* (Ron Howard, 1988).

······

CLOSE ENCOUNTERS OF THE THIRD KIND (1977)

—— RANKING: 16 ——

CREDITS

Columbia Pictures; Steven Spielberg, dir.; Spielberg, Hal Barwood, Jerry Belson, John Hill, Matthew Robbins, scr.; Julia Phillips, Michael Phillips, pro.; John Williams, mus.; Vilmos Zsigmond, John A. Alonzo, cin.; Michael Kahn, ed.; Joe Alves, prod. design; Daniel A. Lomino, art dir.; Ralph McQuarrie, conceptual artwork; Roy Arbogast, Kevin Pike, F/X; Carlo Rambaldi, extraterrestrial realization; Robert Short, alien designer (1980); Larry Albright, mothership neon light effects; Peter Anderson, special visual effects; Gregory L. McMurry, visual effects (1980); Christopher S. Ross, mothership model maker (1980); 135 min. (theatrical print), 132 min. (special edition), 137 min. (director's cut); Color; 2.20:1.

CAST

Richard Dreyfuss (*Roy Neary*); François Truffaut (*Claude Lacombe*); Teri Garr (*Ronnie Neary*); Melinda Dillon (*Jillian Guiler*); Bob Balaban (*David Laughlin*); Cary Guffey (*Barry Guiler*); J. Patrick McNamara (*Project Leader*); Warren J. Kemmerling (*Wild Bill*); Roberts Blossom (*Farmer*); Philip Dodds (*Jean Claude*); Lance Henriksen (*Robert*); Carl Weathers (*Military Policeman*); J. Allen Hynek (*Himself*); Howard K. Smith (*Newscaster*).

MOST MEMORABLE LINE

It looked like an ice cream cone.

ROY NEARY, ATTEMPTING TO DESCRIBE THE ALIEN SPACECRAFT

BACKGROUND

Close Encounters premiered on November 16, 1977, fewer than six months following *Star Wars Episode IV*. Despite the success of Lucas's movie, the film industry held its collective breath. *Star Wars* had, from its opening image, featured not only spacecraft but also action, rating as a space opera; *Close Encounters*, in comparison, offered a realistic sci-fi film, featuring only fleeting glimpses of an alien craft until the spectacular ending. Might a public intoxicated with *Star Wars* find this film, however brilliant, a letdown? The answer was *no*. Shot at

FIRST CONTACT: *Steven Spielberg drew on memories of the kinder, gentler alien invader films from the 1950s, notably* The Day the Earth Stood Still *(1951), for his Disney-like depiction of spiritual star visitors, while employing state-of-the-art F/X for a vivid sense of high-tech grandeur. Courtesy: Columbia Pictures.*

a then-considerable budget (slightly less than $20 million), *Close Encounters* brought in more than $300 million internationally. Clearly, *Star Wars* had not been a one-time phenomenon and the sci-fi renaissance could now proceed.

THE PLOT

Alien spacecraft, circling Earth, are spotted by several people. In the United States, these include an average suburban father, Roy Neary, and Jillian, a single mom whose son has been abducted. Soon a growing number of citizens demand to know what's going on, but government officials remain mum. Gradually, an "elect" group develops, members experiencing mental images of a structure reaching to the heavens. One by one, they realize they've been summoned to Devils Tower, where extraterrestrials will soon make first contact. As the "enlightened ones" attempt to reach the location, only a few arrive to greet the riders from the stars.

THE FILM

Identifying "the film" is difficult in that three cuts are now available. Box office success allowed Spielberg (1946–) to finally film several sequences initially deemed "too expensive" for the original. One, in which a huge ship is revealed to be relocated to the middle of a desert (presumably by aliens), would be hailed as a welcome addition. In another sequence, Spielberg extended the ending, allowing the viewer to see the full interior of the mothership. This produced impressive F/X work, but many fans insisted that less had been more, that the additional footage robbed them of imaginative collaboration as to such details. For the second version, Spielberg listened to critics, cutting much of the "excessive" footage that shows Neary building his own Devils Towers out of everything from mashed potatoes to clay. Yet, the film does not work so well without this charmingly comical sequence. The director's cut offers a compromise between the two earlier versions, and, to this day, sci-fi buffs argue as to which they prefer.

THEME

Spielberg's workaholic father was not around much during his son's childhood, and his parents divorced when he was nineteen. Consequently, Spielberg came to consider his mother the primary influence on his early life. Not surprisingly, then, many of his movies deal with the subject of single motherhood. While Jillian here embodies such a person, similar characters appear in *E.T.* (1982) and *The Color Purple* (1985). Likewise, the plot point of children forcibly removed from their mothers, single or married, recurs in *Poltergeist* (1982), *Indiana Jones and the Temple of Doom* (1984), *Jurassic Park* (1993), and *Schindler's List* (1993). By featuring a continuing personal vision in films that could not be more diverse in subject matter and style, Spielberg achieves the distinction of being honored as a true auteur: the film director who is not only a highly skilled entertainer but also a true artist, with a consistent though evolving vision of life.

TRIVIA

The still relatively young Spielberg relied heavily on homages to films and TV shows that had an impact on his imagination as a child. In *Close Encounters*, the dream-like quality of the boy's experiences during a semi-surreal night in the country recalls *Invaders from Mars* (1953). The descent of an alien craft over Jillian's home is similar to a sequence in which the lead characters are trapped in an isolated house in *The War of the Worlds* (1953). The cloud that then descends on the boy resembles the one in *The Incredible Shrinking Man* (1957). The "normal" neighborhood in which Neary's family lives recalls those in many *Twilight Zone* episodes, particularly "The Monsters Are Due on Maple

Street," which Spielberg has claimed is among his favorites. The cartoon that Neary watches on TV includes the final line of *The Thing from Another World* (1951): "Watch the skies!" The notion of aliens as benign—even perhaps saviors, their arrival a kind of Second Coming—is derived from *The Day the Earth Stood Still* (1951) and *It Came from Outer Space* (1953). Not all of Spielberg's references reach that far back, however: when the mothership first circles Devils Tower, *Star Wars*'s R2-D2 is just barely visible inside.

·······

TIME AFTER TIME (1979)

—— RANKING: 78 ——

CREDITS
Orion Pictures/Warner Bros.; Nicholas Meyer, dir.; Karl Alexander, novel; Meyer, Steve Hayes, scr.; Herb Jaffe, pro.; Miklós Rózsa, mus.; Paul Lohmann, cin.; Donn Cambern, ed.; Edward C. Carfagno, prod. design; Jim Blount, Larry L. Fuentes, Kevin Pike, F/X; Richard Taylor, Chad Taylor, visual/optical F/X; 112 min.; Color; 2.35:1.

CAST
Malcolm McDowell (*H. G. Wells*); David Warner (*John Leslie Stevenson/"Jack the Ripper"*); Mary Steenburgen (*Amy Robbins*); Charles Cioffi (*Police Lt. Mitchell*); Kent Williams (*Assistant*); Andonia Katsaros (*Mrs. Turner*); Patti D'Arbanville (*Shirley*); James Garrett (*Edwards*); Leo Lewis (*Richardson*); Keith McConnell (*Harding*); Corey Feldman (*Little Boy at Museum*); Shelley Hack (*Docent*).

MOST MEMORABLE LINE
Ninety years ago, I was a freak; today, I'm an amateur.
STEVENSON TO WELLS IN 1979

BACKGROUND
Nicholas Meyer (1945–) established his reputation as a science-fiction author in 1973 with his script for *Invasion of the Bee Girls*, a marvelous combination of an alien invasion thriller and a spoof on that 1950s genre. Known for writing three of the best *Star Trek* films, he also worked on two of the best TV films of the

H. G. WELLS VS. JACK THE RIPPER: *In one of Nicholas Meyer's unique spins on the science-fiction genre, the great writer Herbert George Wells (Malcolm McDowell) not only conceives of a time machine but also builds just such a device to pursue the world's most infamous killer through time and space. Courtesy: Warner Bros./Orion.*

1970s with genre themes: *The Day After* (1983), an atomic war drama in the tradition of *On the Beach* (1959), and *The Night That Panicked America* (1975), about the impact of Orson Welles's 1930s radio broadcast of H. G. Wells's *The War of the Worlds*. Meyer's friend Karl Alexander showed him the first few pages of a novel he was writing called *Time After Time*; Meyer optioned the piece, not only selling the project to a major company but also insisting that he direct the film.

THE PLOT

In 1893, H. G. Wells shows something special to his dinner guests: a time machine. The machine is not merely a work of imagination for a new novel but, in Meyer's fictionalized "origination story," it is something that Wells truly did build. What that author/scientist cannot know—at least not yet—is that Stevenson, one of his supposedly respectable friends, is actually Jack the Ripper. When authorities track their suspect to Wells's house, the Ripper escapes in the as-yet untested device. When the time machine returns, owing to a homing apparatus, Wells summons his courage and follows the killer to November 5, 1979, in hopes of putting a stop to any upcoming reign of terror. Wells meets Amy, a bank executive who has seen the Ripper and is willing to help this fish-out-of-water hero track down the villain while also falling in love with Wells.

THE FILM

There is one notable flaw in the plot. Wells and Amy travel into the future so that he can convince her of the truth of his strange story. Then they head back to try and prevent a fourth murder, suggesting it is too late to do anything about the first three. However, if the time machine allows for travel to and from any point in history, why don't they go back several days earlier and prevent all the killings?

The time machine, as envisioned by Wells, could move through time but not space. To make the film more commercial in a Hollywood sense, it was necessary to have the "modern" story take place in California. This was explained by having the film's Wells realize this physical shift occurred because of the eight-hour time difference.

Time After Time includes numerous references to previous thrillers. When Wells and Amy walk among the redwoods, the sequence resembles the shot of James Stewart and Kim Novak in *Vertigo* (Alfred Hitchcock, 1958). When hero, heroine, and villain confront one another at night under huge columns, the sequence recalls the one in which Cary Grant, Audrey Hepburn, and Walter Matthau face off in *Charade* (Stanley Donen, 1963), which Hitchcock was originally slated to direct.

THEME

Meyer's film, like Alexander's novel, contrasts the utopian values of Wells, and his belief in the future perfection of humankind through science and technology, and the dystopian, or negative utopian, form of sci-fi that would evolve after Wells's death. This is established in the symbolic nature of the film's Ripper. If he seemed something of a terrible aberration in the Victorian age, Stevenson self-admittedly fits in beautifully ("I'm home!") in the amoral era that confounds all of Wells's earlier high hopes for humanity.

TRIVIA

The homing device and corresponding key, as well as yet another key that can send a person into a wormhole to oblivion, are not present in Wells's original book, *The Time Machine*. As he built on Wells's book for his own purposes, Meyer added both the device and the key to ensure that the plotting of his own piece could work out successfully in the film's final moments.

Wells here attempts to pass himself off as Sherlock Holmes, the great fictional detective of his era. Five years before penning this screenplay, Meyer wrote a novel called *The Seven-Per-Cent Solution* in which Holmes meets Sigmund Freud, two Victorian-era notables in a parallel pairing to the Wells-Ripper match-up found here.

Amy Robbins was the actual name of Wells's second wife.

· · · · · · ·

ALIEN (1979) AND ALIENS (1986)

—— RANKING: 12 (TIE) ——

ALIEN (1979)

CREDITS

Twentieth Century-Fox/Brandywine Productions; Ridley Scott, dir.; Dan O'Bannon, Ronald Shusett, scr.; Gordon Carroll, David Giler, Walter Hill, pro.; Jerry Goldsmith, mus.; Derek Vanlint, cin.; David Crowther, Terry Rawlings, Peter Weatherley, ed.; Michael Seymour, Roger Christian, prod. design; Christian, Leslie Dilley, set design; John Mollo, costumes; Ron Cobb, concept artist; Nick Allder, Alan Bryce, Clinton Cavers, Brian Johnson, Christian Wolf-La'Moy, Carlo Rambaldi, F/X; Dennis Ayling, Martin Bower, special visual effects; 117 min.; Color; 2.20:1.

CAST

Tom Skerritt (*Dallas*); Sigourney Weaver (*Ripley*); Veronica Cartwright (*Lambert*); Harry Dean Stanton (*Brett*); John Hurt (*Kane*); Ian Holm (*Ash*); Yaphet Kotto (*Parker*); Bolaji Badejo, Eddie Powell (*The Alien*).

MOST MEMORABLE LINE

In space, no one can hear you scream.
ADVERTISING SLOGAN FOR *ALIEN*

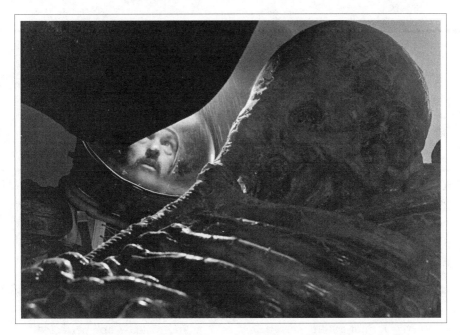

AND THEN THERE WAS ONE: *Effectively mixing two distinct genres, the first* Alien *entry set Dallas (Tom Skerritt) and several futuristic companions within a haunted house in outer space. Courtesy: 20th Century-Fox.*

BACKGROUND

Dan O'Bannon (1946–2009) conceived of making a movie about a bloodthirsty alien while still a student at University of Southern California and working on *Dark Star* (1974) with director John Carpenter and budding F/X expert Ron Cobb. O'Bannon prepared a script titled "Memory"—essentially, *Alien's* first act—but wasn't sure where to take it. He joined forces with Ronald Shusett, who had been highly impressed by the concept of *It! The Terror from Beyond Space* (1958) in which an alien slips aboard a ship. The two collaborators hoped for nothing more than a Roger Corman "quickie," but when the loftier team of David Giler and Walter Hill expressed interest, the project swiftly rose in status. Giler and Hill added the idea of one crewmember secretly being an android.

THE PLOT

Seven blue-collar workers, hauling minerals to Earth, wake from stasis when the receiver in their space vehicle, *Nostromo*, accepts a transmission from a nearby planetoid. They descend to discover the source, a warning from an earlier craft. They find a pod in an immense cave. It smashes against Kane's face, rendering him unconscious. Leader Dallas and others carry him back; Ash insists, over protestations by Ripley, that they disobey quarantine rules and allow re-entry. Once again in transit, everyone is shocked to see a miniature monster rip its way up and out of Kane's chest. An egg had been planted within him. Now the creature, increasing in size, haunts the crew of the *Nostromo*.

THE FILM
O'Bannon's friend Cobb was brought on to design the ship. An H. R. Giger painting, *Necronom*, inspired the design of the creature. The harrowing noir/surrealist approach would prove precisely right for the film. When Hill chose not to direct, the team approached Ridley Scott (1937–), whose cool, distanced approach to the historical tale *The Duellists* (1977) had impressed them. Scott came up with the look for such elements as spacesuits that were halfway between the fantasy approach of *Star Wars* and the ultra-realistic grounding of hard sci-fi such as *2001*.

Alien was shot at Shepperton Studios, England, where Cobb perfected the high-tech, industrial look that would come to characterize future genre work. Carlo Rambaldi, who had worked with Spielberg on extraterrestrials for *Close Encounters*, came up with the iconic head. Scott instructed editor Terry Rawlings to show the creature as little as possible to realize O'Bannon's concept of "*Jaws* in space."

Alien offers sci-fi/horror, mixing the two genres. The concept is a haunted house yarn, here reset in deep space.

THEME
The *Alien* films would prove significant in bringing feminism, the most significant social cause of the 1970s, to the sci-fi genre. Early on in the planning, Ripley was to have been played by a male actor. The part instead went to Sigourney Weaver. The beautiful Ripley is anything but submissive. She is a take-charge person who happens to be female. Audiences assume that Dallas (his name suggests a cowboy hero) would in time save the day. When he fails, then dies, the film effectively deconstructs viewer expectations. We expect a new dragonslayer. It turns out, happily, to be Ripley.

TRIVIA
The name "Nostromo" is taken from a 1904 Joseph Conrad novel about a seafarer lost in unknown and dangerous waters.

ALIENS (1986)

ADDITIONAL/ALTERED CREDITS

James Cameron, dir.; Cameron, David Giler, scr.; Gale Anne Hurd, pro.; James Horner, mus.; Adrian Biddle, cin.; Ray Lovejoy, ed.; Peter Lamont, prod. design; Terry Ackland-Snow, Ken Court, Michael Lamont, art dir.; Emma Porteous, costumes; Ron Cobb, conceptual design; Norman Baillie, Nigel Booth, Ron Burton, Michael Dunleavy, John Richardson, F/X; Stan Winston, alien effects creator; Steven Woodcock, model maker; Jonathan Angell, Dennis Skotak, Robert Skotak, special visual effects; 137 min.; Color; 1.85:1.

ADDITIONAL/ALTERED CAST

Carrie Henn (*Rebecca "Newt" Jorden*); Michael Biehn (*Cpl. Dwayne Hicks*); Paul Reiser (*Carter Burke*); Lance Henriksen (*Bishop*); Bill Paxton (*Pvt. Hudson*); Jenette Goldstein (*Pvt. Vasquez*); William Hope (*Lt. Gorman*); Al Matthews (*Sgt. Apone*).

MOST MEMORABLE LINE

Get away from her, you *bitch*!

RIPLEY TO THE MOTHER CREATURE

BACKGROUND

While waiting for Arnold Schwarzenegger to complete *Conan the Destroyer* (Richard Fleischer, 1984) so that they could start shooting *The Terminator*, James Cameron (1954–) focused on an idea for a possible *Alien* sequel. Fox was in no hurry as they thought the original should have made even more money than it did, but Giler pressed the studio, which finally relented, and the franchise was now in full swing.

THE PLOT

Ripley alone survived, conquering the alien, then drifting in a space-pod for decades. She is finally discovered floating in space, but her story is not believed. The planetoid is now a working colony. Stripped of credentials owing to a corporate desire to remain mum as to any risks, she's informed by Burke of the Weyland-Yutani Corporation. Gorman of the space marines explains that Ripley's status will be restored if she agrees to travel back as a consultant aboard *Sulaco*, a warship. After landing, they discover that the population has been annihilated but for one child, Newt.

THE LAST ACTION HERO: *In an unexpected turnaround, the original's sole survivor (Sigourney Weaver) was re-imagined as a macho babe in a film that reunited her with the monster but revitalized the concept via an emphasis on rough-hewn physical combat. Courtesy: 20th Century Fox.*

THE FILM

The shoot at England's Pinewood Studios did not go well. Many members of the crew remembered Scott warmly and considered Cameron an interloper. Their constant breaks for teatime disrupted the pattern of a director who takes a no-nonsense, straight-ahead approach to filming. Robert and Dennis Skotak, both of whom had worked with Cameron on low-budget Corman films, came aboard for the F/X chores. Most significantly, the director insisted that he was not making "Alien II," but an original film based on the same alien concept. Cameron perfected his unique approach working on *The Terminator* (1984), including the use of state-of-the-art action within the *cinéma fantastique* genre.

THEME

President Dwight Eisenhower, on the eve of stepping down from office in 1959, warned the American public against the military-industrial complex. That sums up Cameron's vision in *Aliens* as the corporate lackey and the marine commander set aside the good of ordinary people for the accumulation of corporate profits and personal power.

TRIVIA

The idea of a mother monster protecting her young had been the premise for *Gorgo* (Eugène Lourié, 1961) and would be re-used by Spielberg for *The Lost World: Jurassic Park* (1997).

· · · · · · ·

ESCAPE FROM NEW YORK (1981)

—— RANKING: 73 ——

CREDITS

AVCO Embassy Pictures; John Carpenter, dir.; Carpenter, Nick Castle, scr.; Debra Hill, Larry J. Franco, pro.; Carpenter, Alan Howarth, mus.; Dean Cundey, cin.; Todd C. Ramsay, ed.; Joe Alves, prod. design; Stephen Loomis, costumes; Arthur Gelb, graphic design; Alan Howarth, special synthesizer sound effects; Roy Arbogast, Pat Patterson, Eddie Surkin, Gary Zink, F/X; James Cameron, special visual effects/matte artwork; 99 min.; Color; 2.35:1.

CAST

Kurt Russell (*Snake Plissken*); Lee Van Cleef (*Hauk*); Adrienne Barbeau (*Maggie*); Ernest Borgnine (*Cabbie*); Donald Pleasence (*The President*); Isaac Hayes (*The Duke*); Season Hubley (*Girl in Chock Full O'Nuts*); Harry Dean Stanton (*The Brain*); Tom Atkins (*Rehme*); John Diehl (*Punk*); Debra Hill (*Computer*, voice).

MOST MEMORABLE LINE

I thought you were dead.
VIRTUALLY EVERY CHARACTER IN THE FILM,
UPON MEETING SNAKE PLISSKEN

BACKGROUND

With his ultra-low-budget *Dark Star* (1974), John Carpenter (1948–) earned a reputation as an edgy indie director with an offbeat sense of humor and a natural feel for sci-fi. The writer-director achieved notoriety with the unexpectedly popular horror movie, *Halloween* (1978). Its success allowed Carpenter to argue successfully for a bigger budget, $6 million, to be allocated for *Escape from New York*.

The idea for the film began to take shape in the early 1970s after he viewed two seminal films, each capturing an aspect of that era: *Death Wish* (Michael Winner, 1974), starring Charles Bronson as the vigilante who sets out to destroy the street criminals who have taken over New York City; and *All the President's Men* (Alan J. Pakula, 1976), a drama about the journalists who uncovered the Watergate scandal and brought about the fall of a president. Carpenter merged the two themes into a dystopian future sci-fi script co-written by Castle, who had played the monstrous "Shape" in *Halloween*. Debra Hill (1950–2005), one of the so-called Movie Brats who had seized control of the industry at this time, had worked her way up from script supervisor and assistant editor on Carpenter's early (and excellent) urban crime drama, *Assault on Precinct 13* (1976), to become a leading producer.

THE PLOT

The crime infestation of Manhattan is so out of control that a decision has been reached from a committee of high-ranking officials: give up trying. A wall has been built around the city, manned by military police, and the government dumps the fiercest convicts into the burned-out ruins of a once-great metropolis. No one who enters ever leaves—at least until a plane carrying the president crashes into these meanest of mean streets. Hauk, a nasty official in charge of engineering a rescue, promises super-convict Snake Plissken that, if he can bring the president (and his all-important briefcase) back within twenty-four hours, he can walk free. If he can't pull off this near-impossible mission within that time limit, he will be exploded from afar by remote control.

THE FILM

As New York City had become too costly for anything but immensely expensive projects, most of the shoot took place in East St. Louis. A devastating fire had turned sections of that city into precisely the sort of wasteland Carpenter needed for his desired look. Most interiors were shot on Los Angeles soundstages, with only one significant image—a helicopter whirring past the most famous skyline in the world—achieved on location in Manhattan.

Carpenter nixed Bronson as the lead, supposedly owing to that actor's age.

ENTER JOHN CARPENTER: *The writer-director, who had previously reinvented urban action (*Assault on Precinct 13, *1976) and slasher cinema (*Halloween, *1978), turned his attention to the action-oriented dystopian subgenre with* Escape from New York, *starring Kurt Russell. Courtesy: AVCO Embassy.*

It is more likely, however, that this decision had to do with the fear that a major star would immediately seize control from a young and relatively inexperienced director. Tommy Lee Jones, Nick Nolte, and Jeff Bridges all turned down the role before Russell finally won it by default. AVCO Embassy executives feared that Russell's long association with light comedy would disqualify him from being taken seriously as an action star, but the public's full acceptance of him proved them wrong. The character as written did not wear an eye-patch; Russell added that detail on the first day of shooting. Co-writer Castle was the one who came up with the idea of Ernest Borgnine's cab driver for comic relief.

THEME

The running gag that has almost every character expressing surprise upon learning that Snake still walks the Earth has resonance beyond its effectiveness as a recurring laugh line. Snake is Carpenter's own incarnation of the Man With No Name as played by Clint Eastwood in the spaghetti Westerns of his early career and *High Plains Drifter* (Eastwood, 1973), the first Eastwood vehicle to imply that his remote character is ghost-like and mythic. In point of fact, despite Carpenter's association with eerie projects, he had always hoped to direct Westerns. To a degree, he had the opportunity to do so here; the irony is that the East Coast city has been reconstituted into a final vestige of the old West in its wildest days. With that in mind, the casting of Lee Van Cleef, Eastwood's friendly enemy in such films as *For a Few Dollars More* (Sergio Leone, 1965), takes on additional meaning beyond the actor's rightness for this role. Here then is a film that, like *Star Wars*, recalls the science-fiction film's identity as a kind of futuristic Western.

TRIVIA

Frank Doubleday and John Strobel respectively play minor characters named "Romero" and "Cronenberg," Carpenter's in-joke way of thanking fellow sci-fi/horror filmmakers George Romero and David Cronenberg for their assistance.

Future "king of the world" director James Cameron, who had been preparing F/X for low-budget films at Roger Corman's Concorde Pictures, created some of the impressive matte shots.

The character "Snake" might have seemed something of a no-brainer for a franchise, but that never quite happened. The belabored sequel, *Escape from L.A.* (1996), struck most fans as too little, too late, despite the considerably larger budget.

Musician-turned-actor Isaac Hayes was picked for the role of Duke owing to his association with the so-called black exploitation flicks of the early 1970s, vividly recalled here. The styles designed for the young stragglers offered an early vision of cyberpunk.

· · · · · · ·

MAD MAX 2: THE ROAD WARRIOR (1981)

—— RANKING: 54 ——

CREDITS

Warner Bros., Kennedy Miller Productions; George Miller, dir.; Miller, Terry Hayes, Brian Hannant, scr.; Byron Kennedy, pro.; Brian May, mus.; Dean Semler, cin.; Michael Balson, David Stiven, Tim Wellburn, ed.; Graham "Grace" Walker, art dir.; Norma Moriceau, costumes; Bob McCarron, special makeup effects; Jeff Clifford, Steve Courtley, Mont Fieguth, David Hardy, F/X; Kim Priest, optical F/X; 95 min., 94 min. (U.S.), 96 min. (director's cut); Color/B&W; 2.35: 1.

CAST

Mel Gibson (*Mad Max Rockatansky*); Bruce Spence (*Gyro Captain*); Michael Preston (*Pappagallo*); Max Phipps (*Toadie*); Vernon Wells (*Wez*); Kjell Nilsson (*The Humungus*); Emil Minty (*The Feral Kid*); Virginia Hey (*Warrior Woman*); William Zappa (*Zetta*); Arkie Whiteley (*The Captain's Girl*); Steve J. Spears (*Mechanic*); Syd Heylen (*Curmudgeon*); Moira Claux (*Big Rebecca*); Kristoffer Greaves (*Mechanic's Assistant*); Harold Baigent (*Narrator*, voice only).

MOST MEMORABLE LINE

I'm just here for the gasoline.

MAX TO THE SETTLERS

BACKGROUND

The Australian New Wave (c. 1975–1985) brought a diverse set of Down Under movies to the attention of cineastes the world over. These included political and poetic works such as *Picnic at Hanging Rock* (Peter Weir, 1975), *My Brilliant Career* (Gillian Armstrong, 1979), and *Mad Max* (George Miller, 1979). *Mad Max* featured an inventive, action-oriented script by James McCausland. The film-making duo of George Miller and Byron Kennedy transformed that vision into

THE AUSTRALIAN CONNECTION: *Recalling John Wayne as "Hondo," crossing the desert with his constant companion Sam, Mel Gibson and "Dog" wander through a devastated terrain.* Mad Max 2: The Road Warrior *brought elements of classic Westerns to the contemporary science-fiction film. Courtesy: Warner Bros.*

a cult phenomenon about an idealistic near-future policeman who gradually becomes a cynical vigilante.

The film's worldwide success paved the way for a sequel with a more ambitious production. Miller determined that his character's emotional arc would take him in the opposite direction, from a rugged individualist caring only about personal survival to a born-again believer in the need for communal responsibility. Miller heightened elements such as the cyberpunk look for villains, biker/bondage black leather costuming, and retro-future costumes that include World War II outfits and gladiator garb.

THE PLOT

An all-out conflict between "two warrior tribes" (apparently, the United States and the Soviet Union, this serving as a Cold War cautionary fable) leads to a victory-less situation in which the ruined world is populated by scavengers. Fuel, rather than gold, has become the universal standard for riches. Loner Max, accompanied by his dog, reluctantly teams with a comical sidekick, a onetime autogyro pilot now surviving as a sand person, living in the isolated dunes, and a snake hunter. They become aware that a monstrous group of marauders led by Humungus plans to raid a peaceful settlement where oil drilling occurs. Initially only wanting to warn the people and take some gas, Max and Gyro find themselves fighting alongside such desert dwellers as the blonde Warrior Woman and the silent Feral Kid.

THE FILM

Road Warrior set the standard for a sci-fi subgenre forever after known as the "post-apocalyptic actioner," its aesthetic based on a maximum amount of stunt work, with rapid-fire editing to draw such sequences into a tight continuum of violence, and a minimalist approach to dialogue. Influenced heavily by spaghetti Westerns from the 1960s, the film drew on Sergio Leone's use of immense desert vistas contrasted with close-ups of faces, accompanied by discordant music and jarring sound effects. The character combines elements of the Man With No Name, played by Clint Eastwood or Charles Bronson in Leone's films, with key qualities of John Wayne in the more traditional Hollywood Westerns. At the opening, as our antihero and his rough-hewn dog cross the prairie toward the camera, the vision recalls *Hondo* (John Farrow, 1953). In the cinematography and editing, the chase during the final third, in which savage hordes on dune buggies and motorcycles pursue the escaping heroes, evokes John Ford's *Stagecoach* (1939) in which the title object is pursued by Apaches.

THEME

Like many George Lucas films, *Star Wars* included, as well as the Indiana Jones collaboration between Lucas and Spielberg, *The Road Warrior* draws heavily on the writings of Joseph Campbell (1904–1987). Max is a warrior hero in the tradition of Han Solo and Indy, believing at first that he is out strictly for himself, but gradually becoming aware that he has, step by step, been drawn into the service of a higher cause. As the story is told by the Feral Kid years later—similar to the narration in the classic Western *Shane* (George Stevens, 1953)—what we experience can be considered an origin myth: the tale of how a society came into being (or how an old, destroyed society was, Phoenix-like, reborn) due to an antihero who saved the day, then disappeared into the wasteland, never to return . . . except in their dreams, and, of course, their legends.

TRIVIA

George Miller (1945–), though an Australian, is of Greek descent. He was working full-time as a medical doctor when several brief experimental films he created as a hobby received serious attention. He quit his day job and embraced what he'd always believed to be an impossible dream: becoming a full-time moviemaker.

Max's sawed-off shotgun is a replica of the weapon carried by Nick Adams as "Johnny Yuma" in the popular American TV series *The Rebel* (1959–1961).

The film was released worldwide as *Mad Max 2*. The only exception was in the United States, where the original had not caught on as a theatrical release, calling for a unique identity: that is, *The Road Warrior*!

· · · · · · ·

HEAVY METAL (1981)

—— RANKING: 97 ——

CREDITS

Columbia Pictures/Guardian Trust/Canadian Film Development Corp.; Gerald Potterton, dir.; Daniel Goldberg, Len Blum, scr.; Ivan Reitman, Michael C. Gross, Peter Lebensold, pro.; Elmer Bernstein, mus. ("Taarna"); Ian Llande, Mick Manning, Gerald Tripp, ed.; Michael C. Gross, prod. design; Pat Gavin, art dir.; Peter Thillaye, sound ed.; John Bruno, F/X; 90 min. (premiere screening print), 86 min. (theatrical release); Color; 1.37:1.

CAST (VOICES)

Don Francks (*Grimaldi*); Caroline Semple (*Girl*); Richard Romanus (*Harry Canyon*); John Candy (*Dan/Den*); John Vernon (*Prosecutor*); Eugene Levy (*Sternn*); Rodger Bumpass (*Hanover Fiste, Dr. Anrak*); Douglas Kenney (*Regolian*); Harold Ramis (*Zeke*).

MOST MEMORABLE LINE

A shadow shall fall over the universe, and evil will grow in its path.
NARRATOR, INTRODUCING THE FILM

BACKGROUND

The French have always been more open to the latest trends in American popular culture than U.S. entertainment critics and social observers. This explains why such forms as the motion picture, rock 'n' roll, and the comic book were

THE MAGIC OF ANIMATION: *Canada's long association with and impressive support for feature-length cartoons were instrumental in bringing* Heavy Metal *magazine to the screen. Here, Gloria and an absent-minded professor are sucked deep inside an alien ship. Courtesy: Columbia Pictures.*

all taken seriously by Gallic enthusiasts, while each was initially considered impossibly vulgar in the United States. Though *Barbarella* has always been best known among the BDs, those European adult comic books that often feature intense eroticism and graphic violence (and, more often than not, a combination of the two), the sexy space fantasy was but one of many graphic novels that appealed to adults, thanks to a satisfying combination of science fiction, surrealism, and sexuality.

The comics anthology, *Métal Hurlant*, offered by artists Jean Giraud and Philippe Druillet from 1974 to 1987, presented cutting-edge graphics with imaginative fantasy tales laced with black humor and noted for their literary value. Also, the anthology published articles on current music—particularly that of evolving heavy metal bands, such as Led Zeppelin and Iron Maiden. This was appropriate considering that the Brit-based heavy metal movement employed aggressively loud electric guitars to convey the hostile, macho values projected in many of the magazine's fictional pieces. While he was in Paris to start a European version of his humor magazine, *National Lampoon*, publisher Leonard

Mogel discovered *Métal Hurlant*. He optioned the American rights, reprinting many of the best existing pieces while bringing in such fresh talent as illustrator H. R. Giger and writer Richard Corben. The U.S. rendition was primed for a film version, as its appeal was always to the smart young set—those very consumers seen as the target audience for most of the then-current movies.

Ivan Reitman (1946–), who had produced the first (and enormously successful) *National Lampoon* film, *Animal House* (John Landis, 1978), committed to producing *Heavy Metal*. Reitman, aware of Canada's government-based commitment to the art of animation, hired fellow Canadian resident and, at the time, National Film Board director Gerald Potterton (1931–) to direct—or, more correctly, oversee—the movie. The aim was to create a contemporary hipster equivalent to Walt Disney's *Fantasia* (1940). In *Heavy Metal*, however, the orchestral music is reserved until the epic segment, "Taarna," proving that rock, like symphonic, music could be artistically fused with appropriate animation.

THE PLOT

In the framing device, a spacecraft descends, releasing a classic Corvette on the order of some celestial birth. Driver Grimaldi enters an isolated hilltop house, similar to the one in Hitchcock's *Psycho* (1960), and presents his innocent daughter with a green sphere, brought back from the far end of the galaxy. This orb, the Loc-Nar, destroys him, then threatens the child with visualized accounts of its far-reaching evil influence. There is "Harry Canyon," a shaggy cab driver from a neo-noir dystopian future who takes a Mickey Spillane-type tough guy cynical view of the jaded world. Then comes "Den," a geeky teenager who wishes himself into a muscular superhero, followed by "Captain Sternn," a Sgt. Rock–type space adventurer who immorally uses the power entrusted to him. "B-17" tracks the fate of a World War II bomber as those in the cockpit realize that the crew has transformed into zombies. The account, "So Beautiful and So Dangerous," focuses on a sexy stenographer whose very presence causes every male, human or robot, to surrender to primitive sexual desire. Only the finale, "Taarna," forsakes science fiction to offer an epic fantasy about an Amazonian avenger. In the epilogue, the menaced little girl deflates the evil green circle and then emerges as a Taarna-like warrior hero for the future.

THE FILM

Artwork for each story was assigned to a specific Canadian company. As each—Atkinson Film-Arts among them—boasted its signature style, the match-ups were carefully considered to create perfect pairings of narrative material and visual orientation. Heavy metal and pop music—including work by Blue Öyster Cult, Stevie Nicks, Journey, Cheap Trick, Sammy Hagar, Black Sabbath, and Devo, among others—used for each of the vignettes was carefully chosen for specific needs at any one point in any particular tale.

THEME
Despite the omnipresent darkness, the film ends, perhaps surprisingly, on an optimistic note. It might be thought of as expressing an "anti-Green" ideology as that color, so associated with innocence and purity in films like *WALL-E* (2008) or *Avatar* (2009), represents demonic forces here. This serves as a reminder that there is no single political sensibility inherent in sci-fi; it is a form that can be used by different artists to express their own social values.

TRIVIA
At one point in the "So Beautiful . . ." segment, we can see the USS *Enterprise* outside the spacecraft's window.

Despite its considerable status in the sci-fi canon, *Heavy Metal* was not a critical or commercial success on release. The self-consciously misogynistic attitude (other than in "Taarna," which presents an intelligent and independent woman) offended females who had embraced the women's movement during the 1970s, limiting the audience considerably. Still, *Heavy Metal* became a cult film, the first motion picture to do so not primarily by screenings on college campuses or exposure on the arthouse circuit but because of home video, which had just recently mushroomed in popularity.

THE GREATEST OF ALL SCI-FI REMAKES: *Many genre aficionados believe that John Carpenter's version of the well-regarded novella* Who Goes There? *rates as greater even than the Howard Hawks–produced 1950s version. Here, T. K. Carter, Kurt Russell, and Donald Moffat prepare to face whatever is "out there." Courtesy: Universal.*

·······

THE THING (1982)

—— RANKING: 30 ——

CREDITS

Universal Pictures, Turman-Foster Company; John Carpenter, dir.; John W. Campbell Jr., short story; Bill Lancaster, scr.; David Foster, Wilbur Stark, Lawrence Turman, pro.; Ennio Morricone, mus.; Dean Cundey, cin.; Todd C. Ramsay, ed.; John J. Lloyd, prod. design; Henry Larrecq, art dir.; Lance Anderson, Rob Bottin, Stan Winston, special makeup effects; Roy Arbogast, F/X; Jim Aupperle, animation effects; 109 min.; Color; 2.20:1.

CAST

Kurt Russell (*R. J. MacReady*); Wilford Brimley (*Dr. Blair*); T. K. Carter (*Nauls*); David Clennon (*Palmer*); Keith David (*Childs*); Richard Dysart (*Dr. Copper*);

Charles Hallahan (*Vance Norris*); Peter Maloney (*George Bennings*); Richard Masur (*Clark*); Donald Moffat (*Garry*); Joel Polis (*Fuchs*); Thomas G. Waites (*Windows*); Norbert Weisser (*Norwegian*).

MOST MEMORABLE LINE
I don't know who to trust.
BLAIR TO MACREADY

BACKGROUND
New Jersey–born John W. Campbell Jr. (1910–1971) became a popular writer of the sort of space fantasies he had devoured as a child, when *Flash Gordon* and *Buck Rogers* were still riding high. During his editorship of *Astounding Science-Fiction* magazine (later *Analog*), Campbell oversaw the creation of a more realistic form for the era of atomic energy and UFO sightings. To distinguish such stories from his earlier work, Campbell created the pen name "Don A. Stuart." His most highly regarded piece was the novella *Who Goes There?* (1938). When Howard Hawks optioned it for *The Thing from Another World* (1951), a film that would capitalize on the postwar fascination with flying saucers, the state of the art of F/X was not sufficient to visualize the transference of an alien's inner being from one earthling to another. After high-tech, big-budget science fiction became popular following the success of *Star Wars*, a true-to-the-original remake struck John Carpenter as logical.

THE PLOT
On what first seems a normal day, members of U.S. National Science Institute Station #4 in Antarctica begin their chores. Suddenly, a malamute rushes into their outpost, pursued overhead by a helicopter full of Norwegians, who fire down on the dog. The Norwegians are killed by accident, and the American crew adopts the dog. Gradually, MacReady, a natural leader, grasps that the Norwegians had unearthed a UFO with an alien being on board. The alien can merge with any animate object and assume the identity of man or beast . . . including the canine that may not turn out to be, in its current guise, man's best friend.

THE FILM
John Carpenter was among the so-called Movie Brats who rose to prominence in the mid-1970s. Their numbers include Steven Spielberg, George Lucas, Brian De Palma, and John Landis. Essentially, they set out to recreate the old (and

now nonexistent) Hollywood product that they loved as youths by endowing such breezy entertainments with a modernist edge. In particular, Carpenter was enamored of the films of Howard Hawks. His first low-budget feature, *Assault on Precinct 13* (1976), reset Hawks's Western *Rio Bravo* (1959) in a contemporary urban situation. Naturally, when the opportunity to remake the Hawks-produced classic, *The Thing from Another World* (1951), came along, Carpenter jumped at the chance. However, despite his close identification with both horror (*Halloween*, 1978) and sci-fi (*Escape from New York*, 1981), Carpenter continued to claim that he most loved the Western. To acknowledge this, he had Kurt Russell wear a sombrero throughout the film.

The Thing was among the breakthrough films in the sci-fi, horror, and fantasy genres, introducing what would come to be called "gross-out/splatter" F/X in which the innards of living creatures, real and imagined, come spilling out. Such a stomach-churning process was largely invented by Rob Bottin (1959–), who had previously contributed to the creature work for the *Star Wars* cantina sequence and the transformations in *The Howling* (Joe Dante, 1981). Before that film, a stop-motion process dating back to Universal's 1940s *Wolfman* features had been employed. Bottin became so exhausted by his endless work attempts to create perfection as to believability that old pro Stan Winston was recruited to help with F/X for the dog cage sequence in *The Thing*.

THEME

However indebted to Hawks, Carpenter's film reverses the ideology of the original movie. In that Cold War parable, the allies, though lackadaisical before the arrival of the carrot-like (therefore "Red") creature, transform into a tight group, able to fight the intruder through loyalty. In Carpenter's version, the opposite occurs: the loose community dissipates the moment that team members realize that the "thing" could be any one of them. The only way to survive is through a reliance on rugged individualism, which may be intended as a commentary on the Reagan era. The ending is ambiguous, with MacReady and Childs facing off, each wary that the other may harbor the parasite. It's possible that the threat has not been destroyed. If so, the arrival of an expected rescue team would introduce the apocalypse that would shortly end the world.

TRIVIA

One major bone of contention during script meetings was whether to include a female team member. In old Hollywood, the inclusion of women in the cast contributed glamour, which was considered essential for box-office appeal.

In more recent films, the woman would be not only beautiful but also strong and smart, as with post-feminist heroine Ripley (Sigourney Weaver) in *Alien*. Concluding that the addition of a woman crewmember would cause their film to resemble Ridley Scott's hit too closely, the filmmakers decided against it. However, they did choose Carpenter's then-wife, Adrienne Barbeau, for the voice of the computer.

· · · · · · ·

E.T. THE EXTRA-TERRESTRIAL (1982)

—— RANKING: 6 ——

CREDITS

Universal Pictures/Amblin Entertainment; Steven Spielberg, dir.; Melissa Mathison, scr.; Spielberg, Mathison, Kathleen Kennedy, pro.; John Williams, mus.; Allen Daviau, cin.; Carol Littleton, ed.; James D. Bissell, prod. design; Jim Gillespie, makeup F/X artist; Ed Verreaux, E.T. sketch artist; Carlo Rambaldi, E.T. designer; Craig Reardon, Robert Short, F/X; Sandra Scott, visual effects pro. (20th anniversary edition); 115 min. (theatrical print), 120 min. (20th anniversary edition); Color; 1.85:1.

CAST

Dee Wallace (*Mary*); Henry Thomas (*Elliott*); Peter Coyote (*Keys*); Robert Mac-Naughton (*Michael*); Drew Barrymore (*Gertie*); K. C. Martel (*Greg*); Sean Frye (*Steve*); C. Thomas Howell (*Tyler*); Erika Eleniak (*Blonde Schoolgirl*); David M. O'Dell (*Classmate*); Richard Swingler (*Teacher*); Debra Winger (*Halloween Zombie-Nurse with Poodle*).

MOST MEMORABLE LINE

E.T. phone home.
E.T. TO ELLIOT WHILE POINTING TOWARD THE WINDOW

BACKGROUND

Spielberg had achieved great success with such larger-than-life spectacles as *Jaws* (1975) and *Raiders of the Lost Ark* (1981), but he wanted to direct intimate films about families. While shooting *Raiders*, he developed an idea for just such a film, dictating his concept to writer Mathison (on the set as Harrison Ford's then-girlfriend). Spielberg's love of fantasy, however, got the best of him: as the script progressed, the small family was suddenly surrounded by evil aliens. At the same time, he felt pressure to do a follow-up to *Close Encounters* (1977), but he did not want to make a conventional sequel. So Spielberg developed two projects simultaneously. In one, attacking aliens were replaced by ghosts; this became the horror/thriller *Poltergeist*. The other, *E.T.*—or, as Spielberg put it, an unofficial sequel to *Close Encounters*, containing the same Disney-like sense of wonderment—is about "the little guy who got left behind" when the aliens returned home.

THE PLOT

Late one night, government officials hurry to close in on several harmless aliens who are exploring California. When they rush back to their spacecraft, one doesn't make it. A little boy, Elliott, finds the creature and takes him home where he and his kid sister Gertie hide and care for him. Elliot comes to realize that the homesick E.T. will die if he doesn't return to his own planet.

THE FILM

While E.T. stays home and watches TV, Elliott is at school, dreaming of kissing the prettiest girl in his class. The movie that E.T. watches and, through telekinetic communication, inspires Elliott to live out his fantasy, is *The Quiet Man* (1952) by John Ford, one of the directors who most influenced Spielberg's style. In it, John Wayne embraces and kisses Maureen O'Hara. If art once imitated life, then here life imitates art, as Elliot does precisely the same thing with his pint-sized inamorata.

Spielberg said that he hoped for an "up cry" ending like those he remembered from Disney films. Far from offering the typical happy ending, many of Disney's most memorable movies, such as *Old Yeller* (1957), end with a simultaneous heartbreaking loss and sense of renewal. Another, more recent Disney film that also influenced the creation of *E.T.* was *The Cat from Outer Space* (1978).

Consciously or not, Spielberg and Mathison modeled the three siblings on those in J. D. Salinger's *Catcher in the Rye* (1951). The older brother is a once-great-guy-turned-teenage-jerk; the little sister, an open-eyed innocent; and the younger boy somewhere between the two, feeling himself becoming more of a young adult every day, but desperately wishing to hang on to the honest and open vision of childhood.

THE REBIRTH OF DISNEY-STYLE MAGIC: *The spellbinding charm that had dissipated from American commercial cinema was brought back by Steven Spielberg in what may just be the greatest family-oriented sci-fi film ever made. Courtesy: Universal.*

THEME

Dr. Phil Lineberger, pastor at the Metropolitan Baptist Church in Wichita, Kansas, pointed out to his congregation that E.T.'s "journey" could, in many ways, be perceived as allegorically resembling that of Jesus and that the concept of atonement was also present in the film. According to this interpretation, E.T.'s telepathic sympathy parallels events in the Gospels. Likewise, E.T. develops a set of disciples, dies, and then rises again, finally ascending. Asked whether he agreed with this religious interpretation, Spielberg noted, "I've been too busy making movies to stop and analyze how or why I make them." He then admitted that his friend George Lucas, when informed of the religious and mythic interpretations of *Star Wars*, came to realize "the meaning of what he had done as much from the critiques he had read . . . as from his own introspection." As to himself and *E.T.*? "I'm the same way."

TRIVIA

In the script, E.T.'s favorite candy was to have been M&Ms. Unwisely, Mars, Inc. turned down a request to use their brand name, clearing the way for Reese's Pieces to reap the benefits.

The little girl in the schoolroom sequence, Erika Eleniak, would some years later pose for *Playboy*.

The image of Elliot and E.T. bicycling across the moon served as the logo not only for the movie, but also for Spielberg's company, Amblin Entertainment. For that image, he drew, consciously or not, from memories of Disney's *The Absent-Minded Professor* (1961) in which Fred MacMurray and his dog ride past the moon in their airborne Model T on a similarly starry night. The mood of *E.T.* was influenced by the post–Walt Disney film *Pete's Dragon* (Don Chaffey, 1977) in which the little boy's dragon is named Elliott, and the lonely child likewise depends on a strange but sweet-spirited visitor that arrives from the sky.

· · · · · · ·

STAR TREK II: THE WRATH OF KHAN (1982), STAR TREK IV: THE VOYAGE HOME (1986), AND STAR TREK VI: THE UNDISCOVERED COUNTRY (1991)

—— RANKING: 28 (THREE-WAY TIE) ——

STAR TREK II: THE WRATH OF KHAN (1982)

CREDITS

Paramount Pictures; Nicholas Meyer, dir.; Meyer, Harve Bennett, Jack B. Sowards, Samuel A. Peeples, scr.; Bennett, William F. Phillips, Robert Sallin, pro.; James Horner, mus.; Gayne Rescher, cin.; William Paul Dornisch, ed.; Joseph R. Jennings, prod. design; Michael Minor, art dir.; Robert Fletcher, costumes; Bob Dawson, F/X; Ken Ralston/ILM, Jim Veilleux/ILM, visual effects; 113 min. (theatrical), 116 min. (director's cut); Color; 2.35:1.

CAST

William Shatner (*Kirk*); Leonard Nimoy (*Spock*); DeForest Kelley (*McCoy*); James Doohan (*Scotty*); Walter Koenig (*Chekov*); George Takei (*Sulu*); Nichelle Nichols

REUNITED AND IT FEELS SO GOOD: *Following years of difficult negotiation, the entire original cast came together again, sporting spiffy new costumes. Standing, from left to right: Leonard Nimoy, George Takei, Walter Koenig, James Doohan, DeForest Kelley, and Nichelle Nichols; seated: William Shatner. Courtesy: Paramount.*

(*Uhura*); Bibi Besch (*Carol*); Merritt Butrick (*David*); Paul Winfield (*Terrell*); Kirstie Alley (*Saavik*); Ricardo Montalbán (*Khan*).

MOST MEMORABLE LINE

Galloping around the cosmos is a game for the young.

KIRK

BACKGROUND

Following the cancellation of *Star Trek* as an NBC prime-time series in 1969, the space opera remained alive in daily syndication. Gene Roddenberry (1921–1991) oversaw a Saturday morning animated version, but his dream of a theatrical film remained elusive until the unexpected, unparalleled success of *Star Wars* provided the necessary catalyst. *Star Trek: The Motion Picture* (Robert Wise, 1979) reassembled the original cast, but the warm relationships of TV's *Enterprise* crew gave way to a clammy, clinical approach. Any sequel would have to be less expensive and more appealing to the fan base.

THE PLOT

Admiral Kirk and Captain Spock train a young crew, led by "Mr." Saavik, to continue the *Enterprise*'s explorations. The untried space cadets are thrown into a crisis situation after Commander Chekov and Captain Terrell beam down to Ceti Alpha V to determine if this supposedly uninhabited world might serve as a suitable test area for the Genesis Device, which can create life forms in barren places. Instead, they discover Khan, a ruthless by-product of previous genetic engineering, and his pirate-like crew, surviving here fifteen years after banishment. Khan plans to exact revenge on his old enemy, Kirk, whose handling of this crisis is complicated by reunions with his lost love Carol and their grown son, David.

THE FILM

Whereas *Star Trek: The Motion Picture* had been budgeted at a then-hefty $35 million, Nicholas Meyer's adeptness at turning out high-quality films on tight budgets convinced Paramount's executives to okay a sequel, albeit cautiously, with an $11 million budget. *The Wrath of Khan* engendered the kind of excitement that its ponderous predecessor had not, and Ricardo Montalbán possessed drawing power as Khan Noonien Singh, the most popular villain in the cult show's history.

THEME

Meyer delved into the non-fantastical idea of aging. In the opening, Kirk admits to melancholia after being kicked upstairs. In the arc of his story, he comes to accept his more mature state, and in part owing to Spock's Vulcan wisdom, he realizes that he does indeed still have a viable place in a changing cosmos. However much it is a cliché, a person really *is* only as old as he or she feels, as Kirk finally learns.

TRIVIA

Khan had appeared in only one TV episode, "Space Seed" (February 16, 1967).

Though Meyer does not take screen credit, he heavily rewrote the scenario, adding his signature literary references. An old-fashioned wooden schooner, much like the *Pequod* from Herman Melville's novel, *Moby-Dick* (1851), sits on display in Kirk's living room. At the movie's midpoint, when the *Enterprise* crew

THE MOST MEMORABLE VILLAIN: *Wisely, the producers brought back bombastic scene-stealer Ricardo Montalbán as "Khan," the franchise's most fascinating foe to Kirk and company. Courtesy: Paramount.*

invades Khan's domain, a copy of *Moby-Dick* is visible. The film's final image features a coffin, a precise parallel to the conclusion of Melville's epic. Also, *The Wrath of Khan* begins and ends with quotations from Charles Dickens's *A Tale of Two Cities* (1859).

STAR TREK IV: THE VOYAGE HOME (1986)

ADDITIONAL CREDITS/ALTERED CREDITS

Leonard Nimoy, dir.; Nimoy, Steve Meerson, Peter Krikes, Nicholas Meyer, scr.; Leonard Rosenman, mus.; Donald Peterman, cin.; Peter E. Berger, ed.; Jack T. Collis, prod. design; Joe Aubel, Peter Landsdown Smith, art dir.; Richard Snell, Rolf John Keppler, special makeup effects; Brian Wade, Klingon and Vulcan prosthetics; George Budd, Alan Howarth, special sound effects; Michael Lantieri, F/X; Mark A. Mangini/ILM, sound effects; 119 min.; Color; 2.35:1.

ADDITIONAL CAST/ALTERED CAST
Catherine Hicks (*Gillian*); Jane Wyatt (*Amanda*); Mark Lenard (*Sarek*); Robin Curtis (*Lt. Saavik*); Robert Ellenstein (*Federation Council President*); John Schuck (*Klingon Ambassador*); Brock Peters (*Admiral Cartwright*).

MOST MEMORABLE LINE
> It's ironic: when man was killing these creatures,
> he was destroying his own future.
> KIRK, AFTER SAVING THE WHALES

BACKGROUND
When *Khan* earned $100 million worldwide, Paramount quickly green-lighted a sequel. However, *Star Trek III: The Search for Spock* (Leonard Nimoy, 1984) fumbled badly. Part of the problem was that Harve Bennett, a former TV producer (*The Mod Squad*) who had assumed control of the franchise, wrote the screenplay, having feuded with the gifted Meyer. Despite a record-breaking opening weekend, owing to high expectations, *The Search for Spock* nose-dived as a result of weak word of mouth. Wisely, Bennett made amends with Meyer before the next film in the franchise.

THE PLOT
Exile on Vulcan provides Kirk and his crew sustenance following their disobeying of direct orders by saving Spock in the previous film installment, *Star Trek III: The Search for Spock* (1984). In that lesser film's storyline, Kirk and his crew had stolen the *Enterprise* in order to rescue the deceased Spock's body and rejoin it with his *katra*, or spirit. In their hearts, though, all wish to return and face judgment. As they near Earth in 2286, Kirk and his crew are warned away by Starfleet Command. A vessel has approached, sending out indecipherable probes and wreaking havoc below. Thanks to Spock's supreme logic, everyone grasps that the only earthlings that could return these calls are humpback whales, long since extinct. In a desperate bid, Kirk diverts the Klingon Bird-of-Prey, which he and his crew had captured in the previous film, through time, landing in the mid-1980s. Their hope is to locate several great sea beasts, their numbers already depleted, then bring them back . . . to the future.

THE FILM
Director Leonard Nimoy (1931–2015) surpassed all expectations by navigating the difficult change of tone from a relatively typical (in fact, darker than usual) opening to the lighthearted humor inherent in the crew's arrival in then-contemporary times. For Meyer, this offered a ripe opportunity to return to themes that deal with the supposed inevitability of history as explored in his more modest *Time After Time* (1979), also set in contemporary San Francisco, and include a similar narrative trope involving women born in the wrong era and more than willing to time travel.

THEME
Most serious science-fiction films are rich with meaning; *The Voyage Home* might be thought of as a message movie, the theme didactically expressed by Kirk in his final line. However much good-natured entertainment this film does indeed offer, the essential idea that comes across powerfully is a need to protect all aspects of our environment, saving the whales included, in order to ensure a better, rather than bitter, future.

TRIVIA
This movie draws on the Moby Dick motif, but it reverses the prejudices of Melville's time, portraying whales as humans' best allies rather than villainous monsters. The first time we see Gillian, offering a tour of two whales in captivity, she corrects all the old misconceptions regarding whales.

The assignment of the film's model design and optical effects to Industrial Light & Magic (ILM), a Lucas company, facilitated the inter-connectedness between the world's greatest science-fiction/space fantasy franchises, *Star Trek* and *Star Wars*.

STAR TREK VI: THE UNDISCOVERED COUNTRY (1991)

ADDITIONAL/ALTERED CREDITS
Nicholas Meyer, dir.; Meyer, Leonard Nimoy, Lawrence Konner, Mark Rosenthal, Denny Martin Flinn, scr.; Ralph Winter, Steven-Charles Jaffe, pro.; Cliff Eidelman, mus.; Hiro Narita, cin.; William Hoy, Ronald Roose, ed.; Herman F. Zimmerman, prod. design; Dodie Shepard, costumes; R. Christopher Biggs, Ed French, Cat'Ania McCoy-Howze, special makeup F/X; John P. Fasal, special

TO BOLDLY GO: *As returning characters met new additions to the cast, a worthy warp-speed backdrop was provided by special effects technicians who, in the post–Star Wars era, added the dazzling visual imagery that fans of the original Star Trek TV series could only dream about. Courtesy: Paramount.*

sound F/X; Terry D. Frazee, F/X; Scott Farrar, visual effects; 110 min. (theatrical print), 113 min. (extended cut); Color; 2.35:1.

ADDITIONAL/ALTERED CAST
Christopher Plummer (*Chang*); Kim Cattrall (*Lt. Valeris*); Iman (*Martia*); Tom Morga (*The Brute Man*); Robert Easton (*Klingon Judge*); Grace Lee Whitney (*Excelsior Crew Member*); Kurtwood Smith (*Federation President*); Rosanna DeSoto (*Azetbur*); David Warner (*Chancellor Gorkon*).

MOST MEMORABLE LINE
In space, all warriors are cold warriors.
CHANG

BACKGROUND
Before the fifth installment, *The Final Frontier*, could be green-lighted, Meyer again stepped away. Shatner meanwhile demanded that he, like Nimoy, get to direct. To save money, Paramount turned over the F/X to a less ambitious company than ILM. The resulting film looks shabby; the story line makes no sense. *The Final Frontier* grossed less than the box office for *The Voyage Home*, prompting the question as to whether the franchise should be put to rest. Fortunately, Meyer returned once again, providing a graceful closing chapter.

THE PLOT
Desperate for energy to continue their civilization, the Klingons over-mine their moon, Praxis, and nature revolts. As a result, they sue for peace with the Federation. Though Kirk, as a result of lingering heartbreak over the death of his son at their hands, does not trust the Klingons, the Federation sends him to escort their representatives to a peace conference. When the *Enterprise* fires at the Klingon vessel, Kirk is blamed for the incendiary incident.

THE FILM
Initially, the film was intended as a twenty-fifth anniversary celebration for the franchise and a prequel, with new, young actors assuming the roles—precisely what would in time emerge with J. J. Abrams's highly successful 2009 reboot.

THEME
The screenplay was always intended as a metaphor for the long-hoped-for end (or so it seemed then) to the Cold War, Mr. Gorbachev heeding President

Ronald Reagan's call to "tear down this wall." Nimoy wondered what would happen if the "wall" came down in space, the premise allowing the filmmakers to comment on the dangers inherent in the then-current situation. Would Kirk, once considered a hero, become an antagonistic troublemaker in the new world order?

TRIVIA

Meyer's screenplay for *Star Trek* IV contained a quote from Shakespeare's *Hamlet* that set up the importance that the author in general, and that play in particular, would have in *Star Trek* VI. In that c. 1599 work, "the undiscovered country," as posited in the "To be or not to be . . . " speech, refers to death itself; in the film, the phrase is reimagined to describe the future.

· · · · · · ·

BLADE RUNNER (1982)

—— RANKING: 7 ——

CREDITS

Warner Bros./Ladd Company; Ridley Scott, dir.; Philip K. Dick, novel; Hampton Fancher, David Webb Peoples, scr.; Scott, Fancher, Michael Deeley, Charles de Lauzirika (2007 final cut), pro.; Vangelis, mus.; Jordan Cronenweth, cin.; Marsha Nakashima, Terry Rawlings, ed.; Lawrence G. Paull, Syd Mead, prod. design; David L. Snyder, art dir.; Michael Kaplan, Charles Knode, costumes; Greg Curtis, Logan Frazee, Terry D. Frazee, Ken Estes, Donald Myers, Robert Cole, Scott Forbes, F/X; Michael Backauskas, Robert D. Bailey, Robert Hall, John C. Wash, Tim Angulo (2007 final cut), visual/optical effects; 118 min. (original cut), 117 min. (2007 final cut); Color; 2.20:1.

CAST

Harrison Ford (*Rick Deckard*); Rutger Hauer (*Roy Batty*); Sean Young (*Rachael*); Edward James Olmos (*Gaff*); M. Emmet Walsh (*Bryant*); Daryl Hannah (*Pris*); William Sanderson (*J. F. Sebastian*); Brion James (*Kowalski*); Joe Turkel (*Tyrell*); Joanna Cassidy (*Zhora*); James Hong (*Hannibal Chew*); Morgan Paull (*Holden*); Kevin Thompson (*Bear*); John Edward Allen (*Kaiser*); Hy Pyke (*Taffey*).

SCI-FI/NOIR: *The carefully designed poster art of this initially misunderstood masterpiece.* Blade Runner *introduced an entire subgenre, fusing the dystopian future elements of traditional science fiction with elements from the pulp-cinema film noirs of the late 1940s. Courtesy: Ladd Company/Warner Bros.*

MOST MEMORABLE LINE

All he'd wanted were the same answers the rest of us want—
"Where did I come from?" "Where am I going?"

DECKARD, ON WITNESSING A DEATH

BACKGROUND

Philip Kindred Dick (1928–1982) was born in Chicago and moved with his parents to San Francisco. During those early years and throughout his adult life, Dick was haunted by the death of his twin sister, Jane, shortly after their birth. Following his parents' divorce, Dick lived with his mother in Washington, D.C., and Berkeley, California. There, at age twelve, he happened upon the pulp magazine *Stirring Science Stories*, and determined to make a living writing just such fiction.

Dick's groundbreaking approach was to create intensely realistic characters, then place them in an impossibly absurd alternative cosmos. Many consider his 1968 *Do Androids Dream of Electric Sheep?* to be his crowning achievement. In that novel, the source for *Blade Runner*, Dick channeled his drug addiction and hallucinatory experiences into an artistic triumph. The antihero's obsession with the mystery woman reflects Dick's own undying obsession with his long-lost "invisible twin." Deckard's attempt to determine whether his inamorata is android or human represents a reflection on Dick's own questionable origins. It also stirred what would soon become one of the key themes of most sci-fi to follow, as well as one of the formative precepts of post-modernism: perception is reality. We can never know anything for certain, only our own individual mental conception of anything "out there."

THE PLOT

In 2019 Los Angeles, Deckard serves as a Blade Runner, a government-backed assassin of a breed called replicants, human-like androids developed to serve as droid slaves in far colonies. Any replicants that illegally return and attempt to pass themselves off as people must be "retired." For some time, Deckard has wanted out; he has come to believe that perhaps these creatures may have a point in their insistence on full integration into society. This makes Deckard's final hit all the more difficult: Rachael, a beautiful advanced form of replicant who believes herself to be human. So . . . like the lead in a 1940s film noir who meets a deliciously duplicitous dame, our antihero Deckard must decide: should he kiss or kill her?

THE FILM

Unlike so many great contemporary sci-fi filmmakers, Ridley Scott did *not* grow up adoring 1950s junk genre films. Among his favorite movies are *Citizen Kane* (Orson Welles, 1941), *Seven Samurai* (Akira Kurosawa, 1954), and *Lawrence of Arabia* (David Lean, 1962). In interviews, Scott has cited Stanley Kubrick as an enormous influence, not only for *2001* but also the costume film *Barry Lyndon* (1975). Scott apparently drew his aesthetic for his 1977 film *The Duellists* from the cool, aloof, purposefully distanced *Barry Lyndon*, which treats a highly emotional human story in a clinically intellectual manner. For Scott, like Kubrick, any appeal (or lack thereof for some viewers) is based on a creative incongruity between subject matter and personal style. Though *Alien* made Scott a huge favorite among genre fans, he agreed to do *Blade Runner* only if he could de-emphasize the expected conventions, offering instead a futuristic film noir.

Scott did not have final cut. The original release print, featuring a heavy-handed voice-over by Harrison Ford, disappointed mainstream viewers and sci-fi buffs alike. Word soon spread that there was another, greater film, lost on the cutting room floor, and fans were eager to see Scott's complete version. The 2007 cut, considered by buffs to be the final word on the subject, has been cited as a genre masterpiece, some aficionados insisting it may well rank as the greatest sci-fi film of all time.

THEME

Though thankfully there are no didactic speeches that might have brought this piece down to the level of a message movie, *Blade Runner* is at heart an existential film about the very nature of what it means to be human. Deckard qualifies as a unique, well-wrought, multi-dimensional character. Also, though, he serves the function of an Everyman: a relatively ordinary face in the crowd who, owing to events, experiences his first thoughts about moral issues. This causes him to question not only what he does but, since his work defines him, also who he actually is. The ambiguousness of the conclusion—is he human, replicant, or a combination of the two?—may confound general viewers. Yet, it is the basis of what those who appreciate the genre at its most complex and demanding love best about *Blade Runner*.

TRIVIA

One disappointing aspect of the theatrical release was that a dance number featuring the replicant stripper Zhora had apparently been cut, presumably for reasons of time. That this scene was not restored in the final cut struck many as odd, since the dance is essential in driving Deckard's repulsion-attraction to this seductive android. According to Joanna Cassidy, the sequence was never actually filmed. She had accepted the relatively small role owing to her interest in revealing her terpsichorean gifts, choreographing and rehearsing the erotic performance. At the last minute, Cassidy was informed that there simply was not enough money and/or time to shoot the number, leaving it the one missing scene that can never be restored.

· · · · · · ·

NAUSICAÄ OF THE VALLEY OF THE WIND/ KAZE NO TANI NO NAUSHIKA (1984)

—— RANKING: 56 ——

CREDITS

Hakuhodo/Nibariki; Hayao Miyazaki, dir.; Miyazaki, scr.; Isao Takahata, Rick Dempsey, pro.; Joe Hisaishi, mus.; Naoki Kaneko, Tomoko Kida, Shôji Sakai, ed.; Mitsuki Nakamura, art dir.; Kazuo Komatsubara, character design/animation; Fukuo Suzuki, color supervisor; 117 min.; Color; 1.85:1.

CAST (VOICES)

Sumi Shimamoto (*Nausicaä*); Mahito Tsujimura (*Jihl*); Hisako Kyôda (*Oh-Baba*); Gorô Naya (*Lord Yupa*); Ichirô Nagai (*Mito*); Kôhei Miyauchi (*Goru*); Jôji Yanami (*Gikkuri*); Minoru Yada (*Niga*); Mugihito (*Mayor of Pejite*); Yôji Matsuda (*Asbel*); Tony Jay (*Narrator*, English language version).

MOST MEMORABLE LINE

All this killing must stop!
NAUSICAÄ

BACKGROUND

Deeply involved in Tokyo's animation industry from an early age, Hayao Miyazaki (1941–) rose through the ranks from humble "in-between" illustrator to full auteur. The first film credited to him as director was the award-winning

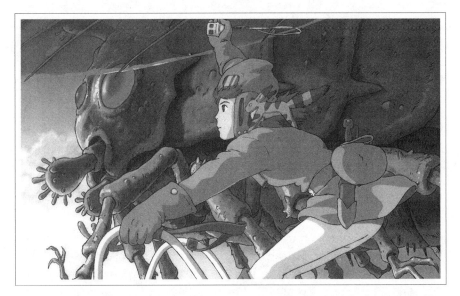

WELCOME TO THE WORLD OF ASIAN SCI-FI/FANTASY: *With the renaissance in genre films for adults, as well as kids, in full swing, some daring entrepreneurs decided it was time to distribute the remarkable anime films, introducing American and international audiences to a whole new world of imagery and ideas. Courtesy: Hakuhodo/Nibarkii/Disney.*

Castle of Cagliostro (1979), the very title revealing this artist's familiarity with horror items from Western culture.

Nausicaä first appeared as a manga (the Japanese term for comic books and, in time, graphic novels) in serialized form in 1982. The book's popularity led to a film offer from Tokuma Shoten, the parent company of *Animage* magazine. The collaborators picked Topcraft as their animation company of choice owing to its artists' unique ability to project visceral action in a delicate manner, resulting in a film experience that combined the best of both worlds—precisely what was needed here. Joe Hisaishi was brought on board to compose the score, taking a minimalist approach that Miyazaki sensed would enhance the work's visual sophistication without challenging the artwork for aesthetic supremacy during the viewing experience.

THE PLOT

Various nests of humans survive in a brave new world in a variety of ways, ranging from war-like retro-behavior to peaceful villages. All are menaced by the great jungle, where gigantic insects roam. These mutations of normal creatures, which existed before a vast war destroyed the techno-metropolises, constantly threaten to break out of their natural surroundings. Fearful that such behavior might imperil their corner of the world, a fierce tribe, Tolmekians, determine to eliminate all such creatures. They believe the best way to do so would be by forcing other humans to join in a mission. The people of the Valley of the Wind, nurtured by their unique child-woman savior/hero Nausicaä, are less than anxious to take such a militaristic approach. Nausicaä attempts to convince them that humans and insects not only can but also must cohabit on an Earth that, if at long last treated with respect, might yet regenerate itself.

THE FILM

Miyazaki's biographers note that, like many of his countrymen, the artist was devastated by the seeming destruction of Minamata Bay following the dumping of wastewater containing methyl mercury by an industrial corporation between 1932 and 1968. Eventually, however, the bay appeared to be overcoming the poison, nature somehow managing to survive humankind's insensitivity. This inspired Miyazaki to want to share such a story with the world. He rejected a realistic, journalistic approach, desiring to move beyond specifics so as to make a universal statement. He sensed that contemporary sci-fi, our equivalent of ancient mythology, should be his "form" for such an ambition. Miyazaki reset the miracle-like recovery (at least for pantheists, who perceive the natural world as God's good garden on Earth) as an enormous epic, drawing on varied texts (Eastern as well as Western) that had intrigued him and combining elements from each in a mix-and-match approach that incorporates them all without obviously imitating any one. Sources for this method include a Japanese folktale, "The Princess Who Loved Insects," as well as the *Earthsea* series by Ursula K. Le Guin, "Nightfall" by Isaac Asimov, and, perhaps most significantly, *The Lord of the Rings* by J. R. R. Tolkien. Here, of course, such a devout quest is lifted out of the alternative realm of epic/fantasy and transformed into science fiction.

THEME

As liberal progressive science fiction/fantasy, *Nausicaä* drives home two points emphatically: an insistence that war never has solved, and never can solve, any issue, and that all of nature, even what appear to be its uglier elements, must be respected and revered for a proper equilibrium to come into being. The base, atavistic human solution known as territorial imperatives—colonizing other races and/or nations while conquering the unknown, including nature, then bending all that has been victimized to dictatorial human power—must be abandoned if a more positive, and less destructive, form of life is ever to be realized. A synergistic approach between races, as well as between the human and the natural, is the first step toward enlightenment.

Nausicaä is, in an almost Hebraic manner, a warrior hero and gentle savior. A radical innocent, she passionately embraces the totality of existence, combining the teachings of Jesus and the Buddha so as to emphasize the similarities between the teachings of those two inspirational figures. Her name was drawn from Greek mythology. The male hero of the *Odyssey* was shipwrecked in a land lorded over by King Alcinous and Queen Arete. Homer emphasizes the combination of gentleness and strength inherent in their daughter Nausicaä. Odysseus, observing this princess, recalls the Greek goddess Artemis, who, alone among the Olympians, had the uncanny ability to communicate directly with animals and fully comprehend their needs. In this greatest of all anime projects, the so-named female is a visionary whose words can comfort people in a pan-cultural manner, though when necessary, her decisive action speaks louder than her soft-spoken edicts.

TRIVIA

Success at the box office convinced Buena Vista, Disney's distribution company, to prepare an English-language version. The film was belatedly released in 1997, at a time when Disney had come to grasp the importance of enhancing its in-studio product with international cutting-edge animation that would appeal to an emergent American audience that was increasingly open to such alternative forms. The official American release title is *Nausicaä of the Valley of the Wind*.

New World Pictures had earlier released a mutilated version (with more than twenty minutes eliminated), called *Warriors of the Wind* (1985).

A common misperception is that Nausicaä was the first film created by Studio Ghibli. In fact, the film's profits were what allowed Miyazaki to co-found his own company.

....

THE TERMINATOR (1984)

—— RANKING: 34 ——

CREDITS

Orion Pictures/Hemdale Film; James Cameron, dir.; Cameron, Gale Anne Hurd, William Wisher Jr., scr.; Hurd, John Daly, Derek Gibson, pro.; Brad Fiedel, mus.; Adam Greenberg, cin.; Mark Goldblatt, ed.; George Costello, Shay Austin, art dir.; Brian Wade, special makeup effects; Stan Winston, Jack Bricker, Ellis Burman Jr., Frank DeMarco, Ernest D. Farino, Roger George, Richard J. Landon, Shane Mahan, David B. Miller, John Rosengrant, Brian Wade, Bob Williams, Tom Woodruff Jr., F/X; Doug Beswick, Phil Huff, Laurel Klick, visual effects; Ken Marschall, matte artist; 107 min.; Color; 1.85:1.

CAST

Arnold Schwarzenegger (*The Terminator*); Michael Biehn (*Kyle Reese*); Linda Hamilton (*Sarah Connor*); Paul Winfield (*Lt. Ed Traxler*); Lance Henriksen (*Det. Vukovich*); Rick Rossovich (*Matt Buchanan*); Bess Motta (*Ginger Ventura*); Earl Boen (*Dr. Peter Silberman*); Dick Miller (*Pawn Shop Clerk*); Shawn Schepps (*Nancy*); Bill Paxton, Brad Rearden (*Punks*).

MOST MEMORABLE LINE

I'll be back.

THE TERMINATOR

BACKGROUND

This little film that no one wanted (at least initially) became one of the great sci-fi franchises. *The Terminator* emerged from an accidental coming together of three talents. James Cameron (1954–) had worked his way up from odd jobs, often for Roger Corman and his low-budget enterprises. Cameron had been the art director on *Battle Beyond the Stars* (1980) and the production designer for *Galaxy of Terror* (1981). This led to F/X work on John Carpenter's *Escape from New York* (1981). Moving back to the Corman fold to work on *Piranha II: The Spawning* (1981) may have seemed something of a comedown. But when the planned director exited, Cameron was offered that position, and he turned this schlock item into an exceptional example of the B movie at its best.

"I'LL BE BACK!" A tightly budgeted science-fiction action flick, which drew
on time travel elements hailing back to Rod Serling and The Twilight Zone,
unexpectedly proved a commercial success, leading to a film series and the
inevitable franchise. *Courtesy: Hemdale/Orion/Carolco/TriStar.*

Cameron then set out to direct his own sci-fi screenplay, meeting with Arnold Schwarzenegger (1947–), who had been searching for an appropriate starring role since *Conan the Barbarian* (John Milius, 1982). Everything coalesced when the third necessary talent, F/X and makeup artist Stan Winston (1946–2008), joined in the enterprise. He would go on to provide such services for *Aliens* (1986), *Predator* (1987), and *Iron Man* (2008).

THE PLOT
Sarah Connor is one more ordinary woman trying to survive in the everyday world until she comes in contact with two strange visitors. Reese, a pleasant fellow, insists he's traveled thirty-five years back in time to protect her from forces in the future that want Sarah dead. The other is a cyborg assassin sent to "terminate" her. Initially, Sarah assumes that all Reese tells her is so much nonsense. But when the emotionless steel-and-machine title character stalks her, Sarah turns to Reese as her only hope for survival.

THE FILM
Orion's original choice to play the title character was O. J. Simpson, but Cameron didn't believe that the public could buy an athlete who, at that time, boasted an all-around nice guy image, as an emotionless killer. Cameron had one of his favorite actors, Lance Henriksen, in mind. Then Schwarzenegger agreed to play the Terminator, rather than, as originally planned, the part of Reese. At that point, Henriksen accepted another part. Both Amy Irving (Mrs. Spielberg #1) and Kate Capshaw (Mrs. Spielberg #2) were considered for Sarah.

An important aspect of the film that is appreciated by women is the manner in which Sarah arcs during the narrative. At first, she appears to be the damsel in distress, needing to be saved from the Terminator time after time. At the mid-point, however, she turns: Sarah becomes Reese's equal partner and, at the end, kills the monster when Reese cannot. Essentially, Sarah is a post-feminist vision included in a sci-fi film—some argue for the first time. Cameron would continue such an enlightened approach in *Aliens* (1986).

THEME
The Terminator was by far one of the best of numerous sci-fi films from its era that attempted to recreate the glory days of *The Twilight Zone*. Shot on a tight budget, the film included many themes that had been introduced to the public at large by Serling's series. Many of the greatest *Zones* dealt not only with the concept of time travel but also with the intellectual exploration of the ideology

involved in such a possibility. If one (or, in this case, more than one) character went back in time, could it be possible to alter things so that the future would turn out differently? Or, is the future set in cement, so that any such attempts only ensure that things turn out precisely the same? As the best of Serling's teleplays demonstrate, that's not an easy question to answer. On the one hand, if Reese had never visited 1984, he would not have impregnated Sarah with the child who will become John, the savior who eventually destroys the Skynet computer world. On the other hand, no matter how powerful the Terminator may be, the creature cannot keep any of this from happening. The answer, then, is yes and no—some things can be changed, though only to keep others from occurring.

TRIVIA

Cameron had a terrible dream while working on a film project in 1981. In it, an indestructible mechanical man showed up on the set and tried to kill him. As soon as he finished that project, Cameron set to work devising the script for what would come to be called *The Terminator*.

Sequels included *Terminator 2: Judgment Day* (Cameron, 1991), *Terminator 3: Rise of the Machines* (Jonathan Mostow, 2003), and *Terminator Salvation* (McG, 2009). Despite increasing F/X budgets, none of these efforts ever quite captured the unique appeal of the original.

· · · · · · ·

BACK TO THE FUTURE (1985)

—— RANKING: 36 ——

CREDITS

Universal Pictures/Amblin Entertainment; Robert Zemeckis, dir.; Zemeckis, Bob Gale, scr.; Gale, Neil Canton, Kathleen Kennedy, Frank Marshall, Steven Spielberg, pro.; Alan Silvestri, mus.; Dean Cundey, cin.; Harry Keramidas, Arthur Schmidt, ed.; Lawrence G. Paull, prod. design; Todd Hallowell, art dir.; Sam Adams, Richard Chronister, William A. Klinger, Kevin Pike, F/X; Andrew Probert, DeLorean designer; 116 min.; Color; 1.85:1.

CAST

Michael J. Fox (*Marty McFly*); Christopher Lloyd (*Dr. Emmett Brown*); Lea Thompson (*Lorraine Baines*); Crispin Glover (*George McFly*); Thomas F. Wilson (*Biff Tannen*); Claudia Wells (*Jennifer Parker*); Marc McClure (*Dave McFly*); Wendie Jo

Sperber (*Linda McFly*); George DiCenzo (*Sam Baines*); Frances Lee McCain (*Stella Baines*); James Tolkan (*Mr. Strickland*); J. J. Cohen (*Skinhead*); Casey Siemaszko (*3-D*); Billy Zane (*Match*); Harry Waters Jr. (*Marvin Berry*).

MOST MEMORABLE LINE

History is gonna change.
MARTY TO MR. STRICKLAND

BACKGROUND

The team of Robert Zemeckis (1952–) and Bob Gale (1951–) had been attempting to score big in Hollywood for some time with youth-oriented films such as *I Wanna Hold Your Hand* (1978) and *Used Cars* (1980). They had hoped to sell this script to the post–Walt Disney (who died in 1966) company but were rejected, even as Spielberg had been with *E.T.* Even then in the process of reinventing old-fashioned family entertainment for an entirely new audience, Spielberg came to the rescue. His top production team of Kathleen Kennedy and Frank Marshall brought *Back to the Future* to the screen with the required nostalgic tone and contemporary spirit. Spielberg is listed as the film's "presenter," precisely the title Disney once received.

This moderately budgeted (less than $20 million) movie grossed more than $350 million worldwide, ranked as the top U.S. box office hit of 1985, and spawned two popular sequels (1989 and 1990). Spielberg knew he could now consistently franchise his unique brand of updated family fun as the reinvented equivalent of the old Disney vision.

THE PLOT

At 1:15 in the morning on October 26, 1985, lovable loser Marty McFly meets his eccentric mentor Doc Brown in the deserted heart of their small town. Doc reveals that he's transformed a DeLorean DMC-12 into a time machine that runs on plutonium. The terrorists who were duped out of the plutonium by Doc attack him and Marty. Marty escapes in the vehicle only to discover that he's gone back thirty years in time to the 1950s.

He prevents a geeky fellow, George, from being hurt in an auto accident. The problem: this is Marty's father as a teenager. If he had been hit, George would have been helped inside the home of Lorraine, and the two would have come together as a couple. Instead, Lorraine falls for Marty. If such a changed situation continues, Marty and his siblings can never be born. Desperate, Marty seeks out the young Doc Brown for help.

THE FILM

The film, along with *Gremlins* (Joe Dante, 1984), was one of the final movies to be shot on the old Universal Studios famed small-town America set that had been used for decades. Spielberg and Zemeckis rightly sensed that if they filmed *Back to the Future* on location, it would look "too real." What they wanted (and fully achieved) was a small town in the movies, rather than in real life, to add a Hollywood fairy-tale aura to the piece.

THEME

Like many films of the mid-1980s, including *The Terminator*, *Back to the Future* was inspired by *The Twilight Zone*, Rod Serling's monumental TV series (1959–1964). One recurring *Zone* theme had been the concept of time travel: could the future be changed if one were to go back? In episode after episode, small things involving individuals who didn't influence history could lead to different conclusions: for example, the bad guys get their just desserts and things turn out better for the downtrodden. Zemeckis and Gale's script might have been titled *Twilight Zone: The Movie*, as it comes closer to recapturing the magic of Serling's show (or at least its light-hearted episodes) than did the failed 1983 film of that name. The McFly family is, as a result of Marty's tinkering with the past, well off when he returns, whereas the dad's 1985 mean boss, who was also his high school bully in 1955, is humbled. All's well that ends well, though it takes some time travel of the type that H. G. Wells first imagined, then Rod Serling effectively updated, to get it all right, both in their classic works and in such classic films as the violent *Terminator* and charming *Back to the Future*.

TRIVIA

Though Zemeckis always wanted Fox for Marty, it seemed all but impossible considering the young star's commitment to his TV series, *Family Ties*. Eric Stoltz worked for four weeks before it was decided he was wrong for the role. At that point, Fox came back on board, shooting his series from early morning to late afternoon, then heading directly to the movie set until late night. Between the firing and rehiring, Ralph Macchio was offered, but turned down, the part.

Characters in 1955 cannot believe the cowboy star from TV's *Death Valley Days* will be president in thirty years. In fact, Ronald Reagan did not take over the hosting job on that series until 1964.

······

COCOON (1985)

—— RANKING: 50 ——

CREDITS

Twentieth Century Fox Film Corporation; Ron Howard, dir.; Tom Benedek, David Saperstein, scr.; David Brown, Richard D. Zanuck, Lili Fini Zanuck, pro.; James Horner, mus.; Donald Peterman, cin.; Daniel P. Hanley, Mike Hill, ed.; Jack T. Collis, prod. design; Aggie Guerard Rodgers, costumes; Brian Penikas, Greg Cannom, special makeup effects; Cannom, alien creatures; Joseph A. Unsinn, F/X; Peter Anderson, creature visual effects; 117 min.; Color; 1.85:1.

CAST

Don Ameche (*Art Selwyn*); Wilford Brimley (*Ben Luckett*); Hume Cronyn (*Joe Finley*); Brian Dennehy (*Walter*); Jack Gilford (*Bernie Lefkowitz*); Steve Guttenberg (*Jack Bonner*); Maureen Stapleton (*Mary Luckett*); Jessica Tandy (*Alma Finley*); Gwen Verdon (*Bess McCarthy*); Herta Ware (*Rosie Lefkowitz*); Tahnee Welch (*Kitty*); Barret Oliver (*David*).

MOST MEMORABLE LINE

Men should be explorers, no matter how old they are.

ART SELWYN

BACKGROUND

Mild, sweet-spirited, and popular with audiences, *Cocoon* had in its time been considered a risky endeavor because of the primary focus: the elderly. Word on the street insisted that, beginning in the 1960s, the age of moviegoers had gradually diminished, and that films now should be produced with an eye to the twelve- to fifteen-year-old market. Any elderly character must, like Obi-Wan in *Star Wars*, serve as a mentor to the young leads. *Cocoon* was originally planned as a sparse chamber drama, and David Saperstein's original story was almost exclusively focused on geriatrics. Richard Zanuck and David Brown, savvy producers, instructed screenwriter Tom Benedek to beef up the role of the young sailor Jack and add a beautiful alien as his romantic interest. Also introduced in the process was the lengthy final chase, not unlike the one that concluded *E.T.*, which was included as a bonus for contemporary audiences. Though the elderly trio remained the center of attention, such commercial sidelights were wise business decisions. The strategy paid off, though at times large-scale excitement does threaten to overpower the nice little fable at the very heart of this big movie's center.

THE PLOT

Despite advanced ages, Florida retirement home residents Ben, Art, and Joe maintain the spirit of the adventurous little boy each once was. When they realize that a gorgeous vacation home not far away boasts an enormous (and, for them, inviting) swimming pool, the codgers secretly plan to slip inside when no one is around. What they don't anticipate is the rejuvenation that occurs. While the old-timers may look the same, their internal systems are re-energized, allowing each to recapture a lost sense, as the poet Wordsworth put it, "of splendour in the grass, of glory in the flower." They frolic in nearby greenery, then return home, where this newfound vitality astounds the women in their lives.

Unwittingly, however, the three have created a serious problem for Walter, a visitor from the planet Antarea. He has arrived to pick up colonists planted here ten thousand years earlier. With the help of a young charter boat skipper, Jack, Walter has collected the cocoons from the adjacent ocean. Water in the pool had been treated with a life-energy force to prepare the ancient aliens for their return trip. Now, however, this top-secret operation may quickly become common knowledge in the nearby town.

THE FILM

By the time he directed his first film, *Grand Theft Auto* in 1977, Ron Howard (1954–) was already famous, known as a gifted child actor on *The Andy Griffith Show* (1960–1968). He successfully navigated the difficult transition to teen idol via *American Graffiti* (George Lucas, 1973) and the television series, *Happy Days* (1974–1984), and he co-starred with John Wayne in that star's final film, *The Shootist* (1976).

Believing that he had already done pretty much everything he could as an actor, the then-twenty-four-year-old aspiring auteur was delighted when his debut film—its very title indicating a drive-in junk movie—won critical praise for its smart humor and assuredness of pacing. As a result, the Disney company Touchstone Pictures offered him a huge opportunity with *Splash* (1984). His seemingly effortless ability to bring that fantasy romance about a mermaid to

THE SPIELBERG-IZATION OF SCI-FI: *Though the famed director-producer had nothing to do with this Zanuck-Brown production, his notion of bringing back a sweet-spirited magic to the genre permeated* Cocoon *and many other genre films of the era. Courtesy: 20th Century Fox/Zanuck-Brown.*

believable life onscreen convinced Brown and Zanuck that Howard was the right director for *Cocoon*. The result is a non-generic sci-fi film driven by warm comedy drama (or "dramedy"), with elements of suspense added for a ticking-clock conclusion. The concept of space travel serves as a catalyst to human interactions, mostly set in the everyday world.

THEME

The desire to conquer the aging process via an elixir of youth has been present in the mythology of humankind since our predecessors first crawled out of caves. If a tale deals with the discovery of such a philosopher's stone, it rates as fantasy; if it is about the invention of such a force, then it is sci-fi. The narrative presented here is borrowed from "Kick the Can" (airdate: 2/9/1962), a classic episode of *The Twilight Zone*. In this episode, written by George Clayton Johnson, elderly people can momentarily regain their lost youth, but only if, in a paradigm that Serling shared with Walt Disney, they truly, fully *believe*. Add *Cocoon*, then, to the already discussed films of the mid-eighties that succeed in achieving *Zone*'s essence—along with a certain warmth that Serling and Disney, different as they might at first seem, had shared. The films appealed to a contemporary cinema hungry for the kind of entertainment that grounds sci-fi/fantasy themes in everyday reality and, better still, uses them for a positive vision. In *Cocoon*, as in *E.T.*, the friendly visitors from another world want to—and get to—go home.

TRIVIA

The role of Susan is played by Linda Harrison, who also played the silent girl in an animal-skin bikini in *Planet of the Apes* and *Beneath the Planet of the Apes* (Ted Post, 1970).

Other veterans from Hollywood's golden age also appear onscreen. Fred Astaire and Ginger Rogers dance in glorious black and white in *The Gay Divorcee* (1934). Stan Laurel and Oliver Hardy are glimpsed in a comedy bit from *The Flying Deuces* (1939), which the film's characters watch with the golden glow of nostalgia on TV.

Howard won the Saturn Award for best director of a science-fiction film. At age five, he had appeared in one of the earliest episodes of *The Twilight Zone*, "Walking Distance."

· · · · · · ·

THE FLY (1986)

—— RANKING: 60 ——

CREDITS

Twentieth Century Fox/Brooksfilms; David Cronenberg, dir.; George Langelaan, short story; Cronenberg, Charles Edward Pogue, scr.; Marc Boyman, Stuart Cornfeld, Kip Ohman, pro.; Howard Shore, mus.; Mark Irwin, cin.; Ronald Sanders, ed.; Carol Spier, prod. design; Rolf Harvey, art dir.; Louis Craig, Ted Ross, Chris Walas, Clark Johnson, F/X; Michael Bigelow, Dennis Dorney, special visual effects; Katherine Kean, Mitchell Rothzeid, special animation effects; 96 min.; Color; 1.85:1.

CAST

Jeff Goldblum (*Seth Brundle*); Geena Davis (*Veronica Quaife*); John Getz (*Stathis Borans*); Joy Boushel (*Tawny*); Leslie Carlson (*Dr. Brent Cheevers*); George Chuvalo (*Marky*); Michael Copeman (*2nd Man in Bar*); Carol Lazare (*Nurse*).

MOST MEMORABLE LINE

I'm working on something that will change the world
and human life as we know it.

SETH TO VERONICA ON FIRST MEETING

BACKGROUND

Playboy, which had premiered in 1953, won a reputation for publishing high-level science fiction along with their then-radical approach to a mainstream presentation of nudity. British journalist George Langelaan (1908–1972) submitted a horror item, which became a huge hit in the June 1957 issue. Fox picked up the film rights and hired James Clavell, later famous for his 1962 novel *King Rat*, to expand the story. The program picture, which came in at a little less than $700,000 ($200,000 more than a typical B movie, owing to color photography) earned a hefty $3 million at the box office, establishing that there was a market for intelligent science fiction.

With the success of John Carpenter's *The Thing* remake in 1982, Fox executives wondered if a remake of *The Fly* might achieve the same success. Edward Pogue's script remained true to the Grand Guignol quality of the original, the lead actually becoming a giant fly. When David Cronenberg (1943–) came on board, he had a different vision and rewrote extensively before production began.

THE PLOT

At a party thrown by Bartok Science Industries to introduce their wide variety of experimental products, Veronica, a reporter for *Particle* magazine, meets klutzy but charming Seth and heads over to his place to check out his landmark invention. Veronica is amazed at a teleportation device, which instantaneously moves any piece of inanimate matter from one pod to another. She becomes intimately involved with Seth. He continues his work, now attempting to move animate matter, though experiments with baboons prove disastrous. Believing he has the problem solved, Seth enters the pod alone. Or so he thinks; a common housefly has joined him.

THE FILM

The Canadian filmmaker retained two key ideas from Pogue's script: a gradual, rather than immediate, metamorphosis from human to monster, and the female lead realizing that she is pregnant. Cronenberg had already, in the low-budget *Rabid* (1977), revitalized vampire films. His beautiful blonde bloodsucker (Marilyn Chambers) is not a spectral figure like the vampires from Hammer Studios

FROM HIGH CAMP TO HIGH REALISM: *Whereas the enjoyably kitschy 1950s film had opted for a melodramatic approach with garish special effects, David Cronenberg's* The Fly *updated the premise with a low-key style. Here, Jeff Goldblum faces his moment of truth. Courtesy: 20th Century Fox.*

horror films, but rather an everyday young woman who, following a highway accident, undergoes a blood transfusion with unexpected results. Cronenberg approaches the ongoing premises of horror, fantasy, and sci-fi, always rethinking them as variations on his most characteristic idea: our unconscious fear of our bodily functions and the unspeakable things that go on just beneath the surface of the skin, which, if any of us happens to be at the wrong place at the wrong time, can transform us into "things." Cronenberg's characters appear to be contemporary, everyday people when we first meet them, speaking in the current vernacular, wearing clothing like everyone else on the street, and living in immediately recognizable homes. When the horror begins, it is effective because the audience associates with the relatively realistic characters they have come to know and recognize as similar to their friends . . . and themselves.

THEME

Debuting only a few years after the AIDS epidemic began, *The Fly* was considered by many critics to be an allegory for that disease. The Oscar-winning makeup by Chris Walas did produce the look of AIDS victims. Others argue against that interpretation inasmuch as sexual relations have nothing to do with the hero's sad fate.

The fear of computers—in particular, the horror that such artificial intelligences might make decisions when programming by humans proves insufficient—is as prevalent here as it is in an entirely different context in *2001: A Space Odyssey*. This anxiety would continue to develop as a theme in the years ahead.

On the one hand, Veronica's insistence on ending the pregnancy after she realizes that the embryo may be a monster prompted many feminists to hail the film as a pro-choice statement. On the other hand, those who have read Cronenberg's script, including sequences that were either left unfilmed or shot and discarded, come away with a different impression: Veronica chooses to have the baby, whatever the outcome.

TRIVIA

Cronenberg appears in a cameo, playing the gynecologist visited by Victoria after she discovers her pregnancy.

Following *The Thing*, this film continued to prove that gross-out effects, with blood and flesh splattering, that previously had been associated with drive-in cult films were now part of mainstream moviemaking.

Unlikely as it may seem, this sci-fi horror/thriller was produced by Mel Brooks's company, Brooksfilms, which mostly turned out broad comedies.

A horrific sequence in which Seth puts a baboon and a kitten into the pod at the same time, resulting in a weird "monkey-cat" creation, was cut from the release print, not so much because of its terrifying impact but because preview viewers felt it diminished any sympathy for the struggling hero.

· · · · · · ·

PREDATOR (1987)

—— RANKING: 62 ——

CREDITS

Twentieth Century Fox Film Corporation/Amercent Films; John McTiernan, dir.; Jim Thomas, John Thomas, scr.; John Davis, Lawrence Gordon, Joel Silver, pro.; Alan Silvestri, mus.; Donald McAlpine, cin.; Mark Helfrich, John F. Link, ed.; John Vallone, prod. design; Frank Richwood, Jorge Sainz, art dir.; Stan Winston, Jim Boulden, James Camomile, Daniel Cordero, Laurencio Cordero, Manuel Cordero, James Balsam, Scott Beattie, Michael Bigelow, Jeff Burks, Paul D. Johnson, F/X; 107 min.; Color; 1.85:1.

CAST

Arnold Schwarzenegger (*Dutch*); Carl Weathers (*Dillon*); Elpidia Carrillo (*Anna*); Bill Duke (*Mac*); Jesse Ventura (*Blain*); Sonny Landham (*Billy*); Richard Chaves (*Poncho*); R. G. Armstrong (*Gen. Phillips*); Shane Black (*Hawkins*); Kevin Peter Hall (*The Predator*, body); Peter Cullen (*The Predator*, voice).

MOST MEMORABLE LINE

If it bleeds, we can kill it.
DUTCH TO HIS MEN

BACKGROUND

As aspiring screenwriters, the Thomas brothers came up with the idea of crossing the two popular genres of the era: one-man army films starring the likes of Arnold Schwarzenegger and Sylvester Stallone and the brilliant and complex

F/X monster films, such as *Alien*. Coming off action hits, including *Lethal Weapon* (Richard Donner, 1987), producer Joel Silver (1952–) hoped to find a different twist and sensed this was it. He hired John McTiernan (1951–), who had all the right stuff to make a top action director; the two would create *Die Hard* in 1988. McTiernan immediately threw out the script's lumbering dog-headed monster, bringing aboard F/X genius Stan Winston from James Cameron's *The Terminator* (1984). While designing an original creature as unique and iconic as the one from that film, Winston conferred with Cameron, who suggested they use mandibles for the jaw. That suggestion provided the necessary final touch that pulled the package together.

THE PLOT

An elite special forces unit, led by veteran Dutch and his CIA contact Dillon, descends via helicopter into a thick Central American jungle. There, they wipe out a guerilla camp, excepting a lone woman, but they cannot find the political captives that Dutch had been ordered to rescue. He realizes the command was only a ruse to manipulate him to commit a massacre. Before the bickering between him and Dillon explodes, a wild card appears: a translucent seven-foot alien that blends with the jungle and turns the tables on the warriors.

THE FILM

Though certainly an action film, *Predator* offered something out of the ordinary by making the combat cerebral as well as physical. Even as Dutch despairs of beating this seemingly super-human creature, he realizes that the mud now covering him keeps the Predator from "seeing" his precise position owing to the natural camouflage of human body heat.

Schwarzenegger had long since proven himself adept at playing brutal men of action, such as the title character in *Conan the Barbarian* (John Milius, 1982). One scene here allowed him to transcend superman typecasting: at his wit's end, Dutch falls down, shivering and shaking, sobbing at his fate. This sense of vulnerability behind the stoic surface suggested for the first time that, perhaps like his idol, John Wayne, Schwarzenegger was capable of emotion, as well as action posturing, in his acting.

THEME

Though hardly intended as a message movie, *Predator* reached classic status in part due to implied themes. After realizing that his supposedly benign government sent him on what appeared to be an idealistic mission to save lives when, in fact, the objective was an all-too-realistic mass murder, Dutch, the true soldier in every sense, feels that his own personal code of honor has been violated. A certain cynicism, typical of the times, lifts the film out of jingoistic simplicity.

However unintentionally, *Predator* might be considered an anti-romantic predecessor to Cameron's *Avatar*, the earlier film suggesting the opposite attitude toward nature. In that more romantic vision, anything that blends with the jungle is "good" and the American military-industrial complex people are all "bad"; in *Predator*, such an idealized vision of the green world is reversed via a vision that equates amoral evil with natural (i.e., uncivilized) land. The film can be thought of as a cinematic predecessor of the controversial book *Iron John: A Book About Men* (Robert Bly, 1990), often perceived as a reaction against the women's movement of the 1970s with its insistence on "real" men recovering their basic instinct for blood combat and asserting their primitive maleness.

TRIVIA

Kevin Peter Hall, who portrays the Predator, also plays the helicopter pilot in the opening sequence.

Martial arts expert Jean-Claude Van Damme was originally slated to play the Predator.

The film was shot in Mexico, explaining why that country's most beautiful and beloved actress, Elpidia Carrillo, was cast as the female lead.

Shane Black, a screenwriter, was cast so that the producer Joel Silver would have him around to work, in their off hours, on future scripts, including *The Last Boy Scout* (Tony Scott, 1991).

Despite a strong start, the *Predator* franchise did not offer the artistic rewards reaped by *Alien*. *Predator 2* (Stephen Hopkins, 1990) is, at best, a routine sequel, lacking the creative imaginative rethinking of, say, *Aliens*. Worse is *Alien vs. Predator* (Paul W. S. Anderson, 2004), a botched attempt to revive the Frankenstein vs. Dracula monster duel classics from Universal during the 1940s.

CALL ME "YAUTJA": *Kevin Peter Hall wears the costume that would lead to a franchise. Writers Jim and John Thomas conceived of the Predator while F/X expert Stan Winston, during the design process, added the perfect final-touch element of mandibles. Courtesy: Amercent Films/20th Century Fox.*

```
.......
```

ROBOCOP (1987)

—— RANKING: 58 ——

CREDITS

Orion Pictures; Paul Verhoeven, dir.; Edward Neumeier, Michael Miner, scr.; Arne Schmidt, Neumeier, pro.; Basil Poledouris, mus.; Jost Vacano, Sol Negrin, cin.; Frank J. Urioste, ed.; William Sandell, prod. design; Gayle Simon, art dir.; Erica Edell Phillips, costumes; Rob Bottin, special makeup F/X; Robert Blalack, Beverly Bernacki, Ed Harker, optical effects; Kevin Kutchaver, Jo Martin, animation effects; George Muhs, visual effects; 102 min.; Color; 1.85:1.

CAST

Peter Weller (*Alex J. Murphy/RoboCop*); Nancy Allen (*Anne Lewis*); Dan O'Herlihy (*The Old Man*); Ronny Cox (*Dick Jones*); Kurtwood Smith (*Clarence J. Boddicker*); Miguel Ferrer (*Bob Morton*); Robert DoQui (*Sgt. Warren Reed*); Ray Wise (*Leon C. Nash*); Felton Perry (*Johnson*); Paul McCrane (*Emil M. Antonowsky*); Jesse D. Goins (*Joe P. Cox*); Del Zamora (*Kaplan*); Donna Keegan (*Rape Victim*); Leeza Gibbons (*Jess Perkins*).

MOST MEMORABLE LINE

He doesn't have a name. He has a program. He's a product.
MORTON TO LEWIS

BACKGROUND

A native of Amsterdam, Paul Verhoeven (1938–) first established a reputation on the continent for artistically rendered, intellectually stimulating films filled with so much graphic violence, explicit sexuality, and excessively rough language that observers were forced to redefine any pre-conceived boundaries separating exploitation and/or pornography and art of the most disturbing order. Apparently, Verhoeven relished that debate—even consciously intended it while designing the edgy love story *Turkish Delight* (1973), the World War II epic *Soldier of Orange* (1977), and the Hitchcock-like thriller *The Fourth Man* (1983). After Hollywood beckoned, Verhoeven surprised ardent fans when, with his second U.S.-financed feature, he turned sharply from reality-based (if highly stylized) movies to science fiction. Though *RoboCop* was produced on a tight ($13 million) budget, its success, critically and commercially, led to ever more elaborate and expensive projects, such as his 1990 classic, *Total Recall*.

"GEOMETRIC": *Rob Bottin, designer of the RoboCop costume featured in the film, numerous sequels, the spin-off, and franchise venues, has stated that this single word was the key to his concept. The costume also had to suggest "speed" and "aerodynamics." Peter Weller is the actor under all that visually astounding baggage. Courtesy: Orion.*

THE PLOT

Street crime and economic collapse have brought the city of Detroit to the edge of financial and social ruin. The constant atrocities, which have become a daily way of life for downtown dwellers, cause city politicians to abandon attempts to maintain law and order. Instead, they sign on with Omni Consumer Products, contracting with the mega-corporation to perform such dirty work. Problems arise when Omni's elderly chairman decides old Detroit cannot be salvaged and plans to level the crumbling downtown. In its place, Omni will build Delta, a city of the future. This creates a conflict of interest. His men-in-suits, who must deal with the urban population, propose genocide of the underclass as a solution. One of these suits, Jones, argues that robot cops are the best option; his competitor Morton prefers to go with cyborgs, half-human androids. When Alex Murphy, a newcomer to the force, is badly wounded in the line of duty, he becomes the subject of an experimental operation to create "RoboCop."

THE FILM

While studying a coming attraction poster for *Blade Runner* (1982), screenwriter Edward Neumeier wondered if the logical follow-up might be a movie about a cyborg cop. *Blade Runner*'s complex scenario suggested that such a conception pre-existed in that film; Harrison Ford's character, like Peter Weller's in *RoboCop*, is forced to face aspects of his own identity not initially obvious even to him. Other sources of inspiration for the RoboCop character, which quickly became a pop culture icon, included the British crime fighter *Judge Dredd* (1995) and *Rom* from Marvel Comics.

At the time of its release, *RoboCop* re-ignited an already heated controversy. A PG-13 rating had been created after a loud and often angry debate about extreme violence in the Spielberg/Lucas "family film" *Indiana Jones and the Temple of Doom* (1984). With *RoboCop*, Hollywood began producing superhero sci-fi that younger kids wanted to see, though the violence and language (if not, in this case, sex) concerned parents, the R rating notwithstanding. In fact, *RoboCop* might have been damned with an X rating if Orion had not trimmed away some sixty seconds of material that was considered over the top. This missing minute would eventually be restored in the director's cut.

THEME

Like most dystopian films, *RoboCop* projects an exaggeration (though hardly unwarranted) of problems already nascent in society. These representations are offered in the hope that heightened awareness of coming dangers might move people to do something about such situations while "there is still time . . . brother," as the final words in *On the Beach* (1959) plead. The bankruptcy of Detroit would become a fact in 2013. That robot warriors could be used not only stateside as Dirty Harry replicas but also in overseas combat, a projection here, has become a reality via the use of drones. The replacement of people by robots in the workplace, here specified as to police work, has in a more general sense been a subject of sci-fi since *Metropolis* (1927).

RoboCop was one of the first genre films to make radical ideology palatable to the mainstream by placing extremist themes in the relatively safe context of a future-world. The cooperation of corporate bigwigs with leaders of organized crime would have been deemed unacceptable within what were considered the respectable limitations of mass-market moviemaking less than a decade earlier. Just as important is the concept of our modern media being held responsible for widespread cynicism, owing to mindless shows: the appropriately titled fictional TV sitcom "It's Not My Problem!" and the "info-tainment" offered by Leeza Gibbons, incarnating a comedic version of herself as Jess Perkins, an ever-smiling purveyor of bad news presented in ten-second "bites" and sandwiched between feel-good stories.

One unintended theme, which emerges from a plot necessity, is an implied attack on underpaid workers who are going on strike. The total breakdown of order occurs after the police force, fed up with working conditions, walks off the job, allowing agents of chaos to take over. It's difficult not to take this as a statement against labor unions and the device of striking as a sometimes-necessary ultimatum when workers' issues aren't properly addressed. Both screenwriters were aghast when this interpretation was pointed out to them as they consider themselves left-leaning in orientation.

TRIVIA

Cashing in on the initial film's success were two sequels (1990 and 1993), four TV incarnations (1988, 1994, 1998–1999, and 2001), as well as video games in 1988, 1990, 1993, and 2003. These, along with the home video market, served to alter the popular notion, then in place, that such genre pieces sharply divided between the family market (*Star Wars*) and a considerably more adult constituency (*Blade Runner*). Once more, as the result of a single remarkable film, the genre itself would have to adjust to a series of new rules.

....•...

THE ABYSS (1989)

—— RANKING: 67 ——

CREDITS

Twentieth Century Fox Film Corporation/Lightstorm Entertainment; James Cameron, dir.; Cameron, scr.; Gale Anne Hurd, Van Ling, pro.; Alan Silvestri, mus.; Mikael Salomon, cin.; Conrad Buff IV, Joel Goodman, ed.; Leslie Dilley, prod. design; Peter Childs, art dir.; Ron Cobb, conceptual designer; Jean Giraud, conceptual artist; Thomas D. Krausz, Joseph A. Unsinn, F/X; Jon Alexander, visual effects; Ken Allen, matte artist; 139 min. (original theatrical print), 171 min. (special edition); Color; 2.20:1.

CAST

Ed Harris (*"Bud" Brigman*); Mary Elizabeth Mastrantonio (*Lindsey Brigman*); Michael Biehn (*Lt. Hiram Coffey*); Leo Burmester (*Catfish De Vries*); Todd Graff (*Alan "Hippy" Carnes*); John Bedford Lloyd (*Jammer Willis*); J. C. Quinn (*"Sonny" Dawson*); Kimberly Scott (*Lisa Standing*); Captain Kidd Brewer Jr. (*Finler*); George Robert Klek (*Wilhite*); Christopher Murphy (*Schoenick*); Adam Nelson (*Ensign Monk*).

MOST MEMORABLE LINE

We all see what we want to see.

LINDSEY, ON THE POSSIBLE EXISTENCE OF UNDERWATER ALIENS

BACKGROUND

Born in Ontario, Canada, James Cameron had always been fascinated with special effects. This interest developed further when his family moved to California. Though he worked as a truck driver, he would visit the University of Southern California on his time off to study on his own the remarkable worlds created by design artists. He also happened to attend a lecture on deep-sea diving and, while listening, conceived of a scenario about a group of undersea scientists.

After seeing *Star Wars*, Cameron decided that he had to find a way into the movie business. He became a miniature-maker for Roger Corman. Even after

OPERATION *UNDERSEA*: *Science fiction dealing with life under the sea—most notably,* 20,000 Leagues Under the Sea—*set the standard for James Cameron's reinvention of this subgenre. Mary Elizabeth Mastrantonio plays the awestruck diver who discovers E.T.-like creatures. Courtesy: Richard Foreman, photographer/20th Century Fox.*

making a breakthrough into major movies, he continued to mull over that early inspiration, realizing that a crew of ordinary guys would be more interesting than the great brains he'd planned for his characters. The success of the Spielberg films, *Close Encounters* (1977) and *E.T.* (1982), influenced the decision to make his aliens appealing rather than menacing.

THE PLOT

Bud is foreman of "Deep Core," an underwater oil platform, leading the search for new sources of energy. Without warning, a call comes in: the USS *Montana*, a submarine carrying nuclear missiles with Trident warheads has inexplicably gone down. As the Russians have already dispatched their crafts, the U.S. government doesn't have enough time to send forces into the area. So a special team of Navy SEALS, commanded by hard-edged warrior Coffey, and the oil platform's designer, Lindsey, will join the civilians to rescue survivors and protect the cargo. All this occurs even as a hurricane tears through the area. That Lindsey and Bud were once married complicates the situation further. While diving, Lindsey discovers something unexpected: underwater life forms she nicknames "N.T.I."—short for "non-terrestrial intelligence."

THE FILM

As with *Aliens*, Cameron broke new ground in terms of drastically redefining the genre. *The Abyss* is another one of those 1980s action-oriented films with a science-fiction twist, but this film also has the earmarks of a Cold War sea thriller such as *The Hunt for Red October* (1990). In the case of Cameron's film, however, the heroes must deal with underwater aliens, as well as Soviets. However, the theatrical print—edited by Cameron, who had final cut—employs those fantasy elements sparingly. The longer cut of the film explains, via inclusion of those originally missing sequences, why the *Montana* sank, why the aliens are playfully encountered by the female lead at mid-movie, and why they appear again to assist the seemingly doomed hero. Throughout much of the narrative, they are absent and, in fact, have been forgotten, by characters as well as by the audience, when Coffey becomes the antagonist. In previous films, once a sci-fi element has entered into the *fantastique*, it dominates; intriguingly, this movie does not divert from its realistic story line, but rather incorporates aliens into it.

The Abyss broke new ground not only within the genre but also in moviemaking. No film had previously been released with the THX LaserDisc format, and no feature film had prior to this featured any effects work achieved by

Adobe Photoshop. Though some Hollywood films had included computer-generated imagery for fantasy imaging, the process was considered crude, suitable only for lower-echelon projects. CGI had just reached a new level of sophistication, convincing Cameron that such effects could appear convincing. Their success here helped prove to Spielberg that for his upcoming *Jurassic Park*, CGI, rather than old-fashioned Ray Harryhausen tabletop models, could be used for the dinosaurs.

THEME

Antiwar in orientation, Cameron had been concerned that audiences had taken *Aliens* as a gleeful celebration of combat. *The Abyss* might be considered a corrective. The militaristic SEALs are portrayed here in a negative light. This decision to portray warriors, even America's own elite corps, in an unflattering manner set the stage for Cameron's upcoming *Avatar*.

TRIVIA

The studio insisted that Cameron's original three-hour print be cut. Current events had an impact on his decision-making. The film was to have included violent conflict between the U.S. military and the Soviets. It was precisely then that the first cracks, symbolic as well as literal, in the Berlin Wall appeared as the Cold War melted down. Realizing that such a battle might date his film, Cameron deleted those sequences.

· · · · · · ·

TOTAL RECALL (1990)

—— RANKING: 48 ——

CREDITS

Carolco Pictures; Paul Verhoeven, dir.; Philip K. Dick, story; Ronald Shusett, Dan O'Bannon, Jon Povill, Gary Goldman, scr.; Shusett, Buzz Feitshans, Andrew G. Vajna, pro.; Jerry Goldsmith, mus.; Jost Vacano, cin.; Carlos Puente, Frank J. Urioste, ed.; William Sandell, prod. design; José Rodríguez Granada, James E. Tocci, art dir.; Erica Edell Phillips, costumes; Ron Cobb, conceptual artist; Rob Bottin/The Bottin Effects Crew, F/X; Eric Brevig, B. J. Rack, visual effects; 113 min.; Color; 1.85:1.

THE WONDROUSLY WEIRD WORLD OF PHILIP K. DICK: *Arnold Schwarzenegger in a far more complex and sympathetic role than the original Terminator had allowed him. Dick's unique vision, augmented with remarkable F/X and elaborate action, created a more commercial project than that edgy author could ever have dreamed of. Courtesy: Carolco/Tri-Star.*

CAST

Arnold Schwarzenegger (*Douglas Quaid/Hauser*); Rachel Ticotin (*Melina*); Sharon Stone (*Lori*); Ronny Cox (*Cohaagen*); Michael Ironside (*Richter*); Marshall Bell (*George/Kuato*); Mel Johnson Jr. (*Benny*); Michael Champion (*Helm*); Roy Brocksmith (*Dr. Edgemar*); Ray Baker (*McClane*); Rosemary Dunsmore (*Dr. Lull*); David Knell (*Ernie*); Alexia Robinson (*Tiffany*); Dean Norris (*Tony*); Debbie Lee Carrington (*Thumbelina*); Robert Picardo ("*Johnnycab*," voice only).

MOST MEMORABLE LINE

If I am not me, then who the hell am I?

DOUG QUAID TO HAUSER

BACKGROUND

The success of their *Alien* screenplay convinced Ronald Shusett and Dan O'Bannon to expand on the Philip K. Dick short story "We Can Remember It for You Wholesale," originally published in 1966. This project had floundered for years. Studio bosses believed that, in the wake of the old-fashioned space-fantasy fun of *Star Wars*, such a thematically complicated piece would prove too obscure for a wide audience, particularly after the critical and commercial failure of *Dune* (1984). Mega-producer Dino De Laurentiis temporarily came on board. He wanted to cast Richard Dreyfuss, in the hopes that this film would serve as an unofficial follow-up to *Close Encounters* (1977). Bruce Beresford was briefly mentioned as a potential director. Then came David Cronenberg, who hoped to make *Total Recall* a more modest, artful, "serious" film, starring William Hurt, with a script that was scrupulously faithful to Dick's vision. When ending that relationship, Shusett stated: "No, no, we want to do *Raiders of the Lost Ark Go to Mars*."

When the rights to the piece opened up once more, Schwarzenegger negotiated a deal whereby Carolco Pictures would develop the work as a vehicle for his muscleman screen image. A fan of *RoboCop*, who at one point had been considered for that film's lead, Schwarzenegger, though not listed in the credits as a producer, controlled almost every element of the embryo project, and he insisted that Verhoeven direct the film. The team then hired special effects wizard Rob Bottin and other key members of his *RoboCop* team. For the forty-third script go-around, Gary Goldman came on board to create the third act that would wrap up all the diverse narratives, both those implicit in Dick's classic and others added along the way.

THE PLOT

Frightful dreams about adventures on Mars with a beautiful mystery woman, Melina, haunt Doug Quaid, a construction worker living in 2084. When Doug attempts to convince his gorgeous, seemingly loyal wife, Lori, that they ought to vacation on that colonized planet, she argues against it, suggesting Saturn as a more appealing destination. Then Doug spots an advertisement for ReKall, a company that has developed technology to implant memories within a person's mind, allowing one the satisfaction of having experienced events that never happened. Doug opts for the Mars trip, with himself cast as a secret agent. During the implantation process, something goes terribly awry. As it turns out, Doug is not Doug but someone named "Hauser," who actually did serve as a government assassin on the Red Planet. The false memories Doug wishes to enjoy are actual memories of his alter ego, making a successful memory implant impossible. Special forces are dispatched to capture Doug, or Hauser, or whoever he may be. His only hope: travel to Mars and live out his wildest fantasies—perhaps for the second time.

THE FILM

If *RoboCop* had pushed all the buttons as to the issue of violence in a mainstream sci-fi film, *Total Recall* in comparison makes that previous work of Verhoeven resemble Spielberg's *E.T.* The final cut (originally rated X until several shots were deleted or altered) contained grotesque F/X, intensely rough language, abundant nudity and sexual material, radical left political views, a demanding ideology, and graphic violence on a level previously unseen in a major studio project. At the time of release, the investors were concerned as to whether they would recoup their then-hefty $65+ million outlay. When *Total Recall* returned close to $270 million at the box office, Hollywood realized that *Blade Runner* had not been an anomaly: disturbing dystopian future films, characterized by intense violence, clearly could now succeed. This was the "new normal," the public flocking to a movie that would have been written off as offensive to middlebrow sensibilities less than a decade earlier. *Total Recall* laid the foundation for such future classics as *V for Vendetta* (2005), altering the shape of sci-fi.

THEME

Far ahead of his time, Dick dared address such issues as the questionable morality of mega-corporations, our society's ruthless exploitation of the working class and the underclass by raw capitalists, and the subjectivity of all existence, from an individual's personality to the surrounding cosmos. His ability to collapse metaphysics and theology into a singular vision crystallized the long-standing yin and yang interests in science and spirituality that have defined this genre from its outset. Also, Dick was among the first to explore now widely accepted ideas such as alternate history and paranoid schizophrenia as the only "normal" reaction to an entirely insane world.

TRIVIA

The day-after-tomorrow underground subway system did not have to be built because Mexico's existing underground almost perfectly suited the filmmakers' needs. Only the TV monitors were added for an even more futuristic look—one that has, from our own perspective, become a part of daily urban travel. Though the creative team chose miniatures over computer-generated effects due to the still primitive appearance of CGI, a mere two years later, the CGI look had advanced so radically that F/X experts embraced it. *Total Recall*, then, was one of the final films shot in the endearing miniature style.

· · · · · · ·

JURASSIC PARK (1993)

—— RANKING: 23 ——

CREDITS

Universal Pictures/Amblin Entertainment; Steven Spielberg, dir.; Michael Crichton, novel; Crichton, David Koepp, scr.; Kathleen Kennedy, Gerald R. Molen, Lata Ryan, pro.; John Williams, mus.; Dean Cundey, cin.; Michael Kahn, ed.; Rick Carter, prod. design; John Bell, William James Teegarden, art dir.; David Lowery, illustrator; Francesca Avila, Kim Derry, Terry W. King, Bruce Minkus, Stan Winston Studio, F/X; Barbara Affonso, chief model maker; Eric Armstrong, computer graphics animator; Christopher Evans, matte artist; 127 min.; Color; 1.85:1.

CAST

Sam Neill (*Dr. Alan Grant*); Laura Dern (*Dr. Ellie Sattler*); Jeff Goldblum (*Dr. Ian Malcolm*); Richard Attenborough (*John Hammond*); Bob Peck (*Robert Muldoon*); Martin Ferrero (*Donald Gennaro*); Joseph Mazzello (*Tim Murphy*); Ariana Richards (*Lex Murphy*); Samuel L. Jackson (*Ray Arnold*); BD Wong (*Henry Wu*); Wayne

Knight (*Dennis Nedry*); Gerald Molen (*Gerry Harding*); Miguel Sandoval (*Juanito Rostagno*); Cameron Thor (*Lewis Dodgson*); Richard Kiley (*Jurassic Park Tour Narrator*, voice only).

MOST MEMORABLE LINE
I'm simply saying that life . . . uh . . . finds a way.
IAN MALCOLM TO HAMMOND ON THE UNEXPECTED ABILITY
OF DNA DINOSAURS TO REPRODUCE

BACKGROUND
Spielberg shot *Jurassic Park* and *Schindler's List* back to back, the former to reassert his status as existing in a dead-heat tie with Lucas as the greatest mass entertainer since Walt Disney, the latter to reveal his ability to make "serious" films and be recognized, finally, as an artist. Universal only agreed to finance *Schindler's List* as a relatively low-budget film ($22 million) if Spielberg signed to direct the more expensive ($68 million) *Jurassic Park*.

THE PLOT
A paleontologist, Grant, his younger team member Ellie, a brilliant mathematician named Malcolm, and a corporate lawyer all arrive on (the mythical) Isla Nublar, off the coast of Costa Rica. They have been summoned by an ecstatic and eccentric entrepreneur, John Hammond, who wants to share the glories of his revolutionary theme park. The park is home to dinosaurs, the DNA for which was drawn from blood found within mosquitoes that had been preserved in amber some 65 million years earlier.

THE FILM
Spielberg originally had been intrigued by the chance to do an exercise with tabletop model dinosaurs on the order of those seen in such films as *King Kong* (1933) and one of his own favorites, *The Valley of Gwangi* (1969), which included a dinosaur presented as part of a public performance, a primitive predecessor to this more up-to-date film involving an actual theme park. Critics had described Spielberg as a maker of theme park movies, the impact of watching an Indiana Jones adventure similar to that of taking a theme park ride—with, of course, future park rides resembling sequences in that movie. *Jurassic Park* fulfilled such a notion: here is a theme park movie about a theme park. Tabletop effects, perfected by Ray Harryhausen in films such as *Gwangi*, were time-consuming and costly, but Spielberg initially chose this option because of his

THE SWEET SIDE OF THUNDER LIZARDS: *Dr. Alan Grant (Sam Neill) convinces Tim (Joseph Mazzello) and Lex (Ariana Richards) that the brachiosaur is not to be feared. Steven Spielberg's film helped erase the false myth that dinosaurs were hulking, dim-witted, slow-moving beasts. Courtesy: Amblin Entertainment/Universal Pictures.*

disdain for the then-tacky look of computer-generated effects. However, when his friend Lucas showed him the incredible advances in F/X, Spielberg reversed his decision, proving that CGI had come of age.

A key reason that Spielberg and Crichton were able to get along well, despite their differing views of the world in general and this film in particular, is that both were dedicated to portraying dinosaurs as highly intelligent creatures, rather than the lumbering dumb beasts of many old movies. Until then, the only time that dinosaurs had been portrayed as able to cleverly solve problems was in Disney's *Fantasia* (1940).

THEME

Crichton was very aware that his own conservative view of life stood at odds with Spielberg's liberal vision and, as a result, the film would not so much present Crichton's ideology as reverse it. In the novel, chaos theory—for humans to impose a simplistically designed system on a complex natural reality can lead only to disaster—mathematically determines that the ending will be dark, humankind doomed to extinction by such terrible experiments. Crichton's pessimism was replaced by Spielberg's Disney-like optimism, leading to a sunny ending in which, despite the horrors, humans can correct their mistakes and, with the danger gone, all's once more right with the world.

TRIVIA

Harrison Ford was the original choice to play the lead. By this time, however, he had become a huge star, with the accompanying huge salary demands. *Jurassic*'s budget experts estimated that, if Ford was hired, considering the limit in terms of the financing, two or three species of dinosaur would have to be eliminated from the F/X budget. As those dinosaurs would be the greatest box-office lure, it was decided to go with the lesser-known Sam Neill in the lead.

In one of the film's most beloved exchanges, Hammond mentions to Ian Malcolm that, on its first day of operation way back in 1956, many of Disney-land's favorite rides broke down. In response, Ian notes, "Yes, but . . . if the Pirates of the Caribbean breaks down, the pirates don't eat the tourists." In truth, the Pirates ride was not a part of the original Disney theme park, but was added some eleven years later.

Crichton modeled Grant on a real paleontologist, Jack Horner (1946–), though the resemblance as to physique and personality is far more emphasized in the book than in the film.

· · · · · · ·

STARGATE (1994)

—— RANKING: 86 ——

CREDITS

Studio Canal+/Centropolis Film Productions/Carolco Pictures/MGM; Roland Emmerich, dir.; Emmerich, Dean Devlin, scr.; Devlin, Oliver Eberle, Ute Emmerich, Mario Kassar, Joel B. Michaels, pro.; David Arnold, mus.; Karl Walter Lindenlaub, cin.; Derek Brechin, Michael J. Duthie, ed.; Holger Gross, prod. design; Frank Bollinger, Peter Murton, art dir.; Joseph A. Porro, costumes; David P. Barton, Jake Garber, special makeup effects; Dave C. Avillo, Paul Barnes, creature art department; Jeff Kleiser, additional creative design; 121 min. (release print), 128 min. (extended version), 130 min. (director's cut); Color; 2.35:1.

THE SPACE TUNNEL: *Lewis Carroll's Alice slipped through a rabbit's hole, down to Wonderland, but in contemporary sci-fi, such portals have been displaced by a wormhole through which travelers can defy the space-time continuum. Carlos Lauchu, as the Egyptian-like Anubis, guards the stargate. Courtesy: Canal+/Centropolis/Metro-Goldwyn-Mayer.*

Kurt Russell (*Col. Jonathan O'Neil*); James Spader (*Dr. Daniel Jackson*); Alexis Cruz (*Skaara*); Viveca Lindfors (*Catherine Langford*); Mili Avital (*Sha'uri*); Jaye Davidson (*Ra*); John Diehl (*Lt. Kawalsky*); Leon Rippy (*Gen. W. O. West*); Carlos Lauchu (*Anubis*); Djimon Hounsou (*Horus*); Erick Avari (*Kasuf*).

MOST MEMORABLE LINE

I created you; now, I will destroy you.
RA TO VISITORS FROM EARTH

BACKGROUND

Stargate (re)introduced the public to a theory that had been discussed at least since the beginning of the twentieth century. Though the term "wormhole" would not be coined until 1957 by American physicist John Archibald Wheeler, the idea of a wormhole, possibly a remnant of the Big Bang, had been conceived by German mathematician Hermann Weyl in the early 1920s. If such a space portal might indeed exist, a person could presumably make a quantum leap, transporting from one corner of the cosmos to another in a split second and avoiding the limitations inherent in the space-time continuum. Also known as the Einstein-Rosen bridge, such a possibility had been included in the writings of such "serious" science-fiction authors as Isaac Asimov.

Though the term "wormhole" had not been used in *2001: A Space Odyssey*, the third act of Kubrick's film approximated such a journey in a then-appropriate 1960s psychedelic style. That classic's first act, in which a monolithic needle descends during prehistorical times, visualized theories that were simultaneously proposed by Erich von Däniken (1935–), grandfather of what today is referred to as "ancient astronaut theory," in *Chariots of the Gods?* (1968). Everything from rock formations at Stonehenge to the pyramids in ancient Egypt might be better understood if one is willing to accept that past extraterrestrial visitors purposefully altered our evolution on planet Earth.

THE PLOT

In 1928, a child, Cathy, is present at a Giza dig in Egypt when her archaeologist father unearths a gigantic ring, dating back to the Fourth Dynasty. Sixty-five years later, the elderly Catherine listens in on a controversial lecture delivered by a young linguistics expert, Daniel Jackson. Dr. Jackson tries without success to convince fellow academics that early societies had to have been influenced by extraterrestrials, re-directing life on Earth for their own purposes. Shortly,

Daniel joins a team working in secret at a restricted U.S. Air Force base. He has been recruited to help them decipher encoded images on "the ring," that portal through space. By stepping inside its confines, Daniel and a military unit, led by Colonel O'Neil, will bypass all preconceived limitations as to space travel and emerge momentarily in a distant world.

THE FILM

Roland Emmerich (1955–) shot most of the outdoor sequences—both those set on Earth and in the alternative realm—in Arizona, not far from where Spielberg grew up. Part of the appeal of *Stargate* derives from Emmerich's ability to convey a full Spielbergian sense of wonderment at the mysteries of the universe as perceived by that rare adult who has held on to "primal sympathy." The poet William Wordsworth used that term to express the vision of childlike acceptance of what most adults have lost the ability to acknowledge in the process of becoming "mature" and jaded. *Close Encounters* had also used the setting of the American Southwest for a sense of a stark, spiritualized beauty that even the greatest of scientific minds cannot explain away. So as to achieve just such a vision of a golden world, Emmerich arranged his shooting schedule so that key sequences were filmed just before sunset, when the desert takes on an appealingly eerie—and quietly profound—aura.

Initially, there were two scripts: in his version, Dean Devlin hoped to play out one of his favorite films, *Lawrence of Arabia* (1962), on a faraway planet; Emmerich's script focused on an ancient spacecraft located beneath the Great Pyramid, similar to *Five Million Years to Earth* (1967). The unique appeal that would come to be represented by the simple term "stargate" (leading to an impressive franchise) emerged when they realized that by combining the two concepts, the writers could satisfyingly flesh out one another's stories.

The striking appearance of the stargate, without which the film could not work as it does, was designed and then built by Jeff Kleiser, his work augmented by a team of more than forty artists and craftsmen.

THEME

Like so much sci-fi, this work attempts to re-explain the concept of God—or, in the case of ancient civilizations, gods—in the scientific terminology that began to develop during the late nineteenth century and has since then challenged earlier beliefs. Here the essential conceit is that those bizarre images we see in relics, in which bodies of men are topped with the heads of beasts, are not artistic or religious conceptions imaginatively designed to symbolically express ideas, but rather realistic depictions of creatures who descended from the stars. A "god," in this reconfiguration, is any being that possesses more knowledge and is further advanced than those who are overwhelmed by the seemingly invincible invaders. Ultimately, a god is not something that does or does not exist but is instead the manner in which a living creature is perceived by inferiors. When sci-fi is used as the conduit for such ideology, an additional theme is invoked: secular scientific vocabulary and religious or mythological language are two unique forms of communicating precisely the same ideas about meaning and mystery in the universe.

TRIVIA

Always open about his homosexuality, filmmaker Emmerich continually searches for some means by which he can add gender identification to any current project. Here, this is manifested in the casting of Jaye Davidson, best known for playing a transgender character in *The Crying Game* (Neil Jordan, 1992).

Alexis Cruz and Erick Avari revived their roles as Skaara and Kasuf for the TV series *Stargate SG-1* (1997–2007).

Egyptology student Omar Zuhdi had, ten years earlier, submitted a suspiciously similar script to Emmerich, which was rejected. Zuhdi sued and received an out-of-court settlement.

· · · · · · ·

STRANGE DAYS (1995)

—— RANKING: 84 ——

CREDITS

Lightstorm Entertainment/Twentieth Century Fox; Kathryn Bigelow, dir.; James Cameron, Jay Cocks, scr.; Cameron, Steven-Charles Jaffe, pro.; Graeme Revell, mus.; Matthew F. Leonetti, cin.; Cameron, Howard E. Smith, ed.; Lilly Kilvert, prod. design; John Warnke, art dir.; Donald Frazee, Terry D. Frazee, Gregor Joackim, James S. Trois, F/X; Ellen Mirojnick, costumes; John Eaves, model maker; Sandina Bailo-Lape, Tom Barwick, Dennis Thorpe, foley; 145 min.; Color; 2.35:1.

CAST

Ralph Fiennes (*Lenny Nero*); Angela Bassett (*Lornette "Mace" Mason*); Juliette Lewis (*Faith Justin*); Tom Sizemore (*Max Peltier*); Michael Wincott (*Philo Gant*); Vincent D'Onofrio (*Burton Steckler*); Glenn Plummer (*Jeriko One*); Brigitte Bako (*Iris*); Richard Edson (*Tick*); William Fichtner (*Dwayne Engelman*); Josef Sommer (*Palmer Strickland*); Joe Urla (*Keith*); Nicky Katt (*Joey Corto*); Michael Jace (*Wade Beemer*); Louise LeCavalier (*Cindy "Vita" Minh*); David Carrera (*Duncan*); Jim Ishida (*Mr. Fumitsu*); Todd Graff (*Tex Arcana*); Malcolm Norrington (*Replay*); Anais Munoz (*Diamanda*); Ted Haler (*Tow Truck Driver*); Rio Hackford (*Bobby*); Kylie Ireland (*Stoned Girl*); Honey Labrador (*Beach Beauty*).

MOST MEMORABLE LINE

Paranoia is just reality on a finer scale.
PHILO TO FAITH

BACKGROUND

Following a two-year marriage, John Cameron and Kathryn Bigelow (1951–) divorced in 1991. Nonetheless, when Cameron began work on his script for *Strange Days*, he knew at once that the phantasmagoric quality associated with Bigelow films—the edgy biker movie *The Loveless* (1982), the vampire thriller *Near Dark* (1987), and the surfer action flick *Point Break* (1991)—was precisely what he needed. The project evolved into the most ambitious example of cyberpunk to appear in a mainstream movie, cinematically conveyed via an aesthetic that portrays a near-future dystopia as the only possible result of high-tech settings filled with low-life characters. In the cyberpunk world, an endless flow of information from more sources than can possibly be comprehended leads in part to a total breakdown in the social order. That scenario serves as this film's starting point.

THE PLOT

Forty-eight hours before New Year's Eve, 1999, street hustler Lenny Nero is marketing illegal wares in a Los Angeles that resembles a nightmare in which the future world of Kubrick's *A Clockwork Orange* (1971) merges with the neon-lit New York decadence that defines Martin Scorsese's *Taxi Driver* (1976). Nero sells discs containing state-of-the-art virtual reality moments. He is devotedly loved by macho woman, limo driver Mace, but he is obsessed with Faith, who left him to live with a record producer who promised to make her a star. Reconnecting with his inamorata, melancholic Nero meets Jeriko, a rap star with heavy-duty connections to the city's downtrodden. A disc that reveals a brutal rape and murder comes into Nero's possession. Realizing that there may be political consequences to a seemingly random crime, Nero enlists the aid of best friend Max, a former cop, to help him identify the killer before Faith becomes his next victim.

NEAR FUTURE: *By setting a story—in this case, in 1999—only a few years after the film was made, the filmmaker can critically comment on "today's" lifestyle by exaggerating current problems to make an audience more fully aware of them. Angela Bassett helps Ralph Fiennes escape in Kathryn Bigelow's dystopian vision. Courtesy: Lightstorm Ent./20th Century Fox.*

THE FILM

As to claims that Bigelow celebrated the coming end of the world as we know it in *Strange Days*, the filmmaker replied: "If you hold a mirror up to society, and you don't like what you see, you can't fault the mirror." Armageddon appears on the horizon every moment in her near-millennial world, a radical version of the fear of atomic oblivion that marked the post-WWII era. Not surprisingly, there are no heroes, only antiheroes in this grunge cosmos. Alienated lone wolves, hard-boiled on the surface if romantic deep down, wander mean streets that resemble exaggerations of those that appeared in the late 1940s in film noirs and cheap paperback bus-station books.

Film critics employed such terms as "ferocious," "kinetic," and "visionary" to describe Bigelow's style. As Janet Maslin of the *New York Times* noted, "No one will ever say she directs like a girl." If a male director had depicted rape in so intense and in-your-face terms—Bigelow insists that we see that the victim is being forced to experience the unspeakable thrills her captor enjoys—it goes without saying that he would have been criticized for creating a sexist cinema of the most exploitive nature. But such a controversial depiction is precisely what Bigelow flirts with in work after work; it is the essence of her unique edge and what makes her not a "woman director," but a director who happens to be a woman. Shortly before Bigelow became the first female ever to receive a Best Director Oscar in 2010 for *The Hurt Locker*, Cameron insisted, "She'll be of a mind that . . . I want to win for the work. [Not] because I'm a woman."

THEME

Early in the film, as Nero listens to an eclectic mix of music, the phrase "every little thing gonna be alright" can be heard. These words from the song "Three Little Birds" first appeared on a 1977 Bob Marley and Wailers album, released as a single in 1980. Here, in a musical nutshell, is the film's social theme. Jeriko is a fictionalized American version of that reggae great, and though his music of choice is rap, he perceives song as a means by which he might incite a revolution. Our own downtrodden, who live in a Third World within the upscale American landscape, could achieve some measure of social justice once their initially marginalized music reaches the mainstream. Like Jeriko in the film, Marley (1945–1981) was shot in 1976, in what many believe was an act of retaliation for his political attacks on fascistic power. Unlike Jeriko, Marley survived his assassination attempt.

The film's title is a tribute to the second album recorded by the Doors, inspired in part by Jim Morrison's views on the radically changing street scene in mid-sixties New York City. The title cut was to have been included in the film, but when legal rights to the Doors version proved too difficult to secure, the cover version by the heavy metal band Prong was used.

· · · · · · ·

TWELVE MONKEYS (1995)

—— RANKING: 29 ——

CREDITS

Universal Pictures/Atlas Entertainment; Terry Gilliam, dir.; David Webb Peoples, Janet Peoples, scr.; Charles Roven, pro.; Paul Buckmaster, mus.; Roger Pratt, cin.; Mick Audsley, ed.; Jeffrey Beecroft, prod. design; William Ladd Skinner, art dir.; Julie Weiss, costumes; Shirley Montefusco, Vincent Montefusco, Anthony Simonaitis, F/X; Richard Bain, Martin Body, Susi Roper, Kent Houston, digital effects; 129 min.; Color; 1.85:1.

CAST

Bruce Willis (*James Cole*); Madeleine Stowe (*Kathryn Railly*); Brad Pitt (*Jeffrey Goines*); Christopher Plummer (*Dr. Goines*); David Morse (*Dr. Peters*); Frank Gorshin (*Dr. Fletcher*); Joey Perillo (*Det. Franki*); Jon Seda (*Jose*); Michael Chance (*Scarface*); Christopher Meloni (*Lt. Halperin*); Joseph Melito (*Young Cole*).

MOST MEMORABLE LINE

Wouldn't it be great if I was crazy? Then the world would be okay.
COLE TO KATHRYN

BACKGROUND

Before the French New Wave introduced greater freedom as to what could and, in the future, would be portrayed onscreen, an earlier coterie of cineastes paved the way with experimental filmmaking. Collectively known as the Left Bank Cinema movement, their company included Alain Resnais, Agnès Varda, and Chris Marker (born Christian François Bouche-Villeneuve, 1921–2012).

AUTEUR AND GENRE: *Every Terry Gilliam film offers a meditation on the meaning of madness.* With Twelve Monkeys, *the filmmaker strikingly presented his highly personal vision within the audience's expectations for an action-oriented sci-fi film. Courtesy: Atlas Entertainment/Classico/Universal.*

Marker's unique projects, often featuring sci-fi plots, pushed film ever closer to the surreal.

Creating visual essays, rather than conventional stories, Marker is best known today for his 1962 *La jetée* (airline portal). The film reveals his intellectual background as a student of philosophy and his workaday experience as a journalist. The latter helped him grasp how essential photographs are to the reception of any article. *La jetée* relates its fantasy in the manner of a documentary, with a succession of still photographs (aka "photo montage") accompanied by a somber voice-over. A boy witnesses the murder of a man at Orly airport in Paris. The memory (or was it but a dream?) haunts him throughout his life—until, in due time, all becomes clear. The man whose death he saw was himself, adult and child incarnations of a person in one place at the same second owing to a trick of fate and the concept of time travel. Though only twenty-eight minutes long (thus not eligible for inclusion here), the film altered everything, its groundbreaking style proving that sci-fi/fantasy could be rescued from abject commerciality and returned to the avant-garde. A serious approach had been restored to the genre.

THE PLOT

In a dystopian future, humans are forced to live underground owing to the poisonous surface. Scientists, having mastered the art of time travel, wonder if it might it be possible to send someone back to 1996, shortly before a deadly virus was released into the atmosphere; locate the about-to-be perpetrator; and obtain a sample of the "super-bug," which might be used to create an antidote. Criminal James Cole agrees to the mission in exchange for a pardon if he is successful. The only real clue is an underground political, apparently terrorist, movement called the "Twelve Monkeys." But as time travel remains imprecise, Cole arrives six years early. Erratic behavior causes him to be institutionalized, alongside Jeffrey Goines, leader of an animal rights movement. Cole's psychiatrist, the gifted and sensitive Kathryn Railly, intuits that there may indeed be something special about this patient, who gives her a sense of déjà vu that they've already met.

THE FILM

The only American-born member of the otherwise all-British comedy ensemble Monty Python, Terry Gilliam (1940–) grew up in Minnesota and Los Angeles. His favorite reading was *Mad* magazine, which guided him toward the off-the-wall humor that would in time characterize his body of work. Moving to England in hopes of avoiding the increasingly threatening social upheaval of the 1960s, Gilliam found work in advertising, which then led to experiments with strip cartooning and animation. As a result of the latter, he began collaborating with Eric Idle, Terry Jones, and Michael Palin. Ever more intrigued with the idea of directing, Gilliam helmed the uneven but appealing sci-fi/fantasy *Time Bandits* (1981), then moved on to dystopian fiction with an Orwellian orientation with *Brazil* (1985).

Gilliam's interest in both these genres was combined in *Twelve Monkeys*, which also provided the filmmaker with an opportunity to create a feature-length homage to his beloved Alfred Hitchcock. At one point in the film, hero and heroine hide in a theater where *North by Northwest*, *The Birds*, and *Vertigo* are playing on a triple bill. The plot of *Twelve Monkeys*, which has a seemingly mismatched couple traveling cross-country, recalls the narrative line in *North by Northwest*. When Bruce Willis and Madeline Stowe stand alone in an abandoned cathedral-like construction, birds fly up and out a broken window in a scene reminiscent of *The Birds*. When Stowe changes from brunette to blonde, she repeats in a ritualistic manner the action in which Judy, played by Kim

Novak, transforms into Madeleine in *Vertigo*, Bernard Hermann's score from the classic used here to emphasize the parallel.

THEME

Like many of Hitchcock's greatest films, *Twelve Monkeys* deals with madness. Cole is considered "crazy" because he perceives reality differently than the majority who constitute the norm. His screams for attention appear identical to those of other would-be prophets, standing on virtually every street corner and being ignored by the public passing by such seeming nutcases. But what if that person who is thrown into a madhouse for claiming to be sent back in time is correct—and the only hope for our planet's survival? As in so much sci-fi and imaginative fiction (dating back at least to Edgar Allan Poe, with many *Twilight Zones* included), madness is posited as a subjective, rather than objective, state. People are neither mad nor sane, but rather considered one or the other according to contexts.

The film's connection to the long heritage of what we now call sci-fi is expressed openly by Dr. Goines: the great responsibility we assume when we experiment can be traced back through the Cold War era of *Dr. Strangelove* to Prometheus's stealing fire from the gods. Never, though, have the threats of the improper use of the technology we develop been as serious as in our time.

TRIVIA

Asian filmmaker Mamoru Oshii admits to having unofficially remade *La jetée* at least twice in his best-known non-anime works: *The Red Spectacles* (1987) and *Avalon* (2001). Director Mira Nair has also said that moments in her *The Namesake* (2006) are "references" to indelible images from the featurette.

······

OPEN YOUR EYES/ABRE LOS OJOS (1997)

—— RANKING: 19 ——

CREDITS

Canal+ España/Las Producciones del Escorpión; Alejandro Amenábar, dir.; Amenábar, Mateo Gil, scr.; Ana Amigo, Fernando Bovaira, José Luis Cuerda, pro.; Amenábar, Mariano Marín, mus.; Hans Burmann, cin.; María Elena Sáinz de Rozas, ed.; Wolfgang Burmann, art dir.; Concha Solera, costumes; Reyes Abades, Colin Arthur, F/X; Alberto Esteban, Ricardo G. Elipe, Luis Guerra, visual effects; 117 min.; Color; 1.85:1.

CAST

Eduardo Noriega (*César*); Penelope Cruz (*Sofía*); Chete Lera (*Antonio*); Fele Martínez (*Pelayo*); Najwa Nimri (*Nuria*); Gérard Barray (*Duvernois*); Jorge de Juan (*Encargado*); Miguel Palenzuela (*Commisario*).

MOST MEMORABLE LINE

Open your eyes!

SOFÍA AND/OR NURIA TO CÉSAR

BACKGROUND

Spanish-Chilean filmmaker Alejandro Amenábar (1972–) teamed with his university friend Mateo Gil (1972–) to co-write screenplays that Amenábar would direct, the style drawing on film classics he adored. Their first collaborative success, *Tesis* (1996), directly addressed the manner in which violent cinema may affect, as well as reflect, ever-escalating brutality in society.

The filmmakers approached their edgy, intellectual concept using the tradition of Hitchcock thrillers as their aesthetic template. That holds true for *Abre los ojos*, which draws heavily from *Vertigo*: two beautiful women become confused and inseparable in the antihero's mind as one beauty morphs into the other. When Sofía steps toward César, the camera assuming the male point of view, she momentarily appears to emerge from a metaphysical plane of existence. The image here is a self-conscious replica of Kim Novak, following her transformation from one character to another, as she approaches James

OFFICIAL
SELECTION
SUNDANCE
FILM
FESTIVAL

eduardo
noriega

penélope
cruz

OPEN
YOUR
EYES

(Abre Los Ojos)

FACE OF A WOMAN: *In a rare move, Penelope Cruz portrayed the female lead in both the original arthouse version of this story and the inferior Hollywood remake, starring Tom Cruise. Courtesy: Redbus/Live Entertainment.*

Stewart. *Abre los ojos* ends with its protagonist's fall from a high building, César expressing his own fear of heights, or vertigo.

THE PLOT

At first glance, César would appear to have it all. Young, handsome, wealthy, and unattached, he's the envy of friends like Pelayo, an ordinary fellow who expresses awe at his pal's conquests of beautiful women. Pelayo has become enamored with Sofía, an artistic free spirit who is infatuated with César. Sofía's refusal to surrender as swiftly as other beautiful women inspires in César emotion that reaches beyond lust: she may just be the great love of his life. As the relationship just begins, César makes the mistake of taking a drive with a cast-off lover, Nuria. Suicidal, she crashes her car, apparently dying. César survives, but his once-attractive face is mutilated. Is it possible Sofía, now a street mime, may yet love César for his inner qualities—if indeed he has any?

THE FILM

Abre los ojos is filled with references to thrillers that reach back at least to *The Cabinet of Dr. Caligari* (1920). In each, the framing device occurs in a mental institution in which the doctors may well be crazier than the patients, and the head doctor—so seemingly sympathetic to the protagonist—may be an evil force obsessed with dominating another human being through mind control. If, that is, César is experiencing this. He may be dreaming all that occurs, the doctor only a character in the nightmarish hospital. If that's the case, then where is César "really"—if reality can truly be calculated, which the film appears to deny. Even the name "César" references *Caligari*, Cesare being the mad psychiatrist's zombie-like servant.

By design or coincidence, *Abre los ojos* recalls individual episodes of *The Twilight Zone*. The concept of characters who believe themselves to be living, breathing human beings but are part of the protagonist's dream recalls "Shadow Play." Similarities in other episodes include: a woman finding herself displaced by a twin/competitor in "Mirror Image"; a man terrified to go to sleep because his nightmares are more real to him than reality in "Perchance to Dream"; the notion of physical beauty as subjective in "The Eye of the Beholder"; and the hiding of one's reality behind a mask in "The Masks." Also referenced is *Star Trek*: César preferring a fantasy of perfection with a lost love following his accident repeats the pattern of Captain Pike's alternative reality and virtual existence in "The Menagerie."

THEME

The preponderance of influences, with nonstop homages to examples from popular culture of the past, eventually moves beyond the limits of simple referencing to become the true theme, as well as a key idea in other post-modern films. What today's leading moviemakers know best is the tradition of movies and television. *Abre los ojos* contains several recurring sci-fi themes: the desire for immortality, as incarnated here by the cryptic Life Extension corporation, and the question of spirituality, apparent in the recurring line of dialogue "Do you believe in God?" Like *Tesis*, if less obviously so, this is a movie about movies: what they are in and of themselves and what they mean to those who consume them.

TRIVIA

In addition to previous films, *Abre los ojos* was in part inspired by Pedro Calderón's play, *Life is a Dream* (*La vida es sueño*, 1635).

Tom Cruise, a fan of the film, picked up the rights to do an American remake. Directed by Cameron Crowe and released in 2001, with Penelope Cruz repeating her role, *Vanilla Sky* succeeded at the box office but lacked the complexity of theme and the iconoclastic style that qualified the original as a true classic with science-fiction aficionados and general audiences.

· · · · · · ·

THE FIFTH ELEMENT (1997)

—— RANKING: 71 ——

CREDITS

Gaumont/Columbia Pictures; Luc Besson, dir.; Besson, Robert Mark Kamen, scr.; John A. Amicarella, Patrice Ledoux, Iain Smith, pro.; Eric Serra, mus.; Thierry Arbogast, cin.; Sylvie Landra, ed.; Dan Weil, prod. design; Ira Gilford, Ron Gress, Michael Lamont, Jim Morahan, Kevin Phipps, art dir.; Jean-Paul Gaultier, costumes; Scott Nicholas Amendolare, model maker; William Aldridge, Nick Allder, Norman Baillie, Neil Corbould, F/X; Thaine Morris, pyrotechnics; Eric Barba, digital artist; Chris Barton, animatronic model designer; Jean Giraud, designer; 126 min.; Color; 2.35:1.

TOMORROWLAND: *Gary Oldman, Bruce Willis, and Milla Jovovich co-starred in Luc Besson's fable about a cabdriver of the future who has more than a little in common with "Harry Canyon" from* Heavy Metal. *Courtesy: Gaumont/Columbia.*

CAST

Bruce Willis (*Korben Dallas*); Gary Oldman (*Jean-Baptiste Emanuel Zorg*); Ian Holm (*Father Vito Cornelius*); Milla Jovovich (*Leeloo*); Chris Tucker (*Ruby Rhod*); Maïwenn (*Diva Plavalaguna*); Luke Perry (*Billy*); Brion James (*Gen. Munro*); Tommy "Tiny" Lister (*Pres. Lindberg*); Lee Evans (*Fog*); Charlie Creed-Miles (*David*); Tricky (*Right Arm*); John Neville (*Gen. Staedert*); John Bluthal (*Prof. Pacoli*); Christopher Fairbank (*Mactilburgh*); Kim Chan (*Mr. Kim*); Sibyl Buck (*Zorg's Secretary*); Indra Ové, Nicole Merry, Stacey McKenzie (*VIP Stewardesses*).

MOST MEMORABLE LINE

Time not important; only life important.

MONDOSHAWAN IN THE 1914 PROLOGUE

BACKGROUND

Luc Besson (1959–) was not, like Lucas or Spielberg (to whom he has been unfairly compared), a "film geek" from childhood. He had hoped to become a marine biologist, an interest that later inspired his 1988 film, *The Big Blue*. He turned to film at age seventeen after a diving accident dimmed his hopes for an oceanic career.

Yet, the comic books that he devoured in his youth, particularly those of Jean-Claude Mézières (*Valérian and Laureline*) and Jean "Moebius" Giraud, would prove influential. Both those BD (European graphic novel) avatars were invited to join *The Fifth Element* team as conceptual designers, though only Giraud's name made it to the final credits. Mézières was then working on a piece called "Circles of Power," featuring a flying cabdriver hero. Duly impressed, Besson added this to his script. Digital Domain created the actual airborne congestion seen in the final cut; those visuals are so highly saturated in detail that each of the "cars" has its own individualized license plate for full verisimilitude.

THE PLOT

In 2263, Dallas, a yellow cabbie of the skies, is stunned when a remarkable beauty, Leeloo, crashes through his roof. She will prove to be manna from above in more ways than one, a perfect embodiment of the Fifth Element, which, when combined with the better-known four, creates the necessary defense against evil incarnate that is about to descend on Earth. The hideous-looking but benign Mondoshawans have delivered her to Earth to ensure everyone's salvation. But their mission may be thwarted by the malevolent shape-shifting Mangalores who have aligned with villainous corporate earthling Zorg. The grubby hero's intentions initially are romantic, but he's persuaded by a priest, his former commanding officer, and Leeloo herself that he must accompany bizarro media star Ruby Rhod on a pleasure cruise, where a performance artist holds the key (four mystic tablets) to humankind's survival.

THE FILM

Despite mixed reviews from mainstream critics, the twenty-four hundred international artists, animators, and craftspeople who are directly involved with onscreen imagery and constitute the Visual Effects Society picked *The Fifth Element* as one of the fifty most influential *cinéma fantastique* films. Intellectual French critic Raphaël Bassan has defended Besson and his work on the grounds that such films constitute a legitimate movement, which in 1989, Bassan labeled *Cinéma du look*—that is, movies attacked for being all style, no substance. In fact, the meticulous attention to onscreen appearances in these films rates as so intense and detailed that the look or style transforms into an alternative substance owing to its very complexity.

THEME

The film, like so many other futurist pieces beginning with *Metropolis*, works on the level of Christian allegory. In the 1914 prologue, a young scientist, Billy, refers to the force of evil as a "snake act." The Garden of Eden fable conveys the Hebraic belief that the snake—worshipped as the most wonderful of all animals by pagan sects because of its ability to form a complete circle with its body—is henceforth to be condemned. Throughout the film, circles are visually presented as symbols of evil, including the gigantic force that arrives from outer space. In almost all images featuring the evil earthling Zorg, actor Gary Oldman is framed onscreen within a circle, as are the wicked Mangalores. In contrast, hero Dallas is framed within images that appear to be pyramids. Similar to the one in which the prologue occurs, these pyramids also resemble the six extensions of a Star of David or the similar four pyramids implied by a cross, if straight lines are added to create a kite-like image of noncircular completion.

TRIVIA

Though Besson has claimed that there are no references to previous movies in this film, some sci-fi aficionados insist they note at least two: Willis's hero shares a last name with Tom Skerritt's character in *Alien*, and his character appears to be modeled in both personality and profession on Harry Canyon, the cabdriver in *Heavy Metal* (1981).

While stopping at a McDonald's, Dallas spots a police officer who is played by actor Mac McDonald, best known for his work in the BBC sci-fi series *Red Dwarf*.

The Fifth Element is never actually identified, but instead merely described as something "perfect." When asked by interviewers, Besson claimed that it is sexual intercourse.

The opera referenced in the Diva's grand performance is *Lucia di Lammermoor*.

· · · · · · ·

MEN IN BLACK (1997)

—— RANKING: 95 ——

CREDITS

Columbia Pictures/Amblin Entertainment/MacDonald/Parkes Productions; Barry Sonnenfeld, dir.; Lowell Cunningham, comic; Ed Solomon, scr.; Laurie MacDonald, Walter F. Parkes, Steven Spielberg, pro.; Danny Elfman, mus.; Donald Peterman, cin.; Jim Miller, ed.; Bo Welch, prod. design; Tom Duffield, art dir.; Cheryl Carasik, sets; Mary E. Vogt, costumes; Mark Alfrey, David LeRoy Anderson, Rick Baker, special makeup effects; Hank Mayo, concept designer; Eugene Gearty, Lewis Goldstein, special sound effects; Peter Chesney, Tom Chesney, F/X; Alia Agha, 3-D matchmove visual effects; Patrick Bonneau/ILM, digital effects; Todd Boyce/VisionArt, computer graphics animation; Derek Thompson/ILM, creature design; 98 min; Color; 1.85:1.

CAST

Tommy Lee Jones (*Kay*); Will Smith (*Jay*); Linda Fiorentino (*Laurel Weaver*); Vincent D'Onofrio (*Edgar*); Rip Torn (*Zed*); Tony Shalhoub (*Jeebs*); Siobhan Fallon (*Beatrice*); Mike Nussbaum (*Rosenburg*); Jon Gries (*Van Driver*): Sergio Calderón (*José*); Carel Struycken (*Arquillian*); Fredric Lehne (*Janus*); Richard Hamilton (*Dee*); Kent Faulcon (*Jensen*).

MOST MEMORABLE LINE

You don't exist. You were never even born. Anonymity is your name. Silence your native tongue. . . . We're "them." We're "they." We are the Men in Black.

ZED TO NEW RECRUITS

BACKGROUND

The first media incarnation of what would become a lucrative franchise appeared in 1990 and 1991, when the once-derided comic book form finally began to gain respectability in the United States, thanks to a new moniker, the "graphic novel." Creator and writer Lowell Cunningham (1959–) envisioned a noir-like near-future not unlike that presented in the influential *Blade Runner* (1982), and Canadian-born illustrator Sandy Carruthers (1962–) possessed the precise talent for designing realistic settings with surreal shadings to realize the dark tone and disturbing themes. The six *Men in Black* comic books appeared likely to become a motion picture on the order of *Watchmen* (Zack Snyder, 2009), with a purposefully unpleasant sensibility. Though the publications were originally published by Aircel Comics, various buyouts and takeovers eventually led to the *Men in Black* becoming part of the Marvel Universe, so a notably different film emerged.

THE PLOT

What initially appears a routine stop to check for illegal aliens reveals something more sinister. Two Men in Black (MiB) agents arrive on the scene, taking over from the border patrol and erasing their memories with neuralyzer devices. Kay and his elderly partner drag a true alien (extraterrestrial) out of the lineup and dispose of this dangerous visitor from the stars. The agents return to New York and their underground headquarters, located in a Battery Park station of the Triborough Bridge and Tunnel Authority. Kay takes on a young York City police officer, Jay, as his new buddy-buddy teammate. He mentors the newcomer as they work on their first case together: pursuing the remains of a redneck farmer whose body now plays host to a killer cockroach. Their fear that something big is about to come down is reinforced by information the two agents learn from Laurel, a doctor at the city morgue.

THE FILM

After Spielberg's Amblin Entertainment acquired the film rights, *Men in Black* underwent a re-invention process not unlike that of the novel *Mary Poppins*, once optioned by Walt Disney. Fundamental to the "Spielberg-ization" of this piece was the elimination of what original *Men in Black* comics fans considered essential to the anxiety-inducing quality: the license to kill that allowed agents to eliminate any ordinary citizen for no better reason than such a bystander might prove cumbersome. The neuralyzer device is now used only to erase memories, rendering witnesses harmless without harming them. Also, the MiB

"LOOK TO THE SKIES!" *Will Smith and Tommy Lee Jones as special secret agents assigned to monitor alien activity in the world around us. The edgy graphic novel by Lowell Cunningham was transformed into a genial crowd-pleaser for greater commercial appeal. Courtesy: Amblin/Columbia.*

would now patriotically monitor the aliens (werewolves and zombies were eliminated from the source's mix) for the good of Earth and its inhabitants, whereas in Cunningham's version, they plan to remake the Blue Planet in their own image, achieving dominance, power, and total control. A cult sensation was transformed into a middlebrow product—and a highly successful one, with Danny Elfman's musical score enticing audiences with the same sort of zany, sweet-spirited tone he created for Tim Burton's *Edward Scissorhands* (1990).

Spielberg chose New York native Barry Sonnenfeld (1953–) to direct because of that filmmaker's previous success with edgy material, neatly turning it into films that appealed to a broad-based audience. Sonnenfeld had reinvented the Burtonesque black comedy with a heart of gold of *The Addams Family* (1991) and the noir nastiness of the novel *Get Shorty* (1995) into smart, glib mainstream movie material—exactly what Spielberg required for *Men in Black* and what

Sonnenfeld delivered in the first film, and both the commercially successful (if, in truth, far less impressive) sequels.

Though this film's budget reached $90 million, the project was always perceived at Amblin as a nostalgic throwback to the glorious B sci-fi films that Spielberg and others his age recalled from Saturday matinees during the 1950s. Most ran for fewer than ninety minutes; the storytelling time for *Men in Black*, minus opening and closing credits, is eighty-eight minutes. Those nostalgia-drenched movies were often hampered by cheap special effects or, in the case of a Harryhausen project, excellent state-of-the-art effects, sparingly employed throughout to keep costs down. Spielberg grew up dreaming about how great those movies might be if first-rate effects were interspersed throughout the tight story line. As the head of Amblin, he had the opportunity with *Men in Black* to make what might be considered the most expensive B movie of all time.

THEME

The idea of insects from space recalls *Five Million Years to Earth* (1967), with its considerably darker vision of aliens entering into humankind's evolution process. Though the film (and its sequels in 2002 and 2012, as well as an animated TV series, 1997–2001) is kinder and gentler than the radical graphic novels, one theme, which runs through all thoughtful sci-fi, continued: human identity. A Man in Black must accept that "you don't exist" and "you were never born." An effective element in the franchise is that the title characters are as "alien" to other humans as are the extraterrestrials!

TRIVIA

When a TV monitor flashes the faces of supposed humans who are actually aliens living among us, among those included are politician Newt Gingrich, Karen Lynn Gorney (the female lead in *Saturday Night Fever*, 1977), Spielberg's friend and sometimes collaborator George Lucas, Spielberg himself, TV weatherman Al Roker, and director Sonnenfeld.

······

THE TRUMAN SHOW (1998)

—— RATING: 37 ——

CREDITS

Paramount Pictures; Peter Weir, dir.; Andrew Niccol, scr.; Niccol, Edward S. Feldman, Scott Rudin, Adam Schroeder, pro.; Burkhard von Dallwitz, mus.; Peter Biziou, cin.; William M. Anderson, Lee Smith, ed.; Dennis Gassner, prod. design; Richard L. Johnson, art dir.; Larz Anderson, F/X; Ted Andre/Cinesite, digital artist; Craig Barron/Matte World, Juliette Yager, visual effects; 103 min.; Color; 1.85:1.

CAST

Jim Carrey (*Truman Burbank*); Laura Linney (*Meryl Burbank/Hannah Gill*); Noah Emmerich (*Marlon*); Natascha McElhone (*Lauren/Sylvia*); Holland Taylor (*Truman's Mother*); Brian Delate (*Truman's Father*); Ed Harris (*Christof*); Paul Giamatti (*Control Room Director*); Harry Shearer (*Mike*); Blair Slater (*Young Truman*).

MOST MEMORABLE LINE

We accept the reality of the world with which we are presented.
CHRISTOF, BEING INTERVIEWED

BACKGROUND

As mentioned numerous times, *The Twilight Zone* (1959–1964) has exerted an incalculable influence on successive generations of imaginative fantasy scribes. Spielberg and Lucas each grew up watching remarkable tales set in the "fifth dimension" during the initial run of the series, but *Zone's* impact also touched younger writers exposed to seemingly endless reruns on cable. Among them, J. Michael Straczynski (1954–), who eventually penned twelve episodes for the 1985–1989 reboot. One, "Special Service," about a couple whose activities are unknowingly videotaped for mass consumption on TV, made an impression on New Zealander Andrew Niccol (1964–). He remained haunted by the concept, which became the inspiration for his next script. Following the release of his *Gattaca* (1997), a low-budget, sci-fi think piece that, like many *Zone* episodes, combined entertaining fantasies with thoughtful ideology, Niccol joined with Scott Rudin to produce *The Truman Show*.

"ALL THE WORLD'S A STAGE . . ." *Or, in the case of writer Andrew Niccol's smart satire on reality TV as it might develop in a near-future, all the world's a theater, and all the women and men, Truman (Jim Carrey) unknowingly, merely players. Courtesy: Scott Rudin/Paramount.*

THE PLOT

Every day, Truman Burbank rises early, shares a pleasant breakfast with his charming wife, Meryl, then gleefully heads off to work at the office. Unbeknownst to Truman, the seemingly solid world around him is a façade. He's the subject (and unwitting star) of a reality TV series. For decades, executive producer and series creator Christof has broadcast Truman's misadventures to an adoring public. Then an odd object—the sort of overhead light used at a studio—drops from the sky, crashing at the feet of the heretofore unsuspecting Truman. Long-repressed fears (particularly of water) and stilted memories (a father's death, a woman's love) prompt Truman to secretly plan a trip to Fiji. However, leaving this island "paradise," actually a faux construction in which he is imprisoned, proves difficult.

THE FILM

The Truman Show offers a case study in how a spec script evolves into an entirely different concept than that originally intended. Hoping to direct and with Gary Oldman in mind for the lead, Niccol planned to mount one more combination of hard-edged action and far-out fantasy, likely with a Manhattan setting that would recall *Escape from New York* (1981). Rudin immediately saw the possibilities to enlarge the scope while narrowing the focus to a sophisticated comedy-fantasy, perhaps starring Robin Williams. Meanwhile Jim Carrey, eager to shed his goofy image by playing in a smart satire, joined the mix. The project's aesthetic altered from tough to tender, and directors renowned for violent thrillers (Brian De Palma) or edgy sci-fi (David Cronenberg) were considered. Australian-born Peter Weir (1944–), who had never worked in this genre but had guided strong character-driven features, such as *Witness* (1985) and *Dead Poets Society* (1989), won the position in part owing to his early arthouse hit *Picnic at Hanging Rock* (1975). That film, an initially realistic mood piece, step by step becomes ever more surreal until the audience wonders if the entire "true story" was actually an elaborate fantasy. This approach was precisely what was needed for the final script by Weir (who contributed anonymously) and Niccol.

THEME

The Truman Show incorporates several *Twilight Zone* influences, particularly the greatest scripts by Rod Serling: "Where Is Everybody?" (10/2/59), dealing with a lonely man who senses the seemingly average town that he walks through is pure fabrication; "A Stop at Willoughby" (5/6/60), examining a modern Everyman's desire to enter into a kinder, gentler place that exists only in nostalgia; "Five Characters in Search of an Exit" (12/22/61), featuring people contained in a metallic dome; and "Showdown with Rance McGrew" (2/2/62), questioning whether reality and TV can ever be separated. Another influence is *It's a Wonderful Life* (1946). Serling once asserted that the Frank Capra classic—with its vision of an ordinary man who, via a fantasy situation, discovers the heroic truth about himself—was one of his templates for *Zone*.

TRIVIA

Weir pictured the re-imagined setting as a combination of Norman Rockwell's sentimental representations of 1940s small-town America and Sir Thomas More's 1516 *Utopia*, in which the ideal world has but a single entrance. Even as filming began, self-contained villages not unlike the one seen here (Disney's master-planned Celebration, Florida, a prime example) emerged in actuality. In an incredible irony, concerns that a vast set would need to be built vanished after Weir's wife suggested he take a look at Seaside, a carefully planned, isolated community in the Florida Panhandle. The location brought to life the film's intended "world of the future." In what Alvin Toffler once described as our "future shock" age, the most difficult problem for sci-fi artists is that reality has a tendency to get there first! Carrey's greatest contribution, besides his convincing performance, was the improvised "Trumania" mirror sequence.

· · · · · · ·

THE MATRIX (1999)

—— RANKING: 32 ——

CREDITS

Warner Bros./Village Roadshow Pictures/Groucho II Film Partnership; Andy Wachowski, Lana Wachowski, dir.; Wachowski, Wachowski, scr; Wachowski, Wachowski, Joel Silver, pro.; Don Davis, mus.; Bill Pope, cin.; Zach Staenberg, ed.; Owen Paterson, prod. design; Hugh Bateup, Michelle McGahey, art dir.; Kym Barrett, costumes; Bob McCarron, Rick Connelly, Sonja Smuk, makeup F/X; Dane A. Davis, special sound design; Steve Courtley, Brian Cox, F/X; Jeff Allen, Lynne Cartwright/Animal Logic, visual effects; Daniele Colajacomo/DFilm Services, CGI; 136 min.; Color; 2.35:1.

CAST

Keanu Reeves (*Neo*); Laurence Fishburne (*Morpheus*); Carrie-Anne Moss (*Trinity*); Hugo Weaving (*Agent Smith*); Gloria Foster (*Oracle*); Joe Pantoliano (*Cypher*); Marcus Chong (*Tank*); Julian Arahanga (*Apoc*); Matt Doran (*Mouse*); Belinda McClory (*Switch*); Anthony Ray Parker (*Dozer*).

MOST MEMORABLE LINE

Ever have that feeling where you're not sure if you're awake
or still dreaming?
NEO, TO HIS LOW-LIFE VISITORS

BACKGROUND

The Whitney Young High School in Chicago, famous for its theater and science programs, allowed Lana (born "Laurence," 1965–) and Andrew Wachowski (1967–) to explore their interests in both, paving the way for careers in which

POST-MODERNISM AT THE MOVIES: *The theory that "truth" is nothing more than an elaborate construction was definitively brought to the screen by the Wachowskis. Laurence Fishburne, Keanu Reeves, and Carrie-Anne Moss attempt to survive the dystopian maelstrom. Courtesy: Warner Bros./Village Roadshow/Joel Silver.*

they would adapt up-to-date scientific research into popular entertainment. An early obsession with the Dungeons & Dragons game revealed their love of fantasy. They decided to drop out of their respective colleges to work as carpenters, while in their spare time writing comic books for Marvel and Epic drawn from the works of contemporary horror avatar Clive Barker (1952–). That creative experience, and the notable quality of their output, eventually earned them entrance to the film business. Though *Assassins* (1995) was so altered by studio executives that the siblings disassociated themselves from their initial project, their next, the edgy if relatively realistic thriller *Bound* (1996), gave them the momentum to move on to the more ambitious work they had been planning.

THE PLOT

In the nearest near-future ever (a few months after the film's release date!), a young man leads a double life, his dual existences connected by computers. By day, Mr. Anthony is one more suited cog in the wheel, developing software. By night, he becomes Neo, a hacker who is oblivious that two powerful forces are closing in. Trinity, a member of a secretive underground army, believes Neo is the one they've been waiting for, a "savior." Then there are the suited government men in glasses, who hope to nab Neo first so he cannot be used by the mysterious Morpheus to reveal a terrible truth to humanity: the supposed reality people walk through every day is a computer-generated replacement for the actual world, destroyed some time ago.

THE FILM

Here is another example of emergent sci-fi incorporating what were previously considered the opposite poles of commercial filmmaking: arthouse cinema, with its complex ideas, and action-oriented adventure, filled with pulp-worthy battle sequences and chases. *The Matrix* contains enough rugged confrontations and explosions to satisfy what previously had been posited as a lowbrow audience, but between such visceral bouts are serious, even intellectual discussions of issues raised by technological advances. When *The Matrix* scored at the box office, a "new normal" emerged. The Wachowskis helped to break down previous barriers, revealing that what had been considered mutually exclusive viewerships could be addressed in one film.

Before *V for Vendetta* (2005), also written by the Wachowskis, *The Matrix* was the most politically radical film ever released by a major studio, inducing mainstream audiences to side with violence-prone "terrorists"—the government's term—though these rebels see themselves as "freedom fighters." Of course, the two terms refer to the same thing, if observed from oppositional ends of the spectrum.

THEME

The vision of computers seizing control of humans has been present in sci-fi since the early 1900s, though never as totally as predicted here. The Wachowskis, while clearly visionaries, draw on themes and images from numerous influences: the inability to distinguish between dream and reality that suffused Rod Serling's *Twilight Zone* scripts; the office cubicles, tangibly representing conformity within the system and threatening to diminish the nameless, faceless quasi-alive workers in Franz Kafka's *The Trial*; the zooming ride through a tubular underground shaft in Lewis Carroll's *Alice's Adventures in Wonderland*; the experience of waking up in another, perhaps better universe from L. Frank Baum's *The Wonderful Wizard of Oz*; and the presence of suited government representatives from *The Men in Black* graphic novels (in this incarnation, posited as villains). Again, Greek tragedy provides a template as Neo must make a choice that will affect not only him, but also the cosmos, and as a desire for free will comes into conflict with a realization of pre-ordained fate. The Oracle's dictate, "Know thyself," guided the Greeks during their golden age, and tragedy emerged as a form to express this as the first step toward grasping the meaning of life. Finally, there is a Christian religious element as the savior Neo dies only to be reborn via a Pietà-like embrace.

TRIVIA

Nicolas Cage was the original choice for Neo. Reeves contributed the gesture in which Neo rubs a thumb and finger across his nose before engaging in martial arts as an homage to the late, great Bruce Lee, who used a similar mannerism.

STAR WARS EPISODE I: THE PHANTOM MENACE (1999), STAR WARS EPISODE II: ATTACK OF THE CLONES (2002), AND STAR WARS EPISODE III: REVENGE OF THE SITH (2005)

—— RANKING: 89 (THREE-WAY TIE) ——

STAR WARS EPISODE I: THE PHANTOM MENACE (1999)

CREDITS

Lucasfilm/Twentieth Century Fox Film Corporation; George Lucas, dir.; Lucas, scr.; Lucas, Rick McCallum, pro.; John Williams, mus.; David Tattersall, cin.; Ben Burtt, Paul Martin Smith, ed.; Gavin Bocquet, prod. design; Phil Harvey, Fred Hole, John King, Rod McLean, Peter Russell, art dir.; Trisha Biggar, costumes; Shaune Harrison, animatronic effects design; Maria Boggi, Monique Brown, animatronic model design; Nick Dudman, creature effects; Geoff Heron/ ILM, Brenda Hutchinson, Peter Hutchinson, F/X; Maurice Bastian/ILM, Andrew Hardaway/ILM, digital effects; Christophe Hery/ILM, Euan K. MacDonald/ ILM, computer graphics; Jeffrey B. Light/ILM, motion capture; Dennis Muren, Amanda K. Montgomery/ILM, visual effects; 136 min.; Color; 2.35:1.

CAST

Liam Neeson (*Qui-Gon Jinn*); Ewan McGregor (*Obi-Wan Kenobi*); Natalie Portman (*Queen Amidala/Padmé*); Jake Lloyd (*Anakin Skywalker*); Ian McDiarmid (*Senator Palpatine*); Pernilla August (*Shmi Skywalker*); Oliver Ford Davies (*Sio Bibble*); Hugh Quarshie (*Capt. Panaka*); Ahmed Best (*Jar Jar Binks*, voice); Terence Stamp (*Chancellor Valorum*); Brian Blessed (*Boss Nass*, voice); Andy Secombe (*Watto*); Ray Park (*Darth Maul*); Sofia Coppola (*Saché*); Keira Knightley (*Sabé*).

MOST MEMORABLE LINE

Fear is the path to the dark side. . . . I sense much fear in you.
YODA TO YOUNG ANAKIN

BACKGROUND

No sooner had *Star Wars* (1977) arrived in theaters than the Big Rumor spread: Lucas would mount two sequels to what, in retrospect, had been subtitled "Chapter Four: A New Hope." Each, word had it, would arrive every three years and, following them, sequel and prequel trilogies. These in due time would sandwich the originals for a sprawling saga that would carry still-youthful fans through their entire lives.

Yet, the years passed and, while the Star Wars Expanded Universe rippled ever further into international pop culture via video games, comic books and graphic novels, TV specials, animated series, toys, and other merchandise, a vast silence loomed so far as more theatrical films were concerned. Meanwhile, the re-release of the originals with enhanced effects split devotees. Roughly half of the fans were convinced that Lucas had been justified in adding the visual verisimilitude he could only dream about in 1977, owing to a tight budget and the limited state of the art for imagery at that time. Just as many others, with a religious devotion to what they accepted as cinematic gospels, allowed no room for departures. When Lucas at last announced that there would indeed be three more films, the initially ecstatic reaction soon turned to widespread anxiety: what if the prequels did not live up to the perceived perfection of the originals?

THE PLOT

There could be no finer Jedi knight than Qui-Gon Jinn, which explains why he's picked for a sensitive mission at a time of crisis for the Republic. Difficulties in the great peacekeeping organization's economic system necessitated taxation of trade routes. This has angered the increasingly powerful Trade Federation, which dares to openly challenge the decision by blockading the planet of Naboo. Hoping for a solution, Chancellor Valorum sends Qui-Gon and his gifted young padawan, Obi-Wan, to meet Nute Gunray and negotiate a compromise. But Nute has been ordered by his superior, Darth Sidious, to kill these ambassadors. Endangered, the heroes hurry away to Naboo, where they encounter Jar Jar Binks, an amiable goofball who agrees to serve as their guide. After saving Naboo's queen, Amidala, they land on Tatooine and, in the spaceport of Mos Espa, come in contact with a brilliant child slave, Anakin.

THE FILM

Whereas in the original trilogy Lucas revealed a true genius as a Walt Disney-type overseer, sparking others to do their best work, he now planned to write the films entirely on his own and personally direct each. Not surprisingly, the result disappointed as many members of the fan base as it delighted. In particular, the addition of Jar Jar so enraged devotees that one viewer used advanced home production devices to prepare an alternative cut in which the character was eliminated. Politically correct types argued that Jar Jar, with his Caribbean accent, could be considered a racist portrait. Ironically, Lucas had been responding to the complaint that his films were not racially diverse enough.

THEME

Though Lucas has always identified himself as a liberal, some observers find conservative values in his work. The portrayal of the Trade Federation as evil was perceived by several critics as an attack on unions. Others, however, argued that the Trade Federation's resistance to necessary taxes by a strong central government portends the Tea Party, as a coterie of rugged individualists insist that the sorely tested old government should do as little as possible.

Political interpretations aside, what clearly works here is the effective setup of Anakin as the *Star Wars* equivalent of the legendary Uther Pendragon, the father of King Arthur. Uther was the great man who might well have become England's once and future king were it not for the hubris that, despite his gifts, eventually brought him down, leaving the epic challenge to his savior-like son. According to Joseph Campbell, Arthur and Luke can be interpreted as variations on "the hero of a thousand faces": the universal warrior-philosopher king who rises from his obscure surroundings to full greatness.

TRIVIA

The film marked a turning point for Hollywood productions in general and sci-fi cinema in particular. Lucas announced that, for several scenes, he had employed the most advanced form of digital video, rather than celluloid film, daring anyone to locate where one left off and the other began. As had been the case with computer-generated effects before Spielberg embraced them for *Jurassic Park* (1993), a once derided form suddenly won industry acceptance and public respectability.

STAR WARS EPISODE II: ATTACK OF THE CLONES (2002)

ADDITIONAL CREDITS

Jonathan Hales, scr.; Lorne Orleans, pro.; Kristelle Gardiner, Sean Genders, special makeup effects; Gab Facchinei, creature effects; Geoff Heron/ILM, F/X;

IN PRAISE OF STRONG WOMEN: *George Lucas listened to feminists' complaints that the females in his original films hadn't displayed equal strength to the men. As this publicity image makes clear, the prequel trilogy remedied any such problem. From left to right, Samuel L. Jackson as Mace, Ewan McGregor as Obi-Wan, Natalie Portman as Padmé, and Hayden Christensen as Anakin. Courtesy: Lucasfilm/20th Century Fox.*

Lleslle Aclaro/ILM, visual effects; Jeffrey Arnold/ILM, digital effects; 142 min.; Color; 2.35:1.

ADDITIONAL CAST
Hayden Christensen (*Anakin*); Christopher Lee (*Count Dooku/Darth Tyranus*); Samuel L. Jackson (*Mace Windu*); Temuera Morrison (*Jango Fett*); Daniel Logan (*Boba Fett*); Jimmy Smits (*Sen. Bail Organa*); Jack Thompson (*Cliegg Lars*); Lee-anna Walsman (*Zam Wesell*); Ayesha Dharker (*Queen Jamillia*).

MOST MEMORABLE LINE
He still has much to learn. . . . His abilities have made him . . . well . . . arrogant.
OBI-WAN, DESCRIBING ANAKIN TO YODA

BACKGROUND
Aware of the criticism directed at Episode I, Lucas pulled back from his decision to write as well as direct each of the prequel films by enlisting Jonathan Hales (1937–) to collaborate. The British-born author had successfully written

the majority of the made-for-TV movies broadcast under the blanket title *The Adventures of Young Indiana Jones.*

THE PLOT

Padmé Amidala now represents her planet as senator. She is dedicated to doing all she can to help hold the increasingly threatened Galactic Republic together. That time-honored system has been challenged by Count Dooku, who abandoned his status as a Jedi to lead a separation movement. When Amidala dares speak out against the coming chaos, an assassin attempts to silence her. The Jedi respond by assigning young Anakin Skywalker, mentored by Obi-Wan, to be her bodyguard. Even as their world threatens to become engulfed in the Clone Wars, the vulnerable young woman is swept into a romance with the boy-man.

THE FILM

Over the three years between the release of Episode I and this follow-up, computer-generated effects improved so vastly that Lucas was able to realize a dream by presenting Yoda through the CGI process. Digital video was used, thanks to rapid improvements at Sony and Panasonic. Lucas could now shoot 24 fps with a high-definition progressive scan camera. These cameras functioned in Tunisian desert locales, the extreme heat of which likely would have destroyed traditional 35 mm film.

THEME

Politically, *Attack* proved prescient as to the movements within red states to secede following the election of Barack Obama. The film served as a cautionary fable of the potential disaster of such a move—here, of course, dramatized in the context of a fantasy film. In terms of a mythic vision, Lucas furthers the comparison of Anakin to Uther by having the potential hero destroy his possibilities for greatness by falling in love with a woman forbidden to him. Likewise, by having Padmé be notably older than Anakin and serving as mother surrogate to the boy, Lucas also invokes the Oedipus myth that will reach full fruition in the third prequel film.

TRIVIA

The massacre of the Tusken Raiders by Anakin, who knows his mother Shmi is held captive in their camp, closely resembles a scene at the end of John Ford's *The Searchers* (1956) in which the character played by John Wayne attacks a Comanche village to rescue his niece (Natalie Wood).

The prequel films, while highly popular and financially successful with an international mass audience, did not engender the same devotion as the originals. *Attack of the Clones* failed to take the number one box-office spot for the year in which it was released.

STAR WARS EPISODE III: REVENGE OF THE SITH (2005)

ADDITIONAL CREDITS

Roger Barton, ed.; Ian Gracie, Peter Russell, art dir.; Katherine Brown, prosthetic makeup artist; Robbie Clot, F/X (model unit); David Young, F/X; Janet Lewin, John Knoll, David M. Gray, Ritesh Aggarwal, Rob Bonstin/ILM, visual effects; Jeffrey Benedict/ILM, digital effects; Doug Griffin, motion capture; 140 min.; Color; 2.35:1.

ADDITIONAL CAST

Keisha Castle-Hughes (*Queen of Naboo*); Peter Mayhew (*Chewbacca*); Silas Carson (*Ki-Adi-Mundi/Nute Gunray*); Matthew Wood (*Gen. Grievous*, voice only).

MOST MEMORABLE LINE

You've become the very thing you swore to destroy.
OBI-WAN TO ANAKIN

BACKGROUND

Lucas's three-month shoot took him and the team to such remote locations as Australia and Thailand, as well as Italy. On release, the last chapter won over the critics, diehard fans, and the public, setting box-office records once word spread that here was a fitting finale.

THE PLOT

After Obi-Wan sets out to track and destroy General Grievous, Anakin finds himself falling under the cunning spell of Supreme Chancellor Palpatine. The threatened youth is too self-involved to grasp that the power offered him by this false father figure has the potential to destroy not only Anakin but also his world. Yet, as Padmé has become pregnant with twins, the would-be hero finds himself drawn to the dark side after Palpatine insists that he possesses the ability to guide Anakin toward a future in which the will of the young Jedi can triumph.

THE FILM

One way of justifying Episodes I and II, despite their uneven quality and narrative flaws, is to posit these as necessary stopgaps on the way to a successful payoff in the third installment. With Anakin's tie to Uther established in *The Phantom Menace*, Lucas set up not only an Oedipal-like desire for the mother in *Attack of the Clones* but also the eventual Laius-like killing of Obi-Wan when Anakin insists he sees this mentor not as an older brother but as a father figure. Episode III allows Lucas to add to the mix a third iconic tragic hero, Shakespeare's Macbeth, who turned to the dark side less out of ambition for the throne than for the sake of the wife he loved deeply, if not wisely.

THEME

Like Macbeth, Anakin sets into motion the invisible machinery of his own destruction by attempting to prove that a man's free will can overcome a

GOOD THINGS COME IN SMALL PACKAGES: *The old adage fits Yoda of the Jedi Order, a Clone Wars hero and later (in narrative time, though earlier as to release dates) mentor to Luke Skywalker. Originally a Frank Oz puppet, Yoda morphed into a CGI creation. Courtesy: Lucasfilm/20th Century Fox.*

destiny set in the stars. Anakin is the latest in a long line of self-doomed figures who do all the wrong things for all the right reasons and fail to see that attempting to avoid one's fate will automatically bring it into being.

TRIVIA

To the surprise of many observers, Lucas—who with the prequel trilogy had exerted more power over the vast project than any other filmmaker in history—did an abrupt about-face in 2012. He sold Lucasfilm to Disney and hence the rights to produce the other three stories that Lucas, in 1977, had implied should be told.

· · · · · · ·

SPACE COWBOYS (2000)

—— RANKING: 80 ——

CREDITS

Warner Bros./Clipsal Films/Malpaso Productions/Village Roadshow Pictures; Clint Eastwood, dir.; Ken Kaufman, Howard Klausner, scr.; Eastwood, Andrew Lazar, pro.; Lennie Niehaus, mus.; Jack N. Green, cin.; Joel Cox, ed.; Henry Bumstead, prod. design; Jack G. Taylor Jr., art dir.; Deborah Hopper, costumes; David Amborn, Ken Ebert, John Frazier, Tom Frazier, Mark Noel, Mark Sheaffer, F/X; Barry Armour, CGI effects; Lisa Todd, visual effects; 130 min.; Color/B&W; 2.35:1.

CAST

Clint Eastwood (*Frank Corvin*); Tommy Lee Jones (*Hawk Hawkins*); Donald Sutherland (*Jerry O'Neill*); James Garner (*Tank Sullivan*); James Cromwell (*Bob Gerson*); Marcia Gay Harden (*Sara Holland*); William Devane (*Eugene Davis*); Loren Dean (*Ethan Glance*); Courtney B. Vance (*Roger Hines*); Barbara Babcock (*Barbara Corvin*); Rade Serbedzija (*Gen. Vostov*); Blair Brown (*Dr. Anne Caruthers*); Jay Leno (*Himself*).

MOST MEMORABLE LINE

Alright, cowboys. Let's round 'em up!
HAWKINS TO HIS "PARDNERS"

BACKGROUND

Immediately after World War II, American pilots like Chuck Yeager and Scott Crossfield set to work attempting to break the sound barrier. Their rough-hewn competitive spirit inspired the press to nickname them "Space Cowboys." But such derring-do did not sit well with the men in suits back in Washington. When President Eisenhower determined that a revved-up rocket program should fall under the jurisdiction of NASA, Yeager, Crossfield, and other rugged individualists—none of whom possessed college degrees—were cast aside in favor of clean-cut "team players" such as John Glenn, Scott Carpenter, and Alan Shepard. The sense of betrayal on the part of those early pioneers—particularly, in their realization that they would not be the first men to walk on the moon, as each had assumed—would be vividly depicted in *The Right Stuff* (Philip Kaufman, 1983), a docudrama based on Tom Wolfe's 1979 bestseller. Clint Eastwood (1930–) drew on that story to create this "fiction about science."

THE PLOT

Retired from the Air Force for more than forty years, Frank Corvin enjoys a middle-class existence. Until one day several NASA representatives arrive at his door, requesting that Frank return to active duty. IKON, a satellite sent into space decades earlier by the Soviets, will soon come crashing down. For reasons not immediately obvious, Russia wishes to intercept the seemingly harmless piece of space junk. For this, they need cooperation from the Americans, Corvin in particular. Following a spy mission, the Soviets "borrowed" the complex if now archaic system that Frank, an engineer, designed. As he's the only person living who understands the inner workings, Frank could oversee a disabling of the satellite in the brief time before it is brought down by gravity. He agrees, but only if allowed to reorganize his original 1958 team—even though he and a member of that team, Hawk, had an ugly falling-out years earlier. A more pressing issue, however, is the real reason why IKON cannot be allowed to simply drop to Earth: it contains six Cold War–era nuclear warheads, which are about to activate.

THE FILM

Following the release of the first *Star Wars* in 1977 and the subsequent theatrical reboot of the *Star Trek* franchise, filmmakers scrambled to create elaborate space operas. But hard sci-fi filmmaking, with its emphasis on everyday realism, was largely jettisoned. Such films take place not in some distant future or far-off galaxy but the day after tomorrow or, in the case of Eastwood's film, today—and they involve adventures that are not only possible but also likely. The mid-section of Kubrick's *2001* adheres to this aesthetic, the effects used not to create imaginative worlds but to bring to the screen a believable vision of what will soon take place. *Gravity* (Alfonso Cuarón, 2013) is perhaps the greatest example of this subgenre.

"WAGON TRAIN TO THE STARS": *That's how Gene Roddenberry pitched his* Star Trek *series at NBC. This film starred actors who were associated with Westerns on TV and in film: from left, James Garner, Tommy Lee Jones, and Clint Eastwood. Donald Sutherland (far right) rounds out the futuristic four musketeers. Courtesy: Warner Bros./Village Roadshow.*

THEME

The image of the astronaut as a futuristic version of the historical frontiersman dates back to the early days of the sci-fi genre. Between gigs as Flash Gordon and Buck Rogers, Buster Crabbe also portrayed Billy the Kid in a series of low-budget oaters, or B Westerns. When Lucas first approached Twentieth Century-Fox with his idea for *Star Wars*, he pitched the project as "cowboys in space." *Battle Beyond the Stars* (Jimmy T. Murakami, 1980), a Roger Corman quickie, cast George Peppard, who appeared in a wide variety of film projects but today is perhaps best known for his roles in Westerns (*How the West Was Won*, 1962), as "Space Cowboy."

TRIVIA

Though critics rightly praised Donald Sutherland's performance as the womanizing member of the team, they noted that, as the Canadian-born actor was usually associated with less erotic, more cerebral roles, he appeared less typecast in his part than the other three stars. In fact, the original choice for O'Neill was Sean Connery, the original James Bond, who was often associated with womanizing roles. Jack Nicholson was the first choice for the role of Tank. Garner, who accepted the part, had played a character with that nickname in the 1984 film *Tank*.

In 1958, the year in which this film opens, Clint Eastwood had just completed the pilot for *Rawhide*, while James Garner ranked as TV's favorite Sunday night cowboy star, thanks to *Maverick*. In one episode of the latter series, Eastwood played the antagonist.

The craft upon which the heroes embark is *Daedalus*, a reference to the mythic Greek hero who glued wings to his arms with wax in order to fly.

······

A.I. ARTIFICIAL INTELLIGENCE (2001) AND MINORITY REPORT (2002)

—— RANKING: 82 (TIE) ——

A.I. ARTIFICIAL INTELLIGENCE (2001)

CREDITS

DreamWorks SKG/Warner Bros./Amblin Entertainment; Steven Spielberg, dir.; Brian Aldiss, story; Spielberg, Ian Watson, scr.; Spielberg, Bonnie Curtis, Jan Harlan, Kathleen Kennedy, Walter F. Parkes, pro.; John Williams, mus.; Janusz Kaminski, cin.; Michael Kahn, ed.; Rick Carter, prod. design; Richard L. Johnson, William James Teegarden, Thomas Valentine, art dir.; Bob Ringwood, costumes; Richard Alonzo, Bill Corso, Kenny Myers, makeup effects; Stan Winston, special robot F/X; Tim Wilcox, digital illustrator; Christian Beckman, animatronics; Jim Rollins, F/X; Dugan Beach/ILM, CGI creature developer: Julie Creighton/ILM, visual effects; 146 min.; Color; 1.85:1.

CAST

Haley Joel Osment (*David*); Jude Law (*Gigolo Joe*); Frances O'Connor (*Monica Swinton*); Sam Robards (*Henry Swinton*); Jake Thomas (*Martin Swinton*); William Hurt (*Prof. Hobby*); Ken Leung (*Syatyoo-Sama*); Robin Williams (*Dr. Know*, voice); Ben Kingsley (*Specialist*, voice); Meryl Streep (*Blue Mecha*, voice); Chris Rock (*Comedian*, voice).

MOST MEMORABLE LINE

To create an artificial man has been the dream
of mankind since the birth of science.
PROFESSOR HOBBY

BACKGROUND

Stanley Kubrick became fascinated with Brian Aldiss's short story "Super-Toys Last All Summer Long" and hired Ian Watson to develop a full narrative. The project bogged down due to Kubrick's inability to decide whether he would employ a child actor or CGI-F/X for the part of David. Apparently, as early as 1995, Kubrick had suggested to Spielberg that the latter might be better suited to this material. No further development occurred until after Kubrick died in 1999, when Spielberg forged ahead to make Kubrick's dream come true.

THE PLOT

Professor Hobby takes the concept of a cyborg to a new level. In addition to creating an artificial intelligence, he endows an android with the ability to give love. This is accompanied by a human-like need to receive in kind. As a test, Monica and Henry Swinton—an ordinary couple who believe they have lost their child—adopt a boy model robot, David, who in time is allowed to play with Teddy, the favorite toy of their "late" biological son. Everything alters when Martin, long held in suspended animation, is cured and sent home. Monica must now choose between her two "boys."

THE FILM

A.I. might be considered Spielberg's joint remake of Walt Disney's *Pinocchio* (1940) and MGM's *The Wizard of Oz* (1939). Spielberg even references himself: Teddy embodies a futuristic version of the simple teddy bear that flew out a car window in his first theatrical feature, *The Sugarland Express* (1974). When a gentle alien reaches out and touches the boy, A.I. visually echoes the end of *Close Encounters* (1977).

THEME

A.I. features another unique variation on the Frankenstein myth as a doctor who hopes to improve the lot of humankind by creating a perfect person instead brings about tragedy for all. Like many sci-fi characters, the doctor invokes religion, asking fellow scientists, "In the beginning, didn't God create Adam to love him?" As in *The Wizard of Oz*, the ultimate "message" here is beautiful in its simplicity: there's no place like home, no experience better than going back there again, if only, in this film's case, for a single perfect day.

TRIVIA

Again, situations are similar to those found in classic *Zones*—not surprising as Rod Serling was one of Spielberg's early mentors. The similarities include: the lead character caged as if subhuman ("People Are Alike All Over"); mannequins surrounding a seeming person ("The After Hours"); the hideous outcast appearing to be normal when returned to his or her own kind ("Eye of the Beholder"); a character coming face to face with a double ("Mirror Image"); an isolated person's attempt to find affection with a robot ("The Lonely"); a cyborg being used to round out a fractured family ("I Sing the Body Electric"); the value that a brief reunion with a lost parent might have on a child ("In Praise of Pip"); and the addictive power of a game designed to ambiguously project the future ("Nick of Time").

MINORITY REPORT (2002)

ADDITIONAL CREDITS
Twentieth Century Fox Film Corporation/Cruise/Wagner Productions; Philip K. Dick, story; Scott Frank, Jon Cohen, scr.; Jan de Bont, Gerald R. Molen, Ronald Shusett, pro.; Alex McDowell, prod. design; Chris Gorak, art dir.; Deborah Lynn Scott, costumes; Michael Lantieri, Tom Pahk, Chiz Hasegawa, F/X; Mark Russell, Marc Varisco/Asylum, Blondel Aidoo/Asylum, visual effects; Barry Armour/ILM, computer graphics; 145 min.; Color; 2.25:1.

CAST
Tom Cruise (*John Anderton*); Colin Farrell (*Danny Witwer*); Max von Sydow (*Lamar Burgess*); Steve Harris (*Jad*); Neal McDonough (*Fletcher*); Patrick Kilpatrick (*Knott*); Jessica Capshaw (*Evanna*); Lois Smith (*Dr. Iris Hineman*); Jessica Harper (*Anne Lively*).

MOST MEMORABLE LINE
You still have a choice.
THE ORACLE

BACKGROUND
If *A.I.* recalls the sweetly melancholic *E.T.* (1982), *Minority Report* resembles *Poltergeist* (1982) with its neo-noir ambience. The color scheme in *Minority Report* features such dark hues of blue that the onscreen image often appears black. Even as, in previous films, Spielberg alternated between mothers and fathers attempting to be responsible to their children, the mother-driven *A.I.* is here complemented by a father-driven tale.

SCIENCE FICTION/TRAGEDY: *Sophocles asked the critical question: are our lives ruled by fate or free will? Over two millennia later, this issue remains at the heart of intellectual genre pieces, particularly those derived from the work of Philip K. Dick. Tom Cruise stars in this Steven Spielberg–directed dystopian future, neo-noir, sci-fi epic. Courtesy: Dreamworks/20th Century Fox.*

THE PLOT

The forces that run America in 2054 employ PreCrime, a private commercial venture, for national police work. A genius, Lamar Burgess has developed a system by which three psychics, the "precogs," predict crimes before they occur. Agents such as John Anderton rush to the scene and apprehend the criminal before violence occurs. Anderton has a deeply disturbing reason to involve himself in such a process: years earlier, his beloved six-year-old son was abducted from a public swimming pool. He hopes to keep such a horrific incident from ever happening to any other parent. Then a psychic predicts that Anderton will murder a man he has never heard of. Convinced he's being framed, he goes on the run, only to realize that, by trying to avoid his fate, he may ensure just such a destiny.

THE FILM

Minority Report is based on a short story by Philip K. Dick, whose angst-ridden worldview inspired *Blade Runner*. Here, Spielberg follows a pattern similar to that of Ridley Scott: create an epic filled with the thrills expected for contemporary science fiction while remaining true to the essence of what Dick attempted to say. The darkness of the film makes sense considering the tragic nature of the story. An emphasis on human eyes from the beginning recalls not only *Abre los ojos* (1997) and Hitchcock's *Vertigo* (1958) but also the central theme of Shakespeare's *King Lear* and Sophocles's *Oedipus Rex*, both of which present physical blindness as a realistic correlative for an inability to perceive obvious truths around us.

THEME

Minority Report illustrates the most basic of all tragic themes: the desire of man to grasp whether predetermination or free will directs his life. The tragic hero always in the end learns that a combination of those forces creates the end result. It makes sense then that the precogs are kept in what appears to be a dolphin pool; in ancient times, such conduits between the fates and humankind (oracles) inhabited a place called Delphi, or Dolphin.

TRIVIA

Minority Report owes much to Spielberg's fascination with Alfred Hitchcock thrillers. The image of Cruise becoming "the wrong man," then finding himself in vertigo-inducing situations recalls *North by Northwest* (1959); the sequence in which Spielberg's camera searches the living spaces of ordinary people owes much to *Rear Window* (1954); and the scene in which an upscale villain inadvertently reveals his guilt to the heroine recalls the near-identical scene between Leo G. Carroll and Ingrid Bergman in *Spellbound* (1945).

SKY CAPTAIN AND THE WORLD OF TOMORROW (2004)

—— RANKING: 93 ——

CREDITS

Paramount Pictures/Brooklyn Films II/Riff Raff Film Productions/Filmauro; Kerry Conran, dir.; Conran, scr.; Jude Law, Jon Avnet, Sadie Frost, Marsha Oglesby, pro.; Ed Shearmur, mus.; Eric Adkins, cin.; Sabrina Plisco, ed.; Kevin Conran, prod. design; Kirsten Conran, art dir.; Gary Pollard, special makeup effects; Judy Bradbury, set design; Jesse D'Angelo, Robert Myers, storyboards; Christopher Brennan, Jimmy L. Dyson, Trevor Wood, Peter Fern, F/X; Stephen Lawes, special photographic process; Mike Navarro, effects animator; Lindsay Adams, Tim Alexander/ILM, visual effects; Jorge del Valle, Duane Floch, James Guilford, Sammy Wong, animators; 106 min.; Color/B&W; 1.85:1.

CAST

Jude Law (*Joseph Sullivan/Sky Captain*); Gwyneth Paltrow (*Polly Perkins*); Angelina Jolie (*Franky*); Giovanni Ribisi (*Dex*); Michael Gambon (*Paley*); Bai Ling (*Mystery Woman*); Omid Djalili (*Kaji*); Laurence Olivier (*Dr. Totenkopf*); Trevor Baxter (*Dr. Jennings*); Julian Curry (*Dr. Vargas*); Peter Law (*Kessler*); Jon Rumney (*German Scientist*); Khan Bonfils (*Creepy*); Samta Gyatso (*Scary*).

MOST MEMORABLE LINE

Couldn't we just for once die without all this bickering?

JOE TO POLLY WHEN IT APPEARS THAT THEIR JIG IS UP

BACKGROUND

Growing up in Flint, Michigan, Kerry Conran (1964–) loved the new breed of sci-fi films initiated by *Star Wars*. He also discovered the pop culture of the 1930s that had inspired Lucas: not only the *Buck Rogers* and *Flash Gordon* series, but also *King Kong* (1933), *Lost Horizon* (1937), the various *Superman* cartoon shorts turned out by Max and Dave Fleischer, and films reaching back to *Metropolis* (1927). He became intrigued with the recording of Orson Welles's infamous 1938 radio broadcast of H. G. Wells's *The War of the Worlds*.

THOSE LIPS, THAT EYE! *Angelina Jolie as the bad good girl (or is it the good bad girl?) in Kerry Conran's ambitious sci-fi pulp-fiction exercise in style about a dystopian past (an alternative 1939). The film was digitally created by situating live actors in a computer-generated world. Courtesy: Filmauro/Paramount.*

Conran attended California Institute of the Arts, where he specialized in animation. His dream project would be a visual pastiche of those nostalgic influences, redone for his generation. Whereas other aspiring filmmakers hoped to go to the expense of constructing alternative world "sets" or employing state-of-the-art computer graphics to achieve such an effect, Conran devised a striking alternative. He would "scrapbook" sights and sounds from the past, then have his actors perform their roles in front of blue screens, afterward combining the two in a computer. Conran shot a six-minute product reel with friends, using a Macintosh IIci. This trailer, which took four years to complete, convinced producer Jon Avnet to back *Sky Captain* as a major film.

THE PLOT

New York City, 1939—or a reasonable facsimile thereof in some parallel/alternative universe. At the same time that the mega-zeppelin *Hindenburg III* arrives at the Empire State Building, intrepid reporter Polly Perkins receives a request to meet a shady scientist in Radio City Music Hall, where *The Wizard of Oz* is playing. Polly learns from Dr. Vargas that an enigmatic figure, Dr. Totenkopf, is about to alter life as we know it.

Momentarily, gigantic robots attack the globe, causing authorities to send for Joseph Sullivan (aka Sky Captain), a man of adventure and mystery who, with engineer and assistant Dex, hurries to the rescue. This super-hero's previous involvement with Polly had ended abruptly owing to his propensity to zip off for exotic adventures without her. The rekindling of their romance is complicated by the arrival of another old flame, the dark and deadly beauty Franky, who may be friend, or foe . . . or a bit of each.

THE FILM

Storyboards, often the essence of *cinéma fantastique*, were used here to a degree never before imagined. A team of approximately ninety animators, digital artists, model makers, and visual compositors worked under Conran's supervision to create the most visually rich film ever produced without a single major set needing to be built. "Animatics" is the term for this process, which recreates sights and scenes of the past. Moreover, the audience is left with the impression that believable characters had entered not only a vision of the past, or even the past itself, but also the past as immortalized by what was once considered the fleeting popular culture of that era. As such, the sensibility of 1930s pulp fiction could be combined with the contemporary tastes for large-scale action. Though it was widely assumed that Conran created new technology for the film's stylized look, he used a combination of Adobe After Effects plug-ins.

THEME

The film, by its very nature, deals with the concept of alternative history, an approach by which any narrative can open as anchored in a tangible past. Yet, as the story develops, the narrative gradually disassociates itself from reality as we know it to have occurred. This is a movie about movies and the manner in which films are appreciated not only on an individual basis but also for the manner in which they all run together in the collective memory, a concept that takes the popular notion of referencing a giant step further.

TRIVIA

The appearance of Laurence Olivier, via reconfigured images from earlier films, marked the first time a deceased actor played a new role in a current film. Even as Conran was creating his vision, two other 2004 films—*Casshern* and *Immortal*—were also being shot using what is now referred to as a "digital backlot." The first such film to prove a success at the box office was the neo-noir *Sin City* (Robert Rodriguez/Frank Miller, 2005).

• • • • • • •

ETERNAL SUNSHINE OF THE SPOTLESS MIND (2004)

—— RANKING: 33 ——

CREDITS

Focus Features; Michel Gondry, dir.; Gondry, Charlie Kaufman, Pierre Bismuth, scr.; Kaufman, Anthony Bregman, Steve Golin, pro.; Jon Brion, mus.; Ellen Kuras, cin.; Valdís Óskarsdóttir, ed.; Dan Leigh, prod. design; David Stein, art dir.; Melissa Toth, costumes; Mark Bero, Drew Jiritano, Thomas Viviano, F/X; Michele Ferrone, Mark Dornfeld, Tricia Barrett/Custom Film Effects, special visual effects; Brent Ekstrand, lead animator; Martin Garner, computer graphics; 108 min.; Color; 1.85:1.

META-MODERNISM: *Science fiction incorporates elements from diverse other genres—notably, serious drama, romantic comedy, and the thriller—as is revealed in this Charlie Kaufman and Michel Gondry collaboration about the meaning of memory. Courtesy: Anonymous Content/Focus Features.*

CAST

Jim Carrey (*Joel Barish*); Kate Winslet (*Clementine Kruczynski*); Elijah Wood (*Patrick*); Thomas Jay Ryan (*Frank*); Mark Ruffalo (*Stan*); Jane Adams (*Carrie*); David Cross (*Rob*); Kirsten Dunst (*Mary*); Tom Wilkinson (*Dr. Mierzwiak*); Ryan Whitney (*Young Joel*); Gerry Robert Byrne (*Train Conductor*); Debbon Ayer (*Joel's Mother*).

MOST MEMORABLE LINE

Meet me in Montauk.
CLEMENTINE TO JOEL

BACKGROUND

French director Michel Gondry (1963–) premiered on the continent as a Oui Oui band member, fashioning the music video for that group. His creation attracted the attention of Björk, who hired Gondry for one of her projects because of his unique ability to visually morph time into space. Gondry's artistic sensibility offered up an original virtual world, one in which the continuum associated with such key elements as time and space appears so conclusively violated that, while watching, we come to doubt its validity even outside the realm of a video, including real-life situations.

If Gondry did not precisely invent the technique that has come to be called "bullet time," he did oversee the evolution of this aesthetic. Initially, bullet time was considered revolutionary when, during this era in sci-fi, the approach was popularized in *The Matrix*. After that introductory presentation to the mass audience, bullet time became accepted as a legitimate narrative device for contemporary *cinéma fantastique*.

Gondry collaborated for the first time with Charlie Kaufman (1958–) on the modestly successful, thought-provoking *Human Nature* (2001). This exercise in Kafkaesque surrealism, like Kaufman's earlier collaboration with Spike Jonze (*Being John Malkovich*, 1999) and their later project *Adaptation* (2002), delved into the mysteries of the human mind. *Eternal Sunshine*, with its emphasis on plot reversals, brought such considerations closer still to the realm of generic science fiction.

THE PLOT

The oddest of odd couples, neurotically shy Joel Barish and outgoing exhibitionist Clementine Kruczynski, meet for the first time (or so we are initially led to believe) during the Valentine's Day holiday. For reasons he cannot grasp, Joel has spontaneously skipped work to board the Long Island railroad, headed east to its final stop in Montauk. Clem never does explain what the lure of that abandoned place might have been on this particular day, though by film's end we have a sense of what motivated her. As opposites that attract, they enjoy a brief period of exultation before beginning to wear on one another's nerves. After a fight, Clem breaks off the romance. She visits a futuristic service, Lacuna, a firm that claims it can erase unwanted memories, freeing their clients to move on. Learning of Clem's decision, Joel approaches that office, planning to likewise remove her. During the process, however, the less-than-professional "scientist" Patrick, assigned to monitor this operation, reveals himself to be Clem's current lover. Further, Mary, a free-wheeling assistant, is not precisely what she appears . . . though this remains a secret even to herself, at least for the time being.

THE FILM

Here is yet another key work that, while pleasing critics and entertaining audiences, also furthered the integration of once-edgy arthouse approaches into mainstream movies. Concerns that thoughtful sci-fi might entirely give way to entertaining space fantasy were allayed when *The Truman Show* performed well at the box office. That Carrey appears in both not dissimilar pieces is but one of several connections. *Eternal Sunshine* is another film filled with intellectual references to, for example, the poet Alexander Pope, from whom the title derives, and philosopher Friedrich Nietzsche, one of the first moderns to question the nature of truth. In no way did this approach—only a decade earlier deemed inappropriate for a mass-market film—interfere with the public's ability to enjoy such a challenging work. Still, *Eternal Sunshine* balances cerebral stylistics with a strong dose of old-fashioned romance, being at heart as much a love story as it is an intellectually provocative film. With its groundbreaking style, *Eternal Sunshine* leaves us with what Spielberg once referred to as an "up cry": a bittersweet ending, optimistic yet not sugary or overly sentimental.

THEME

Eternal Sunshine delves into intellectual areas now referred to as "post-modernism" and "post-structuralism." The film probes what we believe to be the objective world surrounding us only to discover that no one can ever know anything—at least, not for certain. The limitations of the human mind as a functional organ, in tandem with the entirely subjective nature of what we mistakenly call "memory," cause all our perceptions to be precisely that: recreations of what may have once happened, altered each and every time we dredge them up to consider—and re-conceive—those bygone moments once more.

TRIVIA

As a result of this film's success, Gondry returned to France and, with a mostly Gallic cast, filmed a surreal fantasy, *The Science of Sleep* (2006), which contains several plot elements reminiscent of science fiction, if not precisely qualifying as a genre piece. Likewise, Kaufman went on to direct as well as write (with, most critics agree, at best, mixed results) *Synecdoche, New York* (2008).

When Joel rummages through objects that remind him of Clem, we see an immense close-up of a paperweight with a snow scene inside. This is an intentional reference to one of the first shots in Orson Welles's *Citizen Kane* (1941), the first American-made film to raise the issue of a single man's complicated identity (or identities) explored here.

· · · · · · ·

V FOR VENDETTA (2005)

—— **RATING: 44** ——

CREDITS

Warner Bros./Virtual Studios; James McTeigue, dir.; Alan Moore and David Lloyd, graphic novel; Andy Wachowski, Lana Wachowski, scr.; Grant Hill, Joel Silver, Wachowski, Wachowski, pro.; Dario Marianelli, mus.; Adrian Biddle, cin.; Martin Walsh, ed.; Owen Paterson, prod. design; Marco Bittner Rosser, Stephen Bream, Sarah Horton, Sebastian T. Krawinkel, Kevin Phipps, art dir.; Sammy Sheldon, costumes; Gerold Bublak, model maker; Axel Eichhorst, storyboards; Marc Homes, George Hull, concept artists; Rolf Hanke, Uli Nefzer, Marcus Schmidt, Jens Schmiedel, Jürgen Thiel, F/X; Steve Adamson, Andrew Ainscow, Jonathan Fawkner, Mike Bell, visual effects; 132 min.; Color; 2.35:1.

CAST

Natalie Portman (*Evey*); Hugo Weaving (*V*); Stephen Rea (*Finch*); Stephen Fry (*Deitrich*); John Hurt (*Sutler*); Tim Pigott-Smith (*Creedy*); Rupert Graves (*Dominic*); Roger Allam (*Lewis Prothero*); Ben Miles (*Dascomb*); Sinéad Cusack (*Delia*

Surridge); Natasha Wightman (*Valerie*); John Standing (*Lilliman*); Eddie Marsan (*Etheridge*); Clive Ashborn (*Guy Fawkes*).

MOST MEMORABLE LINE

Remember, remember, the fifth of November.
EVEY, ATTEMPTING TO RECALL AN OLD DITTY THAT
SUDDENLY TAKES ON NEW SIGNIFICANCE

BACKGROUND

Author Alan Moore collaborated with illustrator David Lloyd to create a continuing dystopian, futuristic fairy tale for the monthly British comics anthology *Warrior*. The first ten episodes of their black-and-white strip, *V for Vendetta*, appeared from 1982 to 1985, with two additional chapters left unreleased after Quality Communications closed down the publication. Top brass at DC were impressed enough to extend an offer to reprint the stories, now in pastel images, with color provided by Steve Whitaker and Siobhan Dodds and Tony Weare supplying additional artwork. When asked about the concept after V became a cult sensation, Moore stated that the most obvious influences were Orwell and Huxley, both highbrow writers, though *Judge Dredd* comics and the performance art of David Bowie had also made strong impacts, as had the writing of iconoclastic novelist Thomas Pynchon, particularly his best-known book, *V.* (1963).

THE PLOT

In the early 2020s, following a nuclear war, the fascistic political party Norse-fire seizes control of England. Fingermen (Nazi-like policemen) wander the streets, doing pretty much as they please. Their attempt to rape young Evey is interrupted by V, a tall, dark stranger in a frightening mask. He whisks the stunned girl off to his secret hideaway, then insists she watch as he destroys the Old Bailey, the key symbol of once-great London. Even as authorities attempt to apprehend V, he seizes control of the airwaves in a guerilla-like fashion, requesting that people of the city rise up against their oppressors on November 5 to destroy the Houses of Parliament.

THE FILM

The plot resembles a combination of Alexandre Dumas's *The Count of Monte Cristo* (1844) and Gaston Leroux's *The Phantom of the Opera* (1910), with elements from the 1953 3-D *House of Wax* thrown in. As V slips through the city at

RADICAL SCI-FI: *Adapted from a controversial cult graphic novel, this visually elaborate, politically extreme noir parable, starring Natalie Portman and Hugo Weaving as the Guy Fawkes–like title character, rates as the most anarchistic, nihilistic movie ever released by a major studio. Courtesy: Warner Bros.*

night, he bears a striking resemblance to Vincent Price in that richly colored horror film.

Initially, Moore and Lloyd considered fashioning one more conventional superhero. However, they decided that, if their piece was to be taken seriously in its attack on Thatcherism in 1980s English politics, they should reverse expected imagery. So they chose as their model Guy Fawkes (1570–1606), the terrorist who attempted to blow up Parliament as part of the 1605 Gunpowder Plot.

Though James McTeigue (1967–) had never before directed a movie, he won this assignment owing to what the producers lauded as his excellent work as first assistant director on all three *Matrix* movies. Surprisingly to some, McTeigue explained that while the mise-en-scène would be comic bookish, he wanted to recreate the power and passion of Gillo Pontecorvo's *The Battle of Algiers* (1966), a black-and-white docudrama about freedom fighters driving the French out of Northwest Africa.

THEME

Despite the film's adherence to the style and substance of the graphic novels, Moore expressed betrayal at what he saw as a cop-out in the Hollywood-izing of his uncompromising work. At several points in the film, V states outright that the great cause he's fighting for is freedom, a counterpoint to the fascism in the England of his time. Moore insisted that in the comics, the term had not been "freedom" but "anarchy," a far more demanding concept for any writer to ask readers—or viewers—to sympathize with. Still, there can be no question that V is an anarchist from what he does as compared to what he says. Indeed, never has the cause of outright chaos been so openly championed in a big-budget commercial venture.

TRIVIA

Andy and Lana Wachowski, who worked on this screenplay long before they created *The Matrix* (though that series appeared in theaters first), were influenced by the themes and style of Moore's V while creating their own original work.

In the comic books, the future date in which V and Evey meet is November 5, 1997. However, this had to be eliminated for the film version, which did not appear until more than ten years after the events as originally conceived by Moore.

The only actress other than Portman who was seriously considered for the role of Evey was Scarlett Johansson.

·······

CHILDREN OF MEN (2006)

—— RANKING: 9 ——

CREDITS

Universal Pictures/Strike Entertainment/Hit & Run Productions; Alfonso Cuarón, dir.; P. D. James, novel; Cuarón, Timothy J. Sexton, David Arata, Mark Fergus, Hawk Ostby, scr., Marc Abraham, Eric Newman, Hilary Shor, Iain Smith, Tony Smith, pro.; John Tavener, mus.; Emmanuel Lubezki, cin.; Cuarón, Alex Rodríguez, ed.; Jim Clay, Geoffrey Kirkland, prod. design; Gary Freeman, Malcolm Middleton, art dir.; Jany Temime, costumes; Victoria Bancroft, prosthetics; Shaune Harrison, special makeup effects; Richard Beggs, sound design;

Ian Corbould, Paul Corbould, F/X; Nick Dudman, animatronics; Rupert Porter/Double Negative, Lucy Killick, Frazer Churchill, Antony Bluff, Amy Beresford/Framestore, visual effects; Andy Kind/Framestore, CGI effects; 109 min.; Color; 1.85:1.

CAST

Clive Owen (*Theo Faron*); Julianne Moore (*Julian*); Michael Caine (*Jasper*); Clare-Hope Ashitey (*Kee*); Chiwetel Ejiofor (*Luke*); Charlie Hunnam (*Patric*); Danny Huston (*Nigel*); Maria McErlane (*Shirley*); Michael Haughey (*Mr. Griffiths*); Phaldut Sharma (*Ian*); Philippa Urquhart (*Janice*); Tehmina Sunny (*Zara*); Pam Ferris (*Miriam*); Ed Westwick (*Alex*).

MOST MEMORABLE LINE

It's a miracle.

LUKE, SPEAKING OF KEE'S PREGNANCY

BACKGROUND

The films of Alfonso Cuarón Orozco (1961–) run the gamut from updated old-fashioned family movies (*A Little Princess*, 1995) to studies of culture and ethnicity in his homeland, Mexico (*Y tu mamá también*, 2001). A true auteur—director, writer, producer, editor—Cuarón perceives no distinction between a project designed with great commercial potential (*Harry Potter and the Prisoner of Azkaban*, 2004) and one projecting a dark dystopian vision of a future marked by infertility, as is the case with *Children of Men*, so long as story elements allow him to convey his personal truth to the largest number of viewers. A former philosophy student and the son of a nuclear physicist, Cuarón's work conveys serious concerns about science and its potential to destroy the very world it was created to enhance.

A 1992 novel by Phyllis Dorothy (P. D.) James (1920–), who balances her time between serving as a life peer in England's House of Lords and writing smart fiction, mostly of the detective genre, caught Cuarón's artistic attention. A lifelong fan of high-quality contemporary literature, he was particularly attracted to this unique turn on traditional dystopian fiction.

THE PLOT

Civil servant Theo, wandering listlessly through the ruined world around him, is kidnapped by a secret society. The dissident Fishes include his onetime wife Julian, who implores Theo to oversee a clandestine operation. A young woman,

HUMANKIND'S LAST GREAT HOPE: *A young woman (Clare-Hope Ashitey), who is the only female to conceive in a future infertile world, may be a modern Mary. This Saturn Award winner (Best Science Fiction Film) combines the insistence on the need for old-fashioned hope and faith found in* Metropolis *with ultra-contemporary commentary on restrictive immigration laws. Courtesy: Strike Entertainment/Hit & Run/Universal.*

Kee, must be spirited across the country, to the seaside where a ship from the Human Project awaits. Once drawn into the plot, Theo grasps that Kee is pregnant, a rarity as no child has been born for the past eighteen years.

THE FILM

In the novel, it is Julian who is pregnant. Cuarón added the character of Kee to present a woman of color as a potential Mary, mother of the Son of Man. This allowed not only for sensitivity to ethnicity but also an opportunity, via her harassment as a foreigner by British agents, to comment on illegal immigration, a pressing issue at the time of production. In the book, the child is a boy. By making the baby (an apparent savior) a girl, Cuarón was also able to touch on feminist issues.

Searching for a style that would be appropriate to both the narrative and his viewpoint, Cuarón brought the concept of near-future closer to our own time than had ever before been the case in film. Though set in 2027, the onscreen world reveals no attempt at futurization. This is the filmmaker's—and the filmgoer's—own world, driving the social commentary home with added power. For realism, Cuarón opted for a handheld camera, allowing his work to resemble a TV news program. To balance this with the necessary stylization, he drained the spectrum of everyday colors, allowing for an unpleasant industrial blue to dominate the proceedings, an approach that would heavily influence twenty-first-century sci-fi films.

THEME

Cuarón's main concern, in his words, was to express "hope and faith" in even the most tarnished of life situations, highlighting the need for people to believe still in the old cliché that insists that the darkest hour is always just before dawn.

In James's novel, Theo is an Oxford don. Cuarón altered this to make him a common man hero, more in line with the director's desire to reach ordinary people everywhere. James's telling focused more on the political repercussions of the plummeting birthrate: a fascistic dictator seizing control after an increasingly pessimistic public turns its collective back on the democratic process. In the novel, Julian is not the estranged wife of Theo, but married to one of the anti-government radicals. Cuarón replaced these plot points with images of rage in the street, hand-to-hand combat mirroring political upheavals taking place around the globe in our own time, while neatly employing his musical score to imply a religious allegory.

In the novel, male infertility is revealed to be the source of the birthrate problem. Such a premise can be traced back to the 1956 sci-fi film *World Without End* (Edward Bernds). Cuarón reverses that, the majority of women no longer able to become mothers. He leaves the question of a cause—for example, pollution of the environment or exposure to nuclear radiation—ambiguous to suggest that the end of humankind, if that does indeed occur, is not due to any one of society's failings but to *all* of them. Counterpointing this is the possibility of Divine Intervention, a suggestion that qualifies *Children* as a conservative film. The Order of the Fish, a term applied to true believers of more than two thousand years ago, is reapplied to those dedicated to the film's special child. Here, if not in the book, the golden child may be the result of virgin birth, suggested throughout yet never insisted upon, allowing those who wish to accept the film as a new New Testament.

TRIVIA

As grim and post-modern as this film may be, *Children of Men* contains a sly reference to the glamorous, romantic classic *Casablanca* (Michael Curtiz, 1942): each movie begins when an antihero is approached by a beautiful lover from his past, requesting that he use his influence to arrange for letters of transit out of the country.

As a youth, Cuarón was forced to drop out of a Mexican film school owing to his desire to shoot in English and otherwise commercialize his projects. As compared to his mentors, the aspiring filmmaker believed that in so doing, he would not compromise his vision but rather expand the potential audience.

· · · · · · ·

TRANSFORMERS (2007)

—— RANKING: 99 ——

CREDITS
Dreamworks SKG/Paramount Pictures; Michael Bay, dir.; John Rogers, story; Roberto Orci, Alex Kurtzman, scr.; Ian Bryce, Tom DeSanto, Lorenzo di Bonaventura, Don Murphy, pro.; Steve Jablonsky, mus.; Mitchell Amundsen, cin.; Tom A. Muldoon, Paul Rubell, Glen Scantlebury, ed.; François Audouy, Beat Frutiger, Sean Haworth, Kevin Kavanaugh, art dir.; Robin Beauchesne, Howard Berger, makeup effects; H. Barclay Aaris, David Amborn, Ryan Amborn, Sean Amborn, David J. Barker, Robert Bell, F/X; Mimi Abers/ILM, Charles Abou Aad, Ismail Acar/ILM, visual effects; Leigh Barbier, Jason Brown, digital artists; Jeremy Bolan/ILM, Allen Holbrook, animators; 144 min.; Color; 2.35:1.

CAST
Shia LaBeouf (*Sam Witwicky*); Megan Fox (*Mikaela Banes*); Josh Duhamel (*Capt. William Lennox*); Tyrese Gibson (*Sgt. Epps*); Rachael Taylor (*Maggie Madsen*); Anthony Anderson (*Glen*); Jon Voight (*John Keller*); John Turturro (*Agent Simmons*); Michael O'Neill (*Tom*); Kevin Dunn (*Ron Witwicky*); Julie White (*Judy Witwicky*); Amaury Nolasco ("*Fig*"); Zack Ward (*Donnelly*); Rizwan Manji (*Akram*); William Morgan Sheppard (*Capt. Witwicky*); Bernie Mac (*Bobby Bolivia*); Johnny Sanchez (*Clown*); Peter Cullen (*Optimus Prime*, voice); Mark Ryan (*Bumblebee*, voice); Darius McCrary (*Jazz*, voice); Robert Foxworth (*Ratchet*, voice); Jess Harnell (*Ironside/Barricade*, voice); Hugo Weaving (*Megatron*, voice).

MOST MEMORABLE LINE
So you're, like, an alien?

MIKAELA TO A TRANSFORMER

CGI SUPREME: *Two alien races from the planet Cybertron carry their eternal struggle to Earth in Michael Bay's signature film, based on a popular line of toys. As the director has stated, "I make movies for teenage boys."* Courtesy: Dreamworks/SMG/Paramount.

BACKGROUND

Japan's Takara Co. had a huge hit with their Microman and Diaclone series of pliable toys that could be manipulated from motorized vehicles into unique personalities with robotic qualities. In the United States, Hasbro executives wondered if such items might prove successful here, purchasing the molds and rights. Sales to children, teenagers, and adult collectors boomed. In 1984, an animated TV series premiered, followed by a 1986 film. Contemporary franchising led to every conceivable item from cereal brands to video games. As Spielberg was a fan, it made sense that he would eventually executive-produce a spectacular feature film version.

THE PLOT

From a distant galaxy, evil robotic shape-shifters known as "Decepticons" arrive on Earth, searching for the long-missing AllSpark, the creator of their cosmos. Its power will allow their long-frozen leader Megatron to turn Earth's machines against humans. Autobots, the hero Transformers, arrive simultaneously to protect the earthlings. Their leader, Optimus Prime, has his nicest ally, Bumblebee, turn himself into a car, which is purchased by an awkward teen Witwicky, who is hoping to impress a local dream girl, Mikaela. Yet, this purchase owes more to destiny than to accident: more than a hundred years earlier, Witwicky's grandfather made first contact with aliens. Meanwhile, the secretary of defense trusts that a bright young computer hacker can solve the mystery of why Earth is being invaded, and by whom.

THE FILM

After reading a treatment by Don Murphy (producer, *The League of Extraordinary Gentlemen*, 2003) and Tom DeSanto (writer, *X-Men*, 2000) in 2003, Spielberg brought aboard two additional writers, Roberto Orci and Alec Kurtzman, veterans of the TV ventures *Hercules: The Legendary Journeys*, *Xena: Warrior Princess*, and *Alias*, as well as their joint film project, *The Legend of Zorro* (2005). John Rogers contributed to the story line, and as a former stand-up comic, he added its humor. All agreed that theirs would be a freewheeling interpretation, re-inventing the characters' appearances to offer their spin on the origination backdrop. This constituted a risk with Transformers purists. Though initial reviews were mixed, the film became a huge hit, justifying its immense $150 million budget. Even those who don't care for the hard-edged tone of nonstop action and the broad playing of the roles admitted that the fusion of live-action sequences with computer-generated effects was the most sophisticated that had yet been achieved.

THEME

One implied idea is an apotheosis of mainstream movies that appeared during the period in which Transformers became a part of popular culture. This led to numerous Spielberg references, including a boy and his alien pal (*E.T.*), an intergalactic combat (*War of the Worlds*), and even an innocent little girl who wanders through the chaos like the child in a red coat in *Schindler's List*.

TRIVIA

The AllSpark replaces the energon cubes from the animated TV series. Originally called the "Matrix of Leadership," its name was changed to avoid confusion with *The Matrix*. Director Michael Bay altered the make of car that Bumblebee transforms from a Volkswagen Beetle into a Chevy Camaro to limit comparisons with Disney's *The Love Bug* films. The voice of robot hero Optimus Prime is modeled on that of John Wayne.

The relationship of teen hero to his car is derived from *Back to the Future*

(1985) while the idea of a geek who gets the beautiful girl echoes all teen wish-fulfillment flicks made since 1980. The small coterie of heroes are sci-fi versions of *The Magnificent Seven* (1960), and in the script's first draft, there were seven Autobots. The African-American family appears a satire on those in the movies and TV shows of Tyler Perry.

A sequence involving characters struggling in high places has precedent in such Hitchcock films as *Saboteur*, *Vertigo*, and *North by Northwest*. Also essential is Hitchcock's concept of the MacGuffin, a seemingly unimportant object containing great value, the cause of all the activity. Here we have the captain's glasses, a map leading to the AllSpark embedded on the lenses. They also reference the broken glasses in Sergei M. Eisenstein's *Battleship Potemkin* (1925).

· · · · · · ·

WALL-E (2008)

—— RANKING: 27 ——

CREDITS

Pixar Animation Studios/Walt Disney Pictures; Andrew Stanton, dir.; Stanton, Jim Reardon, Pete Docter, scr.; Jim Morris, Lindsey Collins, John Lasseter, pro.; Thomas Newman, mus.; Stephen Schaffer, ed.; Ralph Eggleston, prod. design; Anthony Christov, art dir.; Mark Cordell Holmes, graphic art director; Bruce Zick, visual development; Ben Burtt, sound/character voice design; Neil Blevins, digital artist; Lanny Cermak/ILM, digital artist; Simon Dunsdon, CGI artist; Jeanmarie King/ILM, Richard E. Hollander, Christopher James Hall/Kerner Optical, visual effects; Alan Barillaro, supervising animator; Angus MacLane, directing animator; Bob Scott, end titles; Tom MacDougall, music supervisor; 98 min.; Color; 2.35:1.

CAST (VOICES)

Ben Burtt (*WALL-E/M-O*); Elissa Knight (*EVE*); Jeff Garlin (*Captain*); MacInTalk (*AUTO*); John Ratzenberger (*John*); Kathy Najimy (*Mary*); Sigourney Weaver (*Ship's Computer*); Kim Kopf (*Hoverchair Mother*); Andrew Stanton, Lori Alan, Teresa Ganzel, Laraine Newman (*Additional Voices*), Fred Willard (*Shelby Forthright*).

After 700 years of doing what he was built for . . .
he'll discover what he's *meant* for.
ADVERTISING TAGLINE

BACKGROUND
Andrew Stanton (1965–) pitched the project to Pixar head honcho John Lasseter (1957–) in 1994: "What if mankind had to leave Earth and somebody forgot to turn off the last robot?" Intrigued, Lasseter put the project on a slate that already included *A Bug's Life* (1998), *Toy Story 2* (1999), and *Monsters, Inc.* (2001). When Stanton and Peter Docter (1968–) began work on a script, the original title was *Trash Planet*. During development, the determined little robot emerged as such a distinct personality that the team decided to focus on WALL-E, using the dystopian environment as backdrop. All the same, Steve Jobs (1955–2011), who had become fascinated with and directly involved in the project, had to be convinced to go with the *WALL-E* title (originally spelled *W.A.L.-E.*), which he didn't initially like. Anthony Christov, a native of Bulgaria hired to oversee the art direction, based his concept of the city on Chernobyl. Always, though, everyone involved with the production was aware that, as a Disney family film, *WALL-E* must, despite its cautionary fable quality, end optimistically.

SOMEWHERE, OUT THERE: *Director Andrew Stanton proved that a film created via CGI could contain key human emotions—even when ascribed to young robots in love—on the level of a live-action film. WALL-E also comments on themes as significant as consumerism and ecology. Courtesy: Pixar/Walt Disney Pictures.*

THE PLOT

In 2105, lonely little robot WALL-E methodically continues the project he had long ago been programmed for: compacting trash on a deserted Earth. He has no companions other than a chipper cockroach, the one creature born with the natural protection necessary to survive mankind's trashing of the environment, and, more recently, one green and growing organism, proof of nature's ability to revitalize, at least once humans are gone. Another robot, the probe EVE, beams down and WALL-E is smitten. When EVE is summoned back on board the *Axiom* galacticship, WALL-E follows, putting a new spin on one of the oldest of Hollywood axioms: boy robot meets girl robot, boy robot loses girl robot, boy robot gets girl robot.

THE FILM

The rebellion WALL-E incites on *Axiom* was intended to recall the slave uprising against the Romans inspired by Kirk Douglas in *Spartacus* (Stanley Kubrick, 1960). Once again, by his very presence and determination to live in a free manner, an ordinary man (or robot) inspires others to question their lot for the first time, becoming a hero in the process.

While *WALL-E* and *Inception* (2010) may present the opposite poles of contemporary science fiction—the former delightful in its sweet simplicity, the latter archly demanding in its dark intellectual complexity—these disparate films do share one key element: Édith Piaf's "La Vie en Rose." Key to the soundtrack of both films, the song symbolizes in each a golden age for Earth and man that has somehow slipped away.

THEME

Can robots love, hate, experience emotions? If so, does that mean such manmade creatures are evolving into something that more closely resembles humanity? And, if that is the case, is this for better or worse? These questions have been raised at least since the publication of Isaac Asimov's novel *I, Robot* (1950), though Czech writer Karel Čapek hinted at such a theme earlier in his play *R.U.R.* (Rossum's Universal Robots, 1920). Whereas most cautionary fables about robots stealing control from humans portray a hostile attack, *WALL-E* offers an alternative: the bloodless coup occurs without humans even noticing as people grow lazier and obese after assigning physical activity to their supposed "slaves" and complicated service systems.

The film offers one more unique variation on the green theme, as that first lonely little natural growth leads to the eventual comeback of a green Earth.

WALL-E is thus both romantic in appeal and optimistic in tone, very much in line with the great tradition of Disney products.

TRIVIA

Among the cast members, Fred Willard is unique in that he lends his actual physical presence as well as voice to his character, Shelby Forthright.

Though the film displays the remarkable CGI animation for which Pixar, the company itself and the gifted crew, is renowned, this is very much a Disney film in spirit. The sidekick to the title character might well have been named Jiminy, as the cockroach resembles that cricket in *Pinocchio* (1940).

The film that WALL-E adores, with its idealized image of life in an earlier, happier time, is *Hello, Dolly!* (1969).

Stanton had hoped, at the time, to move on to direct an adaptation of Edgar Rice Burroughs's *John Carter of Mars* pulp fiction novels, though Disney eventually decided to do that as a live-action project. By the time this project reached the screen, with Stanton at the helm, it featured live action with special effects. Whatever the initial dream for the John Carter film may have been, it turned into a nightmare during filming and abruptly ended more than one career.

The visual settings, as well as the narratives that take place within them, became so complex that artists at Pixar had to create a total of 125,000 storyboards, 50,000 more than usual.

Among awards won by WALL-E were the Golden Globe for Best Animated Film, the Nebula Award for Best Script, the Saturn Award for Best Animated Film, and the Academy Award for Best Animated Feature Film.

· · · · · · ·

AVATAR (2009)

—— RANKING: 11 ——

CREDITS

Twentieth Century Fox Film Corporation/Dune Entertainment; James Cameron, dir., scr.; Cameron, Jon Landau, pro.; James Horner, mus.; Mauro Fiore, cin.; Cameron, John Refoua, Stephen E. Rivkin, ed.; Rick Carter, Robert Stromberg, prod. design; Nick Bassett, Robert Bavin, Simon Bright, art dir.; Mayes C. Rubeo, Deborah Lynn Scott, costumes; Alex Alvarez, creature art; Jose Astacio,

STATE OF THE ART: *James Cameron combined criticism of imperialism, colonization, and militarization with a romantic vision of nature in a spectacular viewing experience that changed the nature of moviemaking.* Avatar *rightly netted Oscars for Best Art Direction, Cinematography, and Visual Effects. Courtesy: Dune Entertainment/Ingenious Film Partners/20th Century Fox.*

virtual art; Skywalker Sound, special sound effects; Grant Bensley/Weta Workshop, Dave Booth, F/X; Jim Charmatz/Stan Winston Studio, character design; Shaun Friedberg "Pyrokinesis," Jonathan Fawkner, Laia Alomar/Framestore, visual effects; Ben O'Brien/ILM, digital artist; Richard Baneham, animation supervisor; 162 min. (theatrical release), 171 min. (special edition), 178 min. (extended cut); Color; 1.78:1 (IMAX 3D).

CAST

Sam Worthington (*Jake Sully*); Zoe Saldana (*Neytiri*); Sigourney Weaver (*Grace*); Stephen Lang (*Col. Miles Quaritch*); Michelle Rodriguez (*Trudy Chacon*); Giovanni Ribisi (*Parker Selfridge*); Joel David Moore (*Norm Spellman*); CCH Pounder (*Moat*); Wes Studi (*Eytukan*); Laz Alonso (*Tsu'tey*); Dileep Rao (*Dr. Patel*).

MOST MEMORABLE LINE

Everything is backwards now. Like, out there is the true world.
And in here is the dream.
JAKE SULLY

BACKGROUND

What do you offer as an encore for *Titanic* (1997)? James Cameron took an idea that had haunted him for years, and he used the vast power that was his following the huge financial success of that acclaimed Oscar-winning film. The main roadblock to an immediate start was the F/X necessary to bring Cameron's vision to full life onscreen. He made the decision to delay filming until CGI and other venues reached a new level, allowing for a total realization of his idea.

THE PLOT

By the mid-twenty-second century, earthlings have stretched their territorial imperatives into space to exploit mineral resources, often at the expense of indigenous people. Pandora, a forest-covered moon in the Alpha Centauri system, contains unobtanium, a source of energy mined by astronaut entrepreneurs representing corporate interests. In so doing, they destroy the ecological system and threaten genocide of the local Na'vi. Originally pleased to be a part of this epic conquest, paraplegic Jake Sully finds himself questioning imperialistic attitudes once an extension of himself becomes isolated in a green garden. There, he falls in love with the humanoid beauty Neytiri and comes to share her people's simple, pure values.

THE FILM

In addition to narrative and themes, Cameron always planned to make this a cutting-edge experience for viewers in newly renovated theaters. Pushing back the boundaries of film in what critic Robert Warshow had referred to as "an immediate experience," Cameron conceived the recently improved 3-D process as basic. Rather than use the outdated approach of such nostalgic, though crude, films as *House of Wax* (André de Toth, 1953), Cameron tested RealD 3D, Dolby 3D, XpanD 3D, and IMAX 3D. To maintain secrecy, he tested his advanced process in certain South Korean theaters, employing the revolutionary "4-D" format for a complete stereoscopic effect and qualifying *Avatar* as a technological breakthrough, as well as an artistic endeavor.

THEME

Immediately following the film's release, Pope Benedict XVI, speaking for the Roman Catholic Church, warned against "neopaganism" as tied to the worship of nature, with, of course, *Avatar* being the latest example of precisely that. In its review of the film, the Vatican's official newspaper, *L'Osservatore Romano*, insisted that Cameron's desire to engender a "deification of nature" went against the grain of a Christian tradition that posits the defense of nature rather than its worship.

However one thinks or feels about that perception, a follow-up statement was, simply, incorrect: *Avatar* offered up "a new theology." In truth, the film's religious ideas can be traced back to such popular Westerns as *Little Big Man* (Arthur Penn, 1970), *Dances with Wolves* (Kevin Costner, 1990), and *The Last of the Mohicans* (Michael Mann, 1992); each features an Anglo, hailing from a corrupt civilization, who finds true spirituality in the wide-open spaces with Native American blood brothers. Cameron's views also offer a throwback to the Romantic poets of the early nineteenth century, particularly Wordsworth. His insistence that we celebrate "splendour in the grass" and "glory in the flower" argues in favor of discovering a joyous form of religion in the woods. Such thinking was dismissed as neo-paganism (which indeed it was) by London's classicist minds of that time. No surprise, then, that, thematically speaking, *Avatar* would be damned by contemporary conservatives and hailed by modern liberals owing to its "extreme green" attitude.

TRIVIA

Dr. Paul Frommer, a University of Southern California professor and linguist, invented the unique and entirely original language for the Na'vi. Writer and painter Wayne Barlowe was among those who collaborated with Cameron in creating the look of the Na'vi.

Cameron insisted that his story line was influenced not only by "every science-fiction novel I ever read as a child," but also the jungle adventure romance books of H. Rider Haggard (*King Solomon's Mines*, 1885) and Edgar Rice Burroughs (*Tarzan of the Apes*, 1912).

Though originally budgeted at something less than $250 million, the final cost of completion may have exceeded $300 million. Some industry insiders believed that the film could never come close to earning back its negative cost, but *Avatar* grossed $2 billion internationally, setting the stage for a new era of enormous film production undertakings.

····· ··

STAR TREK (2009) AND STAR TREK INTO DARKNESS (2013)

—— RANKING: 46 (TIE) ——

STAR TREK (2009)

CREDITS

Paramount Pictures/Spyglass Entertainment/Bad Robot; J. J. Abrams, dir.; Roberto Orci, Alex Kurtzman, scr.; Abrams, Kurtzman, Damon Lindelof, pro.; Michael Giacchino, mus.; Daniel Mindel, cin.; Maryann Brandon, Mary Jo Markey, ed.; Scott Chambliss, prod. design; Keith P. Cunningham, art dir.; Michael Kaplan, costumes; Crist Ballas, special makeup effects; William Aldridge, Danny Cangemi, Terry Chapman, F/X; Dan Bornstein/ILM, visual effects; 127 min.; Color; 2.35:1.

CAST

Chris Pine (*James Kirk*); Zachary Quinto (*Spock*); Leonard Nimoy (*Spock "Prime"*); Eric Bana (*Nero*); Bruce Greenwood (*Capt. Pike*); Karl Urban (*Bones*); Zoe Saldana (*Uhura*); Simon Pegg (*Scotty*); John Cho (*Sulu*); Anton Yelchin (*Chekov*); Ben Cross (*Sarek*); Winona Ryder (*Amanda*); Chris Hemsworth (*George Kirk*); Jennifer Morrison (*Winona Kirk*).

MOST MEMORABLE LINE

You are fully capable of deciding your own destiny.
The question you face is: which path will you choose?
SAREK TO SPOCK

BACKGROUND

After NBC cancelled *Star Trek* in 1969, Gene Roddenberry announced to family and friends that he had no intention of giving up on a series that expressed his own unique sense and sensibility. In particular, Roddenberry thought it might be intriguing to return to his original idea for the *Enterprise*'s captain,

Christopher Robin Pike, who was central to the first pilot episode, "The Cage." In 1963, NBC, which had recently cancelled the top-rated Western *Wagon Train*, warmed to the notion that, in the 1960s, the future might provide a canvas similar to that offered by the old frontier in the 1950s. But executives concluded that the intellectual approach of the *Star Trek* pilot had more in common with CBS's *The Twilight Zone* (never high in the ratings) than with the human drama of the number one Nielsen-rated *Wagon Train*. The men in suits asked Roddenberry to return to the drawing board and re-imagine a show rich in romance.

When star Jeffrey Hunter dropped out, Roddenberry decided not to recast the earnest Pike but to create the brash Kirk, a more likely figure to incite action-filled tales. Once the series sold, the chief writer-producer expanded "The Cage" into a first season two-parter, "The Menagerie." In it, the current captain, James T. Kirk encounters the former captain (and more recently fleet captain) Pike as a wheelchair-bound recluse. A three-year series, animated TV episodes, theatrical films, and, finally, a live-action reboot involving Kirk's own successor kept Roddenberry busy. Yet, his dream did belatedly come true when J. J. Abrams (1966–) chose an origination saga in which Kirk at first supports, then supplants Pike.

THE PLOT

The Romulan spacecraft *Narada* attacks a Federation starship. Youthful George Kirk, the acting captain, launches his pregnant wife Winona to safety in an escape vehicle, then courageously makes a frantic last stand against Captain Nero and his Romulan crew. In time, Kirk's son, James Tiberius, grows into a cocky, vain, arrogant youth. He's persuaded to join the Starfleet by his foster father, Captain Pike, who commands the *Enterprise*. First, though, Kirk must attend the academy. There he meets future colleagues, including half-human, half-Vulcan Spock, as committed to logic as Kirk is prone to emotions, and Nyota Uhura, a bright, beautiful linguistics expert. Even as a romantic triangle develops, they are called into action: a distress signal must be answered, and these young people are the only potential crew available to Pike. Kirk alone senses something isn't right, for the supposed lightning storm in space recalls the trap used by Nero on that long-ago day when Jim was born.

THE FILM

One key to the film's spectacular success was Abrams's careful casting and subtle direction of the actors playing Kirk and Spock. To have presented imitations of William Shatner and Leonard Nimoy would have proven disastrous,

THE PERFECT REBOOT: *Though long-time* Trek *fans feared the worst, J. J. Abrams proved them wrong with an origination story that remained true to the essence of Gene Roddenberry's original while adding new textures and dimensions. Here, Zoe Saldana, Chris Pine, and Zachary Quinto prepare for action. Courtesy: Paramount/Spyglass/Bad Robot.*

reducing the reboot to a *Spaceballs*-type parody. Yet, to ignore those iconic portrayals would have also been wrong. Such ingrained portraitures simply had to be acknowledged. Chris Pine and Zachary Quinto's work is informed by physical gestures and vocal intonations that recall the earlier Kirk and Spock, but the younger actors recreated the roles with fresh, original "readings" of the characters.

THEME

Abrams and his writers found themselves in a unique position to add a now-popular sci-fi theme earlier implied by *Star Trek*, beginning with "The Menagerie": alternative reality. This involves human movement beyond the space-time continuum, incorporating wormhole theory. Other versions of actuality other than that presently agreed on are not faux but equally real because all reality is ultimately a mental construction.

STAR TREK INTO DARKNESS (2013)

ADDITIONAL CREDITS

Damon Lindelof, scr.; Bryan Burk, Roberto Orci, pro.; Daniel Mindel, cin.; Ramsey Avery, art dir.; Anne Porter, set design; Burt Dalton, F/X; Ron Ames, Jill Brooks/ILM, Amit Dhawal, Xuzhen An, visual effects; 132 min.; Color; 1.44:1 (IMAX).

ADDITIONAL CAST

Benedict Cumberbatch (*Khan*); Peter Weller (*Marcus*); Alice Eve (*Carol*); Noel Clarke (*Thomas Harewood*).

MOST MEMORABLE LINE

The enemy of my enemy is my friend.
JAMES T. KIRK

THE PLOT

Kirk sets off to capture John Harrison, a fugitive from Starfleet command who committed acts of terrorism, then retreated to Kronos, a planet inhabited by Klingons. The *Enterprise* crew find themselves in a tricky situation, committed to returning Harrison for the legal process while not wanting to inadvertently insult a highly territorial race. A new team member, Carol, wants to help, though things become more complicated when all aboard learn that Marcus, her father and their superior, harbors a hidden agenda.

THEME

Here we encounter science fiction that, far from allowing its audience an easy escape into an enjoyable, fantastical alternative universe, comments on the world that viewers have temporarily left and will shortly re-enter. Abrams revealed himself to be prescient at presenting a situation that would, at the time of his film's release, divide the West into factions as to how escalating violence in the Middle East, particularly Egypt and Syria, should be addressed. Simplistic reaction—to attack or not to attack as extremes—can only make matters worse. To avoid this, leaders must, as Kirk's above quote duly notes, negotiate with enemies. To do so is to prove Einstein correct: everything is ultimately relative.

TRIVIA

The depth with which Abrams developed Khan's dark motivations adds so many dimensions to the character that, by film's end, it seems less appropriate to think of him as a villain than as a tragic character on the order of Shakespeare's Macbeth.

One of the keys to the reboot's success was a decision on the part of Abrams to treat the originals with due respect but not to feel slavishly bound to adhere to every detail for fear of upsetting *Trek* purists. One early example of the effectiveness of this approach is the manner in which Pike becomes wheelchair bound. In the film, it is not identical to the accident that caused his physical problems in "The Menagerie." Yet, the image at the closing of Abrams's *Star Trek* references fans' memories of Pike in such a situation in 1965–1966. In Abrams's version, it becomes clear that Pike was the first person to helm the ship *Enterprise*, whereas in earlier incarnations, Robert April had served as captain for nine years. Torn between loyalty to the source and the need to create a *Star Trek* that would emerge as his own, Abrams opted for the latter.

Roddenberry had always confided to close associates that, as a civil rights activist, he would have loved to create a romantic triangle, with Kirk and Spock vying for the lovely Uhura. However, restrictions on network TV during the mid-sixties were so extreme that he had to fight a major battle simply to win the right to cast African-American actress Nichelle Nichols in the part, much less portray her character involved in an interracial romance.

By making such a relationship the centerpiece of a rebooted *Star Trek*, Abrams finally brought the late Gene Roddenberry's dream to full fruition.

DISTRICT 9 (2009)

—— RANKING: 21 ——

CREDITS

TriStar Pictures/WingNut Films/QED; Neill Blomkamp, dir.; Blomkamp, Terri Tatchell, scr.; Carolynne Cunningham, Peter Jackson, Bill Block, pro.; Clinton Shorter, mus.; Trent Opaloch, cin.; Julian Clarke, ed.; Philip Ivey, prod. design; Mike Berg, Emilia Roux, art dir.; Diana Cilliers, costumes; Jamie Beswarick, Theola Booyens, Donald Brooker, Joe Dunckley, makeup/prosthetics; Andrew Baker, Aaron Beck/Weta Workshop, designers; Grant Bensley, Bruce Campbell/ Weta Workshop, F/X; Trevor Adams, visual effects; 112 min.; Color; 1.85:1.

CAST

Sharlto Copley (*Wikus Van De Merwe*); Jason Cope (*Grey Bradnam/Christopher Johnson*); Nathalie Boltt (*Sarah Livingstone*); Sylvaine Strike (*Dr. Katrina McKenzie*); John Sumner (*Les Feldman*); William Allen Young (*Dirk Michaels*); Mandla Gaduka (*Fundiswa Mhlanga*); Johan van Schoor (*Nicolas Van De Merwe*); David James (*Koobus Venter*); Kenneth Nkosi (*Thomas*); Jed Brophy (*James Hope*); Louis Minnaar (*Piet Smit*); Robert Hobbs (*Ross Pienaar*); Vittorio Leonardi (*Michael Bloemstein*); Tim Gordon (*Clive Henderson*); Eugene Khumbanyiwa (*Obesandjo*).

MOST MEMORABLE LINE

I just want everyone watching right now
to learn from what has happened.
FUNDISWA MHLANGA, ASSISTANT TO WIKUS,
IN AN AFTER-THE-FACT INTERVIEW

BACKGROUND

Born in South Africa in 1979, Neill Blomkamp early on began creating intense imagery for varied media. When he was eighteen, Blomkamp's family moved to Canada, where he attended the Vancouver Film School. There, he developed his signature style, yoking together polar aspects of movies. The *cinéma vérité*, shot-on-the-street, handheld camerawork developed by the French New Wave in the early 1960s could be collapsed into computer graphics, allowing the filmmaker to drastically alter everything he had already shot, transforming reality into a fantasy.

A friend from Johannesburg, Sharlto Copley produced some of Blomkamp's short films. *Landfall* (2007), Blomkamp's live-action Halo 3 trailer trilogy, caught the attention of New Zealand–born and –based filmmaker Peter Jackson (1961–). Between stints on *The Lord of the Rings* trilogy and his remake of *King Kong* (2005), Jackson became a mentor, agreeing to oversee a theatrical version of the Halo video games. When funding fell through, Jackson encouraged Blomkamp to revive an earlier piece, the sci-fi short *Alive in Joburg* (2006). This impressive six-minute film, shot in Johannesburg and employing a documentary-like approach to condemn apartheid, served as a cinematic synopsis for its expanded commercial counterpart, *District 9*.

THE PLOT

After nearly three decades of dealing with unwanted aliens following first contact, and sickened by constant friction between humans and what are derogatorily referred to as useless "prawns," South Africa turns the problem over to a military-industrial conglomerate, MNU. An awkward but honest bureaucrat, Wikus, enters District 9 and delivers eviction notices to ghetto dwellers. He is accompanied by strong-armed mercenary Venter, who would prefer just to kill them all. In contact with alien Johnson, Wikus inadvertently spills on himself a fluid that's been distilled for escape purposes. Soon he begins to morph into a prawn. Executives at MNU see this as a key to total power as previously the aliens' advanced weapons could not be employed by humans. Not wanting to be used for such exploitation, Wikus, now a crossbreed, goes on the run. However, he must face Nigerian gangster Obesandjo, who wants to eat Wikus's alien arm in order to achieve greater power.

THE FILM

In many regards, the Jackson-Blomkamp relationship recalls that of Francis Ford Coppola and George Lucas on *THX 1138*. In both tightly budgeted student films, the approach was to tell the entire story from the point of view of surveillance cameras, consistently conveying that "Big Brother Is Watching You!" Lucas all but eliminated such a technique while shooting the full-length feature. Blomkamp achieved something more complex. *District 9* begins as a documentary, continuing in that mode throughout its first act. During the second act, Blomkamp gradually allows for dramatic scenes to appear, integrating

A NEW KIND OF GENRE FILM: Neill Blomkamp employed a documentary-like sense of immediacy to create his alternative history film, intended to criticize apartheid in South Africa circa 1982. Courtesy: WingNut/QED/Tri-Star.

these so seamlessly that they appear organic in context. With this achieved, the film's second half shifts toward a dramatic presentation of the onscreen events.

The opening sequence, in which the history of the invasion and its aftermath is presented in rapid-fire form, recalls the technique used by Orson Welles to set up his title character in *Citizen Kane* (1941). In that film, Welles presented details through "News on the March," an exact approximation of "The March of Time" newsreel series so popular in the pre-television era. Blomkamp adjusted that approach to employ conventions of today's television news. *District 9* rates as one of the purest science-fiction films in its adherence to the genre's most basic ambition: writing the history of the future as we believe it likely will occur.

THEME

District 9 does not offer an escape from reality but rather a means of comprehending it. The narrative is modeled on an incident that took place in Cape Town, South Africa, during apartheid. Between 1968 and 1982, the government relocated more than sixty thousand residents of District Six to a nearby area on the grounds that interaction between blacks and whites must be halted so as to avoid friction. By transplanting that situation to a genre treatment, Blomkamp transcended the specifics, creating a more universal attack on the meaning of xenophobia.

TRIVIA

The Academy of Science Fiction, Fantasy & Horror Films honored *District 9* with their 2010 Saturn Award for Best International Film. It was also nominated for four Oscars, including Best Picture, one of the rare occasions in which that highly traditional institution has acknowledged a film so radical and cutting edge in style and substance.

INCEPTION (2010)

—— RANKING: 17 ——

CREDITS

Warner Bros./Legendary Pictures/Syncopy; Christopher Nolan, dir., scr.; Nolan, Emma Thomas, pro.; Hans Zimmer, mus.; Wally Pfister, cin.; Lee Smith, ed.; Guy Hendrix Dyas, prod. design.; Brad Ricker, Jason Knox-Johnston, art dir.; Jeffrey Kurland, costumes; Sam Page, digital set design; Chris Corbould, F/X; Pete Bebb/ Double Negative, visual effects; 148 min.; Color; 2.35:1.

CAST

Leonardo DiCaprio (*Cobb*); Marion Cotillard (*Mal*); Joseph Gordon-Levitt (*Arthur*); Ellen Page (*Ariadne*); Tom Hardy (*Eames*); Ken Watanabe (*Saito*); Dileep Rao (*Yusuf*); Cillian Murphy (*Robert Fischer*); Tom Berenger (*Browning*); Michael Caine (*Miles*); Pete Postlethwaite (*Maurice Fischer*); Lukas Haas (*Nash*); Tai-Li Lee (*Tadashi*).

MOST MEMORABLE LINE

Take a leap of faith with me.

MAL TO COBB

BACKGROUND

Born in England, Christopher Nolan (1970–) grew up in London and Chicago. He stands at the forefront of contemporary filmmakers who have shown that the sort of extreme editing techniques, thematic tropes, and surreal imagery that once limited a film to the avant-garde cult cinema market could be used to make mainstream movies. In so doing, he and other proponents of the commercial-arthouse hybrid have dazzled critics with the intellectual complexity of their work. At the same time, their projects feature the expected components of action and violence that have lured an ever-enlarging audience for science fiction at its most satisfying.

A film buff in his youth (and manager of his university film society), Nolan draws from a wide array of influences—from *The Twilight Zone* (particularly episodes that deal with dreaming-as-reality) to high-tone novels such as Marcel

"IF YOU CAN KEEP YOUR HEAD WHEN ALL ABOUT YOU / ARE LOSING THEIRS AND BLAMING IT ON YOU . . . " *Rudyard Kipling's legendary line of poetry might serve as a description for the complex goings-on in this modern masterpiece by consummate crafts-man and visionary artist Christopher Nolan. Courtesy: Legendary Pictures/Warner Bros.*

Proust's *In Search of Lost Time* (7 vols., 1913–1927) and Thomas Pynchon's *Gravity's Rainbow* (1973)—to weave ideology and technique into a cinematic tapestry that is unquestionably his own. Though not precisely sci-fi, *Memento* (2000) dealt with the crucial issue of time as a subjective experience. *Batman Begins* (2005) removed most comic book conventions from the Dark Knight, providing a Hamlet-like youth in search of truth about the world and himself, only to discover the elusiveness of his goal. Nolan's *Inception,* his masterpiece to date, is, in his words, "a contemporary sci-fi actioner set within the architecture of the mind."

THE PLOT

A thief of the future, Dom Cobb makes a living by slipping into the minds of others for a hefty price. He steals ideas, which he turns over to the heads of major corporations who hire him to perform such mind-bending espionage. Cobb, though, cannot get beyond his near-total recall of a past life he shared with a deeply disturbed wife, Mal, and their two girls. Worse, Cobb holds himself responsible for Mal's literal leap of faith into space, a vertigo-inspiring event that caused him to retreat ever deeper into dreams. Such constructions—part memory, part fantasy—allow Cobb to experience an idealized version of the reality that eluded him in actuality. Then comes his last, greatest assignment: enter a man's mind not to take but to give. He is to plant an idea in his target's brain at the bequest of Saito, a mystery man. Saito insists that, following such an inception, Cobb will be able to go home again, recapturing part of what he lost.

THE FILM

Nolan pitched *Inception* to Warner Bros. executives as a follow-up to *Insomnia* (2002). Eight years later, he completed the script to his satisfaction. Character names are all-important: the Fischer father-and-son duo, with their cold, calculated, clinical brand of intelligence, were modeled on chess champion Bobby Fischer. Ariadne, who provides the means for Cobb to escape the virtual labyrinth of another person's mind (and his own alternative reality) references Ariadne of myth, who offers Theseus an escape from the original labyrinth. Mal means evil, often of a seductive nature.

Nolan has stated that he designed this film as a metaphor for the movies. Cobb is a director of dreams (and dreams within dreams); such legendary film historians as Parker Tyler (1904–1974) insisted that watching a movie is akin to dreaming in the daylight. Arthur is the producer, Ariadne handles production design, Eames is employed as the leading man, Saito runs the studio, and Fischer represents to Nolan the audience for their collaboration.

THEME

Inception deals with, among many other issues, the concept of a "lucid" dream: a person experiencing a dream becoming aware that it is indeed a dream, yet not necessarily able to end it or alter events that are in the process of occurring (or seeming to occur) in the dream. The stealing—or, in some cases, sharing—of dreams can be traced back in the popular arts at least to the first great psychological horror movie, *The Cabinet of Dr. Caligari* (1920), then through the aforementioned *Twilight Zone* to the seminal *Star Trek* two-part episode "The Menagerie."

TRIVIA

Issues of "context" and "framing," as defined in *Don't Think of an Elephant!* (2004) by George Lakoff, are included in the complex mix of ideas present here. Simply, the concept holds that if someone orders a person not to think about something, that is the only thing the listener can then think about.

TRON: LEGACY (2010)

—— RANKING: 91 ——

CREDITS

Walt Disney Pictures/Sean Bailey Productions/LivePlanet; Joseph Kosinski, dir.; Edward Kitsis, Adam Horowitz, Brian Klugman, Lee Sternthal, scr.; Sean Bailey, Jeffrey Silver, Steven Lisberger, pro.; Daft Punk, mus.; Claudio Miranda, cin.; James Haygood, ed.; Darren Gilford, prod. design; Sean Haworth, Kevin Ishioka, Mark W. Mansbridge, Ben Procter, art dir.; Michael Wilkinson, costumes; Matthew Aebig, Rick Baker, Julie Beaton-Pachauer, special makeup effects; Steve Boeddeker, sound design; Quantum Creation, F/X; Digital Domain Vancouver, Prime Focus, Prana Studios, compositors; Eric Barba, visual effects; 125 min.; Color; 2.35:1.

CAST

Jeff Bridges (*Kevin Flynn/Clu*); Garrett Hedlund (*Sam Flynn*); Olivia Wilde (*Quorra*); Bruce Boxleitner (*Alan Bradley/Tron*); James Frain (*Jarvis*); Beau Garrett (*Gem*); Michael Sheen (*Castor/Zuse*); Anis Cheurfa (*Rinzler*); Serinda Swan, Yaya DaCosta, Elizabeth Mathis (*Sirens*).

MOST MEMORABLE LINE

I kept dreaming of a world I thought I'd never see. And then, one day . . .
KEVIN FLYNN, TO HIS SON SAM (OPENING)

BACKGROUND

It all began with Pong, which, if not the original video game, was certainly the first to achieve widespread popularity. Following Atari's 1972 release of the simulated tennis game, the resultant industry cinched a connection to the sci-fi genre via such games as Space Invaders (1978) and Asteroids (1979). The audience that now loyally followed such franchises as *Star Wars* consisted of the same people who were soon devoted to video games. Once Pac-Man introduced the maze and edged up the violence quotient in play, Steven Lisberger (1951–), a School of the Museum of Fine Arts graduate renowned for his 1973 short *Cosmic Cartoon*, conceived of formalizing the already existent relationship

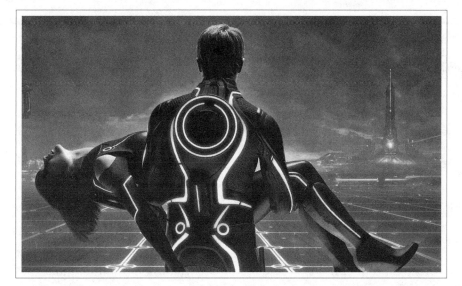

FULFILLING A DREAM: *The desire on the part of Walt Disney Productions to create the first true CGI sci-fi film with the semi-successful* Tron *(1982) was at long last realized with this technically impressive sequel, its other-world conveyed through computer graphics and digital 3 D. Courtesy: Disney/Sean Bailey Productions.*

between games and films. Disney, eager to regain its corner of the mass market for animated projects, green-lighted Lisberger's *Tron*, modifying his concept of a 100 percent computer graphics piece by adding live actors, a Disney tradition.

The resulting 1982 film, *Tron*, featured Jeff Bridges as a young computer programmer who enters the alternative world of software that he has designed, there experiencing a series of adventures. These could also be enjoyed by moviegoers once they bought the Tron game. Those who anticipated what sounded like a perfect film for that precise moment in time were disappointed by the feeble narrative and lack of interesting characters. The film was, at best, a modest success, and there would be no immediate sequel. Yet, *Tron* gained cult popularity via cable TV and home video, and there always remained a sense that a great opportunity had never been fully realized.

THE PLOT

CEO and the primary shareholder of ENCOM International, young Sam Flynn has no financial worries. His father, Kevin, created the software giant shortly before disappearing back in 1989. Like his dad, Sam wants more out of life than money. Financial returns are insignificant compared to the scientific, spiritual, intellectual, and creative gains for humankind inherent in a fascinating alternative universe known as the "Grid." The melancholy Sam can't grasp why his father would have deserted him after promising to share the glories of the Grid. Then Kevin's trusted friend Alan shares significant news: apparently, Kevin did not die or run away, but exists inside the game that began it all. As adventurous as his father, Sam also makes the journey into innerspace.

THE FILM

After Disney executives decided the time was ripe for a belated sequel, they hired writers Brian Klugman and Lee Sternthal to create a story line that would respect the original, so as to please its considerable cult following, while allowing for deeper motives and believably human responses on the part of characters. These include the father-son reunion, which is tempered and challenged by the fact that each has complicated feelings for the beautiful humanoid Quorra. When, several years later, director Joseph Kosinski (1974–) joined the mix, he rejected the then-in-place F/X scheme that borrowed heavily from such landmark films as *The Matrix* (1999). Instead, he opted for state-of-the-art chroma keying to ensure that his first significant feature would project a visual identity all its own.

Kosinski's style is marked by a graceful employment of Vision Research's "Phantom." The camera captures high-speed digital imagery of the sort expected by genre aficionados from the now all-important IMAX 3D Experience. Kosinski dropped the glitzy disco-age phantasmagoric color spectrum of the original in favor of a jet black and gun metal blue palette, enhanced and contained by yellow, orange, and lightning-white framing devices, far more appropriate in the era following *Minority Report* (2002) or *Children of Men* (2006).

THEME

Like many of the best sci-fi/fantasy films, *TRON: Legacy* recalls tales from classical mythology. Sam's journey to rescue his long-lost father parallels, in Homer's *Odyssey*, Telemachus of Ithaca setting out to discover why Odysseus (aka Ulysses) has not returned from the Trojan War. Not surprisingly, in the film, the seductive females who stand in the way of father and son are referred to, in Homeric form, as the Sirens. When Kevin must fight Clu, the double for himself he earlier created, the duel recalls the doppelganger motif: our hero facing off against his evil twin. Mary Shelley's Frankenstein myth is also referenced. Here is a variation on the theme of a father creating a synthetic son to benefit humankind, only to realize that he has potentially set up the destruction of his own race. As with Victor Frankenstein, at least in the original literary incarnation, Kevin appears doomed to an unpleasant fate by having conceived a virtual son without the benefit of a woman only to turn his back on what strikes him as a hideous mistake.

TRIVIA

Kosinski followed up with *Oblivion* (2013), a spectacular based on his own earlier graphic novel of the same name. At the time of publication, his name has been associated with the remakes of such sci-fi franchises as *The Black Hole* and *The Twilight Zone*, as well as a possible sequel to *TRON: Legacy* and a new project, *Archangels*.

· · · · · · ·

RISE OF THE PLANET OF THE APES (2011)

—— RANKING: 69 ——

CREDITS

Twentieth Century Fox Film Corporation/Dune Entertainment/Chernin Entertainment; Rupert Wyatt, dir.; Rick Jaffa, Amanda Silver, scr.; Jaffa, Silver, Peter Chernin, Dylan Clark, pro.; Patrick Doyle, mus.; Andrew Lesnie, cin.; Conrad Buff IV, Mark Goldblatt, ed.; Claude Paré, prod. design; Dan Hermansen, Helen Jarvis, art dir.; Renée April, costumes; Bill Terezakis/WCT, special makeup effects; Aaron Sims, Kazuhiro Tsuji/The Aaron Sims Co., character design; Tony Lazarowich, F/X; Shaun Friedberg "Pyrokinesis"/Weta Digital, visual effects; Simon Baker/Weta Digital, technical effects; Thelvin Cabezas/Weta Digital, digital effects; 105 min.; Color; 2.35:1.

CAST

James Franco (*Will Rodman*); Freida Pinto (*Caroline Aranha*); John Lithgow (*Charles Rodman*); Brian Cox (*John Landon*); Tom Felton (*Dodge Landon*); David Oyelowo (*Steven Jacobs*); Tyler Labine (*Robert Franklin*); Jamie Harris (*Rodney*); Ty Olsson (*Chief Hamil*); Andy Serkis (*Caesar*); Karin Konoval (*Maurice/Court Clerk*); Terry Notary (*Rocket/Bright Eyes*); Christopher Gordon (*Koba*); Devyn Dalton (*Cornelia*).

IN THE BEGINNING . . . *Caesar (Andy Serkis) grows ever more aware of his own identity in this prequel to the 1968 classic. A similar story had been the basis for* Conquest of the Planet of the Apes (1972), *though that B movie cannot boast the technical and dramatic qualities on view here. Courtesy: Chernin/Dune/Big Screen/Ingenious/20th Century Fox.*

BACKGROUND

As Fox's original *Apes* series, production overseen by Arthur P. Jacobs, degenerated from a lofty artistic endeavor into a routine money-making franchise, a single series entry stood out as something special. *Conquest of the Planet of the Apes* (J. Lee Thompson, 1972), fourth in the quintet, revealed in prequel form an explanation as to how the turnaround—apes ruling over man—occurred. Such a vision of rebellion by a mistreated underclass would decades later provide the basis for a reboot. Following the failure of Tim Burton's 2001 remake, Fox had to decide between dumping an outworn project or entirely re-imagining the piece for a new generation. Happily, they chose the latter. *Rise of the Planet of the Apes* proved true to the spirit of the original's still-potent mythology without suffering from slavish devotion to specific details.

THE PLOT

Youthful scientist Will Rodman dedicates his life to a search for the wonder drug that will help regenerate diseased and/or decomposed tissue in a person's brain. He pursues this dream for reasons altruistic (it's the right, that is, idealistic, thing to do for humankind) and personal (his dad, suffering from Alzheimer's, falls deeper into a vegetative state each day). To actualize this agenda, Will has become a workaholic at a major biotech corporation. Gen-Sys accepts his project from a cold, cynical, consumerist point of view: if it works, profits should be huge. All testing is done on chimpanzees. When a female primate whose intelligence has been expanded by doses of the experimental "ALZ-112" is accidentally killed, Will brings her orphan home to raise as a pet. Caesar has inherited the still-uncertain virus strain genetically and is developing a near-human IQ.

THE FILM

The reboot offered one more example of the manner in which, during the early twenty-first century, the invisible walls between avant-garde/indie filmmaking and the commercial mainstream gave way to a new Hollywood cinema. At their best, such hybrids presented intact artistic integrity and provocative ideas while providing the conventional romance between attractive leads and the heavy-hitting action sequences now considered requisite for a box-office success. The English director Rupert Wyatt (1972–) established his reputation with *The Escapist* (2008), an edgy indie that convinced the powers-that-be that such creative directorial achievement could be fused with the elements of a blockbuster to produce an *Apes* reboot.

For the character of Caesar, the husband and wife screenwriting team of Rick Jaffa and Amanda Silver drew on the character of that name in *Conquest of the Planet of the Apes* (1972) and the fifth installment, *Battle for the Planet of the Apes* (1973), both directed by J. Lee Thompson. The female chimpanzee, Cornelia, recalls Cornelius from the original. Jaffa and Silver were inspired to create the story line less from a desire to be the avatars of a franchise reboot than from Jaffa's coincidental reading of a newspaper story about pet chimps. Too smart to exist as simple domesticated pets, the chimps could not completely mesh with the humans around them, experiencing great frustration. The screenwriters realized that such a story, told in a realistic fashion and set in a near-future, could segue at the movie's mid-point into a more fantastical tale of a rebellion that resulted from man's inhumanity to . . . our not-so-distant relatives, the semi-human simians.

The term "performance capture" defines the manner in which artisans at Weta Digital in New Zealand created the ultra-convincing ape characters. Actors were filmed, in motion-capture suits, while performing in natural settings, and then, after a careful study of chimpanzees in the Wellington zoo, the team used digital enhancement for convincing appearance. The person most associated with this approach is Andy Serkis (1964–), who played Caesar and also appeared as Gollum in *The Lord of the Rings* trilogy (2001–2003) and *The Hobbit* prequels (2012–2014) for Peter Jackson. The process, also known as "motion capture," uses a specially designed camera to record, as Serkis describes it, "the actor's movements and expressions (which) are electronically tracked and (then) translated into computer imagery." Essentially, this might be most easily understood as a twenty-first-century state-of-the-art equivalent to the traditional rotoscoping technique.

THEME

Nearly two hundred years after Mary Shelley created the precursor of literary science fiction with her *Frankenstein, or The Modern Prometheus*, *Rise* proved that her original genre theme still remains the most significant idea existing in this form. Once more, a well-meaning scientist, who wants to improve the lot of humankind through state-of-the-art experimentation, creates the possible source of extinction for the human race. As such, *Rise* presents another cautionary fable about the dangers inherent in the very field of study that gives this narrative form its name.

Wisely, Jaffa and Silver added other thematic dimensions, also appropriate for sci-fi, to give the work more gravitas and expand its horizons. This includes genetic engineering in the first half and the increasing danger of pandemic diseases, owing to international travel, toward the end of the film, setting up the sequel. At least by implication, the theme of evolution is explored, the DNA connection of humans to apes being essential to the vision.

TRIVIA

Nominated for five Saturn Awards, *Rise* won in the following categories: Best Science Fiction Film, Best Supporting Actor (Serkis), and Best Special Effects.

········

CLOUD ATLAS (2012)

—— RANKING: 42 ——

CREDITS

Cloud Atlas Productions; Tom Tykwer, Andy Wachowski, Lana Wachowski, dir., scr., David Mitchell, novel; Stefan Arndt, Alex Boden, Grant Hill, pro.; Tykwer, Reinhold Heil, Johnny Klimek, mus.; Frank Griebe, John Toll, cin.; Alexander Berner, Claus Wehlisch, ed.; Hugh Bateup, Uli Hanisch, prod. design; Kai Koch, Nicki McCallum, Charlie Revai, art dir.; Kym Barrett, Pierre-Yves Gayraud, costumes; Uwe Lehmann, Wesley Barnard, F/X; Clare Norman/Bluebolt, Kuba Roth, visual effects; Douglas Bloom/Method Studios, CGI effects; 172 min.; Color; 2.35:1.

CAST

Tom Hanks (*Dr. Henry Goose/Hotel Manager/Isaac Sachs/Dermot Hoggins/Cavendish Look-a-Like Actor/Zachry*); Halle Berry (*Native Woman/Jocasta Ayrs/Luisa Rey/Party Guest/Ovid/Meronym*); Jim Broadbent (*Capt. Molyneux/Vyvyan Ayrs/ Timothy Cavendish/Korean Musician/Prescient 2*); Hugo Weaving (*Haskell Moore/ Tadeusz Kesselring/Bill Smoke/Nurse Noakes/Boardman Mephi/Old Georgie*); Jim Sturgess (*Adam Ewing/Hotel Guest/Megan's Dad/Highlander/Hae-Joo Chang/ Adam*); Doona Bae (*Tilda/Megan's Mom/Mexican Woman/Sonmi-451/Sonmi-351/ Sonmi Prostitute*).

MOST MEMORABLE LINE

Our lives are not our own. From womb to tomb,
we are bound to others, past and present.

SONMI-451

BACKGROUND

Starting with *Run Lola Run* (1998), Germany's Tom Tykwer (1965–) set out to create a personal cinema in which any beginning leads to multiple possible outcomes as a result of minor mishaps, each yielding different results in diverse "real worlds." These affect not only the protagonist and his/her immediate circle but also, as a result of the ripple effect set into motion, everyone in the universe.

Such an approach made Tykwer the right filmmaker to bring David Mitchell's 2004 novel *Cloud Atlas* to the screen. Borrowing the term for a unique style of painting often associated with Georges Seurat, Mitchell described the film adaptation of his novel as a "pointillist mosaic." Lights, shapes, colors, and fleeting images of the human form close up appear only a phantasmagoric blur of bright dots, but focus as clear and concise portraiture. A great fan of the novel, Natalie Portman devoured sections between the filming of sequences for *V for Vendetta* (2005). Her intense interest caught the attention of one of that film's directors, Lana Wachowski.

THE PLOT

In one of six interwoven stories, restaurant server and sex object Sonmi-451 escapes her pre-ordained role as a "fabricant," or clone, when she is rescued by Hae-Joo Chang, a rebel-against-the-class-system intellectual. He mentors her both in radical politics and in the art of love, including (but not limited to) the physical. By chance, Sonmi comes across a film about Timothy Cavendish, the leading character in another of the film's revolving narratives. As a result, she comes to grasp the distinction between who she is and the person (if that is the correct term) this human clone might become. Among the government secrets she learns is one that had been presented in the ambitious though failed 1973 film *Soylent Green* (which concludes with Charlton Heston screaming: "'Soylent Green' is people!"). Only by dying can Sonmi inspire future generations and, hopefully, assure the eventual demise of a system that has doomed her.

THE FILM

During the process of raising the necessary funds for what threatened to become the most expensive independent film of all time (final budget: $111 million), Andy and Lana Wachowski came to realize the impossibility of directing the entire piece. As Tykwer's canon reveals a remarkable ability to underscore seemingly realistic tales with a surreal undercurrent, he opted to do the sequences set in 1936, 1973, and 2012; renowned for imaginative fantasy, the Wachowskis handled the far past (1849) and near (2144) and distant (2321) future.

A series of seemingly disparate but ultimately interlocking incidents occur in 1849 (the South Pacific), 1936 (England), 1973 (San Francisco), 2012 (England), 2144 (Neo Seoul), and 2321 ("The Big Island"), as well as a prologue and epilogue. As two of the tales take place in a spoiled future, *Cloud Atlas* qualifies as dystopian fiction.

Because of the presence of hardware, high-tech and deep impact, this one-of-a-kind film can be considered (if loosely) as an example of generic sci-fi.

THEME

The subjectivity of the individual human personality is at the heart of not only this film's sensibility but also that of a great many other "serious" sci-fi films, particularly those of a post-modernist bent filmed during the early years of the twenty-first century. Here, beloved heroes and despised murderers are not "born" but made. Identity is the result of delicate, even flimsy, twists of fate that, given a split second more or less, could easily have altered—and by doing so, change (even reverse) a person's destiny, as well as his or her supposed identity as "good" or "evil."

Circumstances are the basis of everything, and they are, at best, coincident.

A MISUNDERSTOOD MASTERPIECE: *In their finest film since* The Matrix (1999), *the Wachowskis teamed with Tom Tykwer to create what may be the most emotionally draining and intellectually stimulating science-fiction film of all time. Tom Hanks and Halle Berry headlined the all-star cast. Courtesy: Cloud Atlas/Anarchos/X-Filme/Warner Bros.*

All is relative; therefore, everything is subjective and impermanent. Consequently, outcomes invariably alter as a result of the slightest glitch in the unfolding space-time continuum. Still, *Cloud Atlas* remains not only positive but also faith based, if in a humanistic vein. Nothing is more profound than the smallest act of human kindness; such moments can, will, must lead to great revolutions that, after much pain and suffering, result in the betterment of life.

TRIVIA

Portman was slated to play Sonmi-451. Her pregnancy, simultaneous with the finalization of a production schedule, rendered that impossible. The "451" references the 1953 Bradbury novel (and 1966 Truffaut film) *Fahrenheit 451*. The only previous film to attempt such an ambitious crosscutting over the centuries was D. W. Griffith's *Intolerance* (1916), though that epic contained no corresponding futuristic elements.

Mitchell's essential idea in the novel is that all people are interconnected. The casting of the actors in multiple roles took this literary conceit and presented it via a device uniquely suited to the medium of movies.

· · · · · · ·

THE AVENGERS (2012)

—— RANKING: 25 ——

CREDITS

Marvel Studios/Paramount Pictures; Joss Whedon, dir.; Whedon, Zak Penn, scr.; Kevin Feige, pro.; Alan Silvestri, mus.; Seamus McGarvey, cin.; Jeffrey Ford, Lisa Lassek, ed.; James Chinlund, prod. design; Richard L. Johnson, art dir.; Alexandra Byrne, costumes; Stephen Bettles, John Blake, Roland Blancaflor, Thomas Floutz, Kevin Kirkpatrick/Ironhead, makeup effects; Jane Wu, storyboards; Teresa Eckton, Frank E. Eulner, sound effects ed.; Marc Banich, John P. Cazin, Chris Brenczewski, F/X; Laurenn Reed, Karina Benesh, Sean Cushing/Cantina Creative, Jordan Freda/The Bass Studio, Max Leonard/Lola VFX, Steven Swanson/Luma, Kathleen Lynch, Susan Pickett, Janek Sirrs, Kevin Romond, Garry Runke, visual effects; Derek Bradley, Geordie Martinez/ILM, creature effects; 143 min.; Color; 1.85:1.

CAST

Samuel L. Jackson (*Nick Fury*); Robert Downey Jr. (*Tony Stark/Iron Man*); Chris Evans (*Steve Rogers/Captain America*); Mark Ruffalo (*Bruce Banner/The Hulk*); Scarlett Johansson (*Natasha Romanoff/Black Widow*); Jeremy Renner (*Clint Barton/Hawkeye*); Chris Hemsworth (*Thor*); Tom Hiddleston (*Loki*); Clark Gregg (*Phil Coulson*); Cobie Smulders (*Maria Hill*); Stellan Skarsgård (*Selvig*); Gwyneth Paltrow (*Pepper Potts*); Paul Bettany (*Jarvis*, voice only).

MOST MEMORABLE LINE

Freedom is life's great lie.
LOKI

BACKGROUND

Born Stanley Martin Lieber in New York City, Stan Lee (1922–) collaborated with comic book/graphic novel artists Jack Kirby and Steve Ditko to create the greatest string of superheroes after the golden days of DC. His contributions included Spider-Man, the Hulk, the Fantastic Four, Iron Man, and Thor. While Thor revealed Lee's skills at adapting pre-existing mythological figures to modern-day situations, the other characters demonstrated his abilities to conceive from scratch heroes who precisely fit in with the ever-changing face of American society and the popular culture that reflects it, often in semi-surreal form. Lee's greatest achievement was to veer away from DC's vision of a superhero possessing one flaw: the otherwise perfect Superman, for example, is vulnerable to Kryptonite. Lee presented three-dimensional human beings who happen to possess some single power and choose to walk around in body-clinging cat suits or horned helmets. Each suffers from a strong ego, the result of self-awareness of inborn gifts, and complicated insecurities as a result of forever feeling essentially different. The power of the Avengers concept, beginning with the early 1960s magazine, was to take such diverse and fascinating figures and mix them together to bicker and quarrel—until, of course, it becomes necessary for Iron Man, Captain America, the Hulk, Thor, Black Widow, and Hawkeye to set aside their squabbling in order to save the world. Or, more correctly, Earth-616.

Born in New York City in 1964, Joss Whedon graduated from Wesleyan with a degree in film and headed for Hollywood. He contributed as writer to *Toy Story* (1995), created *Buffy the Vampire Slayer* (1992), and then produced, wrote, and/or directed episodes of the subsequent TV series. Even while *Buffy* remained on the air, Whedon developed *Firefly* (2002–2003) and its film spin-off, *Serenity* (2005). Its critical, if not commercial, success led to Whedon's chance to direct *The Avengers*.

THE MAGICAL WORLD OF MARVEL: *Comics and graphic novels merged with another image-driven narrative form, the motion picture, for what may be the best superhero film ever made. Samuel L. Jackson as Nick Fury (top), Robert Downey Jr. as Tony Stark (middle right), Chris Evans as Captain America (middle), and Scarlett Johansson as Black Widow (bottom right) are among the many favorite cult characters on view here. Courtesy: Marvel/Paramount.*

THE PLOT

An energy source known as the "Tesseract" opens up a wormhole, allowing the exiled god Loki to land on Earth, steal the Tesseract, and then disappear into the portal. Sensing that normal military defenses will not be enough to protect our world, Nick Fury insists that his idea of an Avengers Initiative, rejected earlier by his superiors, be brought into play. The six superheroes, working in tandem, may possibly defeat the coming threat from other planets.

THE FILM

Here is the film that broke down any remaining barriers between what had long been considered the realm of sci-fi and the closely related, if not (at least until now) identical *cinéma fantastique* subgenre known as the "superhero film." With their leader included, the six superheroes constitute a twenty-first-century equivalent of *The Magnificent Seven*, yet one more example of "cowboys in space." The elite group of uniquely gifted individuals, gradually coming together as a community of righteous "gunfighters," provides the last great hope for ordinary people threatened by menacing outlaws, be they from the Old West or the near-future. Several owe their "super" powers almost entirely to scientific and technological progress—most notably, the glib Tony Stark, who becomes Iron Man only when locked into his outfit. At the other extreme stands Thor, a hero from Norse myth re-adapted to the specific needs of the Marvel Universe. As he and his brother, the mischief-maker Loki, enter into a conflict, they are not only legendary characters from old epics but also figures from science fiction. However universally Erich von Däniken may have been derided by experts when his ancient astronaut theories were first published in the 1970s, such thinking remains alive and well (indeed, healthier than ever) today. Endless cable TV specials had made what was once confined to a cult a part of mainstream thinking: the gods of myth may possibly have been visitors from other planets. As a result of such thinking, however puerile it may still be considered by critics, sci-fi and epic fantasy are able to merge.

THEME

Though futuristic in terms of the technology used by the characters, as well as the advanced level of the computers used by the F/X artists working on the project, *The Avengers* is an old-fashioned film. We are often reminded that Captain America is first among equals, if only because he was "the first superhero," at least in the Marvel Universe. Though action sequences dazzlingly display "super" elements, the script hones in on the idea of heroism. How perfect, then, that what infuriates the villain Loki is "sentimentality," a quality he nastily dismisses even as our heroes, no matter how flawed and no matter how superficially cynical—except, that is, Captain America, who always projects a World War II–era aura of simple patriotism—are, in the end, sentimentalists, as the conclusive battle reveals. The film closes with a rebirth of optimism as Loki's fascism (the ultimate non-sentimental form of government) is destroyed by American democracy, our sentimentality the key to ongoing survival.

TRIVIA

Jon Favreau, actor and director, was one of a handful of Hollywood hands who served as executive producer.

The brief but showy role of the security guard is played by Harry Dean Stanton, one of Hollywood's most reliable character actors for more than sixty years and the star of the cult sci-fi film *Repo Man* (1984).

· · · · · · ·

MAN OF STEEL (2013)

—— RANKING: 52 ——

CREDITS

Warner Bros.; Zack Snyder, dir.; David S. Goyer, Christopher Nolan, scr.; Nolan, Emma Thomas, Deborah Snyder, pro.; Hans Zimmer, mus.; Amir Mokri, cin.; David Brenner, ed.; Alex McDowell, prod. design; Chris Farmer, Kim Sinclair, art dir.; James Acheson, Michael Wilkinson, costumes; Michael Ahasay, Alan Lashbrook, F/X; Shaun Friedberg "Pyrokinesis"/WETA Digital, Tom Becker, visual effects; Bernd Angerer, animation supervisor; 143 min.; Color; 2.35:1.

CAST

Henry Cavill (*Clark Kent/Kal-El*); Amy Adams (*Lois Lane*); Michael Shannon (*Gen. Zod*); Diane Lane (*Martha Kent*); Russell Crowe (*Jor-El*); Antje Traue (*Faora-Ul*); Harry Lennix (*Gen. Swanwick*); Richard Schiff (*Dr. Hamilton*); Christopher Meloni (*Col. Hardy*); Kevin Costner (*Jonathan Kent*); Ayelet Zurer (*Lara Lor-Van*); Laurence Fishburne (*Perry White*); Dylan Sprayberry (*Clark Kent*, age 13); Cooper Timberline (*Clark Kent*, age 9); Richard Cetrone (*Tor-An*); Mackenzie Gray

AN AMERICAN HERCULES: *Henry Cavill joins the company of Kirk Alyn, George Reeves, Christopher Reeve, and several others who have played the Man of Steel in movies and on TV. At last, Clark Kent/Superman is treated as a complex character with a dual identity as difficult as Batman's. Courtesy: Warner Bros./Legendary/Syncopy/DC Entertainment.*

(*Jax-Ur*); Julian Richings (*Lor-Em*); Jadin Gould (*Lana Lang*); Rebecca Buller (*Jenny*); Christina Wren (*Maj. Farris*).

MOST MEMORABLE LINE

Son, you're the answer to, "are we alone in the universe?"
JONATHAN KENT TO CLARK

BACKGROUND

Everyone involved in this project understood the goal was not merely to reboot the franchise but also to initiate, as the team would collaboratively present it, "a (new) shared fictional universe" of existing DC characters—in time, providing fresh relationships between old favorites. *Man of Steel* necessarily presented an origination fable that was at once true to the essence of the Shuster and Siegel comic, then seventy-five years old, while offering a clear departure from previous versions. To this end, such reliable standbys as cub reporter Jimmy Olsen and the Achilles heel device of Kryptonite were eliminated—not that either couldn't be retrieved for some future installment. The science-fiction aspect was played as central to the approach rather than, as was the case in *Superman* (1978) and *Superman II* (1980), as a catalyst to the action. A religious aspect was emphasized, owing to Jonathan Kent's fear that his non-biological son, despite his benign savior-like powers, might be misunderstood, even murdered, by an uncomprehending mob.

THE PLOT

As the planet Krypton readies to implode, citizens abandon their ruling council and turn control over to General Zod. Aware that the end is at hand, Jor-El encodes the genetics of his race into his son, then launches the baby into space. Zod and his minions are banished to the Phantom Zone but, after Krypton disappears from the heavens, they wander the solar system, searching for the only other survivor. That special boy has been discovered by the Kents, a Kansas couple, who raise the child as their own. Jonathan Kent insists that, for his boy's well-being, young Clark enact his good deeds only in secret, even allowing innocents to perish in order to remain incognito—a unique spin to the old story that either delighted and fascinated or concerned and troubled longtime fans of the franchise.

THE FILM

Warner Bros. executives were anxious to bring Christopher Nolan on board as "creative consultant." His successes with *Batman Begins* (2005) and *Inception* (2010) were double-barreled proof that he could effectively handle superheroes *and* science fiction. Having penned *Batman Begins*, then co-creating TV's sci-fi series *FlashForward* (2009–2010), David S. Goyer appeared a natural for the screenplay. Completing the team, Zack Snyder (1966–) had revealed with *300* (2006) and *Watchmen* (2009) an ability to darken a fantasy film without turning off a mainstream audience. Despite rumors that he might direct, Nolan planned to launch this project, then move on to *The Dark Knight* (2008) with the assumption that a meeting of these superheroes would emerge from each project's expected success.

THEME

According to Jor-El, "harvesting the core" of Krypton, in response to the exhaustion of energy reserves, is what caused the beginning of the end for their world. Here is a fitting cautionary fable for twenty-first-century earthlings, well aware of our own rapidly depleting reserves and the questionable responses (such as fracking) to the problem. This aspect of the film's ideology can be considered liberal.

Also, at the time of the film's release, the public had recently become more aware of ancient astronaut theories due to dissemination not only in other recent genre films but also in well-received series on cable TV. "Look to the stars," Jor-El begs his fellow Kryptonians, "as our ancestors did, for habitable worlds"—such a line was not heard in earlier Superman films. The wise Jor-El despises genetic engineering, a major topic of contemporary discourse. "What if," he asks, "a child dreamed of becoming something other than what society had intended" for him? He and his wife conceived their son by the forbidden old-fashioned method of natural conception. Here is yet another example of the sci-fi genre's conservative condemnation of the dangers inherent in science and technology contrasting a liberal progressive's dream that these advances will create a better future. The greatest sci-fi films are complex enough to include both liberal and conservative attitudes in a single vision.

TRIVIA

Natalie Portman, Anne Hathaway, and Mila Kunis were among the actresses considered for Lois Lane. Amy Adams's portrayal presented Lois as less the glamorous bitch of so many previous incarnations and more as a contemporary hard-working, post-feminist young woman, projecting the believability necessary to make this fantastical piece play as real, if not narrowly realistic. This was important as the female audience for superhero sci-fi had increased significantly since the late 1970s, when the genre was still considered a part of a boy's fantasy life.

Before winning the lead, Henry Cavill (luckily, according to fans) had been the runner-up to Brandon Routh for *Superman Returns* (Bryan Singer, 2006), which audiences had rejected as a disappointing rehash.

THE RETURN OF "PURE" SCI-FI: *Following a string of sci-fi/fantasy films, Alfonso Cuarón proved that "hard" or pure science fiction remained a viable option even though fantasy films involving action and romance had long dominated the box office. Sandra Bullock is the novice space traveler attempting to survive a space shuttle's destruction in this day-after-tomorrow ultra-realistic adventure. Courtesy: EsperantoFilmoj/Heyday/Warner Bros.*

· · · · · · · ·

GRAVITY (2013)

—— RANKING: 40 ——

CREDITS

Warner Bros./Heyday Films/DC Entertainment; Alfonso Cuarón, dir.; Cuarón, Jonás Cuarón, scr.; Alfonso Cuarón, David Heyman, pro.; Steven Price, mus.; Emmanuel Lubezki, cin.; Alfonso Cuarón, Mark Sanger, ed.; Andy Nicholson, prod. design; Mark Scruton, art dir.; Jany Temime, costumes; Ann Fenton, makeup effects; Julian Caldow, Chris Baker, concept artist; Jim Barr, Pierre Bohanna, modellers; Daniel May, Jamie Martin, 3-D design; Niv Adiri, Ben Barker, Glenn Freemantle, Danny Freemantle, sound design; Vince Abbott, Neil Courbould, Ian Courbould, F/X; Eric Bates/Rising Sun, Benoit Bargeton/Framestore, animation; Chris Watts, Timothy Webber, Richard McBride, visual effects; 91 min.; Color; 2.35:1.

CAST

Sandra Bullock (*Ryan Stone*); George Clooney (*Matt Kowalski*); Ed Harris (*Mission Control*, voice); Orto Ignatiussen (*Aningaaq*, voice); Phaldut Sharma (*Shariff*, voice); Amy Warren (*Explorer Captain*, voice); Basher Savage (*Russian Station Captain*, voice).

MOST MEMORABLE LINE

I *hate* space!

DR. RYAN STONE

BACKGROUND

Despite the long list of intriguing experiments that changed the international moviemaking paradigm during the early twenty-first century, some observers required further proof that the once decisive line between off-beat indie productions and high-profile studio product had gradually disappeared. *Gravity* can be considered the work that they were waiting for—nowhere was the emergence of a mass-market movie containing arthouse elements so obvious as in the once-maligned, now all-important science-fiction genre. Despite attractive A-list stars, director Alfonso Cuarón made no compromises to enhance this as a product. What once might have been considered essential—at least a hint of romance between the two leads, for example—is not present. Instead, *Gravity* subtly portrays a growing respect and a meaningful relationship between two people.

Cuarón's collaborator was his son Jonás. Their unique plan was to create something never before seen: a sparse chamber drama of the type that ordinarily takes place on a bare theatrical stage, but now set against a vast cosmic scope, enhanced by 3-D and, in many situations, IMAX presentation. Had the result not worked, this bizarre juxtaposition of the most intimate of human stories with a gargantuan sense of the galaxy, enhanced by advanced F/X, might have played as a case of style and substance at odds. Instead, the audience is swept up by a striking implied irony: two small people, whose personalities come to seem gigantic, dwarfing the enormity of space with their courage, intelligence, and spirit.

THE PLOT

On what begins as a normal day in space, barely different from what jet pilots experience in our own skies when everything remains calm, Ryan Stone proves that, despite her inexperience as an astronaut, she's a dependable member of the small team aboard a U.S. space shuttle. Suited up for a spacewalk, Stone uses her technical expertise to repair the Hubble Space Telescope, accompanied by the more experienced Matt Kowalski, a glib jokester who expects nothing untoward from this routine mission. Then, without warning, the voice of Mission Control from Houston segues from calm to concerned, informing them that space junk from a Russian missile strike is heading their way, expanding in momentum and size, and they must at once abort. Then, silence—at least from home—even as the heavens explode around them. As Kowalski rescues Stone from floating off into deep space, their companions are killed in the explosions. Once aboard the *Explorer*, the two realize that only the fastest thinking and employment of each person's expertise will allow for even a slight chance to survive.

THE FILM

Like many current motion pictures, *Gravity* references the classics, if in an entirely different way than the films of Spielberg, Lucas, or their followers. Their homages deconstruct the movie we are watching by self-consciously conjuring up precise moments from influential past projects. In this film, the references are so subtle that they might easily slip by without notice. Though the line "I have a bad feeling about this!" recalls *Star Wars*, Cuarón directed George Clooney, then Sandra Bullock, to say similar words in ways that refresh what had long since become stale. Taking as its template the Western classic *High Noon* (Fred Zinnemann, 1952), *Gravity* focuses on a singular person facing an immediate threat, momentarily growing panicky, regaining composure, and then, in a race against time, overcoming what seems a certain fate. Again, cowboys in space. A novice dealing with an overwhelming reality by calling upon memories of a more experienced mentor draws on the relationship between Henry Fonda and Thomas Mitchell in *The Immortal Sergeant* (John M. Stahl, 1943). Sequences in which editing is not employed so as to create an ongoing continuity and a sense of real (rather than cinematic) time—all emotional impact deriving from constant if functional camera movements—recalls *Rope* (Alfred Hitchcock, 1948).

The notion of a single person lost in space while in the process of discovering who he/she actually is describes the essence of *2001: A Space Odyssey* (1968), the film that essentially initiated the post-modernist sci-fi genre. That the person who survives is a woman can't help but remind us of *Alien*, Bullock at one point stripping down to her underwear just as Sigourney Weaver did in the earlier film.

Gravity opened the Venice Film Festival in August 2013 and, shortly thereafter, had its original American screening not at some Hollywood black-tie premiere but rather at the Telluride Film Festival. Its opening weekend in early October of that year topped box-office records, earning more than half of the film's $100 million budget. This justified Warner's ongoing faith in high-quality sci-fi films that appeal to a contemporary audience that appreciates and accepts surface entertainment combined with intellectual content.

THEME

The movie is about survival, analyzing the extremes that a person will go to in order to achieve victory over what may appear to be impossible odds. Despite the near-future setting of space, a viewer may be barely aware of genre, in part because the character of Dr. Stone is so well established, then further developed in a realistic sense. Devoid of elements of either imaginative fantasy or space opera, *Gravity* is a docudrama, or "hard" sci-fi, that recalls those early George Pal classics, *Destination Moon* (1950) and *Conquest of Space* (1955). It is also pure sci-fi in that it tells the history of the future by dealing with the most everyday sort of accident—rather than fabricated gargantuan events—that will, in time, menace astronauts.

Still, this is a highly personal film. One brief religious image reveals the importance of faith, while the oppressively dark surroundings give way, at long last and after much struggle, to an optimism born of brightness, precisely as was the case with *Children of Men* (2006).

TRIVIA

During the film's planning stage, Robert Downey Jr. was slated for the Kowalski role. Likewise, Angelina Jolie hoped to play Stone, but her superstar asking price of $20 million did not match Warner's plans to spend most of the allotted budget on the film's mesmerizing "look." Natalie Portman, Marion Cotillard, and Scarlett Johansson were all at one point or another considered for the lead.

A POST-FEMINIST WOMAN OF SCI-FI: *As in* Gravity, Hunger Games *and its superior sequel,* Catching Fire, *offered a beautiful female lead strong in mind, body, and spirit. Jennifer Lawrence as Katniss is seen here in the first film of the franchise. Courtesy: Color Force/Lionsgate.*

· · · · · · ·

THE HUNGER GAMES: CATCHING FIRE (2013)

—— RANKING: 79 ——

CREDITS

Color Force/Lionsgate; Francis Lawrence, dir.; Suzanne Collins, novel; Simon Beaufoy, Michael Arndt, scr., Nina Jacobson, Jon Kilik, Collins, pro.; James Newton Howard, mus.; Jo Willems, cin.; Alan Edward Bell, ed.; Philip Messina, prod. design; John Collins, Adam Davis, Robert Fechtman, art dir.; Trish Summerville, costumes; Steve Winsett, special makeup effects; Steve Cremin, Christian Eubank, F/X; Andrew Cadey, Paul Butterworth/Fuelvfx, Markus Burki, visual effects; 146 min.; Color; 2.35:1.

CAST

Jennifer Lawrence (*Katniss Everdeen*); Liam Hemsworth (*Gale Hawthorne*);

Jack Quaid (*Marvel*); Taylor St. Clair (*Ripper*); Sandra Ellis Lafferty (*Greasy Sae*); Woody Harrelson (*Haymitch Abernathy*); Josh Hutcherson (*Peeta*); Paula Malcomson (*Katniss's Mother*); Willow Shields (*Primrose*); Donald Sutherland (*President Snow*); Elizabeth Banks (*Effie Trinket*); Bruce Bundy (*Octavia*); Nelson Ascencio (*Flavius*); Philip Seymour Hoffman (*Plutarch Heavensbee*).

MOST MEMORABLE QUOTE

Stay alive.
HAYMITCH'S FINAL ADVICE TO KATNISS

BACKGROUND

Suzanne Collins's (1962–) first *Hunger Games* novel became an immediate phenomenon, particularly with young female readers. Published by Scholastic Press, the book is another example of the emergent young adult fiction that includes the *Twilight* series. Collins's book spoke directly to those girls-to-women (ranging from preteens to young adults, with a notably large following among sixteen-year-old females) who saw their reflection in dystopian fiction form. The target audience related to "Katniss Everdeen" as an idealized vision of their own selves: able to love a boy, if worthy, without handing her life over to him, then turn around and unhesitatingly (if not cold-bloodedly) kill another man she neither likes nor respects. At long last, the New Woman could relate to the New Science Fiction, no longer a boys' adventure genre.

THE PLOT

Katniss Everdeen and Peeta Mellark survive the 74th Hunger Games owing to her strength and smarts. The pair set out on a "victory tour," which has unexpected results. Inspired by their bond, many citizens join together to protest the dictatorial President Snow. Katniss and Peeta are forced to join a special games in which previous victors battle to the death.

THE FILM

The original, released in 2012, scored at the box office, largely as a result of the 2008 book's best-selling appeal and the inspired casting of Jennifer Lawrence, whose combination of talent and beauty brought Katniss to life onscreen. Many critics noted weaknesses: screenwriter-director Gary Ross (1956–), who had written the sweet-spirited fantasy *Big* (1988) and directed *Pleasantville* (1998), didn't sufficiently develop the characters, keep the plotting convincing, or stage action in an inventive manner. The most obvious problem was that the book's serious-minded depiction of intense violence was watered down to make the movie more palatable to a wide audience. For the sequel, Francis Lawrence (1971–), as experienced in high-glamour rock videos as in sci-fi (*I Am Legend*, 2007), was able to realize the sensuality of the dazzling girl-on-fire sequence with action far more vivid and memorable (particularly the Orangutan sequence) than anything in the first film.

THEME

One of the most fascinating motifs in the history of sci-fi cinema is the development of female characters within the genre, which mirrors, in a fascinating manner, changes to the roles of women in society during the twentieth century. *A Trip to the Moon* (1902) focused on male adventurers; a quarter-century later, *Woman in the Moon* (1929) featured a female as a fully accepted group member. As recently as *Star Wars*, the rescue myth (Luke holds Leia while swinging, Tarzan-like, across a technological abyss) remained essential. This image would be countered by Uhura in later *Star Trek* entries as she proved more than capable of taking care of herself. Feminist thinking, seemingly radical during the late 1960s, had been assimilated into the zeitgeist by century's end.

In the early twenty-first century, a challenging concept emerged: post-feminism. An increasing number of women argued that there could be a balance between strong, smart, self-efficient modern women and sexy female girly-girls. No writer did more to promote that post-feminist woman in sci-fi fiction than Suzanne Collins (1962–). A former TV writer, mostly employed on children's shows, Collins created in Katniss a young woman who could switch from a sleek supermodel type to hard-bitten survivalist in a split second.

TRIVIA

Collins knit together a post-feminist sci-fi patchwork quilt from pre-existing genre concepts. The device of a lottery can be traced back to Shirley Jackson's seminal 1948 short story, "The Lottery." A man and woman facing each other in post-apocalyptic survival combat was the essence of "Two," the third season opening episode of *Twilight Zone*. Brutal sports competitions serve as the basis for *Rollerball* (Norman Jewison, 1975) and *The Running Man* (Paul Michael Glaser, 1987), and deadly future games are present in similarly titled films, *Le dernier combat* (Luc Besson, 1983) and *Final Combat* (Menahem Golan, 2003). Readjusting such a premise to teenagers drives the brilliant *Battle Royale* (Kinji Fukasaku, 2000).

GUARDIANS OF THE GALAXY (2014)

RANKING: 39

CREDITS

Marvel Media/Walt Disney Pictures; James Gunn, dir.; Gunn, Nicole Perlman, scr.; Kevin Feige, Jonathan Schwartz, David J. Grant, pro.; Tyler Bates, music; Ben Davis, cin.; Fred Raskin, Hughes Winborne, Craig Wood, ed.; Charles Wood, prod. design; Ray Chan, Ravi Bansal, art dir.; Alexandra Byrne, costumes; Georgia Allen, Paulina Boneva, F/X makeup; Jessica Brooks, prosthetic makeup; Paul Corbould, F/X; Stephane Ceretti, Nicolas Aithadi, visual effects; Emma Ewing, senior animator; 121 min.; Color; 2.35:1; 3-D (optional).

CAST

Chris Pratt (*Peter Quill*); Zoe Saldana (*Gamora*); Dave Bautista (*Drax*); Vin Diesel (*Groot*, voice only); Bradley Cooper (*Rocket*, voice only); Lee Pace (*Ronan*); Michael Rooker (*Yondu Udonta*); Karen Gillan (*Nebula*); Djimon Hounsou (*Korath*); John C. Reilly (*Dey*); Glenn Close (*Nova Prime*); Benicio Del Toro (*The Collector*); Laura Haddock (*Meredith Quill*); Sean Gunn (*Kraglin*); Josh Brolin (*Thanos*, voice only, uncredited).

MOST MEMORABLE LINE

I am Groot.

GROOT

BACKGROUND

As early as 1969, writer Arnold Drake and artist Gene Colan created an initial team of oddball superheroes in space with the name "Guardians of the Galaxy." During the first decade of the twenty-first century, Dan Abnett and Andy Lanning, renowned among comics lovers for re-launching DC's *Legion of Super-Heroes*, seized on the idea of drawing on diverse characters created by various artists and collapsing them into a single (and singular) *Guardians* unit. Such a reboot concept developed during their collaboration on *Annihilation: Conquest* with Marvel editor Bill Rosemann. As the working process on that project reached its conclusion, all realized that what had originally been scheduled as a unique one-shot had emerged, however unconsciously, into an origination narrative. Those few characters "still standing" at story's end all but called out for further adventures.

The idea was unique: an ongoing heroic group that, unlike others that set out to solve existing problems, stops further annihilations before they can even begin. Though Marvel cancelled these comics after two years (2008–2010), all involved realized that their work constituted something special. The finalized team regularly reappeared, most notably in *Avengers Assemble*, a five-book series published in 2012.

THE PLOT

Peter Quill, who prefers to be addressed as "Star-Lord," engages in mercenary ploys on the planet Morag. Quill is seemingly yet one more "space cowboy," perhaps separated at birth from virtual twin Han Solo. A quarter century earlier, back on Earth, Quill's dying mother informed her child that his father had been an angel. An odd but appealing combination of other previous offspring of a god-sent father figure and an earthly mother, such as Hercules and Jesus, Quill (the son) was singled out for abduction by aliens. Now seeking the rare blue Orb for financial gain, Quill discovers that locating this object will not conclude but rather begin his series of unique adventures. Evil Ronan requires this object to destroy a peaceful matriarchy guided by a benign leader. Quill's interests in the Orb evolve as he allows first the warrior woman assassin Gamora, then a rowdy group of misfits, to join him in the seemingly impossible task of ensuring that good will survive—even if this requires self-sacrifice for them all.

THE FILM

Kevin Feige, president of Marvel Studios, was well aware that *Guardians* constituted one of the more "obscure" titles in their considerable library. This perhaps explains why a film version lingered so long in development, even as other works in their in-print galaxy were more rapidly translated into their ever-expanding cinematic universe. Like *Thor* (2011), *Guardians* would only succeed if produced on a big scale to represent what Feige considered "the cosmic side" of their diverse offerings. So he committed an enormous budget, estimated at $170 million, to production, even though the film would not feature any major stars like those who had bolstered box-office expectations for *Avengers* features.

Feige knew he must pick precisely the right director to create a delicate balance: the film must satisfy the diehard *Guardians* fans while playing to the multitudes who had never heard of, much less read, the comics, but would

EXPANDING THE MARVEL CINEMATIC UNIVERSE: *The critical and commercial success of* Guardians of the Galaxy *assured that even somewhat lesser-known elements of the franchise would be embraced in an era when science fiction and space fantasy have become our modern mythology. The characters played by, upper clockwise from left, Vin Diesel, Chris Pratt, Zoe Saldana, Dave Bautista, and Bradley Cooper reveal, in an artist's rendering used as poster art, the manner in which unique individuals can merge into a supportive community. Courtesy: Marvel Studios/Walt Disney Motion Pictures.*

still expect a movie that provided plenty of bang for their buck. He found that director in James Gunn (1970–). A novelist and former rocker, Gunn had made a successful transition to film with his screenplays for the ultra-low-budget *Tromeo and Juliet* (1996) and *Super* (2010), the latter of which he also directed. *Guardians* was shot in England, mostly at the legendary Shepperton Studios, where so many classic science-fiction films had been created. Process shots, particularly for Rocket Raccoon and Groot, were achieved through combinations of CGI, motion capture, and rotomation. The striking rotomation style lends the film an eerie charm reminiscent of the Fleischer cartoons of the 1940s and Ray Harryhausen's *Sinbad* trilogy.

THEME

In her *New York Times* review (7/31/2014), Manohla Dargis described *Guardians* as an "interstellar Western." This sci-fi fantasy, like many cowboy films, is "about a motley group of appealing baddies who rise to the heroic occasion" when inspired by a great cause. *The Magnificent Seven* (1960) rates as the most famous example of such a Western; that legendary film had been adapted from *Seven Samurai* (1954), an Asian action epic. Such parallels establish a continuum for adventure films, which can be set in the past, present, or future and produced virtually anywhere in the world. Though some things do change—for example, now, the group not only can but must contain a strong (and beautiful) woman—other thematic elements remain the same. Ultimately, *Guardians* is a redemption saga, insisting that even those who have fallen into the galaxy's gutter can manage a comeback by pooling their abilities.

TRIVIA

Others who had hoped to direct included Peyton Reed and the filmmaking team of Ryan Fleck and Anna Boden.

Marvel ace Stan Lee appears early in the film as the Xandarian playboy.

"Groot" was the name of John Wayne's sidekick (Walter Brennan) in the Western *Red River* (Howard Hawks, 1948). Many critics noted the similarity of Dunn's direction to that of Hawks: both mixed intense action drama with glib contemporary humor, resulting in films that knowingly wink at their audience while drawing them into the dramatic entertainment elements.

APPENDIX 1

INTERNATIONAL SCIENCE FICTION

From around the globe, fascinating films of imaginative fantasy, each of which almost made the top 100 listing.

1. *Orphée* (Jean Cocteau, 1950): France's cinema poet retells the Greek myth of Orpheus in contemporary settings. A mysterious woman draws the hero (Jean Marais) into a "zone" that predates that of Rod Serling—and perhaps inspired him! This cinematic sonnet was the first film to blur the lines between the avant-garde and postwar sci-fi/fantasy.

2. *Bis ans Ende der Welt/Until the End of the World* (Wim Wenders, 1991): As an out-of-control nuclear-equipped satellite enters the atmosphere, millions panic while a self-serving free spirit (Solveig Dommartin) sets out on a punk phantasmagoria road trip. Imagine Godard's *Breathless* (1960) remade as German sci-fi.

3. *The Quiet Earth* (Geoff Murphy, 1985): From New Zealand, the tale of a scientist (Bruno Lawrence) attempting to create a safe energy grid. He wakes up one morning to find himself alone in the world and realizes his success may have inadvertently depopulated the Earth. Unsettling and eerie, the film was derived in part from Craig Harrison's 1981 novel of the same name.

4. *Aelita: Queen of Mars* (Yakov Protazanov, 1924): Following the Russian revolution, a young man travels to Mars, there organizing lowly workers to stage a rebellion against the Old Order. The fascinating visuals in the final half-hour were shot at the great Mezhrabpom-Rus studio. From Aleksey Nikolayevich Tolstoy's novel of the same name.

5. *Batoru rowaiaru/Battle Royale* (Kinji Fukasaku, 2000): When Japan's young people become increasingly unruly, the government ships a ninth grade class to an isolated island where they will be set free to kill each other. Similar in conception but far superior to *The Hunger Games* (2012).

6. *(These Are) The Damned* (Joseph Losey, 1963): An American tourist (Macdonald Carey), confused and distraught after running into a Brit Teddy Boy biker gang, stumbles upon a strange hospital for children

WHAT A WAY TO GO! In Elio Petri's vision of a near-future, huntress Ursula Andress poses as a stripper to get the drop on her latest victim, then kills him with a pair of bra pistols. In the second image, the femme fatale displays his tie as a makeshift phallic symbol. Courtesy: Embassy.

where unspeakable experiments are conducted. This oddball black-and-white Hammer Films production effectively captures H. L. Lawrence's 1960 book, *The Children of Light*.

7. *Enthiran* (S. Shankar, 2010): Sci-fi, Tamil style, this film filters the timeless Frankenstein myth through an Indian sensibility. A scientist creates an android double only to discover that he may have consigned not only his own life to destruction but also that of the world. Top F/X by the brilliant Srinivas Mohan.

8. *La decima vittima/The Tenth Victim* (Elio Petri, 1965): In a futuristic Italy, violent individuals join The Game, taking turns as hunter and hunted in a duel to the death. Ursula Andress's sexy, deadly bullet bra rates as the eighth wonder of the modern world. From a provocative short story, "Seventh Victim," by Robert Sheckley.

9. *Avalon* (Mamoru Oshii, 2001): Stark buildings in the Polish cities of Wrocław and Warsaw provided the Expressionistic locations for this tale of a daring young woman (Małgorzata Foremniak) becoming the key adversary and player in a deadly video game. *The 10th Victim* by way of *Tron*; mesmerizing.

10. *Santo contra la invasión de los marcianos* (Alfredo B. Crevenna, 1966): Known as "El Santo," Rodolfo Guzmán Huerta (1917–1984) was Mexico's most famous *luchador enmascardo* (masked professional wrestler), as well as the subject of graphic novels and B films. In this film, El Santo takes on invaders from the Red Planet.

APPENDIX 2

THEY CAME FROM BEYOND THE FIFTIES!

The brave new world that Huxley had predicted began to take shape during the postwar years, as did the modern sci-fi genre.

1. *I Was a Teenage Werewolf* (Gene Fowler Jr., 1957): Imagine *The Wolfman* by way of *Rebel Without a Cause* and you've got the best of the low-budget teen sci-fi flicks, with Michael Landon in top form as the victim of a mad scientist (Whit Bissell) and his own hormones. Best sequence: the gym!

2. *Red Planet Mars* (Harry Horner, 1952): Messages that are apparently being beamed down from the title planet suggest that God is, Nietzsche's 1882 dictum aside, alive and well and living on Mars—though the whole thing may just be a Communist plot. The ultimate Cold War sci-fi right-wing message movie.

3. *It Came from Outer Space* (Jack Arnold, 1953): Top-flight Universal release about invaders set the pace for all the Southwestern desert sci-fi flicks to follow, with 3-D heightening the suspense. The ugly but well-intentioned aliens inspired Spielberg to create *Close Encounters*.

4. *Donovan's Brain* (Felix E. Feist, 1953): When a less-than-likable millionaire passes away, scientists keep his brain functional only to discover that its evil power telekinetically controls people in the manner of Germany's old Dr. Mabuse (a super-villain appearing in several early Fritz Lang films). From the influential domestic sci-fi novel by Curt Siodmak.

5. *When Worlds Collide* (Rudolph Maté, 1951): With a star headed directly toward Earth, a rocket ship must be built so that some people may survive. The Oscar-winning film (for Best Effects) is spectacular, but lacks the heart and soul of most George Pal–produced films. From the 1933 novel of the same name by Philip Gordon Wylie and Edwin Balmer.

6. *Rocketship X-M* (Kurt Neumann, 1950): An excellent low-budgeter that was rushed into production to reach theaters before *Destination Moon* (1950), this film still packs a punch. After discovering that an atomic war wiped out civilization on Mars, Lloyd Bridges and his astronaut team attempt a return to warn our own world of the threat.

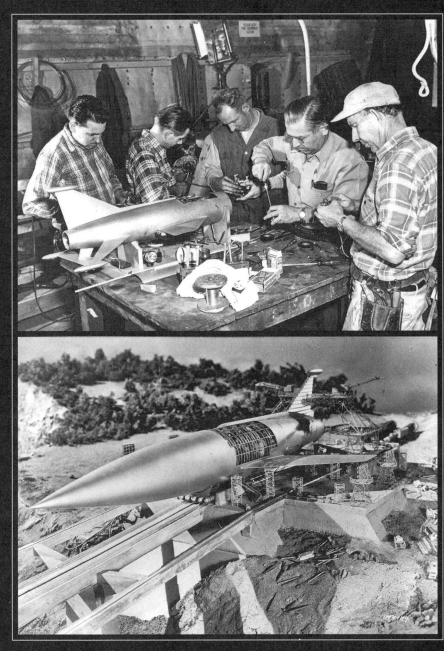

HUMANKIND'S LAST GREATEST HOPE: *Producer George Pal brought an acclaimed novel about Earth's imminent destruction to the screen. When Worlds Collide won the Oscar for Best Special Effects thanks to Harry Barndollar and Gordon Jennings. Here, scientists design and then build a rocket that can spirit at least some humans away to a faraway world. Courtesy: Paramount.*

7. *It! The Terror from Beyond Space* (Edward L. Cahn, 1958): After his rescue from a mission to Mars, the lone surviving astronaut (Marshall Thompson) is accused of murdering his colleagues. Another scary-smart script from the rightly esteemed Jerome Bixby, and the inspiration for *Alien* some two decades later.

8. *The Quatermass Experiment* (Val Guest, 1955): An astronaut returns from space, unaware that he's been overtaken by an alien organism. A bedraggled Brian Donlevy plays England's most famous fictional scientist. The Westminster Abbey conclusion is a classic set piece. U.S. title: *The Creeping Unknown*.

9. *The Fly* (Kurt Neumann, 1958): A scientist (David Hedison) attempting to master teleportation via molecular breakdown makes the mistake of entering a booth that also happens to contain a housefly. Who could ever forget: "Help me! Help me!" From a superb 1957 George Langelaan short story by the same name.

10. *I Married a Monster from Outer Space* (Gene Fowler Jr., 1958): Invaders from a dying planet snatch the bodies of all-American men in hopes of mating with their nubile wives. Cult queen Gloria Talbott in a surprisingly sensitive study of youthful marriage in the uptight Eisenhower era.

APPENDIX 3

CULT SCI-FI

Though far from blockbusters, these diverse films have each found a dedicated following among sci-fi aficionados.

1. *A Boy and His Dog* (L. Q. Jones, 1975): Like John Wayne and Sam on the wild frontier in *Hondo* (1953), a teen (Don Johnson) and his canine pal "Blood" wander the post-apocalyptic West. A self-consciously nasty curio, with an in-your-face chauvinist vision from the ever-ubiquitous Harlan Ellison.

2. *Repo Man* (Alex Cox, 1984): At last, a role worthy of the great character actor Harry Dean Stanton! He cruises around L.A.'s worst neighborhoods with Emilio Estevez, a snarling punk who joins in the automobile abductions—until, that is, the aliens arrive. Makes a David Lynch film feel mainstream.

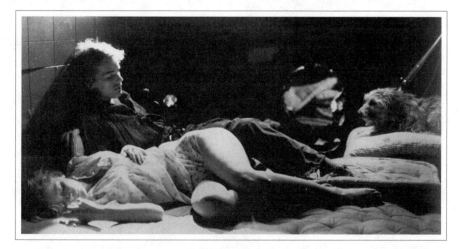

FROM THE UNIQUE PEN OF HARLAN ELLISON: *A 1969 short story, set in a ruined future-world, touches on cannibalism. A Boy and His Dog was the only film ever written and directed by character actor L. Q. Jones. Here, Don Johnson, Susanne Benton, and Blood (the dog's voice provided by Tim McIntire). Courtesy: LQ/JAF-First Run Features.*

3. *Serenity* (Joss Whedon, 2005): "Half of writing history is hiding the truth," Mal (Nathan Fillion) explains in Whedon's worthy follow-up to his short-lived, much-admired TV series *Firefly*. After meeting a psychic nature child, the cynical rebel regains his old idealism and fights the Alliance.

4. *Silent Running* (Douglas Trumbull, 1972): In orbit deep in space, a dedicated environmentalist (Bruce Dern) tends to the last living plants with the help of a trio of Disney-like droids named Huey, Dewey, and Louie. Early Green sci-fi from Trumbull, the wizard of F/X, in his initial directorial effort.

5. *Liquid Sky* (Slava Tsukerman, 1982): The first sci-fi film to boast a soundtrack composed of digital sampler/synthesizer music. Anne Carlisle plays two New Wave models, one male, one female. The movie drew on the already emergent electroclash club culture, then helped to spread that edgy movement.

6. *Capricorn One* (Peter Hyams, 1977): Conspiracy theories that the historic moon landing was staged for the TV cameras led to this similar story about a faked Mars landing, with O. J. Simpson playing an astronaut. A surprisingly smart, savvy, satiric, sophisticated film from a usually inept writer-director.

7. *Robinson Crusoe on Mars* (Byron Haskin, 1964): An astronaut (Paul Mantee), stranded on the Red Planet, gradually comes to realize that his experiences parallel those of Daniel Defoe's hero. Despite the campy premise and over-the-top title, *Robinson Crusoe* is a serious and successful example of B-budget "hard sci-fi."

8. *Donnie Darko* (Richard Kelly, 2001): Jake Gyllenhaal embodies the 1988 equivalent of James Dean's 1950s angst-ridden teenager. Donnie researches time travel after a visitation by a weird man in a rabbit suit who insists that the world has a month left before Armageddon. Purposefully quirky.

9. *The Cat from Outer Space* (Norman Tokar, 1978): When a UFO unexpectedly lands on Earth, the inhabitant turns out to be a cat, longing to rejoin the mothership and go home. Instead, he is adopted by well-meaning earthlings. Sound familiar? Genial Disney comedy provided Spielberg with the template for *E.T.*

10. *Dark City* (Alex Proyas, 1998): A confused man (Rufus Sewell) is pursued, *Les Misérables* style, by an unrelenting detective (William Hurt), as well as a menacing group, the Strangers. Is the amnesiac a serial killer, or the target of a Kafkaesque conspiracy, his world existing in perpetual night?

APPENDIX 4

COMEDY SCIENCE FICTION

Are they comedies with a sci-fi setting or actual examples of the genre, played for laughs? No easy answer to that discussion-inspiring question!

1. *Dr. Strangelove or: How I Learned to Stop Worrying and Love the Bomb* (Stanley Kubrick, 1964): Peter Sellers plays three roles (including the title character) in the greatest black comedy since the Marx Brothers's *Duck Soup* (1933). Several sci-fi bits qualify this genius-level farce to be mentioned here.

2. *Bud Abbott and Lou Costello Meet Frankenstein* (Charles Barton, 1948): Dracula (Bela Lugosi finally returning to the role that defined him) joins the revived Wolfman (Lon Chaney Jr.) and Frankenstein's monster (Glenn Strange) to menace the title duo in this, the greatest film of their careers.

3. *Dark Star* (John Carpenter, 1974): Every technological "advance" that can go wrong does precisely that on a flight into deep space. Shot for less than $60,000, this film launched the careers of Carpenter and screenwriter Dan O'Bannon, who also plays a role and later wrote the screenplay for *Alien* (1979). You gotta *love* that ever-movin' beach ball!

4. *Moon Pilot* (James Neilson, 1962): While an astronaut (Tom Tryon) readies for the first NASA flight to the moon, he meets a girl (Dany Saval) with a foreign accent who comes from considerably farther away than one might guess. Adapted from *Starfire*, the enjoyably light-hearted novel by Robert Buckner.

5. *Frankenweenie* (Tim Burton, 2012): A boy and his dog, Burton style. The nightmare is conveyed through some of the most sophisticated stop-motion photography ever devised. A remake of Burton's own early short subject of the same name, here reaching its full potential for comedy of the most macabre and melancholic order.

6. *Visit to a Small Planet* (Norman Taurog, 1960): Time-space traveler Jerry Lewis lands on Earth to witness the Civil War, but he arrives a century late. A somewhat watered-down adaptation of Gore Vidal's brilliant

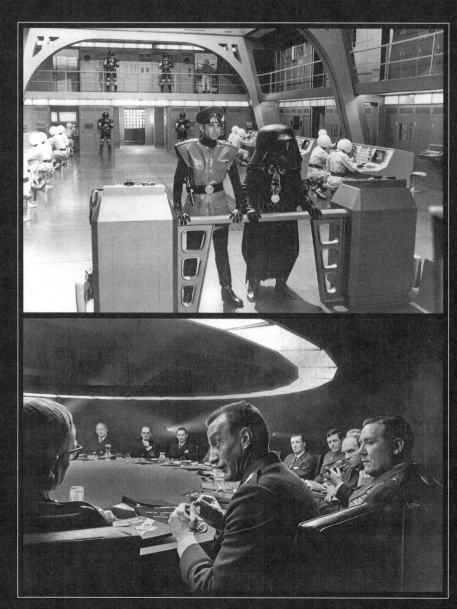

THE BEST MEDICINE: *Comedy sci-fi films run the gamut. Mel Brooks's broad burlesque,* Spaceballs, *spoofs* Star Wars, Alien, *and just about every sci-fi film and stars Rick Moranis as a diminutive Darth Vader type. Courtesy: Brooksfilms/MGM. Stanley Kubrick's darkly humorous* Dr. Strangelove *provides a vision of the world's end, starring George C. Scott as out-of-control General Buck Turgidson. Courtesy: Hawk/Columbia.*

Broadway play, but a surprising amount of the scribe's savage satire on American mores still shines through.

7. *Spaceballs* (Mel Brooks, 1987): A broad burlesque of all the "new" clichés from then-recent sci-fi classics such as *Star Wars*, the *Star Trek* films, and *Alien*. Not, mind you, *Blazing Saddles* brilliant from beginning to end, but most of the gags work, particularly the grotesque Pizza the Hut.

8. *The Brother from Another Planet* (John Sayles, 1984): From the much-lauded indie director, this tale follows a dark-hued, telekinetic spaceman (Joe Morton) hiding out in Harlem. A sly parable about ethnicity and issues dealing with illegal immigration, with this brother "alienated" even from his fellow blacks.

9. *Galaxy Quest* (Dean Parisot, 1999): Aliens abduct the cast of a TV space fantasy, believing that the actors are heroes who will save their planet. The premise recalls ¡*Three Amigos!* (1986), updated from the Wild West to the Final Frontier. A spot-on parody.

10. *Queen of Outer Space* (Edward Bernds, 1958): Astronauts land on Venus and encounter a disfigured Amazonian queen (Laurie Mitchell) and an underground revolutionary leader (Zsa Zsa Gabor). Answer to a long-standing question: with Ben Hecht as co-writer? *Yes* . . . it *was* always intended to be funny!

APPENDIX 5

DYSTOPIAN FICTION

All dystopian films at least flirt with sci-fi. Here are ten that rub right up against the genre's edge.

1. *A Clockwork Orange* (Stanley Kubrick, 1971): Alex (Malcolm McDowell), a juvenile delinquent taken to the nightmare scenario extreme, terrorizes middle-class homes until science and technology are employed to make him conform. Surreal, brilliant version of Anthony Burgess's 1962 novel.
2. *The Trial* (Orson Welles, 1962): In a world that may be our own or some parallel universe, a young man (Anthony Perkins) goes on trial for an unspecified crime. The writings of Franz Kafka are sometimes considered sci-fi; certainly, Welles's shadow-world visually expresses such a descent into madness.
3. *Brazil* (Terry Gilliam, 1985): An ordinary working stiff (Jonathan Pryce) attempts to locate his dream girl in a world that becomes more surreal every day. Visually remarkable, if derivative of *1984* (1949) and *Brave New World* (1932). Theatre of the Absurd playwright Tom Stoppard was among the writers.
4. *La città delle donne/City of Women* (Federico Fellini, 1980): Marcello Mastroianni—here, as in *8½* (1963), playing the great director's alter ego—steps off a train only to find himself in a matriarchal future-world. The ultimate male chauvinist nightmare scenario as only the cinematic genius of Fellini could present it.
5. *Gattaca* (Andrew Niccol, 1997): "Biopunk" entered the realm of sci-fi cinema with this vision of eugenics as the source of a horrific near-future. A young man (Ethan Hawke) who wants to travel to space assumes the identity of a person whose DNA qualifies him for such an adventure. Intense!
6. *The Hellstrom Chronicle* (Walon Green, 1971): A scientist (Lawrence Pressman) realizes that insects are about to take over the Earth. Filmed in a low-key style, without any of the old horror flick clichés or sci-fi conventions. A quietly convincing film bolstered by brilliant "microphotography."

THE LITTLE FILM THAT HIT BIG: *Curious passersby consider entering a theater and catching the small-budget, high-quality indie item that rates as the first American movie to ever depict the aftermath of all-out nuclear warfare. Courtesy: Arch Oboler Productions/Columbia.*

7. *28 Days Later* (Danny Boyle, 2002): A virus, unwittingly allowed to enter our atmosphere, creates a plague of zombies. The brilliant first half draws on *I Am Legend* (1954) and *The Day of the Triffids* (1951). Sadly, the film degenerates into a *Rambo*-style hackneyed conventional action-flick finale.

8. *The War Game* (Peter Watkins, 1965): England attempts to survive following a nuclear attack. Shot in a unique British style known as the "dramatized documentary," in which a fictional tale is delineated as if it were a news story for the BBC. Dazzling and devastating, the film won the Academy Award for Best Documentary Feature in 1966.

9. *Five* (Arch Oboler, 1951): Four men and a woman, well played by relative unknowns, survive a nuclear war. One of the few films from the avatar of the radio program *Lights Out* (a classic, if only dimly remembered, predecessor to TV's *The Twilight Zone*), *Five* is also the first film to depict a post-apocalyptic future.

10. *No Blade of Grass* (Cornel Wilde, 1970): When government officials in London are no longer able to provide food for the rioting masses, a man packs up his family and heads for rural Scotland. A harrowing survivalist drama not unlike maverick Wilde's earlier *The Naked Prey* (1966).

APPENDIX 6

THE NAME OF ACTION

Not all sci-fi films are intellectually stimulating—nor do they necessarily need to be. Thrill rides are appreciated.

1. *Armageddon* (Michael Bay, 1998): Bruce Willis, the Everyman hero of modern sci-fi, saves the world. Scorned by critics, adored by audiences, this typical Bay no-brainer rates as the most consistently entertaining, gut-level, action space fantasy ever. Billy Bob Thornton dazzles in a key supporting role.

2. *Pacific Rim* (Guillermo del Toro, 2013): Immense creatures invade from an undersea portal. Familiar material transformed into something special by the adrenalin rush of stunningly staged action and the director's incorporation of the Asian subgenres of *kaiju* and mecha into a Hollywood blockbuster.

3. *Death Race 2000* (Paul Bartel, 1975): David Carradine vs. pre-*Rocky* Sylvester Stallone in a violent cross-country race. *Rollerball* with cars, but without the pretentiousness. A smart satiric script makes this the best drive-in movie ever from the Corman company. Based on Ib Melchior's story, "The Racer."

4. *Starship Troopers* (Paul Verhoeven, 1997): From a still-hip novel by the great Robert A. Heinlein. Humankind vs. the insects in a nonstop adrenalin rush. The incredible and perhaps unintended irony: no previous cinematic criticism of war ever celebrated violent action quite so openly or so viscerally!

5. *Time Bandits* (Terry Gilliam, 1981): Granada, Wales, and Morocco are but three of the locations in which Gilliam shot his giddily chaotic globe- and time-traveling tale of a little boy's adventures with the most memorable dwarves since Disney's *Snow White*. High point: Sean Connery vs. a minotaur.

6. *Daleks–Invasion Earth: 2150 A.D.* (Gordon Flemyng, 1966): By the mid-sixties, *Dr. Who* had become a staple of British TV, known for its outrageous plots and whimsical humor. In the second theatrical installment, Peter

Cushing incarnates the time-traveling scourge of those miniature invading robots.

7. *The Last Starfighter* (Nick Castle, 1984): *Tron* meets *Star Wars*, plus a preview of *Galaxy Quest*. A video game–addicted child (Lance Guest) is recruited to save a distant world from a supervillain. Child-oriented action adventure pays off for its youthful audience with strong CGI F/X.

8. *Battle Beyond the Stars* (Jimmy T. Murakami, 1980): *The Magnificent Seven*, complete with original cast member Robert Vaughn, reassembled in another galaxy. Lavish by producer Roger Corman's standards; F/X shots were recycled in the schlockmeister's later ultra-low-budget space operas.

9. *Damnation Alley* (Jack Smight, 1977): An intercontinental ballistic missile team retaliates after "some European country" starts a nuclear war, then they fend off killer cockroaches in an armored car that presages George Peppard's *A-Team* van. Peppard also stars in this film. Enjoyable actioner, adapted from a superior novel of the same name by Roger Zelazny.

10. *Starcrash* (Luigi Cozzi, aka Lewis Coates, 1978): A cross between Barbarella and Han Solo, space pirate Stella Starr (Caroline Munro) brings order to the universe while wearing a barely-there black leather bikini. Christopher Plummer looks sadly lost playing an equivalent of Obi-Wan Kenobi.

THE NAME OF ACTION: *One of the many juvenile sci-fi films rushed into production following the success of* Star Wars, The Last Starfighter *had the distinction of being one of the first films to rely heavily on CGI for spectacular F/X, these combined with Ron Cobb's spaceship designs. Courtesy: Lorimar/Universal.*

APPENDIX 7

INVASION OF THE SUPERHEROES

Excepting masked crimefighters sans any superpowers, such adventures are closely related to the science-fiction genre.

1. *Iron Man* (Jon Favreau, 2008): What may rate as Stan Lee's greatest single contribution (that's going some!) stars the pluperfect Robert Downey Jr. as the glib entrepreneur who discovers that clothes sometimes do make the man—that is, if your suit is courtesy of Stan Winston.
2. *Superman* (Richard Donner, 1978): The big one that proved that super-heroes could serve as the centerpiece for A-budget extravaganzas. Chris-topher Reeve charms as the Jerry Siegel/Joe Shuster icon, and Marlon Brando appears as Jor-El. Early Krypton sequences offer sci-fi at its best.
3. *The Incredibles* (Brad Bird, 2004): The superhero syndrome comes to the computer-animation world and, thanks to Pixar's apparently infallible geniuses, results in a slightly edgier than usual, yet still family-friendly, satiric portrait of caped crusaders who balance crime fighting with domesticity.
4. *Watchmen* (Zack Snyder, 2009): The in-your-face comic by Alan Moore and Dave Gibbons finally makes it to the screen as a three-hour, alternative history, Cold War epic. In this world, even superheroes grow old and suffer from cancer. It's the anti-*Incredibles*: brilliant, nasty, memorable.
5. *Spider-Man 2* (Sam Raimi, 2004): Bigger and better than the first, this brightly colored crowd-pleaser balances the humblest superhero's (Tobey Maguire) over-the-top duel against Dr. Octopus (Alfred Molina) with a touchingly intimate tale of his love for an actress (Kirsten Dunst).
6. *The Rocketeer* (Joe Johnston, 1991): In the days leading up to World War II, a would-be hero experiments with a jet-engine backpack. The nostalgia element is played to perfection; Billy Campbell is agreeable as a wide-eyed swain in love with a Bettie Page–type actress (Jennifer Connelly).
7. *The Incredible Hulk* (Louis Leterrier, 2008): More than making up for Ang Lee's dizzyingly disappointing 2003 misfire, this reboot respects both the

TWENTY-FIVE YEARS IN THE MAKING: *After a quarter-century of delays,* Spider-Man *finally reached theater screens in 2002. Tobey Maguire proved the perfect choice for the title role, aided and abetted by David Koepp's smart screenplay and Sam Raimi's sure-handed direction. Marvel Entertainment/Columbia.*

Stan Lee/Jack Kirby source and the seminal 1970s TV series, yet also sets out in satisfyingly different directions, helped along by top acting talent.

8. *The Dark Knight Rises* (Christopher Nolan, 2012): A kidnapped physicist and a fusion reactor add the scientific elements necessary for one of Nolan's exquisite *Batman* films to at last claim a few of the genre's conventions. Christian Bale and Anne Hathaway are perfectly matched as Batman and Catwoman.

9. *Darkman* (Sam Raimi, 1990): *The Phantom of the Opera, House of Wax,* and *The Incredible Hulk* come together in an unsettling neo-noir about a horribly scarred scientist (Liam Neeson) exacting revenge on those who destroyed his life. *Darkman* was the first film to fully capture the visual textures of a 1940s comic strip.

10. *The Toxic Avenger* (Michael Herz, 1984): After being shamed by bullies, a creepy kid takes an inadvertent swim in a vat of hot chemicals, emerging as a monstrous-looking avenger. This early sci-fi/horror entry from Lloyd Kaufman's self-consciously campy Troma Entertainment is among their best.

APPENDIX 8

THE LEAST NECESSARY SCI-FI REMAKES

There's an old saying: Why not leave well enough alone? Some people, however, just don't listen . . .

1. *The Island of Dr. Moreau* (John Frankenheimer, 1996): Marlon Brando and Val Kilmer engage in a contest to see who might do the most damage to what was supposed to be an ambitious new version of Wells's classic novel. The original director Richard Stanley was fired after three disastrous days.

2. *Flash Gordon* (Mike Hodges, 1980): Male mannequin Sam J. Jones stands in for Alex Raymond's space hero with an authentic actor providing his voice in this over-the-top glitz-arama travesty, executed in the low-camp style of TV's *Batman*. The soundtrack by Queen downgrades the story for the disco era.

3. *Planet of the Apes* (Tim Burton, 2001): On paper, the match-up of such beloved material with a quirky cult director must've seemed inspired. The results, however, are dark and depressing, though never profoundly so. Mark Wahlberg (*not* playing Charlton Heston's role) stars in a film at once brooding, shallow, and confusing.

4. *Invaders from Mars* (Tobe Hooper, 1986): Angering remake that eliminates every element so strangely charming in the source via a mean-spirited Dan O'Bannon/Don Jakoby script. The low point: Oscar-winner Louise Fletcher wolfing down a frog. Even Stan Winston/John Dykstra F/X don't help much.

5. *Total Recall* (Len Wiseman, 2012): Once again, the futuristic fall guy discovers he was an adventurer in a previous life. Cutting away the all-important trip to Mars diminishes viewer interest. Lumbering, the elaborate though unconvincing chase and action sequences gradually become numbing.

6. *Village of the Damned* (John Carpenter, 1995): The remarkable purity of vision and understated build-up of suspense that characterized the sublime 1960 version are here replaced by a sledgehammer approach

SPACE OPERA FOR THE DISCO ERA: *With music by Queen, this lavish (and self-consciously campy) production from Dino De Laurentiis pales in comparison to the beloved old movie serials. With Max von Sydow as Ming the Merciless and Ornella Muti as his man-eating daughter Princess Aura. Courtesy: Starling Films/Universal.*

meant to scare, though it more often plays as unintentionally silly. Sadly, Christopher Reeve's final film.

7. *The Blob* (Chuck Russell, 1988): Modern teens go through all the motions in their attempts to warn adults of impending death. Tony Gardner's Grand Guignol F/X, ridiculous rather than horrifying, cannot replace the original's simple appeal, which used the power of suggestion to play to our abiding fear of the unseen.

8. *Godzilla* (Roland Emmerich, 1998): Title aside, this film steals from *The Beast from 20,000 Fathoms* (1953), *Them!* (1954), and *Jurassic Park* (1993) in a futile attempt to concoct something resembling a plot. The dinosaur disappoints, the lead characters annoy, and attempts at humor are nonexistent. Wastes the notable talents of Jean Reno.

9. *The Day the Earth Stood Still* (Scott Derrickson, 2008): In this modernized version, Klaatu arrives on Earth to prevent further destruction of the environment. Great theme, lousy execution. There had to be an actor who could come closer than Keanu Reeves to Michael Rennie's gentle yet mighty Carpenter.

10. *Rollerball* (John McTiernan, 2002): Round and round they go, this time less convincingly than ever. It's one thing to fail to improve on a classic, but how does a remake of the 1975 stinker manage to be every bit as lame as the original? A career killer for McTiernan and star Chris Klein.

APPENDIX 9

THE WORST

No low-budget drive-in junk here. Only those highly ambitious films that promised much and delivered nil.

1. *Battlefield Earth* (Roger Christian, 2000): Alien invaders "Psychlos" subjugate humankind for a millennium. From a novel by L. Ron Hubbard, the film, initially intended as the first installment in a vast epic, is full of shabby, costly F/X. For Dianetics diehards and John Travolta (in dreadlocks, no less) completists only.

2. *Lifeforce* (Tobe Hooper, 1985): A mesmerizing, naked alien (Mathilda May) arrives on Earth. How could the director of *The Texas Chainsaw Massacre* (1974) and Dan O'Bannon, the scribe who would pen *Alien*, collaborate on something so awe-inspiringly awful? From a far better novel, *The Space Vampires* by Colin Wilson.

3. *Zardoz* (John Boorman, 1974): A violent "exterminator" (Sean Connery) zips into the vortex. He comes to harbor second thoughts about his great god, the huge flying head that lends this film its title. Hard to believe the ordinarily impressive director of classics like *Excalibur* (1981) could hit rock bottom.

4. *Dune* (David Lynch, 1984): Among those who appeared likely to successfully adapt Frank Herbert's 1965 philosophical epic, Lynch had to be the leading candidate. Instead, he allowed producers to pressure him into attempting to create another *Star Wars*–type mainstream action franchise. Disastrous.

5. *The Adventures of Pluto Nash* (Ron Underwood, 2002): Remember when Eddie Murphy was the biggest star on the planet? That was before he agreed to headline this loser effort about a supposedly charming rogue who runs a trendy nightclub on the moon. The worst-ever sci-fi comedy with lousy gags and shoddy F/X.

6. *The Man Who Fell to Earth* (Nicolas Roeg, 1976): Glitter rock's David Bowie hopes to find water for his doomed planet, but instead he encounters Earth's techno-corporate capitalism. Roeg's surreal phantasmagoric

approach plays as unrelentingly pretentious. An injustice to Walter Tevis's fine 1963 novel of the same name.

7. *Mars Attacks!* (Tim Burton, 1996): Jack Nicholson is the U.S. president who wonders why earthlings and Martians can't all just get along together. Exhaustingly unfunny spoof of 1950s sci-fi movie clichés wasted lots and lots of money on bizarre F/X. Derived from a popular trading card series.

8. *The Black Hole* (Gary Nelson, 1979): Maximilian Schell is a futuristic Captain Nemo in this expensive Disney film that was supposed to bring back the glory days of *20,000 Leagues*. Instead, it offers talk, talk, talk, most of it boring, followed by a dull climactic entrance into the title empty spot in space.

9. *Sphere* (Barry Levinson, 1998): Samuel L. Jackson, Dustin Hoffman, Sharon Stone in an underwater alien flick, here involving time rather than space travel. A dead-on-arrival dud that combined elements of *The Abyss*, *Alien*, *Solaris*, and *Forbidden Planet*, yet is in no way comparable to those classics. From a 1987 Michael Crichton novel of the same name.

10. *Rollerball* (Norman Jewison, 1975): Overripe treatise on futuristic methods of re-channeling violence while elite leaders of a new world order create the most violent sport ever. Numbingly obvious "message movie" makes its point in the first five minutes, then has absolutely nowhere to go.

SHAKEN, NOT STIRRED? *Former James Bond star Sean Connery enters the vortex (presumably wearing his underwear) in this spectacularly awful film that is preposterous in plotting, pompous in style, pretentious in theme, and ultimately purposeless. Courtesy: John Boorman Productions/20th Century Fox.*

APPENDIX 10

SPACE "CAMP": SO BAD THEY'RE GREAT!

Bad movies, you don't want to watch. Great bad movies, you can't resist. Gleefully indulge in the guilty pleasures.

1. *The Little Shop of Horrors* (Roger Corman, 1960): A nerd (Jonathan Haze) and a masochist addicted to dental surgery (Jack Nicholson) cross paths with a killer plant. This camp classic may have been the first film ever to achieve cult status with college students via late-night TV showings.

2. *Plan 9 from Outer Space* (Edward D. Wood Jr., 1959): Vampira (Maila Nurmi) in her first (and only) sci-fi film; Bela Lugosi in his last. What more could anyone ask for? Flying saucers fashioned from paper plates, perhaps? If Ed Wood had never been born, then Tim Burton would have had to create him.

3. *Invasion of the Bee Girls* (Denis Sanders, 1973): Anitra Ford is a Wasp-like (in every sense of the term) invader who inspires Earth girls to love their men to death. One friend of a recent victim sighs jealously: "Just think! Coming and going at the same time." Savvy script by Nicholas Meyer.

4. *Cat-Women of the Moon* (Arthur Hilton, 1953): Space travelers discover an underground lunar civilization consisting of eight Hollywood hopeful starlets in black leotards. Incredibly, cult queen Marie Windsor doesn't play the queen pussycat but an astronaut. A giant spider, hanging from a visible string, is to die for.

5. *Monster Zero* (aka *Invasion of Astro-Monster*) (Ishirô Honda, 1965): After striking out in Hollywood, Nick Adams played variations on his "rebel" image in international junk movies. Here, Nick—the road company junk-movie answer to lookalike Steve McQueen—goes head to head with Godzilla and Rodan, among others. Eiji Tsuburaya provided the irresistibly tacky F/X.

6. *Robot Monster* (Phil Tucker, 1953): "Ro-Man," a big lug in an unconvincing ape suit with what appears to be an upside-down fishbowl over his head, sets up a bubble machine in Bronson Canyon and attempts to track down and destroy the worst actor who ever lived, George Nader. Originally in 3-D.

THEY DON'T MAKE 'EM LIKE THIS ANYMORE: *Shot in four days on a $16,000 budget, Robot Monster features alien invader Ro-Man (George Barrows) carrying the frantic last woman on Earth (Claudia Barrett) across Bronson Canyon. Courtesy: Astor Pictures.*

7. *Santa Claus Conquers the Martians* (Nicholas Webster, 1964): Concerned that their kids have been so conditioned by technology that they can no longer respond as free individuals, Red Planet parents decide to kidnap the merry old elf and bring good spirits to space. Pia Zadora plays one of the children.

8. *The Horror of Party Beach* (Del Tenney, 1964): The dumping of radioactive waste in the ocean breeds creeps that surge up on shore and menace teenage girls wearing skimpy bikinis by day and lingerie at night. So cheap it makes an American International Pictures quickie look like *Lawrence of Arabia*.

9. *Attack of the Killer Tomatoes!* (John De Bello, 1978): Those fondly remembered 1950s films about deadly carrots are here lovingly spoofed in this purposefully retro-comedy thriller. Several sequels, a TV series, and everything from video games to Viper comics continued this fascinating film's franchise.

10. *Jesse James Meets Frankenstein's Daughter* (William Beaudine, 1966): She (Narda Onyx) moved dad's lab to the American desert but didn't expect a surprise visit from the notorious outlaw (John Lupton). Released as a drive-in doubleheader with another Beaudine film, *Billy the Kid vs. Dracula* (1966).

GENERAL INDEX

210, 216, 233, 242, 266, 286, 308, 329–330, 332, 348–350, 373, 399

Do Androids Dream of Electric Sheep? (novel, 1968), 228

Donner, Richard, 392

Dr. Who (TV), 390

dystopia, xvi, 5, 24, 37, 84, 115, 132, 145, 181, 195, 202, 210, 254, 262, 271, 276, 320, 323, 330, 356, 371, 388–389

Eastwood, Clint, 204, 303–306, *305*

Einstein, Albert, xiv, 46, 101

Ellison, Harlan, 383

Emmerich, Roland, 266, 269–270, 397

Fahrenheit 451 (novel, 1953), 145, 167, 358

Favreau, Jon, 362, 392

Fellini, Federico, 388

Fincher, David, 23

Finney, Jack, 86–88

First Men in the Moon, The (book, 1901), xiv, 2, 8

Fleischer, Max, 3, 126, 143, 312, 375

Fonda, Jane, 153–156, *154*

Ford, Harrison, 183, 216, 226, 227, 229, 266

Frankenheimer, John, 26, 137, 139–140, 395

Frankenstein, or The Modern Prometheus (book, 1818), xiii, 17, 27, 137–139, 308, 341, 350, 354

Frankenstein myth, 14, 23, 25, 52, 152, 165, 308, 350–351, 379, 385, 402. *See also under individual movies*

From the Earth to the Moon (book, 1865), xiv, 2, 8

Fukasaku, Kinji, 372, 377

Gilliam, Terry, 274, 388, 390

Godard, Jean-Luc, 131–134

Gondry, Michel, 315–319

graphic novel. *See* BDs/graphic novels

gross-out/splatter effect, 214, 247

Guest, Val, 111, 113, 382

Gunn, James, 373–376

Hammer Films, 147

Harryhausen, Ray, 65–67, 89–91, 97, 259, 264, 375

Hawks, Howard, 51, 54, 56, 59, 214, 376

Hecht, Ben, 387

Heinlein, Robert A., 47–50, 390

Hero With a Thousand Faces, The (book, 1949), 184

Heston, Charlton, 137, 142, *156*, 164, 356, 395

Hitchcock, Alfred, 29, 98, 124–126, 136, 146, 195, 210, 276, 278, 311, 329, 368

Honda, Ishiro, 95, 97, 400

Hooper, Tobe, 395, 398

Howard, Ron, 241–243

Hunger Games, The (novel, 2008), 371

Huxley, Aldous, 84, 181

I Am Legend (book, 1954), 129–130, 389

I, Robot (book, 1950), 143

Island of Dr. Moreau, The (book, 1896), 24

Jackson, Peter, 341–342, 354

James, P. D., 322

Jewison, Norman, 399

Jolie, Angelina, 312, *313*, 369

Kafka, Franz, 295, 384, 388

Karloff, Boris, 14, 16, *18*, 19, 29, 30–31, 34, 46; as influence, 53

Kaufman, Charlie, 315–317, 319

King, Stephen, xiii, 152

Kneale, Nigel, 147, 149–150

Koepp, David, 263, 393

Kramer, Stanley, 108–110

Kubrick, Stanley, xii, 31, 50, 74, 110, 123, 150–153, 170, 268, 271, 305, 307–308, 385, 386, 388; as influence, 171, 182, 229, 331

Laemmle, Carl, Jr., 14–16, 25, 26–27, 30, 31, 33

Laloux, Rene, 172–175

Lang, Fritz, 3–12, 28, 31, 37

Lasseter, John, 329–330

Laughton, Charles, 23, 24, 25

Lee, Stan, 359, 376, 392, 394

Levinson, Barry, 399

Lisberger, Steven, 348–349

Losey, Joseph, 377
Lost in Space (TV), 94
Lucas, George, xviii, xix, xx, 6, 38, 43, 94, 133, 166–169, 183–190, 207, 213, 217, 223, 265, 288, 289, 296–303, 306, 312, 342, 368
Lugosi, Bela, 16, 19, 23, 24, 26–27, 27, 29, 30, 31, 34, 385, 400
Lynch, David, 383, 398

Mamoru Oshii, 277, 379
Mamoulian, Rouben, 19–20, 22–23
March, Fredric, 19, 21, 22
Marker, Chris, 274–275
Matheson, Richard, 46, 98–101, 127–130
McTeigue, James, 319–321
McTiernan, John, 248–249, 397
Méliès, George, xv, xxvi, 1–3, 10, 12, 28, 42, 45
Menzies, William Cameron, ii, 35–37, 58–60
Meyer, Nicholas, 193–196, 218–226, 400
Miller, George, 205–208
Mitchell, David, 355–356, 358
Miyazaki, Hayao, 230–233
More, Sir Thomas, 23, 291
Mysterious Island, The (book, 1874), 74

Niccol, Andrew, 289–291, 388
Nietzsche, Friedrich, xiv, 318
Nimoy, Leonard, 218, 219, 221–223, 224, 225–226, 336, 337
1984 (novel, 1949), 12, 82–84, 167, 181
Nolan, Christopher, xvii, 345–347, 362, 364, 394

O'Bannon, Dan, 183, 196–198, 259, 261, 385, 395, 398
Oboler, Arch, 389
O'Brien, Willis H., 13, 65–66
Orwell, George, 12, 82–85, 147, 167, 181, 320
Oshii, Mamoru. *See* Mamoru Oshii

Pal, George, 47–50, 61, 63–64, 112–115, 123, 380, 381
Petri, Elio, 378, 379
Pierce, Jack B., 17, 26, 34
Planet of the Apes (book, 1963), 156, 173

Poe, Edgar Allan, 26–27, 28, 30–31, 129–130, 277
Proyas, Alex, 384

Raimi, Sam, 392, 394
Rains, Claude, 31–34
Reitman, Ivan, 208, 210
Roddenberry, Gene, 94, 219–220, 305, 336–337, 340
Roeg, Nicholas, 144, 398–399
Romero, George A., 130, 160–162, 168, 204
R.U.R. (Rossum's Universal Robots, play, 1920), 331

Sayles, John, 387
Schoedsack, Ernest B., 44–46
Schüfftan, Eugen, 3, 5
Schwarzenegger, Arnold, 199, 234, 235, 236, 248–249, 259, 260, 261
Science Fiction Theatre (TV), 100
Scorsese, Martin, 3, 133, 162
Scott, Ridley, 6, 196–198, 215, 226–229, 311
Serling, Rod, xviii, *xix*, 61, 94, 130, 143, 156–157, 159, 235–237, 240, 243, 291, 295, 308–309
Shelley, Mary Wolstonecraft, xiii, 14, 16–19, 27. *See also* Frankenstein myth
Shrinking Man, The (novel, 1956), 46, 100
Siodmak, Curt, 89, 91, 380
Smith, Will, 285, *287*
Snyder, Zack, 362–365, 392
Spielberg, Steven, xviii, 57, 61, 64, 112, 121, 124, 168, 190–193, 201, 207, 213, 215–218, 238–240, 259, 262, 263–266, 285–288, 289, 307–311, 327–328, 380, 384
Stanton, Andrew, 329–330, 332
Star Trek (TV), 93, 135, 143, 165, 219–220, 224, 280, 305, 336–337, 340, 347, 372
Stevenson, Robert Louis, 19–20, 22
Strange Case of Dr. Jekyll and Mr. Hyde, The (book, 1886), 20
Sturges, John, 134–136

Tarantino, Quentin, 133
Tarkovsky, Andrei, 169–171
Time Machine, The (book, 1895), 113, 196

FILM INDEX

ON THE SET: *Author Douglas Brode visits Adrienne Barbeau, Harry Dean Stanton, and Lee Van Cleef during the final day of shooting for Escape from New York. Courtesy: Avco-Embassy.*

AN ENDURING CLASSIC: *For decades, Hollywood producers have talked about a* Forbidden Planet *remake, but it's unlikely that the charm and magic of the 1956 original could ever be recaptured. Courtesy: Metro-Goldwyn-Mayer.*